Mastering Adobe Captivate 2017

Fourth Edition

Create professional SCORM-compliant eLearning content with Adobe Captivate

Dr. Pooja Jaisingh
Damien Bruyndonckx

BIRMINGHAM - MUMBAI

Mastering Adobe Captivate 2017

Fourth Edition

First published: October 2017

Production reference: 1290917

Published by Packt Publishing Ltd.
Livery Place
35 Livery Street
Birmingham
B3 2PB, UK.
ISBN 978-1-78829-528-4

www.packtpub.com

Credits

Authors
Dr. Pooja Jaisingh
Damien Bruyndonckx

Reviewers
Alice Acker
Paul Wilson

Commissioning Editor
Smeet Thakkar

Acquisition Editor
Denim Pinto

Content Development Editor
Nikhil Borkar

Technical Editor
Jijo Maliyekal

Copy Editor
Safis Editing

Project Coordinator
Ulhas Kambali

Proofreader
Safis Editing

Indexer
Rekha Nair

Graphics
Abhinash Sahu

Production Coordinator
Melwyn Dsa

Foreword

Last year, the Government of India withdrew 86% of its physical currency notes in circulation and dramatically changed the trajectory of digital currency adoption in daily transactions. This year, the government did away with almost 20 different sales taxes and compliance regimes, and replaced them with one universal tax called General Sales Tax (GST)--driven and managed by one computer network called GSTN.

In China, Alibaba launched the Hema retail stores, combining mobile app, electronic pay, and data sciences to realize an oxymoron--the hyper-local business.
In US, the quintessential American experience of driving a car is being challenged, first through Uber and now through the driverless car.

As recently as a few years ago, Adobe Flash content was ubiquitous on web properties, including learning content, across the world. Recently, Adobe announced the end of life of Adobe Flash sometime in 2020, meaning that most of the Flash-based learning content now needs to be republished in HTML5.

Machines and algorithms have suddenly sneaked up and are all around us. But the remarkable thing is that most countries continue to add people to their workforce. Young people trained in modern skills or older generation having reskilled themselves are joining to manage and shape the new reality. The cycle of skilling and reskilling, so much at the core of human resilience, is rotating faster than ever in living memory.

People across all demographics, races, and geographies are embracing learning, formally as well as informally. My mother at 75 is learning how to use mobile apps to make payments, Chinese checkout tellers are learning the complexity of managing digital inventory, and US commuters are learning to catch up on their office work on their devices, being driven to work by Uber, or an algorithm! Learning is being delivered digitally, primarily through mobile devices, often on the job, and is increasingly becoming user generated.

Adobe Captivate 2017, as the leader in the space of eLearning authoring tools, continues to push the boundaries of WYSIWYG authoring across devices, while dovetailing productivity with power. Both are important to keep up with the increasing demand for digital learning, especially on mobile, as millennials enter the workforce.

Dr. Pooja Jaisingh and Damien Bruyndonckx, two of the most recognizable and respected names in the field of eLearning, have written an excellent book that not only provides that extra *oomph!* to power users but also helps democratize eLearning authoring by lowering the learning curve for the new entrants in this space. The autoresponsive capabilities in Captivate 2017 spectacularly solve the difficult design and productivity problems of authoring once and publishing across many form factors. However, it also requires a slight change in the design and mindset of content authoring. I am glad to note that the authors have recognized the importance of the problem and opportunity of the capability in Captivate 2017, and have given this topic great importance in their planning of this book.

This book is an essential tool in the chest of tools for anyone in the business of generating compelling eLearning content--from professionals to SMEs.

Happy learning!

Tridib Roy Chowdhury
Sr. Director and G.M.
Adobe Systems

About the Author

Dr. Pooja Jaisingh, the founder of and chief learning geek at LearninGeeks, leads the design and delivery of eLearning and training solutions. She holds a master's degree in education and economics and a doctorate in educational technology. In addition, she is CPLP, ACE (Adobe Captivate), and COTP certified. She has created several award-winning eLearning courses and eBooks, and she regularly conducts workshops and training courses on eLearning tools and techniques. Pooja has authored courses on Adobe Captivate and Captivate Prime for `https://www.lynda.com/` and LinkedIn Learning. She also teaches Captivate courses at IconLogic. Prior to starting her own company, she worked as a teacher trainer, instructional designer, and senior Adobe eLearning evangelist. You can contact her on Twitter at `@poojajaisingh` and via her website at `www.poojajaisingh.com`.

Acknowledgement

I started my eLearning career reading books authored by Dr. Michael Allen. He completely changed my perspective and gave me wonderful ideas on making eLearning engaging and interesting. Though I met him in person only a few years back, his work in the eLearning field has always inspired me. Thank you, Dr. Allen, for everything you do!

Nothing can beat the feeling of being a first-time author, and I'm thankful to my dear friend, Damien, for placing the trust in me and inviting me to be the coauthor of this book. Writing a book can be a daunting task with days and days of nonstop work. I could not have done it without Damien's encouragement and guidance. We crossed each and every stumbling block with a smile on our faces and determination to complete the task. Thank you, Damien--I couldn't have asked for a better coauthor!

I would like to dedicate this book to my friends and colleagues at Adobe for creating an industry-leading eLearning tool and giving us content creation power. Thank you Priyank, Ashish, Shameer, Akshay, Krishnan, Sankaram, Allen, Nipun, Gourav, Shambu, and all the amazing Captivate engineers. And special thanks to Tridib for writing the Foreword for this book and encouraging Damien and me for this initiative.

I would also like to thank Packt, for bringing this book to life, and our friends, Alice Acker and Paul Wilson, for reviewing this book. Your feedback helped us immensely in polishing the content.

Finally, I would like to thank my friends and family for always being there for me through thick and thin.

About the Author

Damien Bruyndonckx has an interest in teaching that dates back to his original training as an elementary school teacher. He began his career in 1998, teaching French as a foreign language in two elementary public schools in Louisiana, USA. In 2001, he came back to Belgium, his home country, and began to work as an IT trainer. He soon acquired the title of Adobe Certified Instructor on various Adobe products, which allowed him to work for a large number of customers and Adobe-authorized training centers across Europe. In 2009, he went back to teaching at IHECS, a higher education school of communications based in Brussels, where he was asked to implement eLearning in the curriculum. Thanks to his work at IHECS, Damien became an Adobe Education Leader in November 2011. Today, Damien is the co-owner and the pedagogical director of DiDaXo, a Belgium-based eLearning company. Damien is the author of four Adobe Captivate books, including *Adobe Captivate 7 for Mobile Learning*, published in August 2013, and *Mastering Adobe Captivate 8*, published in April 2015, both by Packt. You can find him speaking at various Captivate and eLearning-related events around the world. He lives in Thuin, Belgium, with his girlfriend and two children. Damien is a music lover and occasionally works as a sound and lighting technician in the entertainment industry. You can contact him on Twitter at @damienbkx and via his website at http://en.didaxo.be.

Acknowledgement

This is my fifth published book and the fourth edition of the *Mastering Adobe Captivate* series. But this one is very special to me. This is because I'm no longer the only name on the cover. Dr. Pooja Jaisingh has been my *partner in crime* in this project.

Dear Pooja, this book is the first long-term project we undertake together. It has been my privilege to have you as the coauthor of this book. As we progressed into writing, I've discovered a talented teacher, a hard worker, a true Captivate expert, and, above all, a good friend! Thank you so very much for accepting to be part of this crazy adventure. I've enjoyed our endless conversations on Skype and all the jokes we came up with along the way.

This book is also the result of the amazing work of our reviewers. Paul and Alice, I'm so very proud to call you guys my friends. I would like to thank you for the time you have spent reviewing this book. It is great to have you in the Adobe Captivate family.

I would like to dedicate this book to the men and women in the Adobe Captivate team. These are the individuals listed in the Credits section of the About Adobe Captivate menu item. I had a chance to meet some of them and to get a behind-the-scenes sneak peek of developing such an application. Sankaram, Gourav, Mohana, Haridoss, Shambu, and all your colleagues, thank you so much for giving us Captivate and the eLearning community portal.

Thank you to the Packt team that has made this book possible. Special thanks to Nikhil Borkar for his patience, flexibility, and support during the writing of this book.

Finally, I would like to thank the ones that share my life on a daily basis. Without the support, dedication, encouragement, and love of my sweet Céline, none of this would have been possible.

There are a lot of men and women behind this book. They have worked hard to provide you with the best possible resources about Adobe Captivate 2017. We all hope you'll enjoy reading, learning, and working with Adobe Captivate.

About the Reviewers

Alice Acker has worked in training, learning, and development for more than 30 years as a training manager in the U.S. Air Force, a graduate-level university instructor, and as the trainer/author of customer service policies and procedures for a Fortune 500 company. Since 2002, her focus has been on eLearning project management and development. Currently, she is the president of Aptus Learning Design, Inc., a woman veteran-owned small business registered with the Washington Department of Veteran Affairs. Alice has been working with Captivate since Macromedia Captivate (2004), and has been a prerelease tester starting with Captivate 5 (2010) through 2017. Alice has a theatre background and holds a master's degree in public administration (healthcare concentration) from the New York University. She also has a Certificate of Web Design from Olympic College.

Paul Wilson, the owner of Paul Wilson Learning and Design, has been designing and developing with Adobe Captivate for over ten years. Getting into the training field by accident, he has worked as a senior instructional designer for companies such as Bell, Canada, and the Greater Toronto Airports Authority. When he decided to start his own eLearning development company, Paul began creating video tutorials on `http://youtube.com/paulwilsonlearning` to share his knowledge of Adobe Captivate. As of 2017, his videos have been seen all over the world by hundreds of thousands of viewers, and his channel has over 5,600 subscribers. Paul now works with companies all over the globe, consulting and designing eLearning for a variety of learning opportunities, and he loves sharing what he has learned with his fellow designers and developers.

www.PacktPub.com

For support files and downloads related to your book, please visit www.PacktPub.com.

Did you know that Packt offers eBook versions of every book published, with PDF and ePub files available? You can upgrade to the eBook version at www.PacktPub.com and as a print book customer, you are entitled to a discount on the eBook copy. Get in touch with us at service@packtpub.com for more details.

At www.PacktPub.com, you can also read a collection of free technical articles, sign up for a range of free newsletters and receive exclusive discounts and offers on Packt books and eBooks.

https://www.packtpub.com/mapt

Get the most in-demand software skills with Mapt. Mapt gives you full access to all Packt books and video courses, as well as industry-leading tools to help you plan your personal development and advance your career.

Why subscribe?

- Fully searchable across every book published by Packt
- Copy and paste, print, and bookmark content
- On demand and accessible via a web browser

Customer Feedback

Thanks for purchasing this Packt book. At Packt, quality is at the heart of our editorial process. To help us improve, please leave us an honest review on this book's Amazon page at https://www.amazon.com/dp/1788295285.

If you'd like to join our team of regular reviewers, you can e-mail us at customerreviews@packtpub.com. We award our regular reviewers with free eBooks and videos in exchange for their valuable feedback. Help us be relentless in improving our products!

Table of Contents

Chapter 14: Finishing Touches and Publishing

Preface

Adobe Captivate is the industry-leading solution for authoring highly interactive eLearning content that can be delivered on any device. With Adobe Captivate, you can capture onscreen action, enhance eLearning projects, insert SCORM and xAPI-compliant quizzes, optimize content for multiscreen delivery, and publish the work in various formats (including Adobe Flash and HTML5) for easy deployment on virtually any desktop or mobile device.

*Mastering Adobe Captivate 2017, Fourth Edition,*is a comprehensive step-by-step learning guide to creating SCORM-compliant eLearning content including demonstrations, simulations, and quizzes that can be experienced on any device. The sample projects demonstrate virtually every feature of Adobe Captivate, giving you the expertise you need to create and deploy your own professional quality eLearning courses.

This book will guide you through the creation of eLearning projects, including a Demonstration, a Simulation, a Video Demo, a Responsive Project, and a SCORM-compliant Quiz.

What this book covers

Chapter 1, *Getting Started with Adobe Captivate 2017*, introduces Captivate as an eLearning solution. It drives you through the tool icons and panels of the Captivate interface. At the end of this chapter, you will have a chance to visit the finished sample applications that you will build during the course of this book.

Chapter 2, *Working with Standard Objects*, teaches you how to work with the standard objects of Adobe Captivate. These objects include the Text Caption, the Smart Shape, and the Image objects among others. Important Captivate workflows are also discussed in this chapter.

Chapter 3, *Working with Multimedia*, teaches you how to include and edit various types of multimedia elements in your eLearning projects. The tools covered in this chapter include the insertion of animations, video, and audio files in the project.

Chapter 4, *Working with the Timeline and Other Useful Tools*, covers various tools and features (such as the Alignment tools and Smart Guides) used to lay the objects out in the physical space of the slide. The use of the Timeline panel to synchronize the components of the project is also discussed in detail.

Chapter 5, *Working with Interactive Objects*, introduces the objects that bring interactivity to the project. These objects include the Rollover objects, the Drag and Drop interaction, Click Box, Text Entry Box, and Button. Adding interactivity allows you to design branching scenarios, which will be discussed in this chapter as well.

Chapter 6, *Crafting the Graphical Experience with Styles and Themes*, focuses on the aesthetic aspects of your projects. You will learn how to ensure visual consistency, both within a given project and across projects using Styles, Master Slides, Themes, and Templates.

Chapter 7, *Working with Quizzes*, discusses the powerful Quizzing engine of Captivate. You will import questions into your Captivate project using various techniques, review each and every question type of Captivate one by one, and integrate them into question pools to generate random quizzes. In the second part of this chapter, you will see how these interactions can be reported to a SCORM- or xAPI-compliant LMS to easily track your student's performance.

Chapter 8, *Capturing Onscreen Action*, covers the powerful screen capture engine of Captivate. You will learn how to capture interactive demonstrations and simulations using a wide variety of tools and techniques.

Chapter 9, *Producing a Video Demo*, focuses on producing a video tutorial from the start to finish. This chapter covers the specifics of a video project as compared to regular Captivate projects used in the previous chapters.

Chapter 10, *Creating a Responsive Project*, discusses the use of Fluid Boxes to create a Responsive Project. You will learn how to optimize your eLearning content for multiple screens and devices, including the desktop computer, the tablet, and the smartphone.

Chapter 11, *Using Captivate with Other Applications*, explores the relationship between Captivate and other Adobe and third-party applications. First, you will convert a PowerPoint presentation into a Captivate project. You will then export some Captivate data to Microsoft Word in order to localize a Captivate project. You will also import an Adobe Photoshop file and edit audio with Adobe Audition.

Chapter 12, *Creating Accessible eLearning*, discusses how and why it is important to make your eLearning courses accessible for people with hearing, visual, and mobility disabilities. You will learn the steps to add accessibility text, Closed Captions, keyboard shortcuts, and tabbing order to the slides and objects in your Captivate projects to make them accessible for learners with special needs.

Chapter 13, *Working with Variables and Advanced Actions,* unleashes the true power of Captivate by exploring Variables and Advanced Actions. These features will help you design and develop highly interactive eLearning content that offers a unique experience to each and every learner.

Chapter 14, *Finishing Touches and Publishing,* covers project-wide preferences and teaches you how to publish your eLearning content in various formats. First, you will make your projects ready for publishing by modifying the project-level options and preferences. One of these options is the Skin Editor, which lets you customize the playback controls and the table of contents of your projects. In the second part of this chapter, you will make your projects available to the outside world by publishing them in various formats, including Adobe Flash, HTML5, video, and PDF.

What you need for this book

You need the latest version of Adobe Captivate 2017 (available as a free 30-day trial version on the Adobe website) to complete the exercises in this book. Some exercises require the installation of the Adobe eLearning assets and Text-To-Speech voice agents. Both these packages are part of your Adobe Captivate license and are available for free on the Adobe website.

Other requirements are as follows:

- Adobe Media Encoder 2015 (AME 2015 is part of the Captivate 2017 download)
- A modern web browser with the latest version of the Flash Player installed.
- Microsoft PowerPoint 2003 or higher (optional)
- Microsoft Word 2003 or higher (optional)
- Latest version of Adobe Photoshop CC (optional)
- Latest version of Adobe Audition CC (optional)

Who this book is for

If you are a teacher, instructional designer, eLearning developer, or a human resources manager who wants to implement eLearning, then this book is for you. A basic knowledge of your OS is all it takes to create the next generation of responsive eLearning content.

Conventions

In this book, you will find a number of text styles that distinguish between different kinds of information. Here are some examples of these styles and an explanation of their meaning.

Code words in text, database table names, folder names, filenames, file extensions, pathnames, dummy URLs, user input, and Twitter handles are shown as follows: "Video Demo projects use the .cpvc file extension and have a specific user interface."

New terms and important words are shown in bold. Words that you see on the screen, for example, in menus or dialog boxes, appear in the text like this: "Clicking the **Next** button moves you to the next screen."

Warnings or important notes appear in a box like this.

Tips and tricks appear like this.

Reader feedback

Feedback from our readers is always welcome. Let us know what you think about this book—what you liked or disliked. Reader feedback is important for us as it helps us develop titles that you will really get the most out of.

To send us general feedback, simply e-mail feedback@packtpub.com, and mention the book's title in the subject of your message.

If there is a topic that you have expertise in and you are interested in either writing or contributing to a book, see our author guide at www.packtpub.com/authors.

Customer support

Now that you are the proud owner of a Packt book, we have a number of things to help you to get the most from your purchase.

Downloading the example code

You can download the example code files for this book from your account at `http://www.packtpub.com`. If you purchased this book elsewhere, you can visit `http://www.packtpub.com/support` and register to have the files e-mailed directly to you.

You can download the code files by following these steps:

1. Log in or register to our website using your e-mail address and password.
2. Hover the mouse pointer on the **SUPPORT** tab at the top.
3. Click on **Code Downloads & Errata**.
4. Enter the name of the book in the **Search** box.
5. Select the book for which you're looking to download the code files.
6. Choose from the drop-down menu where you purchased this book from.
7. Click on **Code Download**.

You can also download the code files by clicking on the Code Files button on the book's webpage at the Packt Publishing website. This page can be accessed by entering the book's name in the Search box. Please note that you need to be logged in to your Packt account.

Once the file is downloaded, please make sure that you unzip or extract the folder using the latest version of:

- WinRAR / 7-Zip for Windows
- Zipeg / iZip / UnRarX for Mac
- 7-Zip / PeaZip for Linux

The code bundle for the book is also hosted on GitHub at `https://github.com/PacktPublishing/Mastering-Adobe-Captivate-2017-Fourth-Edition`. We also have other code bundles from our rich catalog of books and videos available at `https://github.com/PacktPublishing/`. Check them out!

Downloading the color images of this book

We also provide you with a PDF file that has color images of the screenshots/diagrams used in this book. The color images will help you better understand the changes in the output. You can download this file from `https://www.packtpub.com/sites/default/files/downloads/MasteringAdobeCaptivate2017FourthEdition.pdf`.

Errata

Although we have taken every care to ensure the accuracy of our content, mistakes do happen. If you find a mistake in one of our books—maybe a mistake in the text or the code—we would be grateful if you could report this to us. By doing so, you can save other readers from frustration and help us improve subsequent versions of this book. If you find any errata, please report them by visiting http://www.packtpub.com/submit-errata, selecting your book, clicking on the **Errata Submission Form** link, and entering the details of your errata. Once your errata are verified, your submission will be accepted and the errata will be uploaded to our website or added to any list of existing errata under the Errata section of that title.

To view the previously submitted errata, go to https://www.packtpub.com/books/content/support and enter the name of the book in the search field. The required information will appear under the Errata section.

Piracy

Piracy of copyrighted material on the Internet is an ongoing problem across all media. At Packt, we take the protection of our copyright and licenses very seriously. If you come across any illegal copies of our works in any form on the Internet, please provide us with the location address or website name immediately so that we can pursue a remedy.

Please contact us at copyright@packtpub.com with a link to the suspected pirated material.

We appreciate your help in protecting our authors and our ability to bring you valuable content.

Questions

If you have a problem with any aspect of this book, you can contact us at questions@packtpub.com, and we will do our best to address the problem.

1
Getting Started with Adobe Captivate 2017

Welcome to *Mastering Adobe Captivate 2017, Fourth Edition*. Since its introduction in 2004, Captivate has been the leading solution for authoring interactive eLearning content. In the beginning, it was a very simple screen-capture utility called FlashCam. In 2002, a company named eHelp acquired FlashCam and turned it into a full-fledged eLearning authoring tool called RoboDemo. In 2004, another company called Macromedia acquired eHelp and changed the name of the product once again. **Macromedia Captivate** was born. A few months later, Adobe acquired Macromedia and, consequently, Macromedia Captivate became **Adobe Captivate**.

As the years passed, Adobe released Captivate 2, 3, and 4-adding tools, objects, and features along the way. One of the most significant events in the Captivate history took place in July 2010, when Adobe released Captivate 5. For that release, Adobe engineers rewrote the code of the application from the ground up. As a result, Captivate 5 was the first version to be available on both macOS and Windows. Version 6 was another milestone for Captivate as it was the first version to offer an HTML5 publishing option. More recently, version 8 has introduced the ability to create Responsive Projects, as well as a brand new user interface. A Responsive Project allows you, the eLearning developer, to automatically adjust the layout of your Captivate projects to fit the various screen sizes of tablet and smartphone devices. This makes mobile learning a whole lot easier and more powerful by creating content that looks perfect in different views.

At the time of writing this, the latest version of Captivate is called Captivate 2017. Captivate 2017 introduces many new features and enhancements, including an exciting new approach to responsive design called **Fluid Boxes**. Other new features introduced in Captivate 2017 include the integration of the Typekit font library, the ability to customize Closed Captions on a slide-to-slide basis, a redesigned Slide Notes panel, and tons of other enhancements.

With all this power only one click away, it is easy to overload your projects with lots of complex audiovisual effects and sophisticated interactions that can ultimately drive the learner away from the primary objective of every Captivate course: learning.

While working with Captivate, never forget that Captivate is an eLearning authoring tool. At the most basic level, it simply means that you, the developer, and your audience are united by a very special kind of relationship: a student-teacher relationship. Therefore, from now on-and for the rest of the book-you will not be called *the developer* or *the programmer*, but *the teacher*. The ones who will view your finished applications will not be the *users* or the *visitors*, but will be called *the learners* or *the students*. You will see that this changes everything.

In this chapter, you will:

- Discover the available options to install Captivate
- See the general steps of the Captivate production process
- Tour and customize the Captivate 2017 interface
- Work with panels and workspaces
- View the completed sample applications you will work with during the course of this book

Getting Captivate

Before you can start working with Captivate, you have to download and install the software. In this section, you will discover the three ways that Adobe makes Captivate available to you.

The Captivate perpetual license

This is the old-fashioned way of obtaining the software. You buy Captivate and get a serial number to activate your installation. The serial number is valid for a specific version of Captivate, and for a specific platform (macOS or Windows) only. Once activated, that version of Captivate is permanently available on your computer. With this option, you get all the functionalities of Captivate, and you can start working on your eLearning projects right away! You also get all the patches and bug fixes for the version you bought. This book works flawlessly with the Captivate perpetual license.

See the Captivate page on the Adobe website at
`http://www.adobe.com/products/captivate.html`.

You can download and use this version of Captivate free of charge for 30 days. This should be more than enough time for you to go through the exercises of this book. However, once the trial period is over, you will not have access to Captivate unless you convert your trial to a licensed version. This can be a perpetual or a subscription license.

Download your Captivate 30-day trial from
`http://www.adobe.com/go/trycaptivate/`.

The Captivate subscription

With this licensing model, you subscribe to Captivate on a monthly basis. This means that you pay a certain amount each month to keep using Captivate. The main benefit of the subscription model is that you automatically get all the updates as they are released. The subscription model is the best way to ensure that you have access to the latest version of Captivate. Note that the subscription is just another licensing model; the software itself is identical to the perpetual licensing model.

More information on the various Captivate licensing models can be found at `http://www.adobe.com/products/captivate/buying-guide.html`.

Although the Captivate subscription model is very similar to the way Adobe Creative Cloud works, Captivate is-at the time of writing-*not* a part of the Creative Cloud.

Captivate and the Creative Cloud
If you already have a Creative Cloud subscription, you'll need another subscription for Adobe Captivate.

Captivate in Technical Communication Suite

The **Technical Communication Suite (TCS)** is yet another bundle of applications from Adobe. It is designed to create technical content such as help files and user guides. TCS includes applications such as RoboHelp, FrameMaker, Acrobat Professional, and of course, Captivate. The Technical Communication Suite itself is also available under both the perpetual and the subscription licensing model.

For more information on TCS, visit
`http://www.adobe.com/products/technicalcommunicationsuite.html.`

A first look at a typical production workflow

Creating content with Captivate is a three-step process, or to be exact, a four-step process. However, only three of the four steps take place in Captivate. That's why we like to refer to the first step as *step zero*!

Step zero - the preproduction phase

This is the only step of the process that does not involve working with the Captivate application. Depending on the project you are planning, it can last from a few minutes to a few months. This step is probably the most important step of the entire process as it is where you actually create the scenarios and the storyboards. This is where you develop the pedagogical approach that will drive the entire project. What will you teach the students? In what order will you introduce the topics? How and when will you assess the students' knowledge? These are some of the very important questions you should answer before opening Captivate for the first time. Step zero is where the teacher's skills fully express themselves.

Blog post - Scenario-based training

In this series of posts on the Adobe eLearning community portal, Dr. Pooja Jaisingh shares her experience in creating scenario-based training. These posts clearly stress the importance of *step zero*, and give you a first, high-level approach to the Captivate production process. The first post of the series can be found at
`https://elearning.adobe.com/2012/03/my-experience-with-creating-a-scenario-based-course-part-1/.`

Step one - creating the slides

At the most basic level, a typical Captivate project is a collection of slides, just like a Microsoft PowerPoint presentation. So your first task when creating a new Captivate file is probably to create a bunch of slides to work with. There are several ways to do this:

- First, Captivate has the ability to record any action you perform onscreen. You typically use this ability to create software-related interactive training or simulations. You use your mouse to perform actions on your computer, and behind the scenes, Captivate watches and records any action you do using a sophisticated screen capture engine based on screenshots. Each of these screenshots becomes a slide in your new Captivate project. Using the screen capture feature of Captivate is covered in Chapter 8, *Capturing Onscreen Action*.
- Very often, though, the Captivate project you are working on has nothing to do with software-related skills. In this case, you don't need to use screen capture to take screenshots. You create the slides entirely within Captivate. This is the preferred approach for new training materials that don't require the screen capture capabilities.
- A third solution is to import the slides from Microsoft PowerPoint. You typically use this solution to convert existing training material made with PowerPoint into interactive online training modules, but it is not considered best practice for new training material. Importing PowerPoint slides into Captivate is covered in Chapter 11, *Using Captivate with Other Applications*.

Step two - the editing phase

This step is the most time-consuming phase of the entire process. This is where your project slowly takes shape to become an actual interactive course module.

In this step, you arrange the final sequence of actions, record narrations, add objects to the slides (such as Text Captions and Buttons), arrange those objects in the Timeline, add title and ending slides, develop the advanced interactions, create the Question Slides of the quiz, configure the quiz reporting options, and so on. At the end of this step, the project should be ready for publication. Sometimes, it can take several rounds of edits until you have a project that is ready to publish.

Note that, for most projects, step one and step two overlap. Unless you use screen capture, there is no clear distinction between step one and step two. It is ok to go back and forth between those two steps when developing your next Captivate project.

Step three - the publishing phase

Step three is where you make your project available to your learners. Captivate allows you to publish your course modules in a wide variety of formats. The two formats that you will use most of the time are the Flash and the HTML5 formats.

- Flash is the historical publishing format of Captivate. It is still widely used today. Publishing the project in Flash makes the deployment of your eLearning courses very easy; only the Flash Player plugin is needed. The very same Flash Player that is used to read Flash-enabled websites or YouTube videos is all you need to play back your published Captivate projects. The major caveat of this publishing format is that it is not supported on mobile devices.

- Captivate can also publish your projects in HTML5, which makes the project available on any device, including desktops and laptops, as well as tablets and smartphones. In today's technological landscape, HTML5 has become the preferred format for publishing your online courses for computers and mobile devices.

Note that some features of Captivate are only available either in Flash or in HTML5. For example, a Responsive Project can only be published in HTML5, while a Text Animation object can only be published in Flash. It is very important to know the publishing format you will use before starting the development of a new project.

The end of the Flash Player

As we were writing this chapter, Adobe made an announcement that they would no longer develop and maintain the Flash Player plugin beyond 2020, and that they encourage content developers to migrate to HTML5. This is not a surprise, but it stresses the important evolution that HTML5 represents for our industry. It also clearly states that Adobe Captivate is bound to end up as an HTML5-only authoring tool somewhere in the future. You can see the original Adobe announcement at `https://blogs.adobe.com/conversations/2017/07/adobe-flash-update.html` and the announcement from the Captivate team at `https://elearning.adobe.com/2017/07/flash-the-future-of-interactive-content-for-elearning/`.

Captivate can also publish the project as a standalone application (.exe on Windows and .app on Macintosh) or as video files that can be easily uploaded to YouTube and viewed on a tablet or smartphone.

Step three will be covered in great detail in Chapter 14, *Finishing Touches and Publishing*.

Touring the Captivate interface

In this book, we will cover the three steps of the process requiring the use of Captivate. You will discover that Captivate has specific tools to handle each of these three steps.

Downloading the example code

Before you start reading this section, it is important that you download the sample files we refer to throughout this book. You can download the sample files for all Packt Publishing books that you have purchased from your account at http://www.packtpub.com. If you purchased this book elsewhere, you can visit http://www.packtpub.com/support and register to have the files emailed directly to you.

You will now discover this new interface using the following steps:

1. Open Captivate.
2. If needed, click the **Recent** tab at the top of the Welcome screen.
3. Click the **Browse** button at the bottom of the **Recent** tab of the Welcome screen.
4. Open the Chapter01/encoderDemo_800.cptx file in the exercise folder.

Your screen should look similar to this screenshot:

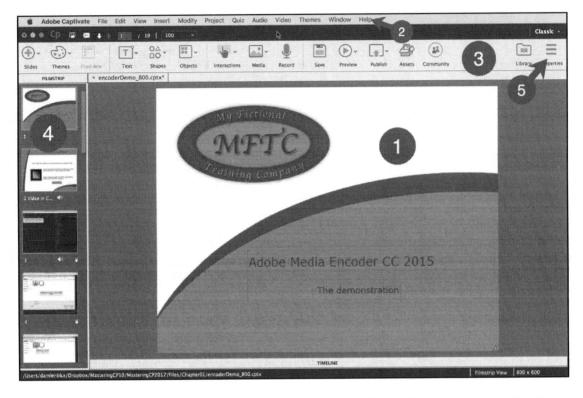

The default Captivate screen looks very simple and clean. The main area is covered by the **Stage** (1). The Stage is where you lay out the objects that make up each slide of the project. The objects on the Stage will appear in your course. The objects in the Scrap Area (the grey area around the slide) will not show in the slide itself.

At the very top of the screen is the **Menu bar** (2). The Menu bar gives you access to a wide range of Captivate features.

Below the Menu bar is the main **Toolbar** of Captivate 2017 (3). The Toolbar is primarily used to insert new slides and new objects into the project, but it also contains important tools for operations, such as previewing, publishing, and saving.

On the left side of the screen is the **Filmstrip (4)**. It shows the sequence of slides in your Captivate project. The primary use of the **Filmstrip** is to let you select the slide(s) you want to work with, but it can also be used to perform basic operations on the slides, such as reordering or deleting slides.

5. At the far right side of the Toolbar, click the **Properties** icon **(5)**.

This action reveals the **Properties** inspector. The **Properties** inspector is one of the most important components of Captivate. It is used to control and adjust the properties of the selected object.

6. Click the **Properties** button on the Toolbar again to hide the **Properties** inspector.
7. Click the **Library** icon located just next to the **Properties** icon to open the **Library** panel.

The **Library** panel is another very important component of Captivate. It maintains a list of all the assets (such as images, audio clips, animations, and so on.) included in the current project.

8. Click the **Library** button on the Toolbar to close the **Library**.
9. Click the **Timeline** button that stretches across the bottom of the screen. This action reveals the **Timeline** panel.

The **Timeline** panel is used to arrange the sequence of objects on the current slide. In short, you use the **Timeline** panel to decide when an object appears on the stage and how long it stays visible. This panel is also used to set up the stacking order of the objects. You will learn more about the **Timeline** in Chapter 4, *Working with the Timeline and Other Useful Tools*.

It is possible to open many panels at the same time.

10. Click the **Properties** button on the Toolbar to reopen the **Properties** inspector.

Both the **Timeline** *and* the **Properties** inspector should now be open.

Because the **Properties** inspector, **Library**, and **Timeline** are the most important panels of Captivate; they are only one mouse click away on the default user interface. However, Captivate contains many other panels that give you access to a myriad of interesting tools. To get the most out of Captivate, you should know how to turn panels on and off.

11. Open the **Window** menu.

The **Window** menu displays a list of all the panels that are available in Adobe Captivate. Note the checkmark in front of the **Filmstrip, Timeline,** and **Library** entries of the **Window** menu. This reminds you that these panels and icons are currently visible on the interface.

12. Click the **Library** menu item of the **Window** menu. This action removes the **Library** icon from the Toolbar.

13. Click the **Window | Library** menu item again to reactivate the **Library** icon of the Toolbar and open the **Library** panel.

14. Click the **Window | Slide Notes** menu item to open the **Slide Notes** panel.

The **Slide Notes** panel appears at the bottom of the screen next to the **Timeline** panel, as shown in the following screenshot:

If you have used Captivate before, the **Slide Notes** panel is one of those areas that has been entirely updated in the Captivate 2017 release. Let's now open one more panel.

15. Use the **Window | HTML5 Tracker** menu item to open the **HTML5 Tracker** panel.

The **HTML5 Tracker** panel lists the features and objects used in the current project that are not supported in HTML5. There should be one unsupported feature listed in the **HTML5 Tracker** panel because the transitions between slides are not supported in HTML5.

Note that this panel is floating on top of the interface. This is very different from the **Slide Notes** panel you opened earlier that was attached (docked) at the bottom of the interface.

Each panel of Captivate is either docked or floating. Also note that in Captivate 2017, it is not possible by default to dock a floating panel or undock a docked panel.

The interface is now very different from what it was when you first opened Captivate.

16. Exit Captivate without saving any changes made to the open file.
17. Reopen Captivate.

When Captivate reopens, you should see the **Recent** tab of the Welcome screen by default. There is a thumbnail showing the last open project(s).

18. Double-click the **encoderDemo_800** thumbnail to reopen the project.

When the project reopens, note that the default Captivate interface is displayed, even though many more panels were open when you exited Captivate.

Thanks to these little experiments, you were exposed to some important basic concepts about the Captivate interface. Before moving on, let's summarize what you have learned so far:

- The Captivate interface is composed of panels laid out around the main editing area called the Stage.
- The grey area around the Stage is called the Scrap Area. Objects on the Scrap Area do not show in your online course.
- By default, most of the panels are hidden, making the interface simple and clean.
- The **Properties** inspector, the **Library** panel, and the **Timeline** are the most important and most commonly used components of Captivate. This is why they are easily accessible from the default interface.
- Some panels of Captivate are not immediately available on the default interface. You must use the **Window** menu to show and hide these panels.
- The panels of Captivate are either docked on the interface or floating on top of it.
- When you close and restart Captivate, the interface returns to its default layout.

Using the Advanced Interface Mode

If you are used to other Adobe tools, such as Photoshop, InDesign, or Illustrator, the default behavior of the Captivate interface probably looks very different. Luckily, there is a way to make the Captivate interface behave similarly to the interface of other popular Adobe tools. This is called the **Advanced Interface Mode**.

1. Use the **Adobe Captivate | Preferences** (macOS) or the **Edit | Preferences** (Windows) menu item to open the **Preferences** dialog of Captivate.

2. In the **General Settings** category of the **Preferences**, select the **Enable custom workspaces/panel undocking** option, as shown in the following screenshot:

3. Click **OK** to validate the new option and close the **Preferences** dialog.
4. As indicated in the **Preferences** dialog box, restart Adobe Captivate to enable the new option (make sure you don't save the eventual changes made to the file).
5. When Captivate restarts, double-click the **encoderDemo_800** thumbnail of the **Recent** tab of the Welcome screen to reopen the project.

Note that the **Properties** and **Library** icons of the Toolbar are no longer displayed.

6. Go to **Window | Properties** to reopen the **Properties** inspector.
7. Use the same procedure to reopen the **Library**, the **Timeline**, and **Slide Notes** panels.
8. Return to the **Window** menu again, this time to activate the **HTML5 Tracker** floating panel.
9. At the bottom of the interface, click the **Timeline** button to reveal the **Timeline** panel.

The interface should now look pretty much the same as when you closed Captivate earlier in this chapter.

10. Restart Captivate one more time without saving the changes made to the project.
11. When Captivate restarts, reopen the project by clicking the **encoderDemo_800** thumbnail on the **Recent** tab of the Welcome screen.

In Advanced Interface Mode, the panel layout is always maintained when you restart Captivate.

In the next section, you will take a closer look at those panels. But first, let's first have a quick summary of what has been covered in this section:

- To make the Captivate interface behave like the interface of other common Adobe tools, you must switch to the Advanced Interface Mode.
- To enable the Advanced Interface Mode, select **Enable custom workspaces/panel undocking** in the Preferences box of Captivate. It is necessary to close and restart Captivate for this change to take effect.
- In the Advanced Interface Mode, the **Library** and the **Properties** icons of the Toolbar are not displayed. Enabling and disabling panels is done exclusively through the **Window** menu.
- In the Advanced Interface Mode, the workspace is always maintained when you restart Captivate.

Working with panels

You already know that Captivate contains a lot of panels and that those panels can be shown or hidden using the **Window** menu. In the Advanced Interface Mode, the Captivate interface offers even more flexibility. In this section, you will learn how to move the panels and create a unique custom screen.

1. Place your mouse on the black line at the top of the floating **HTML5 Tracker** panel.
2. Drag the panel to the right and drop it on top of the **Properties** and **Library** labels in the top right corner of the screen.

When a panel is moved above a possible docking location, a blue outline appears on the screen. Releasing the mouse at that moment docks the panel at the location highlighted by the blue outline.

This action docks the **HTML5 tracker** panel with the **Properties** inspector and the **Library** panel, as shown in the following screenshot:

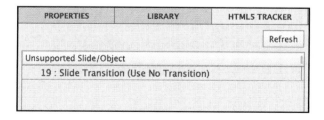

This first action illustrates how to dock the panels that are initially floating on the interface. You will now do the opposite to illustrate that a panel that is initially docked can be turned into a floating panel:

3. Place your mouse on top of the **Library** label on the right side of the screen.
4. Drag the **Library** panel out of the **Library/Properties/HTML5 Tracker** group and drop it on top of the stage.

The **Library** panel is now a floating panel, even though it was docked by default. You have now arranged the panels in a truly unique way. This customized arrangement of your panels is called a **workspace**.

Creating a new workspace

The **Advanced Interface Mode** of Captivate allows you to apply your own unique (custom) workspaces. Depending on the project you are working on, the size of your computer screen, your working habits, and so on, you might want to have several workspaces and quickly switch between them. In this section, you will first learn how to reset the default workspace. Then, you will create and save a new custom workspace.

The default workspace you see when you first open Captivate is called the **Classic** workspace, as shown in the top right corner of your screen.

1. Click the **Classic** button at the top right corner of the screen.
2. Choose **Reset Classic** in the drop down menu, as shown in the following screenshot.

After doing this, your Captivate screen reverts to what it looked like when you opened the application at the beginning of this chapter:

The default **Classic** workspace is an excellent starting point for defining a custom workspace.

3. Use the **Window | Timing Properties** menu item to activate the **Timing** panel on the right side of the screen.
4. Select the **Adobe Media Encode CC 2015** title on the slide and note that the **Timing** panel updates.

Just like the **Properties** inspector, the **Timing** panel always shows the properties pertaining to the object you select. Note that the **Timing** panel of Captivate precisely sets the timing of that object and also applies effects to that object.

5. Use the **Window | Properties** menu item to activate the **Properties** inspector.
6. Drag the **Properties** inspector out of the **Properties/Timing** group and drop it on top of the **Filmstrip** label on the other side of the screen. This docks the **Properties** inspector with the **Filmstrip** panel.

After this last action, your screen should look like the following screenshot:

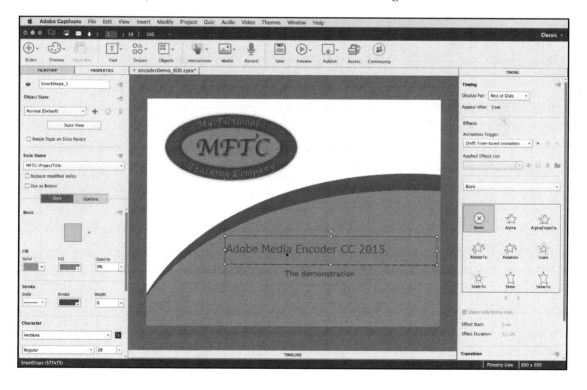

This workspace is very practical when you have to precisely define the timing and apply effects to the selected object. You will now save this panel layout as a new workspace.

7. Click the same **Classic** button you used earlier at the top right corner of the screen.
8. Choose **New Workspace** from the drop down menu.
9. In the **New Workspace** dialog, name your new workspace Timing and click **OK**.

Note that a **Timing** button now replaces the **Classic** button. You can use this button to switch between the Classic workspace and your own custom Timing workspace!

10. Click the **Timing** button at the top right corner of the screen.
11. Select the **Classic** workspace in the drop down menu to reapply the default Classic workspace.
12. Click the **Classic** button and reapply the **Timing** workspace.

This demonstrates how you can quickly switch between your saved workspaces.

Extra credit

You now know all the tools to create custom workspaces. Take some time to experiment with these tools on your own. Try turning panels on and off using the **Window** menu. Explore the other panels of Captivate, such as the **Question Pool** and the **Swatch Manager**. When you feel like you have a great workspace, save it under a name of your choice.

Renaming and deleting custom workspaces

If you ever need to rename or delete a custom workspace, use the following steps:

1. Go to **Window** | **Workspace** | **Manage Workspace**.

Note that the **Window** | **Workspace** menu displays the very same information as the workspace switcher button at the top right corner of the screen.

2. In the **Manage Workspace** dialog, choose the workspace to delete/rename.

Note that the default **Classic** workspace is not listed. This means that this default workspace cannot be renamed or deleted.

3. Click the **Rename** or **Delete** button. In this example, click the **OK** button to close the box without any changes.

4. Open the workspace switcher one more time to reapply the **Classic** workspace before moving on to the next topic.

Updating a workspace

There is no menu item to update an existing workspace. If you want to update an existing workspace, use the **New Workspace** menu item and give the new workspace the name of the existing workspace you want to update.

Workspaces in normal mode

You can return to the normal interface mode using the following steps:

1. Use the **Adobe Captivate | Preferences** (macOS) or **Edit | Preferences** (Windows) menu item to reopen the **Preferences** dialog of Captivate.

2. In the **General Settings** category, deselect the **Enable custom workspaces/panel undocking** and click **OK** to validate.

3. Restart Captivate without saving the changes made to the open project.

4. When Captivate reopens, double-click the **encoderDemo_800** thumbnail to reopen the project.

Confirm that the **Properties** and **Library** buttons are back in the top right corner. This indicates that you are back in normal interface mode.

5. Click the workspace switcher button at the top right corner of your screen. It should currently read **Classic**.

In normal interface mode (that is, when the **Enable custom workspaces/panel undocking** option of the **Preferences** is *not* selected), only the **Classic** workspace can be applied or reset. If you want to use your custom *Timing* workspace again, you first need to return to Advanced Interface Mode and to restart Captivate.

Before moving on to the next topic, these are the key points to keep in mind when creating custom workspaces:

- It is necessary to set Captivate to Advanced Interface Mode to dock and undock panels and create new workspaces.
- Use the **Window** | **Workspace** | **New Workspace** menu item to save the current panel layout as a new workspace. This menu item is also accessible from the workspace switcher at the top right corner of your screen.
- Use the **Window** | **Workspace** | **Manage Workspace** menu item to rename or delete your custom workspaces.
- To update an existing workspace, use the **New Workspace** command to give the new workspace the same name as the workspace you want to update.
- The default **Classic** workspace of Captivate cannot be deleted or renamed.
- In normal interface mode, only the default **Classic** workspace is available.

Join the Captivate community

One of the most recent additions to the Toolbar is the **Community** icon. Clicking this icon opens the Adobe eLearning Community portal inside Captivate.

The Adobe Community portal is a website that is available at `http://elearning.adobe.com` using a standard web browser.

The Adobe eLearning Community Portal is the best place to find information and to interact with other Captivate users. The elLearning Community Portal features the following:

- Blog posts from members of the community.
- Showcases of Captivate course modules.
- A very active forum where you can ask questions and get answers from some of the most influential and popular Captivate users.
- A wide library of video tutorials.
- An agenda of upcoming events, including webinars hosted by members of the Captivate team or members of the community (including us, the authors of this book!).
- And much more!

Performing activities on the eLearning community (such as answering questions, writing blogs/articles, and so on) gives you an opportunity to score points and enhance your level as a product expert. These points can be turned into a wide variety of exciting incentives, including free Captivate licenses and invitations to live events.

See the full listing of levels and incentives at `https://elearning.adobe.com/levels/`.

From newbies to legends, there is a place for everyone on the eLearning portal!

Exploring the sample applications

Now that you know a bit more about the Captivate interface, let's take a look at the sample applications you will build in this book. These applications are designed to showcase almost every single feature of Captivate. Use them as a reference if there is something unclear while you are working through the exercises.

Experiencing the Encoder demonstration

The first application that you will explore is a typical Captivate project. It uses the screen capture feature of Captivate to create a screenshot-based course module.

1. With the `Chapter01/encoderDemo_800.cptx` file still open, click the **Preview** icon on the Toolbar.
2. From the drop down list, choose the **Project** item to preview the entire project.

Captivate generates a temporary file and opens it in the floating **Preview** pane. Follow the onscreen instructions to go through the project. This puts you in the same situation as a learner viewing this eLearning content for the first time.

This first sample project is called a **Demonstration**. As the name suggests, a demonstration is used to demonstrate something to the learner. Consequently, the learner is passive and simply watches whatever is going on. In a demonstration, the Mouse object is shown. It moves and clicks automatically. If the learners move their own mouse, it will not affect the content in any way.

This particular demonstration features some of the most popular Captivate objects, including Text Captions, Highlight Boxes, and Smart Shapes. The audio narration was generated by Captivate's Text-To-Speech tool. We have simply typed the narration in the Slide Notes panel, and Captivate turned it into audio files using the voice of a predefined speech agent. You will learn more about audio and Text-To-Speech in `Chapter 3`, *Working with Multimedia.*

Another popular feature in Adobe Captivate is the ability to add Closed Captions to the audio narration. If you have used Captivate before, this is yet another area of the application that has been completely updated in Captivate 2017. You will learn more about Closed Captions and Accessibility in `Chapter 12`, *Creating Accessible eLearning.*

3. When you reach the end of the project, close the **Preview** pane.
4. Take some time to take a closer look at the **Preview** icon as shown in the following screenshot:

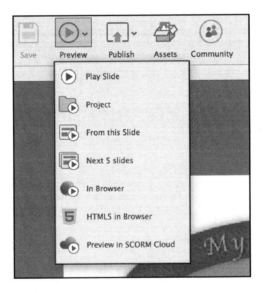

This is one of the icons you'll use the most during this book and when you design your courses. It has seven options that control which part of the project you want to preview and how you want to preview it. Note that each of these options is associated with a keyboard shortcut which will be different depending on the system you work on (macOS or Windows). Place your mouse on top of each of the items to see the associated keyboard shortcut in a tooltip.

Previewing a Responsive Project
When in a Responsive Project, the preview options will not behave exactly as described in the following list. Responsive Projects will be covered in `Chapter 10`, *Creating a Responsive Project*.

Let's now describe the options of the **Preview** icon in more detail:

- **Play Slide**: This option plays the current slide in the Captivate interface. It is the only preview option that does not open the default web browser or a floating preview pane, so the **Play Slide** option is not able to render all the features of Captivate. Previewing a single slide is a good option to quickly test the timing of the objects.
- **Project**: This option generates a temporary Flash file and plays the entire project in the Preview pane.
- **From this Slide**: This option generates a temporary Flash file. Captivate opens the Preview pane and plays the project from the currently selected slide to the end.
- **Next 5 slides**: This is a great option to quickly test a specific sequence of the project. Captivate opens the Preview pane to play a temporary Flash file containing five slides, starting from the currently selected slide.

You can use the **Defaults** category in Preferences to change the number of slides you want to include in the Preview when using this option. To access the Preferences, use the **Adobe Captivate | Preferences** (macOS) or the **Edit | Preferences** (Windows) menu item.

- **In Browser**: Using this preview option, you can see the project in a context very close to the one that will be used by your learners. Captivate generates a temporary Flash file as well as a temporary HTML file. It then plays the entire project in the default browser.
- **HTML5 in Browser**: This option is very close to the previous one. The only difference is that the project is published in HTML5, JavaScript, CSS, and images. It is then played in the default web browser. Note that some features and objects of Captivate are not supported in the HTML5 output. If you plan on publishing your project in HTML5, make sure you use this preview option to ensure that the features, animations, and objects you use in your project are supported in HTML5.

- **Preview in SCORM Cloud**: You can use this preview option to test the reporting features of your course. It generates a temporary Flash file of the project and uploads it to SCORM Cloud. When the upload is complete, you can see your project in a special preview pane, along with a log of all communications exchanged between the LMS and your content. You will learn more about SCORM, LMS, Quiz, and reporting in Chapter 7, *Working with Quizzes*. Note that this preview option is the only one that is not associated with a keyboard shortcut.

Floating and Modal panels

In Captivate, a panel can be floating or docked. When a panel floats, the tools and switches on the other panels are still active. But when the **Preview** panel is open, only the buttons of that panel are active, while the tools of the other panels are no longer active. The **Preview** panel is said to be a *Modal* floating panel because it disables every tool situated on other panels. Also note that the **Preview** panel cannot be docked.

Experiencing the Encoder simulation

You will now open another sample project. Actually, it is not a real *other* project, but another version of the Encoder demonstration you worked with in the previous section:

1. Use the **File** | **Open** menu item to open the Chapter01/encoderSim_800.cptx file situated in the exercises download.
2. Once the file is open, click the **Preview** icon on the Toolbar and choose the **In Browser** option.
3. The project opens in the default web browser and starts playing automatically.

This project is made of exactly the same slides and assets as the demonstration you saw in the previous section. When the project reaches slide 3, it stops and waits for you to interact with the course. This is the main difference between a demonstration and a simulation.

In Captivate, a **simulation** is a project where the learner is active. In a simulation, the Mouse object is hidden, as learners use their own mouse to click around the screen and progress toward the end of the course. The fact that the students are active implies a new level of complexity; the learners can perform either the correct or the incorrect action.

In each case, the course must react accordingly. This concept is known as **branching**. This means that each student experiences the course module based on their own actions.

4. Follow the onscreen instructions and try to perform the correct actions, as described in the demonstration project of the previous section.
5. If you ever perform the incorrect action, a red **Failure Caption** will help you find the right answer. Failure captions are one of the most basic forms of branching. The caption shows only if the student's answer is incorrect.
6. On slide 12, you will fill the new width of the video file. Type 400 and press *Enter* to continue to the next step.
7. When you are done, close your browser and return to Captivate.

This second sample file features pretty much the same Captivate objects as the demonstration you completed in the previous section. Both typing and mouse actions are replaced by interactive objects. The Mouse is replaced by **Click Boxes** and a **Text Entry Box** replaces the typing object on slide 11. These interactive objects can stop the course and wait for the learner to interact. Using the interactive objects of Captivate will be covered in Chapter 5, *Working with Interactive Objects*.

Both the Encoder demonstration and simulation are based on the same screenshots. To create these sample courses, the first two steps of the production process described earlier were used:

- In step one (the slide creation step), the actions were performed in the actual Adobe Media Encoder. They were recorded by Captivate behind the scenes.
- In step two (the postproduction step), the course was edited in Captivate. Audio and Closed Captions were added, the title and ending slides were created, timing was adjusted, and so on.
- Step three (the publishing step) has not yet been performed on these files.

Experiencing the Encoder Video Demo

Video Demo mode is a special recording mode of Captivate that is used to produce .mp4 video files. These files can be uploaded to online services such as YouTube, Vimeo, or Daily Motion for playback on any device (including iPad, iPhone, and other internet enabled mobile devices).

1. Use the **File | Open** menu item to open the Chapter01/encoderVideo.cpvc.

First, note that a Video Demo project does not use the same `.cptx` file extension as a regular Captivate project. It uses the `.cpvc` file extension instead. This is the first indication that this project is going to behave differently than the other ones you have worked with so far. In addition to having a specific file extension, Video Demo projects also have their own unique interface, as shown in the following screenshot:

In the preceding screenshot, note the absence of the **Filmstrip** panel. A Video Demo project is not based on slides. Actually, it is a single big video file. So the **Filmstrip** panel makes no sense in a Video Demo project.

In a video file, interactions are not possible. The file can only be experienced from start to finish in the order defined by the teacher. To use instructional design terminology, a video file gives a *linear* experience to the learner while branch-aware interactive projects provide a *nonlinear* experience where a learner can make choices that change the way the course progresses. Therefore, interactive objects, quizzes, and branching are not available in a Video Demo project.

2. Take some time to inspect the rest of the Video Demo screen. Try to spot the other differences between the regular Captivate interface and Video Demos.
3. When you are ready, click the **Preview** icon. Surprise! Only two options are available in the **Preview** icon!
4. In the **Preview** dropdown, choose the **Play Slide** option.
5. Watch the whole video as if you were viewing it on YouTube!

Experiencing the take The Train sample application

You will now preview the next sample application using the following steps:

1. Use the **File** | **Open** menu item to open the `Chapter01/takeTheTrain.cptx` file.
2. Once the file is open, click the **Preview** icon on the Toolbar and choose the **HTML5 in Browser** option.
3. View the course in your web browser, as a student would.

This sample application is very different from the projects you worked with so far because it is not based on screenshots or screen recording. The Capture tool of Captivate was not used in this example. Instead, all the slides have been carefully crafted in Captivate.

For its audio narration, this project does not use Text-To-Speech. Instead, the narration was recorded and polished in an external audio application (Adobe Audition, in this case) and imported to the project.

This course is also much more involved than the Encoder examples. Advanced Actions and Variables are used throughout the project to power the dynamic features, such as the name of the student appearing in the title of slide 4. This course also features the certificate interaction at the very end (only if you pass the Quiz!), a video is inserted on slide 23 of the project, and it uses the built-in collection of characters to spice up the training with a human touch! But the most impressive feature of this particular project is probably the **Quiz**, one of the most important and most popular tools in Captivate.

The project contains eight Question Slides. Seven of these are stored in the **Question Pool**. Each time the project is viewed, three questions are randomly chosen from the Question Pool and displayed to the student. If you want to experiment with this feature, view the sample project a second time. Because we used the Question Pool to generate the questions, you should not be asked the same Quiz questions as when you first experienced the project.

Experiencing the Adobe Captivate 2017 Training application

The next sample course you will see is not part of the download that comes with this book. Instead, you will use one of the sample applications that are included in Captivate. Use the following steps to open it.

1. Close every open file (without saving) and return to the Captivate Welcome screen.
2. Click the **Sample Projects/Tutorials** icon on the right side of the Captivate Welcome screen (see **1** on the following screenshot).

As shown in the following screenshot, you can access various sample files and tutorials right from the Welcome Screen of Captivate. This is a great resource to learn Captivate and to discover the new and enhanced features of Captivate 2017:

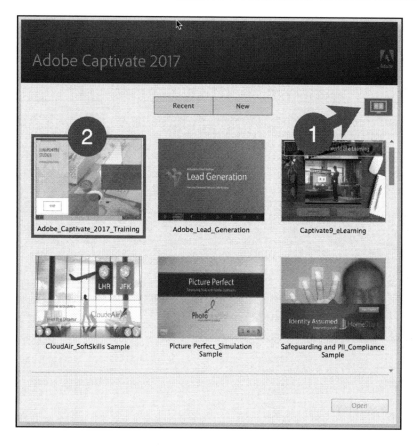

You will now open one of the sample files provided by Adobe:

3. Double click the thumbnail image on the Welcome Screen to open the `AdobeCaptivate_2017_Training` project (see 2 in the preceding screenshot).

4. Click **OK** to clear the message telling you that there are lots of unused assets in the Library.

The project you just opened is a **Responsive Project**. This means that it can adapt itself to the screen it is viewed on. Note the extra toolbar at the top of the stage. This extra toolbar lets you switch between different devices in order to check how the project is displayed on screens of different sizes.

5. In the top left corner of the stage, open the **Custom** drop down menu.

6. Choose **iPhone6** in the list of available devices.

This action resizes the Stage to the size of an iPhone 6 (375 px by 560 px). As shown in the following screenshot, the elements of the current slide are rearranged to fit the new size of the Stage. Some elements (such as the big image that was on the right side of the stage) have even been completely removed to accommodate the reduced real estate of a smartphone:

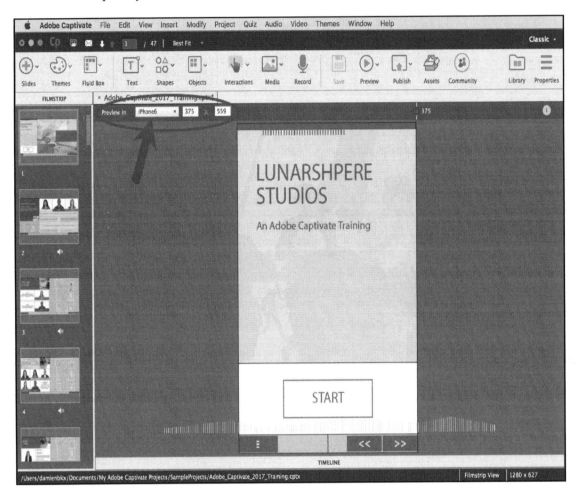

You will now preview this project using the following steps:

7. Click the **Preview** | **Project** icon on the Toolbar.

There are a lot of differences in the way you preview a Responsive Project compared to the way you preview a nonresponsive Captivate project:

- Firstly, the **Preview** icon on the Toolbar contains fewer options.
- Secondly, a Responsive Project is always previewed in the default browser installed on your computer and not in the **Preview** pane of Captivate.
- Thirdly, in the web browser, there is a slider just above the preview to let you change the size of the Stage as you preview your project.

All these changes have a single root cause: a Responsive Project can only be published in HTML5. That's why you need a browser to preview the project.

8. Preview the whole project in the web browser and use the slider above the preview to change the size of the stage (see **1** in the following screenshot). Note how the elements of the various slides of the project are rearranged on the smaller screen sizes.
9. During the preview, also note the very small double arrow icon in the top left corner of the preview (see **2** in the following screenshot). This icon is used to toggle the Table of Contents on and off.
10. When the preview is finished, close the web browser and return to Captivate.

If you have worked with Adobe Captivate before, this project uses a brand new Responsive Design approach. We have used the exciting new Fluid Boxes of Adobe Captivate 2017 to define how the course will look on different devices.

You will learn more about Responsive Projects and Fluid Boxes in `Chapter 10`, *Creating a Responsive Project*.

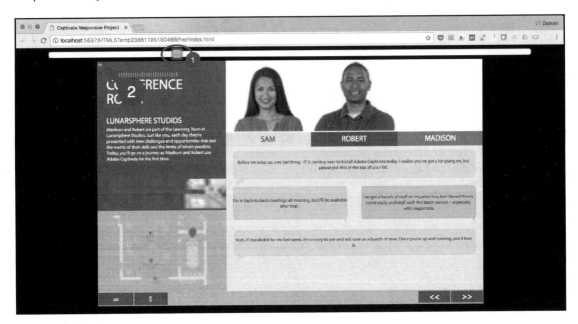

The special previewing features of the Responsive Projects let you test the responsiveness of your project during the development phase, but they have one major disadvantage. Because you preview the project using the default browser of your desktop or laptop computer, you can't experience the course on an actual mobile device.

The best *test drive* for such a project is to view it on a mobile device using a touchscreen and tap actions (as opposed to the mouse pointer). Unfortunately, this requires using special tools such as a web server. Setting up these tools is way beyond the scope of this book, but if you have such a server available, use it to experience your project on your tablet or Smartphone.

Using Browsersync as a testing web server

Browsersync is an excellent tool to test your responsive projects on your actual mobile device. Browsersync can be downloaded for free at `https://www.browsersync.io/`. Unfortunately, Browsersync was designed as a web developer tool. It requires some configuration and the use of the command line to be used.

Experiencing the Introduction to Fluid Boxes project

This is the last sample project for you to experience before wrapping up this chapter. Use the following steps to open and preview this project:

1. Open the `Chapter01/Introduction to Fluid Boxes.cptx` file.
2. Use the **Preview** | **Project** icon on the Toolbar to preview the entire project in the **Preview** pane of Captivate.

This has been entirely developed in Microsoft PowerPoint and converted into a Captivate project using Captivate's ability to import PowerPoint slides. You will learn about importing PowerPoint presentations in Captivate in `Chapter 11`, *Using Captivate with Other Applications*.

3. Use the **File** | **Close All** menu item to close every open file. If prompted to save the changes, make sure you do *not* save the changes to these files.

 The file names on each tab should have asterisks to the left of the name if there are unsaved changes. If there are no asterisks, it means you have saved all the changes.

After viewing these sample applications, you should have a pretty good idea of the tools and general capabilities of Adobe Captivate. Before moving on, let's summarize what you have learned from these sample courses:

- Captivate is able to capture the actions you do on your computer and turn them into slides using a sophisticated capture tool based on screenshots.
- A **demonstration** is a project in which the learner is passive and simply watches the onscreen action.
- A **simulation** is a project in which the user is active.
- Audio and video can be imported to Captivate. The application also features Text-To-Speech and Closed Captioning.
- Question Slides can be created in Captivate. These Question Slides can be stored in Question Pools to create random quizzes.
- Other objects that can be included in a Captivate project include Text Captions, Highlight Boxes, Smart Shapes, Images and more.

- Captivate contains many interactive objects. Some of them are able to stop the course and wait for the user to interact.
- A Video Demo is not based on slides. It is a video file that can be published as a standalone `.mp4` file or uploaded to YouTube or other video applications.
- Video Demo projects use the `.cpvc` file extension and have a specific user interface.
- A Responsive Project is able to adapt itself to the screen on which it is viewed. You can use the new Fluid Boxes of Captivate 2017 to decide how the elements of the slides of the project should be rearranged on various screen sizes.
- Captivate is able to import PowerPoint slides, making it very easy to convert an existing PowerPoint presentation into an interactive Captivate project.

Summary

In this chapter, you were introduced to the four steps of a typical Captivate production process. You toured the application interface and learned how to customize it to fit your needs. Thanks to the Advanced Interface Mode and to the Workspace feature, you were able to save your customized interface as a new Workspace and to reapply your custom panel layout anytime you want to.

Finally, you walked through the sample courses that you will develop in this book, giving you a first, high-level overview of the rich set of features of Adobe Captivate 2017.

In the next chapter, you will start crafting the *Take the Train* project and learn about the basic objects of Captivate 2017.

Meet the community

The title of the book you are reading is *Mastering Adobe Captivate 2017, Fourth Edition*. In order to truly *master* a piece of software, we are convinced that you should be introduced to the community that supports it. The Adobe eLearning community portal (`http://elearning.adobe.com`) makes it easier than ever for you to be a part of the community and to get in touch with the most famous Captivate legends. To help you further, we have provided a *Meet the community* section at the end of every chapter, in which we will introduce you to the key members of the community. By the end of this book, you'll have the names, blog addresses, twitter handles, and other contact details of some of the most influential members. We hope these resources will jump-start your own Captivate career and your involvement in the community.

Allen Partridge

At the end of this first chapter, we want to introduce you to Allen Partridge. Allen is the eLearning Evangelism Group Manager for Adobe. Allen is an awesome speaker and a wonderful teacher. His teaching background makes him an invaluable asset to the Captivate community.

Damien

Allen wrote the foreword of my first book, *Mastering Adobe Captivate 6*. I had the chance to meet with Allen in the summer of 2013 during the Adobe Education Leaders conference in San Jose. It was one of the highlights of my trip to California and I have a vivid memory of that moment.

Pooja

Allen is officially the best colleague a person can get. I've thoroughly enjoyed working alongside Dr. Partridge and have learned a lot from him. When I joined the Adobe eLearning team in 2011, he made me feel comfortable in my new role and environment, and he was always there to help me out. Allen is a Rockstar presenter! If you've not attended his webinars/conference presentations, you are missing something big. I'm proud to have him as a friend, colleague, and mentor!

Bio

Dr. Allen Partridge is the eLearning Evangelism Group Manager for Adobe.
He has written several books and a host of articles on topics ranging from 3D game development to instructional design for new technologies. He is active in the explorations of immersive learning as well as traditional, multimedia-enhanced eLearning and rapid eLearning. He works closely with the eLearning Suite and Captivate teams at Adobe, providing a channel to customer needs and concerns, and helping facilitate communication among the team members.

Contact details

- Blog: http://elearning.adobe.com/
- Twitter: @adobeElearning
- Facebook: http://www.facebook.com/adobecaptivate
- LinkedIn: http://www.linkedin.com/in/doctorpartridge
- YouTube: http://www.youtube.com/adobeelearning/

2
Working with Standard Objects

Now that you have a better understanding of the features of Adobe Captivate, it is time to start exploring them one by one in greater detail. In this chapter, you will begin the development of the *Take the Train* project you experimented with in the previous chapter.

You will begin by creating a new blank project and applying a custom theme to it, so it looks the way you want. Later in the book, you will learn how to create such themes, but for now, you will simply apply it to the project so that you can concentrate on learning the basic standard objects of Captivate.

These objects are the fundamental building blocks of each and every Captivate file. They allow you to enrich your courses with elements such as Text Captions, Shapes, Images, Animations, and more.

In this chapter, we will cover the following topics:

- Create a new Captivate file
- Apply a theme to the newly created file
- Add slides to the project
- Apply Master Slides
- Work with the Properties inspector
- Work with Text Captions
- Insert various types of Images
- Work with Shapes
- Create simple Text Animations
- Apply Text Effects

Throughout this chapter, you will also discover how to modify the properties of these objects. You will see that even though each of those objects is a little different from one another, they all share some common properties and workflows.

But enough talking for now, it is time to start developing your first Captivate project!

Creating a new Captivate project

When starting a new eLearning project, you may be tempted to jump right into Captivate and start adding slides to your course. You learned in Chapter 1, *Getting Started with Adobe Captivate*, that you should extensively research your topic and design the pedagogical approach of your course before opening Captivate for the first time. Starting your course without this understanding may frustrate you and waste a lot of your time. We cannot stress this enough. Captivate is a tool for teaching stuff to people. It helps you in the *craft* of teaching, but not in the *art* of teaching.

That being said, this book is designed to teach you how to use Adobe Captivate, so we have done all the important research and preproduction work for you. This will allow you to concentrate on the *ins* and *outs* of Captivate itself.

When you open Adobe Captivate 2017 for the first time, this Welcome Screen appears:

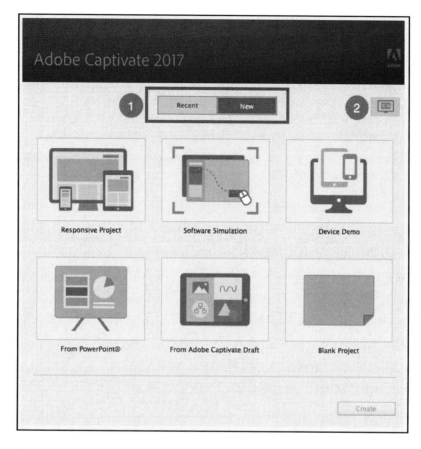

If this is not the first time you're opening Captivate, you may be automatically redirected to the **Recent** tab of this Welcome Screen with a list of recently opened files. Simply click the **New** tab at the top of the screen (marked as **1** in the preceding screenshot) to return to the default Welcome Screen.

Also notice the extra icon on the right corner of the Welcome Screen (marked as **2** in the preceding screenshot). Clicking this icon takes you to a list of sample files and tutorials designed to help you get started with Adobe Captivate.

From this Welcome Screen, you can create different types of Captivate projects. Not all of them are listed though. To see a full listing of all the project types of Adobe Captivate, open the **File** menu in the top-left corner of the screen.

The first two items of the **File** menu contain a comprehensive list of project types. For the most part, these are the same as those listed on the Welcome Screen. However, some project types are only found in the **File** menu:

- The **New Project** menu item lets you create different types of Captivate projects. Notice that some project types present in this menu are not present on the Welcome Screen. The Welcome Screen contains the most common project types. There are a few more options in the **New Project** menu.
- The **Record a New** menu item lets you create a new project using the screen-recording tool of Captivate. This is typically used for software simulations and video tutorials.

The **Device Demo** project type is only available for Mac users. If you are a Windows user, the **Device Demo** icon of the Welcome Screen is replaced by the **Video Demo** icon. If you are a Mac user, you can start a Video Demo recording from the **File** | **Record a New** menu item. You will learn more about Video Demo projects in Chapter 9, *Producing a Video Demo*.

The project you will create in this chapter is a typical non-responsive Captivate project based on slides. For such projects, you use the **Blank Project** icon of the Welcome Screen:

1. Click the **Blank Project** icon of the Welcome Screen.
2. In the **Canvas** dropdown that appears in the bottom-left corner of the Welcome Screen, choose a size of **1024 x 627** for your new project.
3. Click the **Create** button.

Captivate creates a new project containing a single slide. Your next task is to save the project:

4. Click the **Save** icon on the Toolbar to save the project. You can also use the **File** | **Save** menu item or the *Cmd + S* (macOS) / *Ctrl + S* (Windows) shortcut.
5. Save your file as Chapter02/takeTheTrain.cptx within the sample files folder you downloaded in the previous chapter.

Saving your file immediately after creating it is a best practice that ensures your file has a name and actually exists on your hard drive before you attempt to import other elements into it. You can tell that you've saved your file because the asterisk in the file name's tab disappears. Whenever you've made a change and not saved it, the asterisk appears again.

The `Chapter02/final` folder contains the completed project as it should look by the end of this chapter. If you are confused about any of the exercises in this chapter, you can always use it as a reference.

Choosing the right project size

Choosing the right size for your project is the first critical decision you have to make. And you have to make it right because the size of the project plays a critical role in the quality of the student's experience when viewing the project.

Even though it is possible to resize a Captivate project later, you want to avoid it as much as possible because the resize operation always results in a loss of quality. Here are a few things to keep in mind in order to choose the right size for your project:

- Where will the project be viewed? If your Captivate module will be deployed on an intranet site and be watched mostly on a desktop computer, you can safely create a somewhat larger project. If your project will be viewed mainly on tablet devices or Smartphones, you should consider a smaller size.
- The website where your course will be published probably has its own elements to display (logos, links, footer elements, sidebars, and so on), leaving less space on the screen to display your Captivate module.
- A larger project yields to a bigger file size. If your project will be viewed over a fast LAN Ethernet connection, this might not be a big concern. But if the project needs to be transmitted over a WIFI or 4G data link, you should consider a smaller file size.

Knowing your audience and the conditions under which they will experience the finished course is important in choosing the right size for your project.

In this example, the project size is `1024` by `627` pixels. This is the default size proposed by Captivate. It is a kind of *general-purpose* size that looks nice on a desktop computer, while accommodating most tablet devices at the same time.

 Knowing your device size
If you want to know the viewport size of your mobile device, browse to `www.viewportsizes.com/mine`. For a list of common device sizes, you can visit `https://mydevice.io/devices/`.

Applying a theme to the project

Now that you've started your `takeTheTrain` project, your second task is to apply a theme. The theme dictates how the course will look. It brings a set of styles and a set of predefined Master Slides to use and reuse throughout your course development.

Captivate includes many predefined themes that you can apply as-is to your projects. While these predefined themes are a great way to jumpstart your next project, you will probably design and develop your own customized themes. This is what we have done for this project. We have designed my own custom theme.

Later in this book, you will learn how this custom theme was made. But for now, let's focus on applying it to the project:

1. With the new project open, click the **Themes** icon on the Toolbar.
2. Click the **Browse** link in the bottom-left corner of the theme chooser.
3. In the `Chapter02` folder of the exercise files, select the `takeTheTrain_Theme.cptm` file. (Note that a theme uses a `.cptm` file extension, while a regular Captivate project uses a `.cptx` file extension.)
4. Captivate displays a warning message telling you that the current styles will be overridden. Click **Yes** to close the message and apply the custom theme to the project.
5. Save the project when done.

After applying the theme, you will notice a big change in how the first, and currently, the only, slide of the project is displayed. This is due to the Master Slides included in the theme already at work!

You will now take a closer look at the Master Slides included in the theme and choose one for your first slide:

6. Click the **Properties** icon on the right side of the Toolbar to open the **Properties** inspector.
7. At the very top of the **Properties** inspector, in the **Master Slide** section, click the drop-down arrow to reveal a list of the available Master Slides. This operation is illustrated in the following screenshot:

This opens the list of the Master Slides defined in the theme you just applied to the project. A Master Slide is a predefined layout that you can apply to the slides in your Captivate file. The idea is to speed up the development of your courses, while maintaining a strong visual consistency throughout and across your courses.

You will now apply one of these Master Slides to the first slide of your project:

8. With the list of Master Slides open, click the **Title** Master Slide to apply it to the selected slide.

The Title Master Slide is applied to the first slide of your project.

Working with placeholders

The Title Master Slide you just applied to the first slide of the project contains many objects. Some of these objects, such as the blue circle on the right edge of the slide, the blue lines stretching across the slide, or the image background, are aesthetic design elements.

Other objects define the placement and formatting of your content. These objects are called **Placeholder** objects. Your next task is to write some text in the two placeholders present on the slide:

1. Double-click the title placeholder.
2. Write `Take the train` ! in the placeholder.
3. Double-click the subtitle placeholder.
4. Write `A guide to the best way of moving around in Belgium` ! in the placeholder.
5. Click anywhere on the slide or press the *Esc* key to validate your new text.

Using Master Slides and placeholders makes it incredibly easy and fast to develop your eLearning content. It also ensures that the look and feel of your slides and objects is consistent throughout the entire file and across projects.

Adding slides in a project

Now that the first slide of the project is finished, your next task is to add a second slide and apply the appropriate Master Slide:

1. Click the **Slides** icon, which is the first icon on the Toolbar.
2. Click **Content Slide** to add a new Content Slide to the project.
3. In the **Properties** inspector, open the **Master Slide** list.
4. Apply the **Title&text** Master Slide to your new slide.

The **Title&text** Master Slide has a big rectangle that defines the content area of this slide. It also contains two placeholder objects that you will fill with text using these steps:

5. Double-click the title placeholder.
6. Type `Reading the schedule` in the title placeholder.
7. Double-click the caption text placeholder
8. Type `Click on the Next button to explore the various components of the schedule` in the placeholder.
9. Click anywhere on the slide or hit the *Esc* key to accept your new text.

Your new slide should now look like the following screenshot:

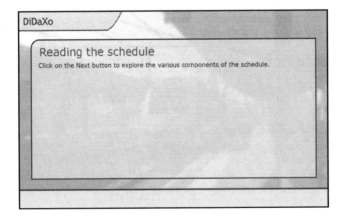

Working with the Properties inspector

The **Properties** inspector is one of the most important and most widely used areas in Captivate. In this section, you will take some time to inspect the **Properties** inspector in more detail.

When you first open Adobe Captivate, the **Properties** inspector is hidden by default, so your first task is to turn it on via the following steps:

1. Click several times on the **Properties** icon situated in the top-right corner of the Toolbar to toggle the **Properties** inspector on and off.
2. Make sure that the **Properties** inspector is turned off before moving to the next step.
3. In **Filmstrip**, double-click on any slide. This also opens the **Properties** inspector.

In Captivate, double-clicking an object opens the **Properties** inspector of the object that has been double-clicked. Double-clicking anywhere on the scrap area around the stage is yet another way to open the **Properties** inspector.

The **Properties** and **Library** icons on the Toolbar are used to toggle the corresponding panels on and off. Make sure the **Properties** inspector is visible before moving on with this exercise.

Panels in the advanced interface mode
Remember that in the advanced interface mode, the **Properties** and the **Library** icons are not present on the Toolbar. Use the **Window** menu to turn these panels on and off.

The **Properties** inspector is dynamic. It means that its content changes depending on the object you select. Let's experiment with this hands-on:

4. With the **Properties** inspector open, click the first slide thumbnail on **Filmstrip** to make it the active slide.

After clicking slide 1, the **Properties** inspector displays the properties of that slide. For example, you can see that the **title** Master Slide is applied to the currently selected slide:

Take some time to examine the available properties and options in the **Properties** inspector.

The **Properties** inspector is actually a group of two panels: the **Properties** and the **Timing** panels:

5. At the very top of the right column, click **Timing** to make it the active panel (see the arrow in the preceding screenshot).
6. Take some time to examine the properties of the **Timing** panel. When you are done, return to the **Properties** inspector.

The **Properties** inspector itself is divided into three different tabs: **Styles**, **Actions**, and **Options**.

7. Take some time to examine the content of each of these tabs.
8. In **Filmstrip**, select the second slide to make it the active slide. Notice that the **Properties** inspector now displays the properties of that slide.

The selected slide contains two objects. You will now use the **Properties** inspector to examine the properties of these two objects:

9. Click the **Reading the schedule** title to make it the active object.
10. Take some time to examine the **Properties** inspector. It now displays the properties relevant to the selected object. Most of these properties should be self-explanatory.
11. Don't forget to examine the **Options** tab of the **Properties** inspector as well as the **Timing** panel. Look at their properties and controls.
12. Click the second text to make it the active object.
13. Take some time to examine the **Style** and **Options** tabs of the **Properties inspector**. Note that the displayed properties are not exactly the same as when the title object was selected.
14. Also, examine the **Timing** panel of the selected object and compare it to the **Timing** panel of the title object.

Even though both the objects of the slide are used to display text, these are two very different objects in Captivate. The title object is called a **Smart Shape**, while the second text is a **Text Caption**. This explains why the controls in the **Properties** inspector are a little different for each of these two objects.

Also, notice that the **Options** tabs and the **Timing** panel contain the very same options and properties for both the objects. Only the **Style** tab of the **Properties** inspector is a little bit different.

To work with the **Properties** inspector, remember the following:

- In the normal interface mode, the **Properties** inspector is not displayed by default. Use the **Properties** button on the right side of the Toolbar to toggle its visibility on and off. In the advanced interface mode, use the **Window** menu.
- You can also double-click any object to open the **Properties** inspector of that particular object. This object can be a slide in **Filmstrip** or any object present on a slide.
- When clicking the **Properties** button on the Toolbar, you actually reveal both the **Properties** inspector and the **Timing** panel.
- The **Properties** inspector and the **Timing** panel are both *dynamic*. This means that they show the properties relevant to the *active* object. Consequently, selecting another object updates the content of these panels.
- The **Properties** inspector is further divided into tabs.
- Usually, the **Style** tab is specific to the selected object while the **Options** tab is more or less the same for all the objects.

Now that you know how the **Properties** inspector works, you will learn about the basic objects of Captivate.

Exploring the objects of Captivate

Captivate offers more than a dozen objects. In this section, you will learn about the standard non-interactive objects of Captivate. Later in this book, more complex objects will be covered. The first object you will focus on is the **Text Caption** object.

Working with the Text Caption object

The Text Caption is the most basic object in Captivate. It is typically used to display text on the screen. In its most basic form, the Text Caption is a text item that appears and disappears from the screen according to its position on the **Timeline**.

The second slide of your project contains a Text Caption. Let's select it and examine what you can do with it.

There are two editing modes available when working with Text Captions:

- First, you can consider the Text Caption as *an object*. In this case, eight white squares appear around the Text Caption. These white squares are the *handles* used to resize the Text Caption. In this mode, you can move the Text Caption around and resize it, but you cannot edit the text inside the Text Caption.
- To edit the text you must be in the text editing mode. In the text editing mode, the eight white handles disappear and a blinking cursor appears in the Text Caption.

To switch from the object mode to the text editing mode, you simply double-click the Text Caption. To switch from text editing mode back to object mode, use the *Esc* key.

You will now modify the height of the Text Caption on slide 2:

1. Click once on the Text Caption on slide 2. Note that even though there is just one line of text in the Text Caption, it is almost as high as the content area defined on the Master Slide.
2. Reduce the height of the Text Caption by dragging the bottom handle upward. You will see a double-sided arrow when you are resizing. Make sure the Text Caption is only as high as needed to properly enclose the text.

Creating new Text Captions

The Text Caption you just worked with was created by adding some text in a placeholder object defined on the Master Slide. You will now create and modify a *brand new* Text Caption.

1. While still on slide 2, click the **Text** icon on the Toolbar and select the **Text Caption** item.
2. Type `Click on Continue when done.` in the new Text Caption object.
3. Hit the *Esc* key to leave the text-editing mode. The new Text Caption should still be selected.

When adding a new Text Caption, note the following:

- By default, the new Text Caption is inserted in the middle of the slide. In fact, this is the case every time you add any new object on a slide, regardless of it being a Text Caption or anything else.
- By default, the Text Caption was placed in the text editing mode, allowing you to type in some text right after inserting the object.

Resizing and moving Text Captions

In Captivate, resizing and moving an object is very easy and can be done in two different ways: using the white handles, or using the **Options** tab of the **Properties inspector**:

1. While still on the second slide of your project, use the resize handles to resize the Text Caption so that the text you just typed fits into a single line.
2. Open the **Options** tab of the **Properties** inspector.

The **Options** tab contains the properties that control the size and position of the selected object. **W** indicates the Width of the object, while **H** stands for the Height. Both dimensions are expressed in pixels:

3. On the stage, use the white handles to make the Text Caption a bit bigger.
4. Take another look at the **Properties** inspector. The height and width fields of the **Options** tab reflect the new size of the object.

If you want to give your objects a specific size, you can enter the Height and the Width in the **Properties** inspector directly. If the **Constrain proportions** checkbox is selected, Captivate automatically calculates the new **Height** of the object when you modify the **Width** (and vice versa) so that the Height/Width ratio of the object does not change:

5. With the Text Caption still selected, take a look at the **X** and **Y** values in the **Options** tab of the **Properties** inspector.

6. Use your mouse to move the Text Caption around the slide.

See how the **X** and **Y** values of the **Options** tab change as you move the Text Caption. The **X** coordinate is the distance (in pixels) between the left edge of the selected object and the left edge of the slide. The **Y** coordinate is the distance (in pixels) between the top edge of the selected object and the top of the slide. You can manually enter the **X** and **Y** coordinates in the **Options** tab to give the selected object a pixel-precise position on the slide:

7. Use your mouse to move the new Text Caption and place it approximately under the first one.

8. As you do so, notice the vertical and/or horizontal dotted green lines that appear on the stage. Use them to properly position your Text Caption under the first one.

These dotted green lines are called **Smart Guides**. They automatically appear and disappear from the stage as you move objects around. Their aim is to help you align the object quickly and precisely.

You can turn the Smart Guide feature on or off by going to the **View** | **Show Drawing / Smart Guides** menu item. The aforementioned procedure assumes that the Smart Guide feature is turned on, which is the default value.

After this simple procedure, your slide should look like the following screenshot:

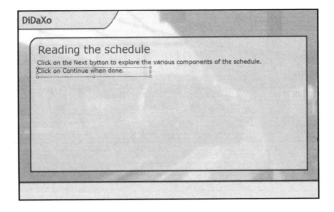

Formatting a Text Caption

You will now examine some of the formatting capabilities of the Text Caption object. To do so, make sure that the Text Caption you just inserted is selected before performing the following steps:

1. If necessary, open the **Properties** inspector by clicking the **Properties** icon on the Toolbar.
2. In the **Style** tab of the **Properties** inspector open the **Caption Type** dropdown and choose the **Adobe Green** item.
3. Directly under the **Caption Type** dropdown, experiment with the five **Callout** types.
4. Open the **Caption Type** dropdown again and choose the **Transparent** item at the top of the list.
5. Experiment with the other properties. For example, change the color of the text, the font family, or the size. For the most part, these properties should be self-explanatory.
6. When you are done, click the little icon just above the **Style Name** drop-down list and click the **Reset Style** item, as shown on the following screenshot:

Your last action resets the style applied to this Text Caption to its default formatting.

In Chapter 6, *Crafting the Graphical Experience with Styles and Themes*, you will learn how to create these Styles and how to apply them to the other Text Captions of the project. But for now, this exercise concludes your first exploration of the Text Caption object.

Before moving on to the next object, let's summarize what you have learned about Text Captions:

- The Text Caption object is used to display text to the learner
- Changing the size or moving an object with the mouse also changes the corresponding values in the **Options** tab of the **Properties inspector** and vice versa

- Apply a **Caption Type** to the object to quickly format it
- Captivate provides five **Callout Types** for each **Caption Type**
- Most of the formatting properties of Text Captions can be found in the **Style** tab of the **Properties** inspector

As you can see, the Text Caption object is very simple to understand and manipulate. In earlier versions of Captivate, it was the only means of displaying text to the learner. In the more recent versions of Captivate, you can also display text using a much more powerful object called the Smart Shape.

Working with Smart Shapes

Smart Shapes are a predefined collection of shapes, including rectangles, circles, banners, stars, arrows, and many more. Before working with Smart Shapes, let's add another slide to the project using the following steps:

1. In **Filmstrip**, select the first slide of the project.
2. Click the **Slide** icon, which is the first icon on the Toolbar.
3. Click the **Content Slide** icon to create a new content slide.
4. With the new slide selected, use the **Properties** inspector to apply the **contentBkg** Master Slide to the new slide.

Note that Captivate adds a new slide *after* the currently selected slide. In this case, Captivate has added the new slide as slide 2 because slide 1 was selected when you added the new slide. It is therefore not possible to add a slide at the very beginning of a project. Hopefully, you can drag and drop slides in the **Filmstrip** panel to reorder them the way you want.

Drawing a simple Smart Shape

You will now draw a simple rounded rectangle Smart Shape via the following steps:

1. Make sure that you are on the newly created slide.
2. Click the **Shapes** icon on the Toolbar. Take some time to examine the list of available shapes.
3. Select the rounded rectangle shape in the **Basic** section of the list of shapes.
4. Click and drag your mouse to draw a rounded rectangle shape in the top-right corner of the content area of the slide. Resize and move the shape as necessary.

In the top-left corner of the shape, you should see a yellow handle in addition to the eight white handles that surround the shape. This yellow handle is one of the features that make a Smart Shape smart. It is used to modify the shape. In this case, the yellow handle is used to adjust the roundness of the rectangle.

Other Smart Shapes might display multiple yellow handles allowing you to customize multiple aspects of the selected shape. The number of yellow handles actually depends on the shape:

5. Use the yellow handle to adjust the roundness of the rectangle to your taste.

Don't worry about the exact positioning and formatting of the rounded rectangle. These elements will be adjusted later.

Formatting Smart Shapes

As you might expect, you use the **Properties** inspector of Captivate to format your Smart Shapes. In this section, you will discover the main formatting properties of the Smart Shapes object via the following steps:

1. On slide 2 of the `Chapter2/takeTheTrain.cptx` project, select the rounded rectangle shape you created in the previous section.
2. Look at the **Style** tab of the **Properties** inspector.
3. In the **Fill** section, open the **Solid** drop-down menu

This menu is one of the many reasons why I love Smart Shapes, because it offers you so many possibilities. Let's review these options one by one:

- **Solid Fill**: This is the default value. It allows you to define a single plain color as the background color of your Smart Shape. Simply use the **Fill** property next to the dropdown you just opened to choose a color with the color picker.
- **Gradient fill**: This lets you arrange two or more colors in a gradient. This capability is unique to the Smart Shape object. The gradient editor is very similar to the one found in other Adobe applications, such as Photoshop, Illustrator, and InDesign.
- **Image fill**: This lets you choose an image to be used as the background of the Smart Shape.

As you can see, this drop-down menu opens a world of formatting capabilities, making the Smart Shape object the most versatile object of Captivate. (And you just opened a single drop-down menu!) Let's dig deeper into the formatting capabilities of the Smart Shape object:

4. In the **Fill** section of the **Style** tab of the **Properties** inspector, open the **Opacity** drop-down menu.
5. Change the **Opacity** value to 10% and look at your Smart Shape on the stage.
6. Reopen the same drop-down menu and change the **Opacity** value to 100%.
7. Select the **Opacity** value and type 85 with your keyboard. Don't forget to apply the new value by using the *Enter* key.

The opacity property lets you create objects that are more or less transparent. With a lower value, your Smart Shape is more transparent, letting more of the background image show through the object. With an opacity value of 0, the Smart Shape is fully transparent. With a higher value, your Smart Shape becomes more and more opaque. With a value of 100%, the Smart Shape is completely opaque, and the background image is completely invisible.

The opacity property is also unique to Smart Shapes. Remember that this level of control was not available when a Text Caption was selected. A Text Caption can only be completely transparent or completely opaque. This is one of the key differences between a Smart Shape and a Text Caption.

You will now reset the formatting properties of the selected Smart Shape and add a small border to your rounded rectangle:

8. With the rounded rectangle Smart Shape of slide 2 still selected, click the small icon on the right side of the **Style Name** label in the **Properties** inspector.
9. Click the **Reset Style** item to return to the default formatting.
10. Now, find the **Stroke** section of the **Style** tab of the **Properties** inspector.
11. In the **Style** dropdown, make sure you choose a solid border.
12. In the **Stroke** dropdown, choose a white stroke.
13. Open the **Width** dropdown and choose a width of 3 pixels for your stroke
14. You should now have a solid white stroke of 3 pixels all around your Smart Shape.

The ability to create highly customizable strokes around a shape is yet another formatting capability that makes the Smart Shape object so powerful.

Your slide should now look like the following screenshot:

Creating your own Smart Shapes

In addition to predefined shapes, Captivate allows you to draw your own Smart Shapes and save them for later use. In the following exercise, you will experiment with this feature hands-on, via the following steps:

1. In slide 2 of the `Chapter02/takeTheTrain.cptx` project, click the **Shapes** icon on the Toolbar to open the Smart Shape menu.
2. Choose the Polygon tool in the Smart Shapes menu. It is the line that ends with a star at the top of the menu. With the Polygon tool selected, the mouse pointer turns into a crosshair.
3. Click anywhere on the slide where you want the first point of the Polygon to be located.
4. Click a second time at another location to create a second point. Captivate automatically connects the two points with a dotted line.
5. Use the same technique to add other points of the shape.
6. To close the shape, click a second time on the first point you created. Captivate displays a small circle next to the mouse pointer to indicate that the shape can be closed.

You now have your very own custom shape on the slide. Don't worry if the shape is not exactly like the one you intended to create! In the next subsection, you will learn how to modify the shape you just created.

Modifying a custom shape

A Smart Shape is a **vector object** similar to those you can draw with Adobe Illustrator. To create these shapes, designers use the *Pen tool* of Illustrator to draw Bezier points and Bezier curves. Even though Captivate is not equipped with a full-fledged pen tool, you can, however, access these Bezier points and modify your shape via the following steps:

1. Right-click the shape you created and choose the **Edit Points** item in the contextual menu. This action reveals the points that you defined when you created the polygon.
2. Move those points to modify the shape. You can also move the green handles to modify the curvature of the connecting lines, as shown in the next screenshot.
3. When you are happy with the shape, hit the *Esc* key on your keyboard to leave the point-editing mode and to select the shape.

Note that you can only move the defined points or modify their curvature, but you cannot add or remove points to and from the shape:

Converting predefined shapes to freeform

Another way to create your own Smart Shapes is to start with a predefined shape and modify it using the very same technique as the one that was just described. Simply right-click a Smart Shape and choose the **Convert to freeform** item in the contextual menu to access the Bezier points. Have fun!

Saving a custom shape

Captivate gives you the ability to save your custom shapes and add them to the list of predefined shapes. In this exercise, you will save your custom shape and insert a second instance of it via the following steps:

1. In slide 2 of your project, make sure that your custom shape is selected (with white selection handles around it).
2. Locate the **Custom** section at the very top of the **Style** tab in the **Properties** inspector.
3. Click the icon in the top-right corner of the **Custom** section and choose the **Save Shape** item, as shown in the following screenshot:

4. Type myShape in the **Rename Item** dialog and click **OK** to save your custom shape.

By saving your custom shape, you actually make it a part of the collection of predefined shapes, so you can reuse it in the future. Perform the following steps to draw a second instance of the same shape:

5. Click the **Shapes** icon on the Toolbar to open the Smart Shapes panel.

Note that your new shape is present in the **Recently Used Shapes** section at the top of the drop-down menu. If you did not use that shape recently, it would not be a part of the menu. In that case, here is how you can draw that shape:

6. Choose the Polygon tool (the dotted line that ends with a star).
7. Randomly add a few points to the slide in order to create a new custom shape. The actual shape you come up with is of no importance.

8. Make sure that the new shape is selected, and look at the **Custom** section at the top of the **Style** tab in the **Properties** inspector.

9. Click on the little black arrow to reveal a list of additional shapes.

10. Choose your custom shape in the list of additional shapes, as shown in the following screenshot:

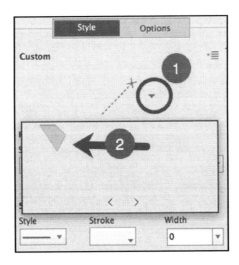

You should now have two instances of your custom shape on the slide, demonstrating how you can save and reuse the custom shapes you create. Since these two shapes were added for demonstration purposes only, your next task is to remove them from the slide:

11. Select both your custom shapes and hit the *Delete* key on your keyboard to remove them from the slide. You can also right-click a shape and use the **Delete** menu item.

12. Save the file when done.

You should now be back to the original situation with only one rounded rectangle in the top-right corner of the slide.

Adding text inside Smart Shapes

The awesomeness of Smart Shapes does not end here! In this exercise, you will explore another creative option available in the Smart Shape object, by adding text inside a Smart Shape. This means that you can create an entire project without ever using Text Caption objects. You will still use Text Caption objects though, because they are so quick and easy to create. However, most of the time, you will probably only use the transparent Caption Type. For all your other text needs, the Smart Shape object gives you much more power, flexibility, and opportunities to be creative.

Make sure you are still on slide 2 of your newly created Captivate project and select the rounded rectangle Smart Shape:

1. In the **Properties** inspector, the **Style** tab should contain four sections: the **Basic** section at the top, the **Fill** and **Stroke** sections, and a collapsible **Shadow and Reflection** section at the bottom.
2. Double-click the rounded rectangle. This action brings a blinking cursor in the middle of the shape.
3. Type `Liege Guillemins` inside the Smart Shape. When done, use the *Esc* key to leave the text editing mode and select the shape as an object.
4. Take another look at the **Properties** inspector.

By adding text inside your Smart Shape, the **Character** and the **Margin** sections have been automatically added to the **Style** tab. These two sections are the same as those used to format the text inside a Text Caption object. It means that you have the exact same text formatting capabilities on a Smart Shape as on a Text Caption.

 Liège Guillemins is the main train station of the city of Liège in the eastern part of Belgium. A great place to visit on your next European trip!

Extra credit - duplicating objects

Currently, you have a single rounded rectangle Smart Shape on your slide. However, you need three of those in this slide. These three rounded rectangles will be very similar. Actually, they should be exactly the same, except that each rounded rectangle will contain different text.

Instead of drawing two brand new rounded rectangle Smart Shapes, you will build on what you've already created by duplicating the existing rounded rectangle and changing its text. Follow these steps:

- Select the rounded rectangle Smart Shape.
- Use the *Ctrl + D* (Windows) or *Cmd + D* (Mac) shortcut to duplicate the existing shape.
- Double-click on the newly created shape and replace the text with `Bruxelles - Midi`.
- Hit the *Esc* key to leave the text editing mode while keeping the Smart Shape selected.
- Repeat the procedure to create a third shape. Write `Oostende` in the third Smart Shape.
- Arrange your Smart Shapes so that the slide looks like the following screenshot:

 Bruxelles-midi is the main train station of Brussels, the capital city of Belgium, and *Bruxelles* is how you spell Brussels in French. *Oostende* is a city situated at the far west of the country, along the coast.

 To duplicate an object, you can also drag it with the mouse while holding down the *Ctrl* (Windows) or *Cmd* (Mac) key. This gives you the ability to duplicate an object and to position the copy on the stage in a single action.

Extra credit - creating additional Smart Shapes

In this extra credit section, you will draw two additional Smart Shapes on your slide. This will give you the opportunity to experiment with another predefined shape. Follow these steps to draw two arrows pointing downward between the rounded rectangles:

- Make sure you are still on the second slide of your new Captivate project.
- Click the **Shapes** icon on the Toolbar to open the list of available shapes.
- In the **Arrows** section, click the Down Arrow shape.
- Draw a downward pointing arrow between the first two rounded rectangles.
- With the new arrow selected, experiment with the three yellow squares to see how each affects the shape of the arrow.
- When the arrow has the desired shape, move it into place. Use the green dotted Smart Guides to align the objects accurately.
- With the new arrow selected, open the **Style Name** drop-down list of the **Properties** inspector and apply the **shape_As_HB** style to the selected arrow. This style is part of the theme that you applied to your project earlier in this chapter.
- Use the *Ctrl + D* (Windows) / *Cmd + D* (Mac) shortcut to duplicate the arrow.
- Move the second arrow between the second and the third rounded rectangles. Use the green dotted Smart Guides to properly align the shapes.

After these steps, your slide should look like the following screenshot:

Remember that Smart Guides can be turned on and off using the **View |
Show Drawing / Smart Guides** menu item.

In this section, you learned a lot about Smart Shapes. Before moving on to the next section,
let's summarize what was covered in this section:

- Smart Shapes are a collection of predefined shapes that can be manipulated in
  many ways with the tools of Captivate.
- The collection of Smart Shapes includes rounded rectangles, banners, triangles,
  arrows, callouts, and more.
- When a Smart Shape object is selected, special yellow handles allow you to
  modify the Smart Shape.
- Use the **Polygon** tool to draw your very own custom shapes that you can save for
  reuse.
- Smart Shapes are vector objects similar to those you create with Adobe Illustrator.
  Use the **Edit Points** or the **Convert to Freeform** menu items to access the Bezier
  points and curves of your shape.
- The **Fill** of a Smart Shape can be a **Solid Fill**, **Gradient Fill**, or **Image fill**.
- You can control the **Opacity** of a Smart Shape. An opacity of 0% means that the
  object is completely transparent, while an opacity of 100% means that the object is
  completely opaque.
- Text can be added inside a Smart Shape.
- When a Smart Shape contains text, additional text formatting properties are
  displayed in the **Style** tab of the **Properties** inspector.
- These text formatting properties are the same as those found in a Text Caption
  object.

I must admit that I love Smart Shapes! In Chapter 5, *Working with Interactive Objects*, you
will discover even more capabilities of this very flexible Captivate object. For now, let's
move on to the next feature of this chapter.

Working with images

The next object to learn is the **Image** object. Captivate lets you insert various types of
images on any slide. Once an image is inserted, you can modify and format the image using
the image editing tools of Captivate.

Keep in mind, though, that Captivate is not an image editing application. To guarantee the best possible results, you should always prepare your images in a dedicated image editing application (such as Adobe Photoshop or Adobe Illustrator) before inserting the image into Captivate. However, if you don't have access to these programs, you can do some basic image editing inside Captivate.

Inserting an image

Your first task of this chapter is to insert an image on a slide.

An image is worth a thousand words

Images play an important role in eLearning, as an image can be a tremendously efficient way to convey a strong meaning without using a single word! In our modern world where learners are more and more reluctant to read (especially on a screen), this old saying takes on a whole new dimension. The more I progress into eLearning, the more I use images. Another benefit of images is that they don't need to be translated when creating a multilingual course. You can save on translation costs while creating a more efficient and appealing eLearning module!

Adding images to your project is very simple to do in Captivate, and is very similar to what is found in other applications. Follow these steps to insert an image into a slide:

1. Make sure that you are still on the second slide of your Captivate project.
2. Click the **Media** icon on the Toolbar, and then, click the **Image** option.
3. Navigate to the `Chapter02/` folder of your exercise files and choose the `belgiumRailroadMap.png` file.

The image is inserted in the middle of the slide. Obviously, it is way too big! Your next task is to resize and position this image so that it integrates nicely with the other elements of the slide:

4. Make sure that the image is selected on your slide.
5. Use your mouse to change the size of the image by clicking and dragging the white handles. This will most likely distort the image.

You can avoid distortion by pressing and holding the *Shift* key on your keyboard while using a corner handle to resize (scale) the image.

6. In the **Style** tab of the **Properties** inspector, click the **Reset To Original Size** button to restore the image to its original aspect.

You will now use the **Options** tab of the **Properties** inspector to resize this picture:

7. Switch to the **Options** tab of the **Properties** inspector.
8. Make sure that the **Constrain proportions** checkbox is selected and change the width of the picture to 480 pixels. Captivate calculates the new height of the image (393 pixels) so that its height/width ratio does not change.
9. Move the image to the left side of the slide, next to the Smart Shapes you created in the previous section.

Your slide should now look like the following screenshot:

About image types

Captivate lets you insert many different image types in your projects, including .jpg, .gif, and .png images. If you want to know more about these image formats, visit

http://www.sitepoint.com/gif-jpg-png-whats-difference/.

Using the image editing tools

Inserting an image in Captivate is very easy! You will now explore some of the image editing tools available in Captivate:

1. Make sure that the newly imported image is selected, and take a look at the **Style** tab of the **Properties** inspector.
2. Click the **Edit Image** button.

This action opens a dialog box showing the image on the left and a set of control sliders on the right:

3. Move the sliders to see how each affects the image.
4. When done, click the **Reset All** button in the bottom-right corner of the dialog box.
5. Take some time to inspect the other controls available in the dialog box. Note that the image can also be flipped, resized, and cropped.
6. Click **Cancel** to close the dialog box without saving the changes.

These image editing capabilities are a great convenience to fine-tune the images you insert in Captivate. However, let's reiterate the fact that these tools are not meant to replace actual image editing software, such as Adobe Photoshop or Adobe Illustrator. If you have access to a dedicated image editing application, it is usually better to prepare your image in one of those external applications before inserting it into Captivate.

Inserting a picture slide

Inserting images into existing slides is one of the many possibilities offered by Captivate. Another nice feature is the ability to create a new slide with an image as the background. In this example, you won't actually use this feature because all the slide layouts you need are included in the theme you have applied to your project earlier in this chapter.

But if you want to use an image as the background of a slide, here is the general process:

1. Use an external image editing application (such as Adobe Photoshop) to prepare an image with the same size as your project.
2. Use the **Insert | Image Slide** menu item and select an image on your computer.
3. A new slide is inserted after the selected slide. This new slide uses your picture as its background.

Even though the use of Themes and Master Slides is a much better way of creating reusable slide layouts, the ability to create a new slide based on an image is a nice little feature of Captivate that is worth mentioning.

You will learn more about Master Slides and Themes in Chapter 6, *Crafting the Graphical Experience with Styles and Themes*.

Inserting Character images

Characters are a collection of images that can be inserted in your Captivate projects. These images represent male and female characters in various postures and expressions. Inserting such pictures in your eLearning projects brings in a human and sometimes humorous touch.

Downloading the eLearning assets
These characters are part of the eLearning assets available with your Captivate license. These eLearning assets are not part of the main Captivate installation package. A separate package must be downloaded and installed to use the characters. You can find these extra installers at http://www.adobe.com/go/Cp2017_win_assets_installer (for Windows) or http://www.adobe.com/go/Cp2017_mac_assets_installer (for macOS). Make sure you download and install this additional package before moving on with this section.

You will now create a new slide and insert a Character image using the following steps.

1. In the **Filmstrip**, select the first slide of your project.
2. Click the **Slide** icon on the Toolbar to insert a new **Content Slide**.
3. Use the **Properties** inspector to apply the **2Cols Text right** Master Slide to the newly created slide.
4. Click the **Media** icon of the Toolbar.
5. In the **Media** dropdown, click **Character**.

This opens the **My Assets** dialog box, as shown in the following screenshot. You can use it to insert various types of assets from various sources into your Captivate projects:

This dialog box is one of the treasures of Adobe Captivate. So, before moving on with the exercise, you should spend some time examining its features.

The top row of buttons (marked as **1** in the preceding screenshot) lets you decide where you want to look for assets:

- The **My Assets** button lists the assets that are stored on your computer. These can be assets that are part of the Captivate installation or assets downloaded after the installation of Captivate using the other features of this dialog box. These assets are further arranged and sorted by types. They are accessible through the second row of icons (marked as **2** in the preceding screenshot).

- Use the **Get Adobe Stock Assets** button to download stock images and videos from Adobe Stock. Adobe Stock is a huge online library of stock images and videos. You can use this online library in almost every Adobe application, including Photoshop, Illustrator, Premiere, and others, and, of course, in Captivate. Adobe Stock is not included with your Captivate license and requires an extra subscription. More information can be found at
`https://stock.adobe.com/`.

- The **Get Free eLearning Assets** button lets you access the online assets library of eLearning Brothers. *eLearning Brothers* is a company that teamed up with Adobe to offer you a huge library of free assets. Access to this online library is part of your Captivate license. It contains thousands of eLearning assets including cutout people, templates, themes, interactions, scenarios, and more. All you need to do is create a free account to access the library.

Don't hesitate to spend some time browsing these online resources. Remember that this is part of your Captivate license (except Adobe Stock), so don't hesitate to browse the library and use those assets. Once you download an asset from the eLearning Brothers library, you can access it via the **My Assets** button of this dialog box.

In this exercise, you will use an image asset already stored on your computer, so make sure that you return to the **My Assets** button before continuing with this exercise:

6. In the row of buttons, marked as **2** in the preceding screenshot, make sure that you are in the **Characters** assets.
7. Open the **Category** drop-down menu (marked as **3** in the preceding screenshot).
8. Select the **Casual** category.
9. In the left column of the dialog, choose the last character.
10. In the center column, take some time to examine the available poses for the character you selected. When done, select the very first pose at the top of the list.
11. Notice that you can choose three different shots for the chosen pose. (See **4** in the preceding screenshot.) In this example, choose the **Full** shot.
12. Click **OK** to insert the chosen pose in your slide.

From now on, the newly inserted character behaves just like another image. In fact, it actually *is* a .png image. This means you can move and resize it just like any other image (don't forget to hold down the *Shift* key while resizing the image to prevent the image from being distorted by the resize operation). You can also use the buttons of the **Properties** inspector to further edit this image, as discussed in the previous section.

The **Flip image horizontal** option of the **Image Edit** dialog box is an easy way to double the number of available postures!

Make sure your slide looks like the following image before moving on:

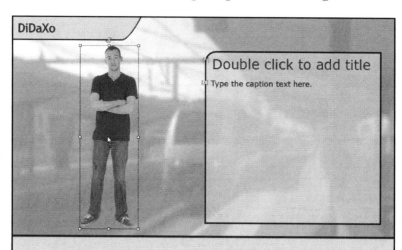

Working with SVG images

The image files you have been working with so far in this section are all *bitmap* images. This means that they contain pixels. Each pixel is a tiny little dot of a certain color and it is the collection of all these tiny little colored dots that recreates the picture as you see it.

Bitmap images are great, but they have one important limitation. To guarantee the best possible image quality, you must consider that a bitmap image is designed for a specific size. You should use an external application (such as Adobe Photoshop) to generate the image. You should not resize the image after you insert it in Captivate.

A bitmap image is composed of a fixed number of pixels. Imagine, for example, an image of 300 pixels in width and 200 pixels in height. This image contains 60,000 pixels (the multiplication of 300 by 200). So, what happens if you enlarge this picture after you insert it in Captivate? Well, you basically ask those 60,000 pixels to cover a bigger area, so there is no other choice than to make each pixel a little bigger. If you enlarge the picture just a tiny bit, this is barely noticeable, but if you want to make a tiny picture much bigger, you start to see each pixel, because you need to enlarge them too much.

SVG stands for *Scalable Vector Graphic*. SVG images are different, because they do not contain any pixels! Instead, they are made of a collection of shapes defined by mathematical coordinates and formulas. Without going into too many details, let's say that an SVG file contains the information necessary for the computer to calculate the image when it is viewed. The biggest advantage of this approach is that an SVG image is not tied to a specific size. If you resize it, the computer will simply recalculate the image for the new size. It means that an SVG image stays crisp and focused, whatever its size! Let's experiment with this hands-on via the following steps:

1. Return to slide 3 of your Captivate project.
2. Click the **Media** icon on the Toolbar and choose the **SVG** option.
3. Browse to the `Chapter02/mapSymbolPin.svg` file and insert it into your slide.

At first sight, this looks just like any other image. Now, let's experiment with the magic of SVG files:

4. Reduce the size of the picture (remember to hold down the *Shift* key to resize it proportionally).
5. Move the pin so that it points to the yellow area in the center of the map of Belgium.
6. Now, place your mouse pointer on top of one of the corner handles of the SVG image you just imported.
7. Hold down the *Shift* key and dramatically enlarge the image, but do not release your mouse button just yet.

You should see that the more you enlarge the image, the more it gets pixelated. When the image is dramatically bigger than the original, the deterioration is unacceptable:

8. Release the mouse button and see how your SVG file reacts.

This is where it gets interesting! When you release the mouse button, Captivate recalculates the image for its new size. After a short delay, you will see that the image is again nice and crisp even though you have enlarged it dramatically! This is illustrated in the following screenshot:

Of course, you don't need the image to be that big, so let's return to a more reasonable size that fits nicely into this slide:

9. Hold down the *Shift* key and resize the SVG image so that it fits on top of the map of Belgium, pointing to the yellow area at the center.

After this short experiment, you should understand the huge advantage of SVG images over bitmap images, especially when developing responsive eLearning content (that is, content that has the ability to adapt itself to any screen size, from large desktop computers to tiny smartphones).

Before moving on to the next section, let's quickly summarize what you learned in this section by comparing SVG files to their bitmap counterparts in the following table:

	SVG images	**Bitmap images**
File extension	`.svg`	`.png`, `.jpg`, and `.gif`
Contains	Vector shapes and paths used to calculate the picture	A fixed amount of pixel
Size	Resolution independent as the picture is recalculated for each size	Because it contains a fixed amount of pixel, a bitmap image is designed for a specific size

Authoring tool	Adobe Illustrator	Adobe Photoshop
Limitation	Cannot reproduce an actual photographic image	Cannot be easily enlarged; usually much bigger file size
Typical use case	Drawings, illustrations, logos, buttons, and other interface elements.	Photographic images

In modern-day eLearning, where the demand for responsive content increases by the day, SVG files are just awesome! They can be scaled to any size without losing their quality and the file size is usually much smaller than that of a bitmap file. This makes SVG images easy to transmit to mobile devices over WiFi or 4G connections. You will learn more about responsive eLearning in Chapter 10, *Creating a Responsive Project*.

Seeing the content of an SVG file

If you are curious about the inner workings of an SVG file, you can use Windows Explorer (Windows) or the Finder (macOS) to navigate to the SVG file you inserted in the previous exercise. Open it with a text editor, such as Notepad (Windows) or TextEdit (macOS). You should see a bunch of tags coordinates and color codes that represent the individual vector shapes and paths that compose the SVG image. But... no trace of any pixel in this file!

This concludes your first exploration of images in Adobe Captivate. Before moving on to the next topic, let's summarize what you learned in this section:

- You can easily insert many types of images in Captivate.
- Captivate provides some image editing capabilities. These are found in the **Image Edit** dialog accessible through the **Image Edit** button situated in the **Style** tab of the **Properties** inspector.
- It is best to prepare the image in another image editing application before inserting it into Captivate.
- If needed, use the **Reset To Original Size** button to change the picture back to its original size.
- Use the **Insert | Image Slide** menu item to create new slides with an image as the background.
- Captivate gives you access to thousands of free and paid assets that you can use within your Captivate course. Use the **Assets** button on the Toolbar to access the assets libraries.

- **Characters** are a collection of pictures (photographs and illustrations) that you can use in your eLearning projects.
- The installation of an extra package is required to use the Characters.
- `jpg`, `png` and `gif` images are all Bitmap images. This means that they contain a fixed number of pixels. This also means that they are designed for a predefined and fixed size.
- SVGs contain vector images that are resolution independent and very lightweight. This makes them well adapted for responsive projects, but they can also be used in regular (non-responsive) projects.

Working with Text Animations

The next object you will focus on is the Text Animation object. You won't need it in your final project, so this exercise is for demonstration purposes only. You will create a new slide to experiment with the object and delete it when you are finished:

1. In the `Chapter02/takeTheTrain.cptx` file, select the last slide in the **Filmstrip** panel.
2. Use the **Slide** icon on the Toolbar to create a new **Content Slide**.
3. Use the **Properties** inspector to apply the **Blank** Master Slide to your new slide.

Now that the stage is set, let's add a Text Animation object to the slide and explore its properties:

4. Click the **Text** icon on the Toolbar and choose the **Text Animation** item in the list.
5. In the **Text Animation Properties** box, type `Experimenting with Text Animations`.
6. Change the **Font** type to **Verdana** and the **Size** value to **62**.
7. Click the **OK** button. The new object appears in the middle of the slide.

With the new Text Animation object selected, take some time to inspect the **Style** tab of the **Properties** inspector. Most options are self-explanatory.

The new Text Animation is a little too wide to fit in the slide. If this happens with a regular Text Caption, you would use the white resize handles or the **Options** tab of the **Properties** inspector to resize the object:

8. Make sure the Text Animation is the selected item.
9. Switch to the **Options** tab of the **Properties** inspector.

As usual, the **X** and **Y** coordinates as well as the rotation **Angle** are available in the **Options** tab. But where are the width and height properties? And where are the white resize handles when the object is selected on the stage?

Actually, Captivate automatically calculates the size of a Text Animation object based on the text content and the font size. So, your only options to modify the size of a Text Animation object are to modify its text content and/or its font size. In this example, you will add a line break just before the **Text Animation** part of the content:

10. Make sure that the Text Animation object is still selected.
11. Return to the **Style** tab of the **Properties** inspector.
12. Click the **Animation Properties** button. Alternatively, you can also double-click the **Text Animation**.

This action reopens the **Text Animation Properties** box where you can change both the text content and the font size of your Text Animation object:

13. In the upper area of the **Text Animation Properties** box, use your mouse to place the cursor between **With** and **Text Animation.**
14. Hit the *Enter* key to create a line break at the location of the cursor.
15. Click the **OK** button to confirm the change.

The **Text Animation Properties** box closes and the Text Animation object is updated:

16. If necessary, use your mouse to move the Text Animation to the middle of the slide.
17. In the **Style** tab of the **Properties** inspector, choose an effect in the **Effect** drop-down list.

Use the preview area at the top of the **Properties** inspector to control the selected effect:

18. To test your new Text Animation, use the **Preview** icon on the Toolbar to preview the **Next 5 Slides**.
19. When you are done, close the preview pane to return to the authoring environment of Captivate.

In this exercise, you experimented with Text Animations. This is a somewhat old object of Captivate that isn't very popular anymore. The main reason why people don't use this object anymore is that Text Animations are based on Flash and they cannot be used in an HTML 5 project. Today, most Captivate projects are published in the HTML 5 format, and so, the Text Animation object is often obsolete.

That being said, if you publish your project in Flash, the Text Animation object is a great addition to your toolbox providing that you use it with care. It is a great effect if you use it every once in a while. But if you use it too often, it overcharges your projects, giving an unprofessional impression.

You will now delete the slide containing the Text Animation and return to the original situation:

20. In **Filmstrip**, right-click the last slide of the project.
21. Click the **Delete** menu item and confirm the deletion in the dialog box.
22. Save the file when done.

Let's now summarize what you have learned about the Text Animation object:

- The Text Animation object can be created entirely in Captivate. There is no need to use an external application (such as Adobe Animate or Adobe After Effects) to create the animation!
- To resize a Text Animation, change its content, add a line break into the text, or change the font size.
- Use the Text Animation object with care. You don't want to overcharge your projects with unnecessary distractions.
- The Text Animation object is not supported in HTML5 and is not very popular anymore.

Working with Text Effects

The Text Effects feature lets you create and apply some sophisticated visual effects to the Text Captions and Smart Shapes containing text. If you are a Photoshop user, you'll be in familiar territory because Captivate's Text Effects feature shares most of its functionalities with the effects of Photoshop.

Follow these steps to experiment with Text Effects:

1. Return to slide 2 of the `Chapter02/takeTheTrain.cptx` file.
2. Double-click the Title placeholder and type `Jan` as the title text.

3. Double-click the Text Caption placeholder and type the following text (hitting the *Enter* key after each line of text):

```
Nationality : Belgian
Lives in : Brussels
Occupation : Student
Takes the train : Everyday!
```

4. Hit the *Esc* key to leave the text edit mode and leave the Text Caption object selected.

5. Reduce the height of the Text Caption so that it takes approximately half the available space.

6. Select the Title Smart Shape.

Now that you have some text on the slide, you can start experimenting with Text Effects:

7. With the Title Smart Shape still selected, look at the **Properties** inspector.

8. In the **Character** section of the **Properties** inspector, click the **Effects** icon next to the **Color** and the **Highlight** properties.

9. Click on any of the effects in the drop-down menu.

10. Repeat the preceding operations to apply other predefined effects and get a feel of what is possible.

11. When you are done, reopen the Text Effect menu, and click the **Clear** button to remove the applied effect.

In addition to applying predefined Text Effects, Captivate also lets you create your own custom Text Effects. Let's create one and save it for later use.

12. Make sure the Title Smart Shape (containing the text **Jan**) is still selected.

13. Reopen the Text Effect dropdown and click the first available + icon. This operation is shown in the following screenshot:

The **Text Effects** window opens. The left side of the window contains nine effects. You can easily turn these effects on and off by clicking their checkbox. The right side of the window displays the options of the effect selected on the left. Currently, no effect is applied:

14. In the left column of the **Text Effects** window, select the **Drop Shadow** checkbox.

A Drop Shadow effect is added to the selected text object. For this example, accept the default settings of the Drop Shadow effect:

15. In the left column of the **Text Effects** window, select the **Outer Glow** checkbox.

The **Outer Glow** effect is also applied to the Text Caption and the options of the **Outer Glow** effect are displayed on the right side of the **Text Effects** window. To make your effect more appealing and visible, modify the color of the **Outer Glow** effect:

16. On the right side of the **Text Effects** window, click the **Color** option of the **Outer Glow** effect.

17. In the color picker on the right side of the window, choose any bright green color. The **Text Effects** window should now look like the following screenshot:

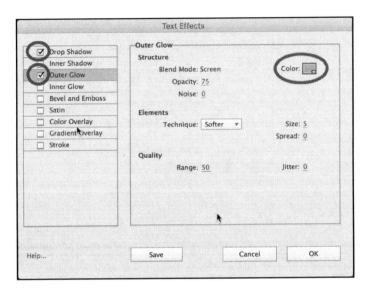

Hey! It looks like you just came up with a very nice effect. Let's save it for future use:

18. At the bottom of the **Text Effects** window, click the **Save** button.

The **Text Effects** window closes and your effect is applied to the selected Text Caption. Because you have saved your nice effect, it is easy to apply it to another text object of the project:

19. Select the Text Caption object located just below the title on which you applied an effect.
20. In the **Properties** inspector, open the **Effects** icon one more time.
21. There should be a new predefined effect in the drop-down menu! Apply your new effect to the selected Text Caption.

In this section, you have experimented with Text Effects. You have also created a custom Text Effect and you have you have saved it for later use. Finally, you have applied the same custom effect to another text object. Note that a Text Effect must be applied to the entire text content. It is not possible to select a portion of the text and apply the effect to the selected portion only.

You will now remove those effects and return to the initial situation:

22. Select the title Smart Shape containing the text **Jan**.
23. In the **Properties** inspector, reopen the **Effects** icon.
24. Click the trash can icon to remove your custom effect from the menu.
25. Now, click the **Clear** button to remove the effect from the selected object.
26. Select the Text Caption object and repeat the above action to remove your Text Effect from the Text Caption.

You should now be back to the initial project and your slide should look like the following image:

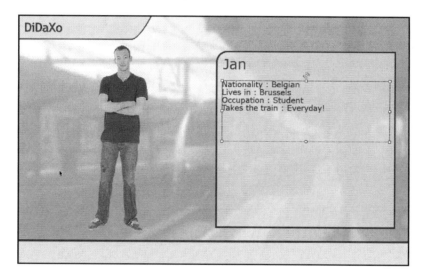

Before wrapping up this chapter, let's summarize what you learned about Text Effects.

- There are nine basic effects (such as Drop Shadows and Outer Glows) that can be mixed and combined in order to create complex visual effects
- Text Effects can be applied to both Text Captions and Smart Shapes objects (provided that the Smart Shape contains text)
- It is possible to save a custom Text Effect and reuse it later
- The Text Effect window of Captivate looks like the Effects window of Photoshop. (Actually, it is the same technology at work behind the scenes!)
- Use the **Effects** icon of the **Properties** inspector to define and apply a Text Effect to the selected Text Caption or Smart Shape.

Summary

In this chapter, you learned a lot about some of the standard non-interactive objects of Captivate. Although very simple to use, these objects are the fundamental building blocks of every single eLearning project that you will build with Adobe Captivate.

Among all the objects you studied in this chapter, one of them stands out. The Smart Shape object lets you draw custom or predefined shapes in your project. These shapes can be used in such a wide variety of situations that they can advantageously replace the Text Caption object in most situations

Another important object is the image object. You have learned that there are two very different types of images. The bitmap images contain a fixed number of pixels and are therefore designed for a predefined size. Scalable Vector Graphic (or SVG) images contain vector paths and shapes used by the computer to regenerate the picture each time its size changes. SVG images are therefore resolution independent and very lightweight.

Now let's be honest. You are not there yet! There is still a lot of work left to be done before sharing the project with your learners.

In the next chapter, you will build on your new skills and learn about other objects that are used to incorporate multimedia elements into your eLearning content.

Meet the community

In this section, we would like to introduce you to Anita Horsley, one of the most active members of the Captivate community and an awesome Captivate Certified Instructor. She authored the *Fast Track to Adobe Captivate 6* video series by *Packt* (see `http://www.packtpub.com/fast-track-to-adobe-captivate-6/video`).

Damien

Anita has been a reviewer for two of my previous Captivate books. We finally met in October 2014 during the Adobe learning summit in Las Vegas. I was completely jetlagged by the trip, but Anita was kind enough to offer me a gigantic cup of coffee!

Pooja

I've got the privilege to co-present with Anita at various conferences in the past few years, and she is a delight to work with. She always comes up with fantastic ideas to present the content during the sessions. My daughter is very fond of Anita, and wants to be a Fire Fighter like Anita one day!

Anita Horsley

During Anita Horsley's tenure as a firefighter, she initiated, developed, and managed the health and safety program. At the Oregon State Fire Marshal, she founded the eLearning track as well as implemented and coordinated the eLearning team and internal training. She managed the learning management system and chaired the Oregon State Captivate User Group. She is the founder and President of CALEX Learning Consultants, LLC. She is a full-time eLearning developer and instructor. She often presents at conferences nationally. She authored the video tutorial series *Fast Track To Adobe Captivate 6* by *Packt*. She also has a blog named *Crazy About Captivate* that provides tips and tricks on Adobe Captivate. She holds a Master's in Education, an Adobe Certified Expert in Captivate, and is an Adobe Captivate instructor.

Contact details

- **Web**: http://calex-llc.com
- **Blog**: http://captivatecrazy.blogspot.com
- **Twitter**: @captivatecrazy
- **LinkedIn**: http://www.linkedin.com/in/anitahorsley
- **Google +**: https://plus.google.com/u/0/+CALEXLearningConsultantsLLCCharleston/posts
- **Facebook**: https://www.facebook.com/CALEXLearningConsultantsLLC

3
Working with Multimedia

In this chapter, you will continue to experiment with the objects and features of Adobe Captivate 2017. You will now focus on the objects and features used to transform your eLearning content into a compelling multimedia experience.

Multimedia means that you will use various media and technologies to convey your message to your learner. This includes static text and images (already covered in the previous chapter) as well as audio, video, and animation.

Some of this animated content can be created entirely within Captivate, while other rich content is developed in external applications, such as Adobe Animate CC, and imported in Captivate when ready.

In this chapter, you will cover the following topics:

- Inserting Flash and HTML 5 animations in your course
- Inserting video files in the project
- Adding sound effects to objects
- Adding background music to the project
- Recording narration to the slides
- Importing external sound files into Captivate
- Editing a sound clip in Captivate
- Generating narration with Text to Speech

These are a lot of exciting things to cover, so let's get started by inserting some animations in your course module.

Preparing your work

Before jumping into inserting animation, prepare Captivate and open the project files of this chapter using the following steps:

1. Open (or restart) Captivate.

If you are using the default interface mode (as described in Chapter 1, *Getting Started with Captivate 2017*), restarting Captivate resets your workspace to default. If you are using the advanced interface mode, be aware that the screenshots in this book and the step-by-step instructions were created using the default interface. To switch back to the default interface mode refer to Chapter 1, *Getting Started with Adobe Captivate 2017*.

2. Use the **File** | **Open** menu item to open the *Chapter03/takeTheTrain.cptx* file. You can also use the *Ctrl + O* (Windows) / *Cmd + O* (Mac) shortcut to open a file.
3. Take some time to look at this project and its objects.

The project you just opened contains 20 slides, including those you worked with in the previous chapter. After reading the previous chapter, you have the skills to complete everything in this sample file. We've only added a few slides into the project, applied Master Slides, and inserted standard objects such as Text Captions, Images, and Smart Shapes.

Using the exercise files

In this chapter, you will use the sample files in the Chapter03 folder. In the Chapter03/final folder, you find the sample files as they should be at the end of this chapter if you follow all the step-by-step instructions. If you get confused by any of the step-by-step instructions, look at the final folder. Also, be aware that you'll have a fresh set of files to work with at the beginning of each chapter, so don't hesitate to experiment and mess up with the files while performing the exercise.

Inserting external animations into the project

In this exercise, you will import animations into the course. These animations are Flash and HTML5 animations that have been created in external applications such as Adobe Animate CC. The main difference between a Flash animation and an HTML5 animation is where and how these animations can be played back.

To read and play a Flash animation, your browser needs the Adobe Flash player plug-in and the Captivate file needs to be published in Flash. While there is nothing wrong with Flash technology, remember that it is not available on mobile devices. Flash is a no-go if you want to deploy your eLearning courses on tablets and Smartphones. HTML5 animations use technologies that are natively supported by web browsers. So an HTML5 animation does not need any plug-in to be played back and is therefore supported on any device.

When it comes to creating these animations, the preferred solution is Adobe Animate CC, which is available as part of the Adobe Creative Cloud subscription. Adobe Animate CC creates and publishes both Flash and HTML 5 animations.

The animation authoring tools from Adobe

There have been a lot of changes with Adobe's authoring tools lately. When it comes to animations, the historical application was *Adobe Flash Professional*. Although the latest versions of this application generated both Flash and HTML5 animations, it was mainly used as a Flash authoring tool. In 2011, Adobe launched another application called *Adobe Edge Animate* that was used to create HTML5 animations. From 2011 to 2015, the two applications (Adobe Flash Pro and Adobe Edge animate) coexisted. One was used mainly to create Flash animations, while the other one was used to create HTML animations. As of November 2015, Adobe decided to merge Flash Pro and Edge Animate into a new application called *Adobe Animate CC*. In this book, we only refer to the actively developed applications at the time of writing. That's why we refer to Animate CC and not to Flash Pro or Edge Animate. That being said, if your organization still uses these applications, you can still access them from your Creative Cloud subscriptions. For more details, visit `https://helpx.adobe.com/creative-cloud/kb/why-has-adobe-stopped-developing-my-app-.html`.

Importing Flash animations

The first type of animation you will focus on is Flash. The external application for generating these animations is Adobe Animate CC (formerly Adobe Flash Professional) and the file imported in Captivate is the compiled `.swf` file. If you do not have Animate CC installed, don't worry, all the necessary animations have already been created for you.

The file extensions of Adobe Animate CC

When saving a file with Adobe Animate CC (formerly Adobe Flash professional), the file extension used is .fla. The .fla file contains every object, animation, timeline, filter, and so on, needed for the animation to work properly. Consequently, it can be a very large file. Once the .fla file is finished, it is necessary to export it (the technical term is *compile*) to another format. Usually, you compile your Animate CC project either in the .swf format (for Flash) or in the HTML5 format. If compiled in .swf, you need to publish your Captivate file in .swf also, and the student will need the Adobe Flash Player to play the animation. If compiled in HTML5, you generate an entire HTML/JavaScript/CSS application that can be played without any plugins on any device. The important takeaway is that you always import a *compiled* version of your animation in the Captivate project. Make sure you keep the original source file (with a .fla file extension) in your archives in case you ever need to modify your animation later. Converting a .swf or HTML5 animation back to .fla (an operation known as *reverse engineering*) is not possible (well actually, it is with specialized workaround, but you will never get back to the *original*.fla file!).

In the next exercise, you will import a Flash animation into the *Take the Train* project. Because the final project will be published in HTML5, the next exercise is for demonstration purposes only. First, you will insert a new slide into the project and you will insert a Flash animation into it. At the end, you will delete the new slide. Perform the following steps to do so:

1. In the **Filmstrip**, select the last slide of the project (slide 20).
2. Use the **Slide** icon on the Toolbar to insert a new **Content Slide**. The new slide should be inserted at the end as slide 21.
3. Use the **Properties** inspector to apply the **contentBkg** Master Slide to the newly inserted slide.
4. Use the **Media | Animation** icon on the Toolbar to insert a new animation on the current slide.

The **Open** dialog box appears to let you locate the animation to insert.

If you do not have Adobe Animate CC or if you do not know how to use it, don't worry! To get you started, Captivate ships has a **gallery** of many objects that you can use. This gallery is located in:

- **Windows**: The `C:\Program Files\Adobe\Adobe Captivate 2017 x64\Gallery` folder
- **macOS**: The `/Applications/Adobe Captivate 2017/Gallery` folder

The `Gallery` folder is further divided into several subfolders containing various types of assets. One of these folders is the `SWF Animations` folder.

5. Browse to the `SWF Animations/Arrows/Orange arrow/down.swf` file in the gallery and click the **Open** button.

The animation is imported in the middle of the slide just like the Text Caption you added in the previous chapter. Note that only `.swf` and animated `.gif` files can be inserted like this in Captivate.

The animated `.gif` format is supported in both the Flash and the HTML5 output of Captivate.

6. With the newly inserted animation selected, look at the **Properties** inspector.
7. Switch to the **Timing** panel situated just next to the **Properties** inspector.
8. At the top of the **Timing** panel, open the **Display For** drop-down menu.
9. Select the **Rest of Slide** option. This operation is illustrated in the following screenshot:

You will now use two techniques to preview the animation you just inserted.

10. Switch back to the **Properties** inspector.
11. In the **Style** tab of the **Properties** inspector, click the **down** button.

The inserted animation plays into the **Select animation from the library** box.

12. When you're ready, click **OK** to close the box.
13. Use the **Preview | Next 5 Slides** icon on the toolbar to get a sense of what this animation looks like in your slide.
14. Close the **Preview** panel when you're done.
15. Delete the animation from the slide when you've finished.

During the preview, pay attention to the way the orange arrow is animated, and keep in mind that the general timing of the slide hasn't been set yet.

Animations like this liven up your slide, but remember that it has one major limitation. Because it is Flash based, it is supported in the Flash output of Captivate only, but not in HTML5.

Flash animations in HTML 5

When viewed in HTML5, Flash based animations, such as the Orange Arrow that you inserted in this exercise, gracefully degrade into a static image displaying only the first frame of the animation. The concept of graceful degradation lets you design the optimal experience (here an animated arrow). In case this optimal experience is not completely supported it is degraded in such a way that the content is preserved (in this case, the arrow is present as an image in the HTML5 output, but is not animated). The progressive enhancement concept takes the opposite approach. It lets you design a satisfactory basic experience, which you enhance depending on the capabilities of the browser.

Fortunately, Captivate supports another type of animation made entirely in HTML5 and supported on any desktop or mobile device.

Importing HTML5 animations

In this exercise, you will import an HTML5 animation into the project.

Since this project does not require any HTML5 animation, the next exercise is for demonstration purposes only, and you will delete it at the end of the exercise. The animation you will import comes from another project. It has been created in Adobe Animate CC, and compiled into an HTML5 animation.

If you have Adobe Animate CC installed on your computer, the source file of the animation you will use in this exercise is available in the `Chapter03/sources` folder of the exercises. Feel free to take a look at that file to see how the animation was made.

Use the following steps to import an HTML5 animation in your course:

1. Make sure you are still on slide 21 of the `Chapter03/takeTheTrain.cptx` project.
2. Click the **Media | HTML 5 Animation** icon on the Toolbar to start the import.
3. Navigate to the `Chapter03/SpeedLimit_120.oam` file and import it into your slide.
4. When the animation has finished loading, hover over the newly imported object to preview it on the slide.

An `.oam` file is a special package created by Adobe Animate CC. It works more or less like a `.zip` file. That is, the `.oam` file is a wrapper that contains all the HTML, CSS, and JavaScript resources needed to make the animation run properly.

Inspecting the content of a OAM file

If you want to inspect the actual content of an `.oam` file, here is a simple trick: just change the `.oam` extension to `.zip`. Then, unzip the resulting file and inspect its content. Make sure you change the extension of the package back to `.oam` before continuing with this exercise.

You will now adjust the properties of the newly inserted HTML5 animation, so it integrates nicely with the slide. The most obvious thing to do is to adjust the size of the object. When inserting these kinds of animation Captivate creates a container of 400 pixels in width by 300 pixels in height, regardless of the actual size of the animation.

5. With the HTML5 animation still selected, look at the **Options** tab of the **Properties** inspector.
6. Deselect the **Constraint proportions** checkbox.
7. Change the Width to 500 px and the Height to 100 px. Use the *Enter* key to validate the new values.
8. Return to the **Style** tab of the **Properties** inspector and look at the available options. They should be self-explanatory for the most part.
9. Deselect both the **Border** and the **Scrolling** checkboxes.

The size of the animation is 500px by 100px. If you have access to Adobe Animate CC, you can open the `Chapter03/sources/SpeedLimit_120.fla` file and confirm this size in the Properties panel of Adobe Animate CC.

You will now preview your new HTML5 animation using the **Preview** icon on the Toolbar.

10. Use the **Preview | Next 5 slides** icon on the Toolbar to open the preview pane.

Well, it looks like you have a problem! Your HTML5 animation is not showing in the preview pane. Don't worry! There is nothing wrong with your project. The preview pane shows a temporary Flash file of whatever portion of the project you want to preview. But the HTML5 animation you just inserted is not supported in Flash, and this is why it is not playing in the preview pane. To test your HTML5 animation, it is necessary to preview the HTML5 output of the content in a web browser.

11. Close the preview pane and click the **Preview** icon on the Toolbar one more time.
12. Choose the **HTML5 in Browser** item in the list of options.

This preview option only works for the entire project. There is currently no way to preview the HTML5 output of the next five slides in the browser. When the preview reaches slide 21, make sure your HTML5 animation is displayed as expected.

During the preview, keep in mind that the project is not yet finished. The arrangement of the objects on the slides as well as the overall timing is yet to be defined.

Since this project does not need any HTML5 animations, you will now delete slide 21 and return to the original project.

13. In the **Filmstrip**, right-click on slide 21.
14. Click the **Delete** menu item and confirm the deletion of the slide in the dialog box.

This concludes your overview of inserting external animations into Captivate. It is time to summarize what you have learned:

- Captivate lets you insert external `.swf`, `.gif` and HTML5 animations in your projects.
- `.swf` animation requires the Adobe Flash Player plug-in. They are typically created in Adobe Animate CC and are not supported in HTML5.

- Captivate ships with an extensive Gallery containing various types of assets that you can use in your courses. Regarding animations, the Gallery only contains `.swf` animations.
- With Adobe Animate CC, you can create animations and compile them either as `.swf` or as HTML5 animations.
- Use Adobe Animate CC to package your HTML5 animations into `.oam` files before inserting them in Captivate.
- Captivate has the ability to import the `.oam` packages directly into your project.
- Those HTML5 animations are not supported in Flash and therefore do not appear in the Flash based preview pane of Captivate. It is necessary to test the project in a web browser to see these animations.

In the next section, you will continue learning about the multimedia capabilities of Captivate by inserting video files into your project.

Working with video

It's time for the next object in this chapter: the **Video** file. Captivate allows you to insert various types of video files, including `.flv`, `.avi`, `.mov`, and `.mp4` files. However, Captivate will always convert your videos to `.mp4` upon publishing, because the `.mp4` video file format is compatible with both the HTML5 and the Flash player.

 It is not Adobe Captivate that handles the conversion of your video files to the `.mp4` file format. This task is taken care of by the Adobe Media Encoder CC 2015 behind the scenes. Adobe Media Encoder CC 2015 is included in Adobe Captivate 2017 installation package.

In this exercise, you will insert a new slide in the Take the Train project and add a video file to it:

1. Return to the `Chapter03/takeTheTrain.cptx` file.
2. Use the **Filmstrip** to go to slide 19.
3. Click the **Slide | Blank Slide** icon on the Toolbar to create a new blank slide.
4. If necessary, use the **Properties** inspector to apply the **contentBkg** Master Slide on the newly created slide.

The new slide is inserted as slide 20. Remember that new slides are always inserted *after* the active slide. You will now import a video file onto this new slide.

5. Go to the **Media | Video** icon on the Toolbar. Alternatively, you can also use the **Video | Insert Video** menu item.

The **Insert Video** dialog opens. At the top of the Insert Video dialog, you have to choose either an **Event video** or a **Multi-Slide synchronized video**. The following table lists some of the differences between these two options:

	Event Video	**Multi-Slide synchronized video**
Sync	Cannot be distributed over several slides.	Can be distributed over several slides or not.
Timeline	The Timeline of the video is independent from the Timeline of the project.	The video plays in sync with the slide or slides it appears on.
Playback controls	Event videos can have their own playback controls.	Have no specific playback controls associated because it uses the same playback controls as the project.
Closed Captions	Cannot be closed captioned	Can be closed captioned.

In this case, you want the video to show on slide 20 only, something that both the **Event Video** and the **Multi-Slide Synchronized Video** can achieve. But in Chapter 12, *Creating Accessible eLearning* you will add Closed Captions to the video; something that only the **Multi-Slide Synchronized Video** can do.

6. At the top of the dialog box, choose the **Multi-Slide Synchronized Video** option.
7. Click the **Browse** button and navigate to the Chapter03/departure_sequence_EN.mp4 file of your exercises folder.
8. Click **open** to insert the video onto the slide.
9. In the lower area of the **Insert Video** dialog, select the **Modify slide duration to accommodate video** option.
10. Make sure the **Insert Video** dialog looks like the following screenshot and click the **OK** button:

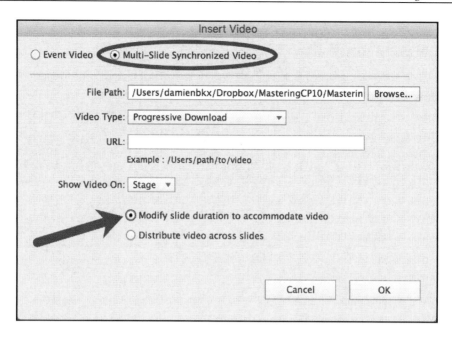

The video is inserted in the center of the slide. You can see that the video is a little bit too large to fit on the slide. Therefore, your next task is to adjust the size of the video using the following steps:

11. Make sure the video is selected and look at the **Options** tab of the **Properties** inspector.

Notice the message **Proportions are locked**. It means that you cannot change the Width of the video independently from its Height. This is made to ensure that the proportions of the video are respected and your video does not appear distorted when the size is changed.

12. In the **Properties** inspector, change the Width of the video to 550 px.
13. Note that Captivate calculates a new height for the video so that the Width/Height ratio of the video does not change.
14. For the position of the video, change the **X** coordinate to 237 px and the **Y** coordinate to 107 px. This should place the video at the center of the stage.
15. Take a look at the **Timeline** and notice that the duration of the slide matches the duration of the video file.
16. Save the file and use the **Preview | Next 5 slides** icon on the Toolbar.
17. When the preview is finished, close the **Preview** pane.

In this exercise, you have inserted an external video into your Captivate course. It is time to summarize what you learned about inserting videos in Captivate:

- There are two options available to insert videos in Captivate: **Event Video** and **Multi-Slide Synchronized Video**.
- Captivate allows you to insert various types of videos in your project, but will always convert your files to .mp4 video upon publishing.
- The *Adobe Media Encoder* is an external application. It is part of Adobe Creative Cloud and part of the default Adobe Captivate package. The **Adobe Media Encoder** (**AME**) automatically converts any video file to .mp4, so it can be used in Captivate.

In the next section, you will start looking into the audio support in Adobe Captivate.

Working with audio

In this section, you will discover how audio can be used in a Captivate project. In Captivate, you can add sound at three different levels:

- **Object level**: The audio associated with an object plays when the object appears on the screen. This is a great place to add small sound effects (Whoosh, clings, bangs, tones, and so on) to the project.
- **Slide level**: The audio clip plays in sync with the slide. Most of the time, this option is used to add voiceover narration.
- **Project level**: Most of the time, project level audio is used to add background music to the entire course module.

You will now cover these three options in greater detail.

Adding audio to the objects

Sound can be added on each and every object in Captivate. The audio clip associated with an object plays when the object appears on the stage.

While object level audio is the preferred place to add sound effects, nothing prevents you from adding narration or any other type of audio content at object level. It may be used, for example, to read aloud descriptive text or to pronounce a difficult word. This book only shows the typical use case, but experiment and be creative in how you actually use this feature.

In the next exercise, you will associate a sound effect with one of the Character images present in the Take the Train project using the following steps:

1. Return to the `Chapter03/takeTheTrain.cptx` file and use the **Filmstrip** to select slide 2.
2. Select the Character image on the left side of the slide.
3. Refer to the **Properties** inspector and switch to the **Options** tab.
4. Click the **Add Audio** button.

Clicking the **Add Audio** button on the **Options** tab of the **Properties** inspector is one of the many ways you can add audio to an object. You can also use the **Audio | Import To | Object** menu item or right-click the object and choose the **Audio | Import to** contextual menu. Whichever way you use, you will always end up in the following dialog box:

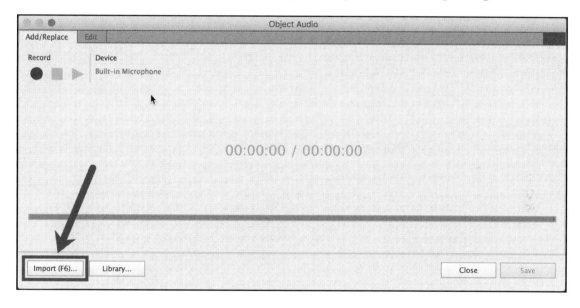

5. At the bottom of the **Object Audio** dialog, click the **Import** button (see the arrow in the preceding screenshot).

By default, the window that opens displays the content of the `Sound` directory of the Gallery. Remember that the **Gallery** is a collection of assets that ship with Captivate. You already used the Gallery earlier in this chapter to import the animated orange arrow.

If the **Import Audio** dialog does not show the content of the `sound` directory by default, remember that the gallery is located in the `C:\Program Files\Adobe\Adobe Captivate 2017\Gallery` folder (Windows) or in the `Applications/Adobe Captivate 2017/Gallery` folder (Mac).

6. At the end of the list, choose the `Whoosh 2.mp3` file and click **Open**.

The audio clip is imported into the project and the sound wave is loaded in the **Object Audio** dialog.

7. Click the **Play** button in the top left corner of the **Object audio** dialog to control the imported sound.
8. Click the **Save** button at the bottom right corner of the box.
9. Click the **Close** button to close the **Object Audio** box.

The audio clip is now associated with the selected Character image. If you open the **Timeline** panel, you will see a loudspeaker icon on the image layer indicating that an audio clip is associated with that particular object (see the following screenshot).

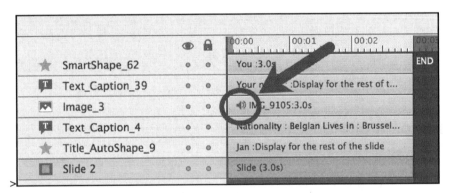

The sound effect plays in sync with the object. This means that you hear the sound effect whenever the Character image appears on the screen. You will now use the **Timing** panel to modify the timing of the selected image and give it a try.

10. Make sure the Character image you associated the audio clip with is still selected
11. Open the **Timing** panel. Remember that the **Timing** panel is associated with the **Properties** inspector and appears on the right side of the screen.
12. At the top of the **Timing** panel, change the **Appear After** property to 5 seconds. Your object is now displayed for a **Specific Time** of three seconds and **Appears After five** seconds.

If the **Timeline** panel is open at the bottom of the screen, you see this change reflected in the **Timeline** panel. This is illustrated in the following screenshot (you can use the **Window** | **Timeline** menu item to open the **Timeline** panel if needed):

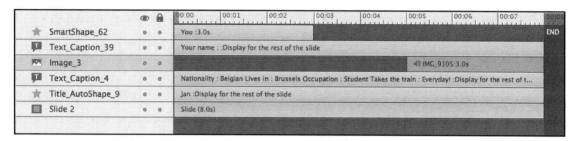

Even though we will discuss the **Timeline** in detail in Chapter 4, *Working with the Timeline and Other Useful Tools*, it is quite easy to see that the character image is scheduled to appear five seconds into the slide and to be displayed for three seconds. It also means that your sound effect should play five seconds after the slide begins, in sync with the object. Let's check this out using the Preview feature of Captivate.

13. In the **Filmstrip**, select the first slide of the project.
14. Use the **Preview** icon on the Toolbar to preview the **Next 5 Slides** and test the sound effect.
15. When slide 2 displays in the preview pane, make sure the sound effect is played in sync with the Character icon, five seconds after the beginning of the slide.
16. Close the **Preview** pane when done.
17. Don't forget to save the file when you are finished.

This concludes your overview of object level audio in Captivate. Let's summarize what you have learned:

- You can associate an audio clip with any object. The audio plays when the object appears on the stage.
- Usually, object level audio is used to add sound effects to the course.
- Only sound clips in .wav or .mp3 format can be imported into Captivate (but try to use .wav files whenever possible).
- When a sound clip is added to an object, a loudspeaker icon appears in the corresponding layer of the **Timeline**.

Adding background music to the entire project

In this section, you will associate an audio clip with the entire project. Usually, project level audio is used to add **background music**, but again, nothing prevents you from adding other types of audio content at that level. To make sure that the music plays during the entire project, you will use a 15 to 30 second sound clip (called a sample) and make it loop for the duration of the course.

In the next exercise, you will add background music to the Take the Train project:

1. If needed, return to the `Chapter03/takeTheTrain.cptx` file.
2. Use the **Audio | Import To | Background** menu item.
3. Choose the `Loop Acoustic.mp3` file from the `/Sound` directory of the Captivate `Gallery` and click **Open**.
4. The **Background Audio** dialog box opens.

The **Background Audio** dialog informs you that the duration of the `loop Acoustic.mp3` sound clip is 16 seconds (see the arrow in the following screenshot).

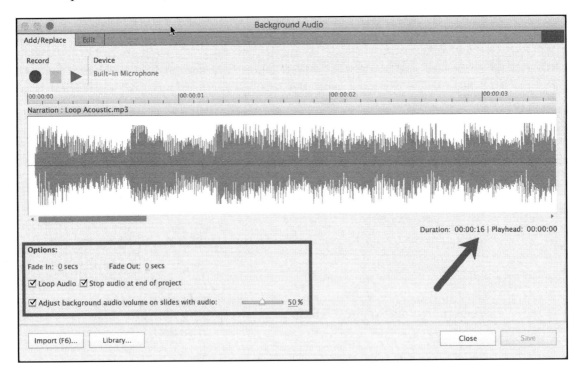

Some interesting options are in the lower part of the **Background Audio** dialog (see the rectangle in the lower left area of the preceding screenshot):

- When the audio clip is finished, the **Loop Audio** option makes it start over, so the sound clip plays for the entire project.
- The **Stop audio at end of project** option should be selected at all times. If it is not selected, the background audio will keep playing even after the end of the course.
- The **Adjust background audio volume on slides with audio** option automatically lowers the volume of the background music on slides with associated slide-level audio. This option ensures that the slide audio is always louder than the background audio.

Most of the time, leaving these options at their default settings works just fine.

5. Accept the defaults and click **Close** to close the **Background Audio** dialog.
6. Use the **Preview** icon on the Toolbar to preview the entire **Project**.
7. Close the **Preview** pane when you are done

If you need to modify the **Background Audio** or one of its associated options, use the **Audio | Edit | Background** menu item to reopen the **Background Audio** dialog. Use the **Add/Replace** tab of the **Background Audio** dialog to use another sound clip and the **Edit** tab to modify the current sound clip.

When to use background audio?

I have never used background audio in a Captivate project! I find it annoying and distracting. It drives the students away from what I want them to focus on. That being said, there are probably some use cases for which background audio would be useful. If you run into one of these use cases, don't hesitate to use the feature. There is only one thing to keep in mind: *you are teaching*, so the background music you use, as well as any other features of your Captivate project, *should serve the student's learning*.

You will now remove the background audio that you have added to the project.

8. Use the **Audio | Remove | Background** to remove the background audio.
9. Confirm you want to remove the audio clip.
10. Save the file when you are done.

Before moving to the next section, this is a summary of what you have learned about background audio:

- Audio can be added at the project level. Most of the time, this feature is used to add background music to the project.
- Use the **Audio** menu to add, edit, and delete the background audio.
- To make sure the background music plays for the entire duration of the course, use a short sample of music and make it loop.
- Captivate has an option to lower the volume of the background audio when a slide with an associated sound clip plays.
- Use background audio with care! It should not distract your students!

Also remember that Background Audio does not have to be music. It can, for instance, be the background sounds you may hear in a hospital setting when learning about hospital procedures. It can also be used in an introduction slide where students can check if they have audio or if it is a good volume. Again, this book shows the most typical use case. It is your imagination and instructional design that will ultimately define how this feature is used.

Adding audio to the slides

Adding audio to the slides is, by far, the most interesting place to use audio in Captivate. Typically, slide level audio is where you add voiceover narration. Slide level audio is also the only audio where you can apply closed captioning. You will learn more about closed captioning in Chapter 12, *Creating Accessible eLearning*.

There are three ways to add audio at slide level:

- The narration can be produced entirely within Captivate
- The narration can be produced in an external application and imported into Captivate
- Text-To-Speech can generate the audio clips

In this section, you will experiment with these three options one by one.

Recording narration with Captivate

The first way to insert audio at the slide level is to record your audio clips with the tools of Captivate. First, you have to make sure that your microphone or system audio communicates with Captivate.

The following exercise requires a microphone. If you do not have a microphone available, just read through the steps. You'll have a chance to catch up in a subsequent exercise.

Setting up the sound system

The exact setup procedure depends on your audio equipment and your operating system, but basically, setting up a sound system can be divided into three phases:

- **Phase 1**: Plug the microphone in the audio input port of your computer (usually it is the red plug of your sound card). If you have a USB microphone, plug it into any available USB port.
- **Phase 2**: Check out the audio options of your operating system (see the following screenshot):
  - **macOS**: In the **System Preferences**, use the **Input** tab of the **Sound** section
  - **Windows**: Use the **Manage Audio Devices** link in the **Hardware and Sound** section of the **Control panel**
- **Phase 3**: Check out the audio options of Captivate.

Once the audio options of the operating system are properly set up, you can adjust Captivate's audio settings:

1. Return to the `Chapter03/takeTheTrain.cptx` file.
2. Use the **Audio | Settings** menu item to open the **Audio Settings** dialog box.
3. Open the **Audio input Devices** drop-down list and select your microphone or audio interface.

If your computer has multiple audio input devices (such as a microphone-in and a line-in), the **Audio Input Devices** drop-down list instructs Captivate on which device it has to use. This is the single most important part of the procedure. If the wrong device is selected, the audio data will never reach Captivate. In the following screenshot, I instruct Captivate to listen to the audio stream coming from the **Yeti Stereo Microphone**, which is an external microphone plugged to my computer with a USB cable. The actual content of the drop-down menu depends on the audio equipment installed on your system.

For the **Bitrate** option, the default should be fine. If you later decide that the default audio quality is not good enough, you can test a new recording with a higher **Bitrate**. Be aware that the higher the **Bitrate**, the bigger the file. When choosing the **Bitrate**, you have to find the most appropriate balance between the quality of the sound and the size of the resulting file.

4. Leave the **Bitrate** option at its default and click the **Calibrate Input** button.

Calibrating the input is finding the right sensitivity for the microphone. If it is set too high, you'll have a saturated sound with lots of clipping, but if it is set too low, the recorded narration will be lost in the background noise. To help you out, Captivate provides an auto-calibrating feature. All you need to do is to say a few words into the microphone and let Captivate evaluate the input sensitivity to find the right value. Let's give it a try!

5. In the **Calibrate Audio Input** dialog box, click the **Auto Calibrate** button.

6. Speak normally into your microphone until you have a message saying that the microphone has been calibrated (if you don't know what to say, just tell a joke! Don't worry it is not recorded!).

7. Click the **OK** button to validate the sensitivity value and to close the **Calibrate Audio Input** dialog.

8. Close the **Audio Settings** dialog box as well.

Recording the narration

Now that both your computer system and Captivate are properly set up, it is time to concentrate on the actual recording of the voice over narration:

1. Still in the `Chapter03/takeTheTrain.cptx` file, use the **Filmstrip** to go to slide 2.

2. Use the **Audio | Record To | Slide** menu item to open the **Slide audio** dialog.

This is one of the many ways to start a slide audio recording. Another option is to click the **Add Audio** button in the **Options** tab of the **Properties** inspector when a slide is selected.

 Make sure you use the **Audio | Record To | Slide** menu item with slide written with no **s**. If you **click Slides** (with an **s**), you'll end up in a very similar, but slightly different dialog box.

The next step of the exercise is the actual recording of the sound clip. Before you press the record button, it is necessary to take some time to rehearse the narration.

The following text is the script that you will record:

Hi there! My name is Jan. I'm a student in Brussels, the capital city of Belgium. I'll be your guide during this short training on how to take the train in Belgium. Before we get started, I'd like to know a bit more about you. Please, type your name in the box below and click on the submit button.

Read those sentences aloud a few times. When you feel ready, you can move on to your first audio take!

3. Click the red **Record Audio** button at the top left of the **Slide Audio** dialog. After a short countdown, read the preceding sentences aloud at a normal speed and with a normal voice.

4. When the recording is complete, click the **Stop** button.

5. Control the quality of your take by clicking the **Play** button. If you are not satisfied, start over with another take.

6. When you are satisfied with the result, click the **Save** button and **Close** the **Slide Audio** dialog.

If the recorded sound clip is longer than the slide, you will be prompted to extend the duration of the slide to the length of the sound clip as shown in the following screenshot. Click **Yes** to finalize the integration of the new sound clip into the slide.

7. Take a look at slide 2 in the **Filmstrip** panel and notice the small loudspeaker icon below the slide thumbnail.

8. Click the **Timeline** button at the bottom of the screen to open the **Timeline** panel.

In the **Timeline** panel, the new sound clip is displayed as an additional layer below the slide layer. If needed, you can move the sound clip on the **Timeline** to better synchronize it with the rest of the slide. But you cannot use the **Timeline** to change the duration of the sound clip. Now, don't worry too much about the proper syncing of the narration and the slide just yet. You will finalize this in Chapter 4, *Working with the Timeline and Other Useful Tools*.

To test the slide, use the **Play** button at the bottom left corner of the **Timeline** panel. This button plays only the current slide without opening the preview pane. This preview option does not let you test every single feature of the slide, but it is a quick and easy way to do some basic testing and synchronization.

Recording narration is not an easy task, especially if you are not used to speaking into a microphone. Here are some basic tips and tricks to help you out:

- Write the script that needs to be recorded and rehearse it a few times before the recording.
- Keep in mind that you don't have to be perfect the first time. Try as many times as needed.
- Speak slowly, especially if you have an international audience where all the students do not speak the same language.
- Have a glass of water ready to avoid the dry mouth effect. Remember that lots of students will hear the narration through a headset.
- Position the microphone within four to six inches of your mouth and slightly to the side to avoid pops and hisses on the letters S and P.
- Standing up and gesturing while speaking can help you speak more clearly and confidently, and add more energy to your voice.
- Remove any objects that could get picked up in the audio, such as jewelry, or a squeaky chair.
- A well-insulated room will give you better, warmer quality than a large cavernous room, which could add echo or distort your voice.
- etc.

With these simple tips and tricks, a basic computer microphone, and a bit of practice, you should be able to record some pretty good audio clips right away!

Whose voice should be recorded?

If you can afford it, it is best to hire a voiceover talent, but most of the time you will be recording your own voice or the voice of a colleague or a friend. When choosing the person who will read the lines, always have your students in mind. For my very first big Captivate project, I had to develop a course in English, but most of the students were not native English speakers. We met with the customer and agreed to record the voice of a non-native English speaker (it was an employee from the next-door office who was into theater). The recorded English was not perfect, the accent was a bit strange, but it was not important because it was adapted to the audience.

Editing a sound clip in Captivate

Even though Captivate is not a fully-fledged audio editing application, it does have some basic audio editing capabilities. You will now explore these capabilities with the audio narration that you just recorded.

If you did not succeed in producing a great audio recording, you can use the `Chapter03/takeTheTrain_audio.cptx` file for the next exercise. It contains my own audio recording made with the techniques described in the previous section (please forgive my strange sounding voice; I had a bad cold on that day).

Use the following steps to finalize the audio you have recorded in the previous section:

1. Return to the second slide of the `Chapter03/takeTheTrain.cptx` file.
2. Use the **Audio | Edit | Slide** menu item to edit slide level audio. You can also use the **Edit Audio** button in the **Options** tab of the **Properties** inspector (when the slide is selected).

This action opens the **Slide Audio** dialog box on the **Edit** tab (see the arrow in the next screenshot). It is the same dialog box you used when recording the audio in the previous section. The only difference is that you used the **Add/Replace** tab when recording the audio.

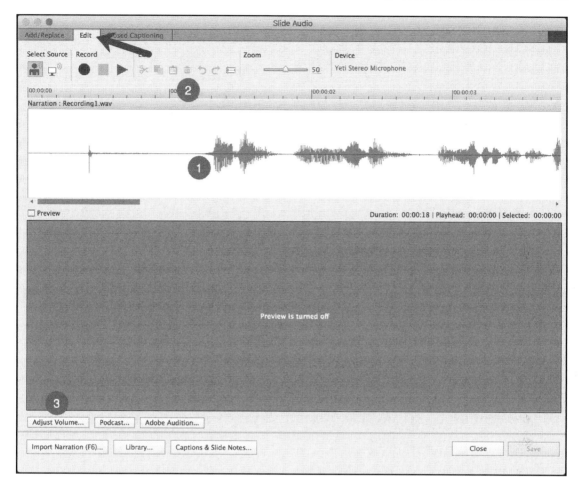

When recording the audio narration in the previous section, chances are you did not start speaking right after clicking the **Record** button. Consequently, you certainly have some silence between the beginning of the recording and the actual beginning of the narration. In the preceding screenshot, you can see that the actual audio waveform (the graphical representation of your audio file) is not at the very beginning of the audio clip (see **1** in the preceding screenshot). You will now select this silence and remove it.

3. Click the **Play** button to listen to the entire audio clip. Try to associate what you hear with the graphical representation of the waveform as displayed in the **Slide Audio** dialog.

4. Use your mouse to select from the beginning of the clip up to the actual beginning of the narration.

5. When done, hit the *Delete* key of your keyboard, or click the trash icon in the **Edit** section at the top of the **Slide Audio** dialog (see **2** in the preceding screenshot).

6. Repeat this operation with the silence at the end of the audio clip.

7. Click the **Play** button to test the new version of the clip.

Congratulations! You just took your first step into the fascinating world of audio editing! Another thing that you can do is to adjust the audio volume of the audio. You will now use the **Adjust Volume** feature of Captivate to normalize the volume of your audio narration.

8. In the bottom-left corner of the **Slide Audio** dialog, click the **Adjust Volume** button (see **3** in the preceding screenshot).

9. Take some time to review the options of the **Adjust Volume** box, but do not change any of them at this time.

10. In the **Audio Processing** section of the **Adjust Volume** dialog box, select the **Normalize** option and click the **OK** button.

Normalizing an audio clip means finding the best audio level for that particular sound clip.

Blog post

If you want to know more about the normalization process, I've written an entire blog post on this topic. It can be found at
`http://en.didaxo.be/blog/producing-high-quality-audio-content-fo`
`r-captivate-part-1-normalization/`.

11. Click the **Save** button at the bottom right corner of the **Slide Audio** dialog.

12. Click the **Close** button to close the **Slide Audio** dialog.

In the next chapter, you will position this audio clip on the **Timeline** to sync it with the other slide event.

Round trip editing with Adobe Audition CC

Audition CC is the audio application from Adobe. It is available as part of a Creative Cloud subscription. Adobe Audition (formerly Cool Edit) is an awesome yet easy to use audio application. If Adobe Audition CC is available on your system, the **Adobe Audition** button of the **Slide Audio** dialog will be enabled. Clicking this button opens the audio clip in Audition, where you can use specialized and dedicated audio tools to edit your clip. When you're done editing, just save the file in Adobe Audition and return to Captivate to update it.

Importing an external sound clip

The second way to add audio at slide level is to import the needed audio clips into the course. When taking this approach, the audio clips are recorded and produced in a dedicated audio application.

In this exercise, you will delete the audio narration recorded in the previous section and replace it with an imported audio file:

1. Return to the second slide of the `Chapter03/takeTheTrain.cptx` file.
2. Use the **Audio | Remove | Slide** to remove the audio clip associated with the selected slide.

Note that this action removes the audio from the slide, but not from the **Library** of the project. You will learn more about the **Library** in `Chapter 4`, *Working with the Timeline and Other Useful Tools*.

3. In the **Options** tab of the **Properties** inspector, click the **Add Audio** button. The **Slide Audio** dialog box opens.
4. Click the **Import Narration** button in the bottom left corner of the dialog box.
5. Browse the files on your computer and select the `Chapter03/Slide02.wav` file in the download associated with this book.
6. Click **Open**. The selected file is imported into the project.
7. Click the **Play** button to test the imported audio.
8. Save the changes by clicking the **Save** button in the bottom right corner of the **Slide Audio** dialog.
9. It is possible that the duration of the slide has to be increased to match the duration of the new audio file. Click **Yes** if prompted to do so.
10. Close the **Slide Audio** dialog box.
11. Save the file when done

After these steps, the audio file appears in the **Timeline** panel as an extra layer at the very bottom of the stack.

Yes, it is that easy to import external sound clips into Captivate! In the next chapter, you will import the remaining audio clips and learn how to use the **Timeline** panel to synchronize the audio with the other slide elements.

Using Text-To-Speech to generate narration

The third way to insert audio at slide level is to use Text-To-Speech. The idea is to type the voiceover narration into the **Slide Notes** panel and have Captivate convert it to a sound clip. To convert typed text to sound clips, Captivate uses preinstalled voices packages called **speech agents**.

Installing the Captivate speech agents

Due to their very large size, Adobe decided to make the installation of the Text-To-Speech agents optional. Adobe Captivate 2017 ships with one voice package that installs several speech agents for various languages. Note that Captivate is also able to pick up third-party Speech Agents installed on your system.

The Speech agents of Captivate can be downloaded from the following locations:

- For Windows 64 bit:
  `http://www.adobe.com/go/Cp2017_win64_voices_installer`
- For Mac: `http://www.adobe.com/go/Cp2017_mac_voices_installer`

 It is required to install the Text-To-Speech agents in order to go through the steps of the next exercise.

Working with the Slide Notes panel

The basic idea of Text-To-Speech is to transform a piece of typed text into a sound clip. In Captivate, you use the **Slide Notes** panel to type the text you want to convert to speech. The **Slide Notes** panel is not displayed by default, so your first task is to turn it on:

1. Go to slide 3 of the `Chapter03/takeTheTrain.cptx` file.
2. Use the **Window | Slide Notes** menu item to show the **Slide Notes** panel.

By default, the **Slide Notes** panel appears at the bottom of the screen next to the **Timeline** panel.

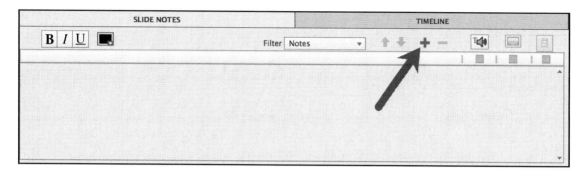

At the far right side of the panel, the **+** icon is used to create a new note.

3. Click the **+** icon to add a new note.

4. Type `Thank you! It's great to know you!` in the new note.

5. Click the **+** icon to add a second note after the first one.

6. Type `Congratulations on your decision to come visit us in Belgium. It's a great country to visit, full of historical places, tourist attractions, awesome landscapes, and great food!` in the second note.

7. Add a third note to the **Slide Notes** panel and type `And to get around, the best way is the train! I take it every day, and I just love it!`

8. If needed, use the up and down arrows in the top right corner of the **Slide Notes** panel to reorder the notes.

When typing the text into the **Slide Notes** panel, keep in mind that a program will soon convert it to an audio clip. This program will not work correctly if the spelling and punctuation aren't perfect, so double-check (and even triple-check) your typing. If it is wrong, you'll get unexpected (and sometimes hilarious!) results.

9. Use the **Filmstrip** to browse the remaining slides. Notice that the necessary Slide Notes have been added where appropriate.

Converting Slide Notes to speech is one of the many goodies of the **Slide Notes** panel. Before moving to the next section, take some time to experiment with the **Slide Notes** panel and notice the icons, boxes, and switches that surround it. In `Chapter 12`, *Creating Accessible eLearning*, you will return to this panel and use it to generate the Closed Captions.

Now that the Slide Notes have been correctly typed and carefully ordered, you can safely convert them to audio using Text-To-Speech.

Converting text to speech

Converting the text typed into the **Slide Notes** panel to speech is not difficult. All you need to do is choose the note(s) to be converted, assign a speech agent to each note, and generate the audio file:

1. Make sure you are on slide 3 in the `Chapter03/takeTheTrain.cptx` file.

2. At the top of the **Slide Notes** panel, click the **TTS** checkbox to select all three notes as shown in the following screenshot:

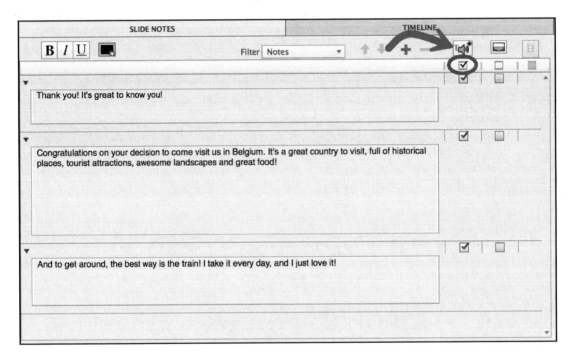

Most of the time, you'll want to convert all the notes to speech. But, if needed, you can deselect the notes that don't need to be converted to speech.

3. Click the Text-To-Speech button at the top of the **Slide Notes** panel (see the arrow in the preceding screenshot). The **Speech Management** window opens.

The **Speech Management** window is where you assign a speech agent to each of the note(s) you selected for Text-To-Speech conversion. The number of available speech agents depends on the voice packs installed on the system (see the *Installing the Captivate speech agents* section for more details).

For this exercise, you will use the speech agent named **Paul**. This speech agent is designed for US English text only, and is included in the voices installer of Captivate.

> 4. In the **Speech Management** window, use the drop-down menus in front of each note to assign the speech agent **Paul** to all three notes.

While assigning the speech agent to the Slide Notes, there are some interesting things to notice:

- You can assign a different speech agent to each Slide Note. This means that you can use different speech agents on the same slide. It is very handy to generate conversations, for example.
- Notice the **Speech Agent** drop-down menu at the very top of the **Speech Management** window. You can use it to assign the same speech agent to all the selected notes instead of going one note at a time.
- In the top right corner of the **Speech Management** window, notice the same icons as those found in the **Slide Notes** panel. Use them to type new notes, delete existing notes, or reorder notes directly from the **Speech Management** window.

Now that you have assigned a speech agent to each note of the slide, it is time to generate the audio file.

> 5. Click the **Generate Audio** button at the bottom left corner of the window. A progress bar appears on the screen as the audio is generated.
> 6. When the progress bar disappears, click the **Close** button to close the **Speech Management** window.
> 7. At the bottom of the screen, switch to the **Timeline** panel.

Surprise! The **Timeline** panel now shows an audio layer beneath the slide layer.

> 8. Use the **Play** button of the **Timeline** panel to test the audio clip.

Great! The Slide Notes of slide 3 were successfully converted to speech using a speech agent named Paul. You will now repeat the same procedure on the other slides, but using a slightly different method.

9. Use the **Audio | Speech Management** menu item to reopen the **Speech Management** window.

Note that opening the **Speech Management** window this way displays the Slide Notes of the entire project rather than those of the selected slide.

10. In the top left corner of the **Speech Management** window, switch to the **Slide notes** tab (see **1** in the following screenshot).

11. Use the **Speech Management** window to browse the Slide Notes in the project. As you do so, select them for Text To Speech (see **2** in the following screenshot) and assign the speech agent **Paul** to all of them (see **3** in the following screenshot).

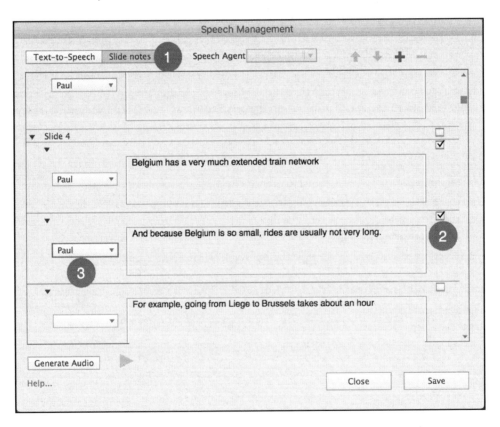

12. When this is completed for all the Slides Notes of the project, click the **Generate Audio** button.

13. When the audio generation is complete, click the Play icon just next to the **Generate Audio** button. This allows you to control the audio that was generated.

14. When you are ready, close the **Speech Management** dialog and switch to the **Timeline** panel.

With this technique, you can generate the audio of the entire project in a single operation! When Captivate has finished generating the audio files, examine the results and notice the following:

- Captivate has generated audio files for almost all the slides of the project. These can be identified easily thanks to the loudspeaker icon visible under each slide thumbnail in the **Filmstrip** panel.

- Text-To-Speech cannot reproduce every single word correctly. It is the case of the URL www.sncb.be on slide 15, for example.

- Text-To-Speech is very sensitive to any spelling or typing mistake (including punctuation and grammar!).

- You can always return to the **Slide Notes** panel of any slide, correct the typing, spelling, punctuation (or adjust the text in any way), and regenerate the audio files using the techniques covered earlier in this section.

- Captivate has matched the length of the slides with the length of the generated audio files as necessary.

Tweaking the speech agents
There are ways to have the speech agents correctly pronounce the words they initially mispronounce, such as technical terms. A thorough explanation is way out of the scope of this book. Kevin Siegel discusses it well in the following blog post: http://iconlogic.blogs.com/weblog/ 2016/05/adobe-captivate-train-the-text-to-speech-agents.html. You can also use the VTML language in your Slide Notes as described in the following documentation https://media.neospeech.com/document/vt_eng-Engine-VTML-v3.9.0-3 .pdf. Note that these techniques only apply to the speech agents included with Captivate. Third-party speech agents might have their own custom mechanisms.

You have now worked with all the options that can be used to insert audio at slide level. Here is a summary of the key points that have been covered:

- There are three ways to insert audio at slide level: recording audio with Captivate, importing an audio file produced in an external application, or generating the audio clips with Text-To-Speech.
- When recording audio with Captivate, ensure that the audio interface is correctly set up both in the operating system and in Captivate.
- The first time you record audio with Captivate, it is necessary to calibrate the sensitivity of your microphone. Captivate has an easy to use auto calibrating feature.
- Captivate provides some basic audio editing tools that allow you to perform simple operations, such as trimming the beginning and the end of your audio files or adjusting the volume of the audio.
- Audition CC is the dedicated audio application of Adobe Creative Cloud. If it is available on your system, use it to produce your audio clips.
- The basic idea of Text-To-Speech is to convert a piece of text into an audio clip. To do it, Captivate uses speech agents.
- Captivate ships with a bunch of speech agents packed into an extra installer available for free on the Adobe website.
- Captivate also recognizes third-party speech agents installed on your system.
- Each speech agent is designed for a specific language.
- The **Slide Notes** panel is used to type the text to be converted to speech. You can choose to convert every Slide Note to speech or just some of them.
- A different speech agent can be assigned to the different notes of the same slide.
- The **Speech Management** window provides a quick and easy way to convert all the notes of the project to speech at once.

Most of the slides of your project now have an associated voice over narration. Even though there is a lot of work left to be done, your course is definitely starting to provide a genuine multimedia experience.

Text-To-Speech versus manual voice-over recording

Is Text-To-Speech better than an actual recording? A real recording takes a lot of time and, consequently, costs a lot more money. But the result is perfect and can be tailored to fit the specific needs of a particular project. Text-To-Speech is fast, easy, and cheap, but the result may sound like an old Game Boy (for millennials, a Game Boy is a 20th century Video Game console), depending on the quality of the speech agents that you use. Another thing to consider is how easy it is to update the project. Updating a Text-To-Speech audio file is easy. Just change the text in the Slide Notes panel and regenerate the audio to make your updates. Modifying a human recorded sound is much more difficult and costly. You may have to rent a sound studio, hire the voiceover talent a second time, and so on. No solution is perfect. The choice is yours...

Using the Advanced Audio Management window

The Advanced Audio Management window provides a high level overview of all the audio in your project. In the following exercise, you will open the **Advanced Audio Management** window and take a look at the tools it provides using the following steps:

1. Make sure you are still in the `Chapter03/takeTheTrain.cptx` file.

2. Use the **Audio | Audio Management** menu item to open the **Advanced Audio Management** window.

The **Advanced Audio Management** window contains a list of all the slides in the project along with their associated audio file(s) if any.

3. In the bottom left corner of the **Audio Management** window, select the **Show object level audio** checkbox (see **1** in the following screenshot).

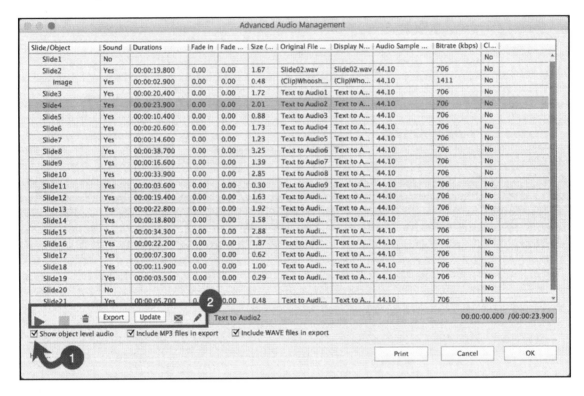

By selecting the **Show object level** audio checkbox, the list of audio files displayed in the **Advanced Audio Management** window includes the audio associated with the Character image on slide 2.

4. Select any of the audio files in the list.

When an audio file is selected in the **Advanced Audio Management** window, the buttons in the bottom part of the window are enabled (see **2** in the preceding screenshot). These buttons allow you to play the selected audio file, export it to a .wav and/or .mp3 file, edit the audio file, add Closed Captions, and more.

5. Inspect the controls of the **Advanced Audio Management** window. They should be self-explanatory.

6. Close the **Advanced Audio Management** when you are done.

7. Save and close the `takeTheTrain.cptx` file.

There really is nothing more to say about the **Advanced Audio Management** window. It is just a nice and easy way to have a general overview of all the audio used in your course module.

Summary

In this chapter, your project took on a whole new dimension. With the addition of multimedia elements, your eLearning is much more fun and dynamic to look at and your message is more powerful than ever.

You first learned how to import external animations in to your project. These can be Flash animations (`.swf` files), or HTML5 animations packaged in `.oam` files. Remember that HTML5 animations are supported both in the Flash and in the HTML5 output of Captivate, while the Flash based animations will play only if the Captivate project is published in Flash. Adobe Animate CC is the external application that was used to produce those animations.

You also learned how to insert video files into your course module. You can insert them as Event Videos or as Multi-Slides Synchronized Videos. Captivate lets you import various types of video files, but will always convert them to `.mp4` videos upon publishing.

Finally, you studied the audio options in Captivate. You learned that sound can be added at object level, slide level, or project level. To produce the audio files, Captivate offers the ability to record your own clips, but you can also import audio clips produced in an external application or convert text typed into the **Slide Notes** panel to speech using one of the speech agents provided by Captivate or already present on the system.

There is still a lot of work to do before your course module can be made available to the learners. One of the most obvious things to be done is the synchronization of the newly inserted audio files with the other elements of the slide. This process, along with many other tools, will be covered in the next chapter.

Meet the community

In this section, we would like to introduce you to Dr. Ray Jimenez, who has authored several books on scenario-based learning and micro-learning. His workshops and training sessions are informative, effective, and, at the same time, very entertaining. The example scenarios he showcases during his training sessions are a class apart!

Ray E. Jimenez, Ph.D.

Ray Jimenez started his career as a management consultant at Coopers Lybrand in the areas of learning design and technologies. Currently, he is the chief learning architect at Vignettes Learning and `TrainingMagNetwork.com`, with over 100,000 members. He is the creator of the *Story-Based Learning Design* and *Micro-Learning for Disruptive Results* concepts. Ray is the author of *3-Minute eLearning* (2011), *Scenario-Based eLearning* (2014), *Micro-Learning Impacts Special Report*, and an upcoming book, *Micro-Learning for Disruptive Results*. He is a frequent speaker at the Association for Talent Development (ATD), eLearning Guild, Training Magazine, EduBerlin, Open University in Hong Kong, Civil Service of Singapore, and others. He assists clients such as Ashford University, Edison International, LyondellBasell Industries, and Caltech, NASA, to name a few.

Contact details

- **Web**: `http://www.vignetteslearning.com/`
- **Twitter**: `@RayJimenez`
- **LinkedIn**: `http://www.linkedin.com/in/vignettes`

4

Working with the Timeline and Other Useful Tools

You've done a lot of work on the project you started two chapters ago. But you're not done yet! Some of the remaining things to be done include the proper alignment and positioning of the objects and the synchronization between the audio and the other elements of the slide.

In this chapter, you will primarily focus on using the **Timeline** panel to synchronize the elements you already added with the audio. You will also learn about various tools and features used to manage the objects of the project and how to lay them out in the physical space of the slide.

In this chapter, you will learn the following:

- Using the Library to manage the assets of the project
- Using the Smart Guides to accurately arrange the objects
- Using the Ruler and creating custom Guides
- Learning how to group and ungroup objects
- Using the Align toolbar to perfectly arrange the objects on the slides
- Using the Timeline to synchronise the various elements of the slide
- Applying Effects to the objects

At the end of this chapter, you will better understand how the features and objects discussed in the previous two chapters come together to build an actual eLearning course.

Preparing your work

To get the most out of this chapter, you should first reset your workspace. If you are using the default interface mode, restarting Captivate also resets your workspace to default. If you are using the advanced interface mode, use the **Window** | **Workspace** | **Reset 'Classic'** menu item to reset the classic workspace to default.

In this chapter, you will use the exercise files in the Chapter04 folder. If you get confused by any of the step-by-step instructions, look at the Chapter04/final/takeTheTrain.cptx file, which is the project as it should look at the end of this chapter.

Working with the Library

The first tool you will explore in this chapter is the **Library**. The **Library** contains a list of the assets in your project. These assets include the background used on the Master Slides and all the external files imported into the project (images, video, sounds, and so on). Perform the following steps to open a project and explore its library:

1. Open or restart Captivate.
2. Open the Chapter04/takeTheTrain.cptx file.

When using default interface mode, a **Library** icon appears at the far right side of the Toolbar, just next to the **Properties** icon.

3. Click the big **Library** icon situated at the far right side of the Toolbar. Alternatively, use the **Window** | **library** menu item.

When the **Library** panel opens, it looks like the following screenshot:

As shown in the preceding screenshot, the **Library** is composed of the following elements:

- At the very top of the **Library** panel is the name of the file the library belongs to (**1**). This means that the library is associated with the currently active project only. If you switch to another project, you will also switch to another library.
- The preview area (**2**) gives a preview of the selected item. In the preceding screenshot, we have selected the **Slide02.wav** audio clip you imported in the previous chapter. Note that by default, nothing is selected when you open the **Library** panel.
- Just below the preview area, the library toolbar (**3**) displays a row of icons. These are the tools used to manage the assets in the **Library** panel.
- The main area of the **Library** panel (**4**) lists the assets of the project organized by type.

The main area of the **Library** panel is further divided into folders representing the type of assets stored in the library. You may not have files of each type in each project, but Captivate organizes the Library with these folders in case you add these types of files later. You will now take some time to further explore the **Library** using the following steps.

4. Take some time to scroll down the **Library** panel and see the available folders. Take note of the assets already present in the library. Can you associate them with the exercises of the previous two chapters?
5. In the **Audio** section of the **Library**, select the Slide02.wav audio clip. It is the audio file you imported in the project during the previous chapter.
6. Click the sixth icon on the **Library** toolbar. This icon is called **Usage**.
7. A box pops up and informs you that this particular audio clip is used as the background audio of slide 2.
8. Click **OK** to close the **Usage** dialog box.

The only purpose of the **Usage** window is to inform you about where the selected asset is used in the project.

Using the Library to remove assets from the project

In the previous chapter, you used Text-to-Speech to generate background audio. You will now replace these audio files with actual recordings made in an external audio application (in this case, the external application was Adobe Audition, but it could have been any external audio application).

Alternatives to Adobe Audition CC

If you do not have Adobe Audition CC on your computer, you can use any other dedicated audio application, such as Apple Logic, Steinberg Cubase, ProTools, and so on. If you don't want to spend any money on a dedicated audio application, Audacity (http://www.audacityteam.org/) is a great open source audio editing application.

You will now use the library to remove the audio clip generated by Text-to-Speech using the following steps:

1. In the **Audio** section of the **Library**, select all the *Text to Audio...* files (select the first one, hold down the *Shift* key, and select the last one. This should select all the needed files).

2. Click the last icon on the **Library** toolbar (the trash can icon) to delete the selected files from the **Library**.

3. Confirm your intention to remove the selected files from the **Library** by clicking **Yes** on the message that pops up.

4. A second message tells you that the selected file is currently used as the background audio of a slide. Click **Yes To All** to remove all the **Text to Audio** clips from the **Library**.

The selected audio files have been removed from the project. In the **Filmstrip**, notice that the loudspeaker icon that was associated with these slides was removed, indicating that there is no more audio associated with these slides (except for slide 2, which uses the Slide2.wav file as background audio). This is shown in the following screenshot:

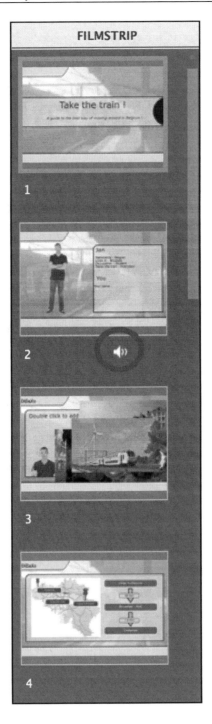

Using the **Library**, it has been easy to remove several assets from the project. Note that you have performed this operation without going to any individual slide to manually remove each audio narration. Using the **Library** is a big time saver!

Importing external assets in the library

Now that you have removed the Text to Audio files, you will replace them with actual recordings created with an external audio application. You could select each slide of the project and import the new audio files one by one, but again, the library will speed up the work and make it easier.

Using the following steps, you will import the audio files into the project and associate them with the corresponding slide:

1. In the `chapter04/takeTheTrain.cptx` file, make sure the **Library** panel is open.
2. Click the second icon on the **Library** toolbar. This icon is named **Import**.
3. Browse to the `Chapter04/audio` folder of the downloaded exercises and select all the `.wav` files it contains.
4. Click the **open** button and let Captivate import the selected audio files into the **Library** panel.
5. When the import process is finished, you will see a message that **18 items has been successfully imported**. Click **OK** to acknowledge the message.

All the required audio files have been imported into the project. Your next task is to associate each of the imported files with the corresponding slide.

6. Use the **Filmstrip** to go to slide 3 of the current project.
7. Drag the `slide03.wav` file from the **Audio** section of the **Library** and drop it on top of slide 4. Make sure you drop it on the slide itself and not on one of the objects present on the slide.
8. If the **Audio Import Options** dialog pops up, choose to extend the duration of the slide to match the length of the audio file.

Yes, it is that easy to import external assets into the **Library**! If you take a look at the **Filmstrip**, you'll notice a loudspeaker icon next to the slides you just added audio to.

Now, the rest of this exercise is simple! You will use the exact same drag and drop technique to associate the remaining audio clips to their corresponding slides. Use the name of the sound clip to know which slide to associate it with (the `Slide10.wav` audio clip goes on slide 10, and so on). Naming the audio clips that way is a best practice and helps you to know which audio clip is associated with which slide. The only potential thing you have to be mindful of is to drop the audio clip on top of the slide, and not on top of one of the objects sitting on the slide.

 To avoid any problems during the drag and drop of audio files to the slides, you can drag the audio clips from the **Library** panel to the slide thumbnails in the **Filmstrip** or to the scrap area (the grey area around the slide). This makes the process go even faster and avoids the potential for associating the audio file with an object instead of the slide.

After this exercise, all the audio files have been added to the project and associated with the correct slide. It is time to move to the next section and discover another feature in the **Library** panel.

Reusing library items

One of the main benefits of the Library is the fact that you can reuse the same asset multiple times without reimporting it in the project. In this section, you will learn to reuse the assets already in the project library using the following steps:

1. In the `Chapter04/takeTheTrain.cptx` file, use the **Filmstrip** to navigate to the slide.
2. Select the Character image on the left side of the slide.
3. Right-click the image and click the **Find in the Library** menu item.

This action selects the IMG_9105.png image in the **Library**, as shown in the following screenshot:

Renaming library items
The default name of an item in the Library panel is the name of the file that was imported in the project. If you want, you can right-click a library item to rename it and give it another, more meaningful name.

If you want to use the same image again, there is no need to import it a second time. It can be taken directly from the **Library** panel and reused as many times as needed throughout the entire project. Using multiple instances of the same file helps to keep the file size as low as possible. You will now drag and drop another instance of the same image elsewhere in the project.

4. Use the **Filmstrip** to go to slide 8.
5. Drag the **IMG_9105.png** file from the **Images** section of the **Library** and drop it on the left of Slide 8.

6. Move and resize the image so your slide looks like the following screenshot:

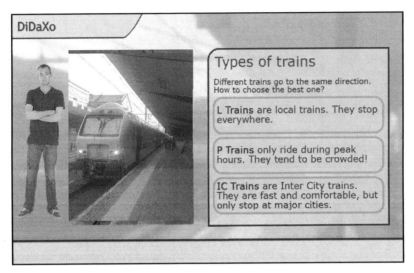

In this exercise, you have reused an image from the Library. If you look at the **IMG_9105.png** file in the **Images** folder of the **Library** panel, you should notice that the usage count of this asset is now 2.

Importing objects from another library

Another great feature is the ability to open the library of another file. This makes it easy to share assets across different Captivate projects.

In the next exercise, you will open the library of another Captivate file and insert one of the assets it contains into the Take the Train project:

1. In the `Chapter04/takeTheTrain.cptx` file, use the **Filmstrip** to go to slide 7.
2. In the **Library** panel, click the first icon on the library toolbar. This icon is named **Open Library...**

3. Navigate to the exercises folder and open the `Chapter04/library.cptx` file. The **Library** panel of this file appears as an extra floating panel.

Make sure the `Chapter04/library.cptx` file is closed when doing this operation.

4. If needed, enlarge the external **Library** panel. It contains a single image called `inAmsterdam.jpg`.

5. Drag the `inAmsterdam.jpg` image from the external library to the middle of slide 7.

6. Close the external library when done.

Oops, wrong image! Sorry folks, this is an image of me in Amsterdam a few hours before the AC/DC show during their 2009 Black Ice world tour! Well, even though this is not the intended picture, I've made my point: the library can be used to share assets between Captivate files. Notice that the `inAmsterdam.jpg` image is now present in the **Images** folder of the **Library** of the current project.

7. Still on slide 7, select and delete the newly inserted image.

Take another look at the **Library** panel after you deleted the image. Notice that even though it is no longer used in the project, the image still appears in the **Images** folder of the **Library** panel.

Deleting unused items from the library

The unused items are the assets that are present in the project library, but are no longer used in the project. To control the size of the .cptx file, it is a good idea to remove these items from the library. In this exercise, you will use the tools of the **Library** panel to quickly identify and delete these unused items:

1. In the **Library** panel, click the **Select Unused Items**. It is the second to last icon in the library toolbar as shown in the following screenshot:

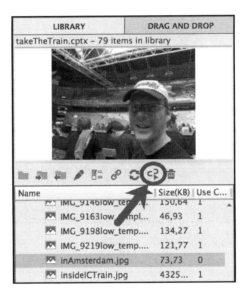

The unused items, including the inAmsterdam.jpg image, are now selected in the **Library**.

2. Click the last icon on the library toolbar (the trash can icon) to delete the selected assets.
3. Click **Yes** to confirm the deletion.
4. Save the file when done.

That's it! Thanks to the **Library** panel, it has been quick and easy to identify and delete the unused assets. This will help you keep the size of your .cptx file as low as possible.

Be careful when deleting assets from the Library. Once an item has been removed from the Library, there is no way to get it back without reimporting it from outside of the project. Make sure you have a copy of the important files if you ever need to import them again later.

You will discover a few more features of the **Library** panel later in the book, but for now, let's make a quick list of what you already know:

- The **Library** panel appears on the right side of the screen, next to the **Properties** inspector.
- The primary purpose of the **Library** is to maintain a list of all the assets in the active project. These assets include the pictures, audio files, videos, animations, and so on, imported into the project.
- The **Library** panel provides the necessary tools to let you manage the assets used in the project.
- You can use the **Library** panel to insert multiple instances of the same asset in your project. This helps in keeping the project size as low as possible.
- It is possible to share assets across projects by opening the library of other `.cptx` files and importing the assets they contain in the current project.
- When you delete an asset from a slide, it is not deleted from the library. As a result, you may end up with a library containing many unused items. Captivate will alert you to many unused Library items when you open a file.
- You can easily select and delete the unused items with the tools of the **Library** panel.
- Right-click any item in the **Library** panel to discover additional functionalities, including the ability to rename the item you right-clicked.

Laying out the objects on the slides

In this section, you will examine a few practical tools to help you quickly and easily arrange the objects on your slides.

Using Smart Guides

The first of these tools is the **Smart Guides**. These Smart Guides make it very simple to align various objects together. In this section, you will return to slide 8 of the `takeTheTrain.cptx` file and precisely align the Character image so it is located exactly in the vertical middle of the train image that sits on its right:

1. Return to the `Chapter04/takeTheTrain.cptx` project and use the **Filmstrip** to navigate to slide 8.

2. Open the **View** menu.

3. Make sure the **Show Drawing/Smart Guide** option of the **View** menu is enabled. If not, enable it now.

4. Select the Character image you imported in the previous section and move it slowly towards the top of the slide.

When the Character image is aligned with another object, you will see a horizontal and/or vertical green dotted line. The Character image will briefly snap to that line, allowing you to align the two objects together. This dotted green line is a Smart Guide. These Smart Guides appear automatically when some kind of alignment is possible, as shown in the following screenshot:

5. Release the mouse to place the Character image at the location defined by the Smart Guide.

6. Move the same Character image again. Move it slowly towards the bottom of the slide.

7. At some point you will see a horizontal Smart Guide extending from the middle of the Character image to the middle of the train picture on the right.

8. Release your mouse when that Smart Guide is displayed to properly align these two images.

Using the Smart Guide, it is simple and fast to align an object with the other objects on the same slide. At the end of this exercise, slide 8 should look like the following screenshot:

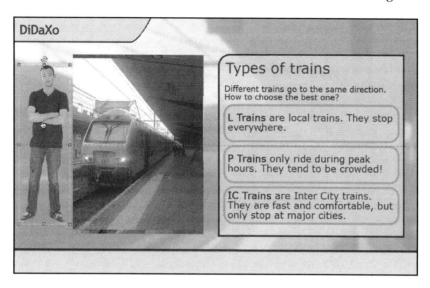

Using the rulers and the guides

Other features that will help you properly position objects on a slide are the rulers and the guides. The difference between the guides you will use in this section and the Smart Guides discussed in the previous section is that you will now draw the guides and decide where to position them. In the previous section, Smart Guides were temporary guides automatically generated by Captivate.

In the next exercise, you will properly position the images of slide 9 using the rulers and custom guides that you will place on the slide yourself. Your first task is to turn the ruler on and to draw the guides using the following steps:

1. In the `Chapter04/takeTheTrain.cptx` project, use the **Filmstrip** to navigate to Slide 9.
2. Select the **Getting a ticket** title shape to see its boundaries and its resize handles.
3. Use the **View | Show Ruler** menu item to turn both the vertical and the horizontal rulers on.
4. Place your mouse on top of the vertical ruler, at the left edge of the stage area.

5. From there, drag a vertical guide. Place the guide so that it touches the left edge of the **Getting a Ticket** title Smart Shape.

6. Select the image of a train ticket on the right side of the slide to reveal its boundaries and its resize handles.

7. Place your mouse on top of the horizontal ruler at the top of the stage.

8. From there, drag a horizontal guide. Place the guide so that it touches the top edge of the selected image.

As shown in the following screenshot, you should now have two guides on your slide: one vertical guide and one horizontal guide:

In the preceding screenshot, the guides have been purposely exaggerated to help you properly spot them. In real life, these guides are much thinner than on the image.

Before moving on with this exercise it is important that you fully understand the operations that you can do with these guides:

- First, you can move the guides by placing your mouse on top of a guide until the mouse pointer turns into a double arrow. This allows you to fine-tune the position of an existing guide.
- To remove a guide, you can drag a horizontal guide back to the top ruler, or drag a vertical guide back to the vertical ruler at the left edge of the screen.
- Open the **View** menu to discover some more operations, such as Hiding all the guides, Clearing (removing) all the guides, Locking the guides, and so on.

In this exercise you want to move the train image (on the left-hand side of the slide) so that its top left corner matches the intersection of the two guides. To help you out, you will activate the **Snap To Guide** feature before moving the image into position.

9. Use the **View | Snap to Guide** menu item to turn the Snap to Guide feature on.
10. Select the train image on the left side of the slide.
11. Slowly move the image so that its top left corner matches the intersection of the guides. When the image touches the guides, these should turn purple.

Thanks to those guides, you properly positioned the image on the slide.

Extra credit - aligning the image legend

Now that the train image is in place, you can move the **Inside an IC train** Smart Shape into position. The bottom edge of the Smart Shape should touch the bottom edge of the train image. Move the Smart shape around and use the Smart Guides to position it properly.

Alternate ways to create guides

In the previous exercise you used your mouse to drag vertical and horizontal guides from the top and the left ruler. This is just one of the available methods of creating guides. In this section, you will explore the other ways of creating guides:

1. Use the **Filmstrip** to return to slide 8. Note that the guides you created on slide 9 are also displayed on slide 8. This means that guides are not tied to a particular slide layout, but are added on top of the stage for the whole project.
2. Use the **View | Clear Guides** menu item to remove all the existing guides.

3. Use the **View | New Guide** menu item to open the **New Guide** dialog box.

4. In the **New Guide** dialog, choose to generate a **Horizontal** guide located precisely at 89 pixels from the top of the slide. Click **OK** to validate and create the guide.

The **New Guide** dialog allows you to create new guides and to position them precisely on your slide.

You will now explore yet another way of creating guides in Captivate.

5. Use the **View | Create Multiple Guides** menu item to open the **Create Multiple Guides** dialog.

This box allows you to create a lot of guides in a single operation. Designers use it to generate a grid of guides that they use to layout their slides in Captivate. These grids are very common among graphic designers because they simplify things and help in creating slick and flawless designs. You will now generate a grid of 12 columns by 3 rows using the following steps:

6. In the **Create Multiple Guides** dialog, select both the **Column** and the **Row** checkboxes.

7. In the **Columns** section of the box, you want *12* columns with a gutter of 20 px between each column (the gutter is the empty space between the columns).

8. In the **Rows** section, you want three rows.

9. Select the **Margins** checkbox and ask for margins of 50 px on all four sides.

10. Finally, select the **Clear Existing Guides** checkbox to remove the current guides and replace them by those you are generating.

Make sure the **Create Multiple Guides** dialog looks as follows before clicking the **OK** button:

In the preceding screenshot, notice that the **Width** of both the columns and the rows is set at 0. It means that Captivate will calculate the width of those elements so that the slide is divided into 12 columns of equal width (with a space of 20 px between each columns) and in 3 rows of equal height.

A grid of 12 columns is very popular among designers, because it allows for a lot of combinations. For example, if you want three elements side by side, you will give each of them a width of four grid columns (because *4 * 3 = 12*), but if you want two elements side by side, you shall give each element a width of six grid columns (because *6 x 2 = 12*), and so on. Thanks to the *20* pixels gutter between each column, the elements you hang on the grid will be separated from each other by a margin of *20* pixels.

In the case of this particular project, we did not use this grid system to lay out the slides of the project, so you will now delete the guides that you have created.

11. Use the **View** | **Clear Guides** menu item to delete the existing guides.

Using the Align toolbar

If you are looking for pixel perfect alignment and positioning, the Align toolbar is the best tool. It contains the necessary icons to align, distribute, and resize the objects of your slides. By default, the Align toolbar is not displayed in the Captivate interface, so your first task is to turn it on:

1. Use the **Window | Align** menu item to turn the Align toolbar on. By default, it appears in the top left area of the screen.

As shown in the following screenshot, the Align toolbar contains 14 icons. During the next exercise, you will use many of these 14 icons. To make it clearer to know which icon to click, they are numbered from 1 to 14:

The Align toolbar actually contain 18 icons, but only the 14 first are used to align items on the stage. The remaining four icons are used to arrange the stacking order of objects. Arranging the stacking order will be covered later in this chapter.

By default, none of the icons of the Align toolbar are available. The set of available icons depends on your selection.

2. Navigate to slide 4 of the `chapter04/takeTheTrain.cptx` file and select the **Liège Guillemeins** Smart Shape on the right side of the slide.

With one object selected on the slide, only the **Center horizontally on the slide** (icon **7**) and the **Center vertically on the slide** (icon **8**) icons are available.

3. With the **Liège Guillemins** Smart Shape still selected, hold the *Shift* key down while clicking the **Bruxelles -Midi** Smart shape to add it to the current selection.

With two objects selected, most of the icons of the align toolbar are available. Only the **Distribute Horizontally** (icon **9**) and the **Distribute Vertically** (icon **10**) icons are still disabled.

4. Hold the *Shift* key down while clicking the **Oostende** Smart Shape to add it to the current selection.

With three (or more) objects selected, all the icons of the Align toolbar are available.

You can also access the tools of the align toolbar by right-clicking an object and opening the **Align** menu item. The content of that menu depends on the current selection and will always match what is available on the Align toolbar.

Selecting multiple objects

Most of the tools of the Align toolbar require that at least two objects be selected. Selecting multiple objects is not difficult and it works the same way in Captivate as in most other applications. But Captivate has one important particularity when multiple objects are selected. This is what you will explore in this section:

1. Still on slide 4 of the `Chapter04/takeTheTrain.cptx` file, click anywhere in the scrap area (the grey area around the slide) to deselect all the objects.
2. Click the map of Belgium to select it.
3. Hold the *Shift* key down while clicking the **Liège Guillemins** Smart Shape.

You now have two objects selected on your slide. The first object you selected (the map of Belgium) is surrounded by white selection handles while the **Liège Guillemins** Smart Shape is surrounded by black selection handles.

In Captivate the first selected object is the **key object** of the selection. It means that the tools of the Align toolbar are calibrated based on the size and the position of that object. To make it recognizable, Captivate displays white selection handles around it and black handles around all the other objects of the selection.

4. Click the **Align top** (icon **4**) button of the Align toolbar.

This operation aligns the top edge of the **Liège Guillemins** Smart Shape to the top edge of the map of Belgium (remember that the map of Belgium is the Key Object).

5. Hold down the *Shift* key and click the **Liège Guillemins** Smart Shape again to remove it from the current selection.
6. Click the **Oostende** Smart Shape in the right side of the slide while holding down the *Shift* key to add it to the selection.

Once again, you have two objects in the selection. The Key Object (with the white handles) still is the map of Belgium. The second object is the **Oostende** Smart Shape.

7. Click the **Align bottom** (icon **6**) button of the Align toolbar.

This operation aligns the bottom edge of the **Oostende** Smart Shape to the bottom edge of the map of Belgium, which is still the Key object.

Now that the top and the bottom Smart Shapes are in place, you will place the **Bruxelles-Midi** shape right in the middle of the other two using the following steps:

8. Hold down the *Shift* key and click the map of Belgium to remove it from the current selection.

Because the map of Belgium was the Key Object, Captivate automatically chooses another object of the selection as the Key Object. In this case, since the **Oostende** Smart Shape was the only other object selected, it becomes the new Key Object and is therefore surrounded by white selection handles.

9. While holding down the *Shift* key, click the **Bruxelles-Midi** Smart Shape and the **Liège Guillemins** Smart Shape to add them to the current selection. After this step, you should have three objects selected.
10. Click the **Align Left** icon (icon **1**) of the Align toolbar to align the left edges of the three selected Smart Shapes to the left edge of the Key Object.
11. Click the **Distribute Vertically** (icon **10**) icon of the Align toolbar to space the three selected objects equally.

With these operations completed, these three Smart Shapes are in their final position.

Extra credit - aligning the other objects of the Slide

You now have all the skills you need to perfectly align the remaining Smart Shapes of this slide. Here is what you need to do:

- Select the objects you want to align, paying close attention to the first one you select. Remember that the tools on the Align toolbar are calibrated based on the first selected object.
- Use the tools on the Align toolbar to move the objects of the slide to their intended position.

- Remember that the three blue Smart Shapes are already at their final position. Use them as reference.
- Save the file when finished.

At the end of this extra credit section, your slide should look like the following screenshot:

Grouping objects

The next tool discussed in this chapter is the ability to group objects together. When objects are grouped, you can manipulate them as a single entity. This means that you can, for example, move the entire group of objects without breaking their alignment to each other. You can also apply effects to a group (rather than applying effects to each object of the group) and control the visibility of an entire group of objects using actions and variables.

 Applying effects will be discussed later in this chapter. Variables and actions will be covered in Chapter 13, *Working with Variables and Advanced Actions*.

In the following exercise, you will group the seven Smart Shapes you aligned in the previous section. Use the following steps to do so:

1. Make sure you are on slide 4 of the `Chapter04/takeTheTrain.cptx` file.
2. Click one of the seven Smart Shapes present on the right side of the slide.
3. Holding down the *Shift* key, click the other six Smart Shapes one by one to add them to the selection.
4. With all seven objects selected, use the **Edit | Group** menu item to group them together. Alternatively, you can use the *Ctrl* + *G* (Windows) or the *Cmd* + *G* (Mac) keyboard shortcut.

Now that these Smart Shapes have been grouped, they can be moved together without breaking their respective alignment.

5. Experiment with moving the group of seven Smart Shapes around the slide and confirm that these objects are moving together as a single entity.
6. When finished, use the green dotted Smart Guides to put the group of objects back into place.

Even though these objects have been grouped, you can still access each of them independently and modify the properties of one of the group members only.

7. Click an empty area of the slide to deselect any active object. The **Properties** inspector should display the properties of the slide.
8. Click once on the group to select it.

When a group is selected, the outline and the white handles surround the entire group. But, within the group, thin grey dashed lines identify the members of that group.

9. While the group is selected, click on one of the objects within the group.

This action sub-selects the object you clicked within the group. Note that the white selection handles now surrounds the selected object, while the group it belongs to is identified by green handles as shown in the following screenshot:

The **Properties** inspector shows you the properties of the currently selected object, in this case, the object you sub-selected within the group. If needed, you can use the controls and switches of the **Properties** inspector to modify the properties of the selected object without affecting the other objects of the group.

 If you want to ungroup the grouped objects, all you need to do is select a group and use the **Edit | Ungroup** menu item. You can also use the *Ctrl + Shift + G* (Windows) or the *Cmd + Shift + G* (Mac) keyboard shortcut to ungroup the selected group. Finally, you can also right-click a group and select **Ungroup** in the contextual menu.

In this section, you learned about four Captivate features you can use to easily position objects on your slides. These four features are the Smart Guides, the Ruler and Guides, the Align toolbar, and the ability to group objects. Before moving on to the next section, let's summarize what you learned in this section:

- Smart Guides are dotted green lines that automatically appear and disappear as you move objects around. These guides are used to help you align objects together. These are temporary guides that are automatically generated by Captivate.
- Smart Guides can be turned on and off using the **View | Show Drawing/Smart Guides** menu item.
- Use the **View | Rulers** menu item to turn both the horizontal and the vertical rulers on and off.
- When the rulers are on, you can drag custom horizontal and/or vertical guides from the rulers to the slide. These guides are meant to help you properly position the objects on the stage.

- Use the **View** | **Create Multiple Guides** menu item to create a grid of guides on your slides. Use this grid to layout the objects on your slides. Many designers use this grid technique.
- Use the **View** | **Clear Guides** menu item to remove all the guides.
- The Align toolbar is not part of the default interface. It is necessary to turn it on using the **Window** | **Align** menu item.
- There are 14 icons on the Align toolbar. The number of enabled icons depends on the number of objects selected.
- It is possible to select multiple objects in Captivate using the same techniques as in most other applications.
- The first selected object of a multiple selection is known as the key object of the selection. The tools on the Align toolbar are calibrated based on that key object.
- Captivate displays white selection handles around the key object and black selection handles around the other objects of the selection.
- Different objects can be grouped into a single entity. When grouped, these objects can be moved together without breaking their relative alignment.

With a bit of practice, the Smart Guides, the Align toolbar, the Rules and Guides, and the Group feature will soon count among your most commonly used tools in your Captivate toolbox!

Working with the timeline

By default, the **Timeline** is hidden from the Captivate interface. To reveal it, click the **Timeline** bar at the bottom of the screen. The primary purpose of the Timeline is to organize the sequence of events on each slide, but the **Timeline** panel can be used for other purposes as well. This is what you will explore in this section.

Using the timeline to select objects

Sometimes, the objects are so close to each other that you might have a hard time selecting the correct one. The objects can also be stacked on top of one other so that selecting an object that is not on top of the stack can be very tricky. Using the **Timeline** panel, you can make sure that the object you select is the one you actually want to select!

1. If necessary, return to the `Chapter04/takeTheTrain.cptx` file.
2. Click the **Timeline** bar at the very bottom of the screen to open the **Timeline** panel.

3. Use the **Filmstrip** to navigate to slide 3. This slide contains several images stacked on top of each other.

4. Look at the **Timeline** panel at the bottom of the screen.

In the **Timeline** panel, each line (layer) represents an object (with the exception of the bottom most line, which represents the audio clip associated with this slide).

The line just above the audio clip represents the slide itself. Looking at that line, you learn that duration of the slide is currently **21.7 sec**, which matches the duration of the associated audio clip (see the ellipse in the following screenshot). The other lines represent the objects inserted on top of the slide. The brown line is the placeholder title Smart Shape that currently reads **Double click to add a title** (see the arrow in the following screenshot). The remaining lines represent the images that you see on the stage.

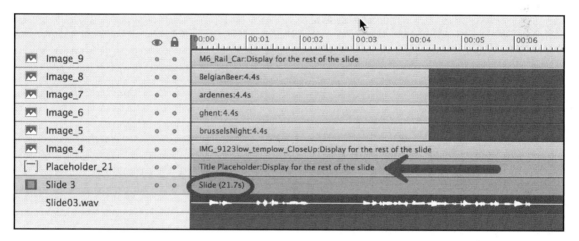

Counting the remaining lines, you learn that there are six images in this slide. One of them is the Character image in the bottom left corner of the slide.

4. Click the Character image on the slide to select it.

5. Take another look at the **Timeline** panel. You should see that the line corresponding to the Character image is also selected.

6. In the **Timeline** panel, click the topmost layer to select it. Notice that the corresponding image is also selected on the stage.

Selecting an object on the **Timeline** panel selects it on the stage and vice versa. This helps you to figure out which layer of the **Timeline** corresponds with which object. Using the **Timeline** panel to select an object is also a great way to select objects that are difficult (or even impossible) to select with the mouse. This is the case when the objects are very close to each other, or when they overlap.

Labeling the objects

The **Timeline** panel also shows the name of the objects. You can use the text field at the top of the **Properties** inspector to label your objects. The name you give in the **Properties** inspector also appears on the **Timeline** panel. Giving your objects a meaningful and custom name is considered best practice.

Using the timeline to lock and unlock objects

Hiding and locking objects is another feature that will help you select the correct one. It also prevents you from accidentally modifying something you've already completed. To illustrate this, you will now lock the group of objects you created in the previous section using the following steps:

1. Use the **Filmstrip** to return to slide 4 of the `Chapter04/takeTheTrain.cptx` file.
2. Click once the group of Smart Shapes you created in the previous section.
3. Turn your attention to the **Timeline** panel and notice that the group has its own line and that this line is selected.
4. If needed, click the disclosure triangle located in front of the group label in the **Timeline** to expand the group and see its components (see **1** in the following screenshots).

5. Still in the **Timeline** panel, click the Lock icon associated with the group layer (see **2** in the following screenshot).

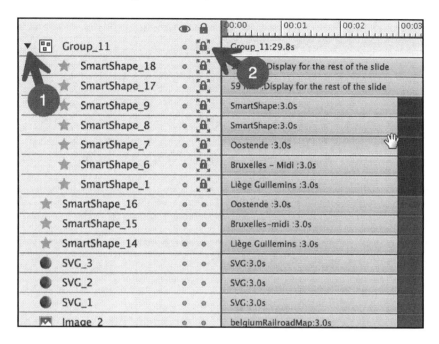

6. On the stage, click the group to select it. Note that Captivate allows you to select the group even though it is locked. In the **Properties** inspector, the properties of the group are displayed as usual.

7. Try to use the mouse to move the group around the slide. Captivate does not let you move the group.

8. With the group still selected, switch to the **Options** tab of the **Properties** inspector.

In the **Options** tab of the **Properties** inspector, note that the **Lock Size and Position** checkbox is selected. When a lock icon with arrows is displayed in the **Timeline** panel (as shown in the preceding screenshot) only the size and the position of the objects are locked. The objects can still be selected and their other properties (such as fill color, opacity, and so on) can still be accessed as usual.

9. Click the lock icon associated with the group (marked as **2** on the preceding screenshot) again. Notice that another type of lock (without the arrows) now appears next to the group layer.

10. On the stage, try to click the group to select it. Because the group is locked, Captivate does not allow you to select the group. In the **Properties** inspector, the properties of the group are no longer accessible.

11. Click the same lock icon again to disable all the locks. There should be no lock icon on the group layer.

Clicking the lock icon several times circles you through three lock states:

- If no icon is present in the Lock column of the **Timeline**, the object is completely unlocked and all its properties are accessible.
- If a lock icon with arrows is present only the size and the position of the object are locked. The other properties (such as the Fill and the Stroke properties) are not locked and can be modified as usual.
- If a standard lock icon is displayed (without the arrows), then the object is completely locked and cannot even be selected.

The lock feature of Captivate is a nice tool that prevents you from accidentally selecting or moving objects that have been already taken care of.

The Lock icon at the very top of the **Timeline** panel allows you to lock and unlock all the objects of the slide in a single click! The lock command can also be accessed from the right-click menu, but for unlocking, you'll need to use the **Timeline**.

Using the timeline to show and hide objects

In the **Timeline** panel, next to the *Lock/Unlock* icons, are the *Show/Hide* icons (the eye icons). These icons work the exact same way as the Lock icons covered in the previous section. You can use them to hide objects from the slide. When the slide contains a large number of objects, the Show/Hide option can help you select and work with the correct objects while keeping the others out of the way. Note that hiding an object with this tool hides it **from the Captivate interface only**, not from the final project that will be viewed by the students.

Using the timeline to change the stacking order of the objects

The stacking order decides which object goes in front of or behind the other objects. In the **Timeline** panel, the topmost object is in front of any other objects. It means that in case objects overlap, the topmost object covers the one(s) below it. The slide always is at the very bottom of the stack since it serves as the background.

1. Use the **Filmstrip** to navigate to slide 3 of the `Chapter04/takeTheTrain.cptx` file.

2. In the **Timeline** panel, click the topmost line to select the corresponding image on the stage.

Note that you have selected the image with the train and the wind turbines. It is the topmost image of the stack. It covers all the other images that are behind it.

3. In the **Timeline** panel, use your mouse to drag the topmost line down. As you do so, look at the stage and notice that the corresponding image now goes behind the other ones.

4. Still in the **Timeline** panel, right-click the image you just moved down and use the **Arrange | Bring to Front** menu item.

This action brings the image back to the top of the stack, both on the stage and in the **Timeline** panel.

5. If needed, use the **Window | Align** menu item to turn the Align toolbar back on. Notice that the last four icons of the align toolbar also allow you to control the stacking order of the selected object.

The main takeaway of this section is the fact that the stacking order of the lines in the **Timeline** panel matches the stacking order of the object on the stage. To change this stacking order, you have four possibilities:

- You can drag the layers up and down in the **Timeline** panel
- You can right-click an object and use the **Arrange** menu
- You can use the last four icons of the **Align** toolbar
- Finally, you can use the **Modify | Arrange** menu item

Extra credit - aligning images

Before moving on to the next section, you will put your new skills to work by aligning the images on slide 3.

On the right side of the slide; there are five images of Belgium. These images are exactly the same size. Your assignment is to use the tools described in the preceding sections (Smart Guides, Rulers, Align Toolbar, and Timeline panel) to position these five images exactly on top of one other and to place them on the right side of the slide, without changing their stacking order.

At the end of this assignment, your slide should look like the following screenshot:

Using the timeline to set the timing of the objects

The primary purpose of the **Timeline** is to let you control the timing of the objects on the active slide. For each object, you can choose when it appears on the stage and how long it stays visible. By carefully and precisely arranging the objects on the timeline, you'll be able to achieve great visual effects with minimal effort. This is what you will explore in this section, using the following steps:

1. Use the **Filmstrip** to navigate to slide 5 of the Chapter04/takeTheTrain.cptx project.
2. Look at the **Timeline** panel and notice how the six objects of the slide are organized.

3. Click an empty area of the slide or the scrap area around the slide to make it the active item. The **Properties** inspector updates and displays the properties of the slide. In the **Timeline** panel, Slide 5 will be blue highlighted.

4. Switch to the **Timing** panel.

5. At the top of the **Timing** panel, change the **Slide Duration** property to **16** sec. This change is reflected in the **Timeline** panel.

6. In the **Timeline** panel, drag the right edge of the slide layer to the **14** sec mark. This change is reflected in the **Slide Duration** property of the **Timing** panel.

The changes made in the **Timeline** panel are reflected in the **Timing** panel and vice versa. This gives you two methods to organize the timing of your objects.

Adjusting the zoom level on the Timeline

At the very bottom of the Timeline panel, you will find a horizontal slider that you can use to adjust the Zoom level of the Timeline. Adjust the Zoom level of the Timeline until you get a view that works best for you.

7. Click the map of Belgium image to make it the active object. The **Timing** panel updates and shows the timing properties of the selected image.

The **Timing** panel states that the image **appears after 0** seconds and stays visible for a **specific time** of **3** seconds. The **Timeline** panel is a visual representation of this situation.

You will now adjust the timing of the audio file that was imported into this slide.

8. In the **Timeline** panel, place your mouse on top of the audio file layer until the mouse pointer turns to a grabbing hand.

9. Move the audio file to the right so it begins at the 0.5 sec mark.

Sound can be very intrusive, so you must use it with care. One of the things I always do on slides with voice-over narration (such as the one you are working with) is to move the sound clip on the **Timeline** half a second to the right, to make the audio narration begin half a second into the slide. This simple trick dramatically diminishes the intrusive and aggressive feeling that sound can induce without affecting the general rhythm of the project.

You will now adjust the timing of the map of Belgium image so that it shows for the entire duration of the slide.

10. On the stage, select the map of Belgium image.
11. In the **Timing** panel, open the **Display For** drop-down menu and change its value to **Rest of Slide**.

This operation is reflected in the **Timeline** panel. The layer representing the map of Belgium image has been extended to the end of the slide. This image should now **Appear After** 0 sec and be **Display**ed **For** the **Rest of** the **Slide**.

Adjusting the default timing of the objects

When a new object is added to the stage, its timing is set to three seconds by default. This default timing can be adjusted for each type of object separately. Simply go to **Edit** | **Preferences** | **Defaults** (Windows) or **Adobe Captivate** | **Preferences** | **Defaults** (Mac), choose an object in the **Select** drop-down list, and adjust the default timing of the selected object type.

You will now arrange the timing of the five circle Smart Shapes using the following steps:

12. At the bottom of the **Timeline** panel, click the Play icon to hear the audio narration.
13. Stop the playing when the narration says *"Click on the map to see..."*.
14. If necessary, use your mouse to move the red playhead approximately to the **8** sec mark. This location corresponds to a silence in the audio clip.
15. In the **Timeline** panel, place your mouse at the very beginning of the **SmartShape_29** object. This object is one of the five blue circles on top of the map. The mouse pointer will turn into a double arrow.
16. Use the mouse to drag the beginning of this object to the 8 seconds mark, where the red playhead is located.

17. Look at the **Timing** panel and confirm that the selected object is scheduled to **Appear After 8 sec** and will **Display For** the **Rest of** the **Slide**.

18. Use the same technique to change the timing of the other blue circles. Make them begin half a second apart from each other.

When you are finished, the **Timeline** panel of slide 5 should look as follows:

Finally, you will test your work using the preview feature of Captivate.

19. Use the **Preview | Next 5 slides** icon of the Toolbar to test your sequence in the **Preview** pane.

Everything looks fine and syncs well. The **Timelime** shows exactly what you saw in **Preview**. Before moving on to the next section, let's fine-tune one small detail:

20. On the stage, select the map of Belgium image.

21. At the bottom of the **Timing** panel, open the **Transition** drop-down menu.

22. Change the **Transition** to **Fade In Only**.

23. Use the **Preview | Next 5 Slides** icon of the Toolbar again to test your change. You should see that the map of Belgium appears on the stage with a nice fade in effect.

In Captivate, it is possible to apply a *Fade In* and/or a *Fade Out* effect on (almost) every object. By default, this **Transition** effect lasts half a second, but you can adjust its timing in the **Transition** section of the **Timing** panel.

Keep the **Transition** effect in mind when setting up the timing of your objects. Imagine a Text Caption set to stay visible for a specific time of three seconds with a default Fade In and Fade Out transition applied. The first half a second is used for the Fade In effect and the last half a second is used for the Fade Out effect. It effectively leaves only two seconds to the learner to read the text contained in the Text Caption!

Congratulations! You just synced your first slide in Captivate using the **Timeline** and the **Timing** panels. This is a bit tedious, but it is straightforward. With a bit of practice, it will soon become second nature for you. Before moving on to the next section, let's summarize what you have learned so far:

- The primary purpose of the timeline is to define the timing of the objects.
- The timeline can also be used to select the objects, to lock them, to modify their visibility in the Captivate authoring environment, and to modify their stacking order.
- The **Timeline** panel is a visual representation of the properties found in the **Timing** panel. Changing the timing of the objects in the timeline updates the **Timing** panel and vice versa.
- It is possible to apply a Fade In and/or a Fade Out effect on an object using the **Transition** drop-down menu on the **Timing** panel. The default transition time is **0.5** sec, but this can easily be changed in the **Timing** panel.

Tips and tricks for great syncing

When it comes to syncing the objects of your project, the Timeline is your best friend. But it is when combining different features of Captivate that you will go the extra mile and achieve great syncing. In this section, we would like to share with you some of the techniques we use when syncing the projects we work on. These techniques have one thing in common. They use many Captivate features that work together to produce the final effect.

Using the Sync with Playhead feature

The first trick is to use the Sync with Playhead feature. You will use it to sync slide 3 of the `Chapter04/takeTheTrain.cptx` file. The steps are as follows:

1. Return to or open the `Chapter04/takeTheTrain.cptx` file and use the **Filmstrip** to navigate to slide 3.
2. If needed, click the **Timeline** bar at the bottom of the screen to open the **Timeline** panel.

Remember that Slide 3 contains five images of Belgium that are the same size. Normally, these five images are positioned exactly on top of each other on the right side of the slide.

The first step of the workflow is to define the beginning and the ending of the slide.

3. In the **Timeline** panel, move the audio clip to the right so it begins at the **0.5** sec mark.

4. Go to the end of the Timeline and extend the duration of the slide to the **23** sec mark. If you prefer, you can also modify the slide duration in the top section of the **Timing** panel.

The next step is to make each of the five images appear when the corresponding comment is said.

5. In the **Timeline** panel, select the **brusselsNight** layer. This layer represents the image that is at the bottom of the stack.

6. Click the Play icon in the bottom right area of the **Timeline** panel.

7. Stop the playback when the narration says "*Congratulations on your decision...*" (around the **3.5** seconds mark).

8. With the red playhead in position, right-click the **brusselsNight** layer and choose **Sync with Playhead** in the contextual menu.

This action makes the selected Text Caption appear at the current position of the playhead. Since you'll be performing this kind of synchronization often, it's good to know the keyboard shortcut associated with the **Sync with Playhead** feature (*Ctrl + L* on Windows and *Cmd + L* on the Mac).

9. At the bottom of the **Timeline** panel, click the play icon again to listen to the next part of the audio clip.

10. Stop the playhead when the narration says "*..full of historical places..*" (around the **9.5** sec mark).

11. In the **Timeline** panel, select the **ghent** layer. It is the layer that is immediately above the one you just synced.

12. Use the *Ctrl + L* (Windows) or the *Cmd + L* (Mac) shortcut to sync the selected image with the current position of the playhead.

13. Repeat the same sequence of actions for the remaining three pictures, using the following table as a reference:

Image	Narration	Approximate timing
Ardennes	...awesome Landscape...	12.8 sec
BelgianBeer	...and great food...	14.7 sec
trainWindmills	...the best way is the train...	18.5sec

By now, all the images should appear on the stage, in sync with the audio narration. Let's check it out using the preview feature of Captivate.

14. Use the **Preview | Next 5 slides** icon on the Toolbar, to test your sequence.

During the preview, pay close attention to how and when the images appear on the stage. You should see that the timing is correct, but a few remaining details remain. The most obvious issue is the duration of the first image, which is too short.

15. Close the preview pane when you are finished.
16. Back in the **Timeline** panel, use your mouse to drag the right edge of the **brusselsNight** image to the 10.5 sec mark. Alternately, you can achieve the same result by changing the value of the **Time** property at the top of the **Timing** panel with that image selected.
17. Finally, use the **Timeline** to select all five images one by one. At the end of the **Timing** panel, make sure they all use the same **Fade In Only** transition.
18. Use the **Preview | Next 5 slides** icon of the Toolbar, to test your synchronization once again.

During the preview, make sure that the images are correctly synced with the audio. If necessary, return to the slide and adjust the timing of the images before testing again.

At the end of this exercise the **Timeline** panel of slide 3 should look similar to this screenshot:

Notice that because all the images are the same size and share the same position, you see a cross-fade effect between the images. Remember that the default *Fade In* and *Fade Out* transitions last 0.5 sec. So, if you extend the duration of an image by at least 0.5 sec (make that 1 sec just in case) you ensure that the images disappear from the stage when the next one is already visible on top of it. The Fade In Only Transition brings the final touch to this effect.

To achieve the desired result, you applied several features together in this section:

- You used an image-editing tool (such as Adobe Photoshop) to ensure that all the images have the exact same size (this has been done for you before the images were inserted into the slide)
- You used the Align toolbar to position all five images in the exact same place
- You used the Smart Guides and/or the Rulers and Guide to align the image stack
- You used the default 0.5 sec **Fade In Only** transition on your images
- You used the **Timeline** panel and the **Sync with Playhead** feature to sync the images with the narration
- You extended each image by at least 0.5 sec to make sure an image disappears after the end of the Fade In transition of the next image to create a cross-fade effect

This exercise demonstrates that the power of these tools is optimized when they are used together.

Extra credit - adjusting the timing of the other slides

Now that you know the tools and techniques used to set the timing and the stacking order of objects, browse the other slides of the takeTheTrain.cptx project to adjust the timing of the objects on each slide. Refer to the Chapter04/final/takeTheTrain.cptx file of your exercise folder for examples and inspiration.

These are some tips to keep in mind before you get started:

- Use the **Timeline** panel whenever possible. It is the most intuitive and visual way to adjust the timing of the objects.
- If you require super-precise timing, use the **Timing** panel.
- Remember the **Sync with Playhead** feature and its associated keyboard shortcut (*Ctrl + L* on Windows and *Cmd + L* on the Mac).
- Use the tools of the **Align** toolbar to resize and relocate the objects on the slide. Proper size/location combined with precise timing can lead to strong, yet easy to achieve, visual effects.
- Finally, keep in mind that some objects (for example, buttons) are still missing and will be added in the next few chapters.

Not too fast and not too slow

When creating an online course with Captivate, you'll quickly discover that one of the most difficult aspects is to find the right pace for your instruction. When there is some audio narration, it is quite easy, because the narration dictates the overall pace of the project. When there is no narration, here is a simple trick. For text objects, use the stopwatch function of your cell phone and *slowly* read the content of the text aloud, then round up the timing to the upper half a second. For example, if it takes you 5.7 seconds to read the text aloud, make that object stay on the stage for a specific time of six seconds. If your audience is multilingual, add up to one second to that timing so that the students taking the course in a language other than their native language will be allowed some extra time to read and understand. You can also use the **Calculate Caption Timing** preference of Captivate. When this preference is turned on, Captivate automatically calculates the length of the Text Captions based on their content. You can find this option under the **Defaults** category of the Captivate preferences.

Working with Effects

Effects can be added to any Captivate objects. Since so many animations can be created within Captivate, you may find you do not need to import external animations. In this section, you will use these effects to animate some of the objects of the project.

Applying and removing effects

Use the `Chapter04/takeTheTrain_synced.cptx` file if you didn't sync during the last exercise.

1. Use the **Filmstrip** to navigate to slide 2 of the `Chapter04/takeTheTrain.cptx` file.
2. Select the Character image on the left side of the slide.
3. If needed, open the **Properties** inspector, and then, switch to the **Timing** panel.

The **Effects** section of the **Timing** panel is where you find the built-in effect of Captivate. The main area of this section (see **1** on the following screenshot) is comprised of the list of available effects.

Take some time to inspect the **Timing** panel and get used to its icons before continuing with this exercise.

4. In the main area of the **Timing** panel (see 1 in the preceding screenshot), move your mouse to the top of the effects, and look at the selected Character image on the stage. You will see a preview of the effect you hover on.

5. Click the effect you like the most to apply it to the Character image.

6. Use the **Preview | Next 5 Slides** icon on the Toolbar to test your effect in the Preview pane. Close the **Preview** pane when done.

Now that you know how to apply an effect to an object, you will learn how to remove an effect. Then, you will explore additional effects available in Captivate.

7. With the Character image still selected, click the trash can icon on the **Timing** panel to remove the applied effect from the Character image (see **3** in the preceding screenshot).

8. In the **Effects** section of the **Timing** panel, open the **Basic** drop-down menu.

9. Take note of the five families of effects available in Captivate (**Basic**, **Emphasis**, **Entrance**, **Exit**, and **Motion Path**).

10. When ready, click the **Entrance** category. The list of Entrance effects appears in the main area of the **Timing** panel.

11. Click the arrow marked as **2** in the preceding screenshot to discover even more Entrance effects.

12. On the last page of the Entrance effects, click the **Fly In From Left** effect to apply it to the Character Smart Shape.

13. Use the **Preview | Next 5 Slides** icon on the Toolbar to test your effect in the Preview pane. Close the **Preview** pane when done.

With this effect applied to the Character, you see a horizontal line starting with a green triangle and ending with a red square. This line is a Motion Path. It shows the movement of the character image on the slide. The beginning of the movement is the green triangle and the end of the movement in the red square. Note that you can move these two points with the mouse if you ever want to edit this path.

14. Place your mouse on top of the green triangle and move it to the right. This shortens the Motion Path. The Character will now do a shorter movement.

Moving the green triangle in a straight line
Hold down the *Shift* key while moving the green triangle, to move it in a straight line.

Make sure the effect is as shown in the following screenshot:

With this configuration, the Character image starts its motion outside the stage, enters the stage in a sliding movement from the left to the right, and ends its motion at its current location. You will now modify the duration (and thus the speed) of the movement using the **Timeline** panel.

15. With the Character image still selected, look at the **Timeline** panel.
16. Click the small disclosure triangle in front of the selected layer of the **Timeline** (see **1** in the following screenshot). This reveals the timing of the effect applied to the Character image.
17. Reduce the duration of the effect to the first half a second of the duration of the object (see **2** in the following screenshot).

This action is shown in the following screenshot:

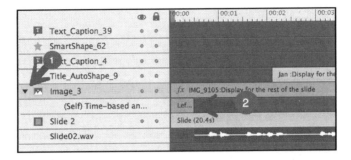

Congratulations! You just applied your first Entrance effect to one of the objects of your Captivate file! Use the **Preview | Next 5 Slides** icon on the Toolbar to test your new effect in the **Preview** pane.

Applying other effects

Still on the same slide, you will now apply another effect to the Text Caption describing, Jan, the Belgian student:

1. Still on slide 2 of the `Chapter04/takeTheTrain.cptx` file, select the Text Caption situated just under the title **Jan** on the right side of the slide.
2. In the **Character** section of the **Properties** inspector, increase the **Spacing** to **1.5**. This adds some space between the lines of text within the Text Caption.
3. With the Text Caption still selected, switch to the **Timing** panel.
4. Open the **Basic** drop-down menu and choose the **Entrance** family of effects.
5. Use the right arrow just below the list of available entrance effects to browse through the three pages of available effects.
6. On the third page, click the **StretchFromTop** effect to apply it to the selected Text Caption.
7. At the bottom of the **Effects** section of the **Timing** panel, change the **Effect Duration** to **0.5** sec.
8. Open the **Timeline** panel if necessary.
9. In the **Timeline** panel, open the little triangle at the beginning of the selected Text Caption layer (see the preceding screenshot for the exact location of that triangle). You should see your effect applied to the first half a second of the Text Caption.

Once again, the **Timeline** panel is a visual representation of the properties found in the **Timing** panel. Changing the effect duration can be done on the **Timeline** and the **Timing** panel.

10. Use the **Preview** | **Next 5 slides** icon on the Toolbar to preview your effects in the Preview pane

When watching the preview, notice how these two simple effects make the slide much more dynamic and visually appealing, without overshadowing the content. This is the key aspect in using effects. It has to enhance the content, to make it more appealing and meaningful. But if it ever takes precedence over the content of the slide, then you missed the point of adding effects. To help you out in using effects more effectively, here is a list of simple considerations to keep in mind:

- Never forget that you are teaching. Just like any other feature you use in Captivate, effects must *serve the student's learning*.
- While there are a lot of built-in effects available, you will probably end up using the same two to five effects. That's perfectly fine!
- Don't add an effect to every object. Instead, carefully choose the objects you want to attract the student's attention to, and apply an effect only to those objects. Sometimes, you'll even have an entire slide without any effects applied. That's OK, too!
- Sometimes, a simple Fade In or Fade Out transition (found at the very end of the **Timing** panel) is just enough to make the slide stand out.

The key words when using effects are *simplicity*, *subtlety*, and *efficiency*!

Extra credit - adding effects to the remaining slides

Now that you have applied effects to the objects on slide 2, browse through the remaining slides. When you feel like an effect would be useful, use the **Timing** panel to apply the effect you feel is the most appropriate.

This is a good opportunity for you to familiarize yourself with the built-in effects of Captivate and to experiment with how they work. While doing this, you will certainly discover some features that were not covered in the previous section, such as:

- The ability to add multiple effects on the same object.
- The ability to combine effects together to create new ones.

- The ability to fine-tune the parameters of the effects. The actual parameters you can edit depend on which effect you apply.
- The ability to trigger an effect with an action rather than with the timeline (actions will be covered in `Chapter 13`, *Working with Variables and Advanced Actions*).

Look at the `Chapter04/final/takeTheTrain.cptx` file to see how we have used effects in this project.

This Extra Credit section concludes your overview of effects in Captivate. Feel free to experiment more by applying other effects to other objects and to your own projects. The possibilities are endless, and this book only shows a few examples of what is possible.

Before wrapping up this chapter, this is a list of what you have learned about effects:

- It is possible to add effects to any Captivate object.
- Use the **Timing** panel to apply and manage effects.
- The available effects are sorted into five categories: **Basic**, **Entrance**, **Emphasis**, **Exit**, and **Motion Path**. These categories are available in the **Timing** panel.
- A Motion Path describes a movement that is applied to an object. Captivate contains many pre-defined motion paths, but you can also define custom motion paths.
- You can see the effects applied to an object by opening the disclosure triangle on the **Timeline**.
- Effects can be combined to create sophisticated animations.
- Use effects wisely, keeping in mind that they should serve the content and facilitate the learning of the student.

Summary

At the end of this chapter, use the **Preview** | **Project** icon on the Toolbar to take a look at the whole project and let yourself be amazed at the job you have already accomplished!

In this chapter, you learned how to use various tools to lay out, animate, and synchronize the elements of your eLearning project. These tools include the Library, the Smart Guides, the Align toolbar, the Effects and, most importantly, the **Timeline**.

Used individually, these tools are great, but it is when used in combination that they reveal all their power and flexibility.

By syncing the elements of the slides, you reached another milestone in the creation of your eLearning course. But the road is still long before the project can be considered finished.

One of the most impressive capabilities of Captivate is its ability to generate highly interactive animations. In the next chapter, you will learn how to build this interactivity, taking your projects to an even higher level.

Meet the Community

In this section, we would like to introduce you to Josh Cavalier. He had a secret identity in the Captivate community, which, for years, had been a well-guarded secret. But now, we all know that *Captain Captivate*, the superhero of the Captivate community, was in fact Josh Cavalier! Even though he has announced his retirement as Captain Captivate, he will still be around and active in the community using his real name.

> *"I may have retired the cape, but Captain Captivate will always live on. I absolutely love where Adobe is taking Adobe Captivate, and I enjoy every opportunity to train eLearning developers on the tool."*

Josh Cavalier

Josh Cavalier, who founded Lodestone in 1999, is in charge of Lodestone's eLearning consulting services and leads the overall direction and operations of Lodestone's eLearning team. He brings 23 years of eLearning development experience, technology implementation, and vision to his clients. Prior to Lodestone, he was an art director for Handshaw, a leading eLearning services company. He was one of the key resources leading the effort to streamline Handshaw's eLearning development process and transition from CD-ROM delivery to the web. He holds a bachelor's degree in Fine Arts from Rochester Institute of Technology.

Contact details

- Website: www.lodestone.com
- Twitter: @joshcav

5
Working with Interactive Objects

In this chapter, you will continue developing your Captivate project by adding interactivity. This will make it even more interesting, engaging, and fun to use for your students.

This interactivity is created by the interactive objects of Captivate. Three of those objects (Button, Click Box, and Text Entry Box) can stop the playhead and wait for the learner to do or type something. Captivate also provides other means of building interactivity. The Rollover Objects don't stop the playhead, but they do provide some kind of interactivity. They are hidden by default and revealed when the student rolls the mouse over a sensitive area. The **Drag and Drop Interaction** provides an easy way to build highly engaging interactions. Finally, the new **Multi-States Objects** make it simpler than ever to build sophisticated interactions without any programming.

This interactivity introduces a new level of complexity to your projects, as the students will receive feedback that is dependent on the action they perform. So, you will have to account for multiple possible answers from your students and act accordingly. This concept is known as **branching**.

Thanks to these interactive objects and features, your online courses will soon provide a great interactive experience that drives student engagement and retention.

In this chapter, you will learn how to:

- Insert different kinds of buttons that give students more control over the timing of the project
- Use Text Entry Boxes to capture the student's typed answers
- Experiment with Rollover Captions, Rollover Images, and Rollover Slidelets

- Convert a Smart Shape into a Rollover Smart Shape
- Use the Drag and Drop Interaction to add exciting interactivity to your content
- Use the Object State to build highly engaging interactions without any programming

These will combine to create another chapter full of surprises and discoveries.

Preparing your work

To get the most out of this chapter, you should first reset your workspace. If you are using the default interface mode, restarting Captivate also resets your workspace to default. If you are using the advanced interface mode, use the **Window | Workspace | Reset 'Classic'** menu item to reset the classic workspace to default.

In this chapter, you will use the exercise files in the `Chapter05` folder. If you get confused by any of the step-by-step instructions, look at the `Chapter05/final` folder, which contains a copy of the exercises as they should look at the end of this chapter.

Working with Buttons

The **Button** is the first interactive object of Captivate you will study. A Button can stop the playhead and wait for the student to click it. This triggers an action. Despite its apparent simplicity, the Button is an essential part of every Captivate project as it lets the student control the overall pace of the course.

You will now return to the `takeTheTrain.cptx` project and add a button onto slide 3:

1. Open the `Chapter05/takeTheTrain.cptx` file.
2. Use the **Filmstrip** to navigate to slide 3.
3. In the Toolbar, use the **Interactions | Button** icon to insert a new button in the middle of the slide. Alternatively, you can also use the *Shift + Ctrl + B* (Windows) or the *Shift + Cmd + B* (Mac) keyboard shortcut.
4. With the new button selected, open the **Properties** inspector.

When a button is selected on the stage, the **Properties** inspector shows the properties that are relevant to a Button object. Look at the three tabs (Style, Actions, and Options), as shown in the following screenshot:

The **Actions** tab is displayed in addition to the usual **Style** and **Options** tabs. This tab only appears when an interactive object is selected.

5. In the **Style** tab of the **Properties** inspector, change the button **Caption** to `Continue.`

6. Inspect the other properties available in the **Style** tab of the **Properties** inspector, but do not change any of them at this time.

7. Switch to the **Actions** tab of the **Properties** inspector.

8. Open the **On Success** drop-down list and review the available options. When you are done, choose the **Go to the next slide** option.

9. Use the resize handles to increase the size of the button so the new text fits in the object.

When increasing the size of the button, consider the learners that will take the course on a mobile device with a touch screen. They will appreciate the bigger tap target offered by a bigger button.

10. Position the new button in the bottom-right corner of the slide below the images (don't forget that you can use the Smart Guides to better align the button).

11. If needed, click the **Timeline** label at the bottom of the screen to open the **Timeline** panel.

Now that the button is in place and performs the correct action, you need to arrange it on the **Timeline**. There are a few more options than usual to take care of since the button is an interactive object that stops the playhead.

On the **Timeline** panel, the button object is separated into two areas. As shown in the following screenshot, the separator between the two areas is a *Pause* symbol. It represents the exact moment when the button will stop the playhead:

When the button is clicked, the action you selected in the **On Success** drop-down menu of the **Actions** tab in the **Properties** inspector occurs. In this case, the action is **Go to Next Slide**. It means that when the learner clicks the button, the playhead jumps from the pause symbol directly to the first frame of the next slide. Consequently, your students will never see the frames of slide 3 situated in the **inactive** area, after the pause symbol of the button.

12. Use the **Timeline** or the **Timing** panel to:
   - Make the Button **Appear After** 20.5 **sec**
   - Have the Button **Pause After** 1.5 **sec**
   - Have the Button **Display For** the **Rest of** the **Slide**
13. Use the **Preview | Next 5 Slides** icon on the Toolbar to test the new button.

The button appears just before the audio narration ends and pauses the playhead when the narration is over. When you click the button, the playhead jumps directly to the next slide and the project continues as usual.

Formatting the Buttons

In this section, you will use the **Properties** inspector to explore some of the properties available on the Button object using the following steps:

1. Still on slide 2 of the `Chapter05/takeTheTrain.cptx` file, make sure the new button is selected.
2. Return to the **Style** tab of the **Properties** inspector and open the **Text Button** drop-down menu.

This drop-down menu lists the three button types available in Captivate:

- **Text Button**: This is the default. It is a simple button whose text can be customized in the **Caption** field of the **Properties** inspector.

- **Transparent Button**: This is a sensitive area that serves as a button. The Transparent button may serve many purposes and may not even be transparent. It is typically added on top of a background picture.
- **Image Button**: This is an image (actually a set of three images) that is used as a button. Captivate provides a few predesigned image buttons. But you can also create your own buttons in an image editing tool and import them in Captivate.

In this exercise, you will create a button from a set of images stored on your computer using the **Image Button** option:

3. Choose the **Image Button** option in the drop-down menu.
4. Inspect the list of pre-defined buttons provided by Captivate.
5. Next to the **Image Button** dropdown, click the folder icon. Choose the Chapter05/images/buttons/btn_continue_en_up.png file of the exercises.

When browsing for the image file, note that the Chapter05/images/buttons folder contains three versions of the image:

- One version ends with _up. It is the normal state of the Button.
- Another version ends with _over. It is the Rollover State of the button. It is used to change the appearance of the button when the student rolls the mouse over the button.
- The third version ends with _down. It is the down state of the button, used when the student has the mouse over the button and presses the mouse button at the same time. The action occurs when the student releases the mouse button.

Captivate is able to recognize these three states providing that all three images are stored in the same location and share the same name with _up, _over, or _down added as a suffix:

6. Save the file and use the **Preview | Next 5 Slides** icon of the Toolbar to test the button.
7. When the button appears on the stage, the _up image is used by default.
8. Pass your mouse over the button without clicking to see the _over state of the button.
9. Click and hold on the mouse button to see the _down state.
10. When you release the mouse button, the action specified in the **On Success** menu of the **Actions** tab of the **Properties** inspector (in this case, **Go to the next slide**) occurs.
11. Close the **Preview** window and save the file when you are done.

Keep in mind that the button states will not behave the same way on a touch device (Tablet or Smartphone). On such devices, the RollOver state is not visible. The Down state is briefly displayed whenever the student taps on the button.

This exercise concludes your first overview of the Button object of Captivate. In the next section, you will discover yet another feature of the Smart Shape object.

Finding the Images Buttons

When choosing **Image Button** in the **Style** tab of the **Properties** inspector, Captivate proposes a list of pre-defined Image Buttons you can choose from. The image assets pertaining to these buttons are located at `[Captivate install Path]/Gallery/buttons`. This folder also includes a `more` subfolder, which contains a few extra **Image Buttons** that do not appear in the **Properties** inspector by default.

Using Smart Shapes as Buttons

Back in `Chapter 2`, *Working with Standard Objects*, you learned about Smart Shapes. If you are still not convinced by the awesomeness of **Smart Shapes**, this section will give you yet another argument to convince you after all!

1. Return to the `Chapter05/takeTheTrain.cptx` file.
2. Use the **Filmstrip** to navigate to slide 4 of the project.
3. Use the **Shapes** icon on the Toolbar to open the Smart Shape menu.
4. Select the rounded rectangle shape and draw a rounded rectangle in the lower-left area of the slide.
5. Double-click the Smart Shape and write `Continue` in the rounded rectangle.
6. Use the **Style Name** dropdown of the **Properties** inspector to apply the **shape_As_Button** style to the rounded rectangle shape.

Remember that this style, along with all the other styles currently in use in the project, is defined in the Theme you applied in Chapter 2, *Working with Standard Objects*. When done, your slide should look like the following screenshot:

You will now turn your new Smart Shapes into a Button:

7. Look at the **Properties** inspector when the Smart Shape is selected. It contains the usual **Style** and **Options** tabs as for any other standard Captivate objects.
8. At the top of the **Properties** inspector, select the **Use as Button** checkbox. Notice that the **Actions** tab appears.
9. Switch to the **Actions** tab of the **Properties** inspector.
10. Make sure that the **On Success** action is set to **Go to the next slide**.
11. Look at the **Timeline** panel. If necessary, click the **Timeline** button at the bottom of the screen to open it.

In the **Timeline** panel, notice that the rounded rectangle Smart Shape now has a pause symbol, just like the Buttons you worked with earlier in this chapter.

12. Move the Smart Shape to the end of the **Timeline** so that the pause symbol corresponds to the end of the audio narration.

Make sure the end of the **Timeline** panel of slide 4 looks like the following screenshot. Then, use the **Preview | Next 5 slides** icon on the Toolbar to test your new button:

In this section, you have learned that any Smart Shape can be used as a button. This means that any shape can be turned into a sensitive area you can attach an action to. This, of course, includes the custom shapes that you can draw using the polygon tool. Still not convinced by the awesomeness and flexibility of Smart Shapes?

Branching with Buttons

Branching refers to providing a customized experience to the learners based on their actions in the project. In this exercise, you will create the sequence explaining the types of train tickets to the student. What you want to achieve is allowing the student to view the ticket types in any order and as many times as needed. To do it, you will create a slide with three buttons, one for each ticket type. You will also send the student back to this slide after viewing each ticket type.

Preparing the buttons

The first step is to prepare the necessary buttons. There are several ways to do it in Captivate. Here is one of them:

1. Use the **Filmstrip** to go to slide 11 of the `Chapter05/takeTheTrain.cptx` file.

2. Use the **Media | Image** button of the Toolbar to import the `Chapter05/images/ticket.png` image file into the slide.

3. Repeat the same operation to import the `Chaper04/images/subscription.png` and the `Chapter04/images/pass.png` images into the slide.

4. Move, resize, and rotate the images so that your slide looks like the following screenshot.

Rotating the images can be made in the **Options** tab of the **Properties** inspector, or using the rotate icon that appears on top of the selected object:

When resizing the images, don't forget to hold down the *Shift* key to make sure the original aspect ratio of the images is maintained during the resize operation.

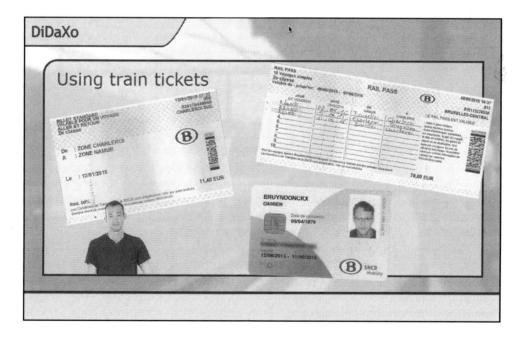

Now, you will add a legend on top of each image using three semi-transparent rectangle Smart Shapes:

5. Use the **Shapes** icon on the Toolbar to create a rectangle.
6. Double-click the new Smart Shape and write `Using standard tickets` in it.
7. Select the `ticket.png` image on the slide. White resize handles appear around it.
8. Hold down the *Shift* key while selecting the new rectangle. This adds the rectangle to the selection with black resize handles.
9. Use the tools of the Align toolbar to give the rectangle the same width as the image (it may be necessary to turn the Align toolbar on using the **Window | Align** menu item).
10. Also align the rectangle to the vertical and the horizontal center of the image.
11. Finally, use the **Properties** inspector or the rotate icon to give the rectangle the same rotation as the image.
12. Repeat this sequence of actions with the other two images. Write `Using passes` on top of the `pass.png` image and `Using Subscriptions` on top of the `subscription.png` image.

At the end of this procedure, your slide should look like the following screenshot:

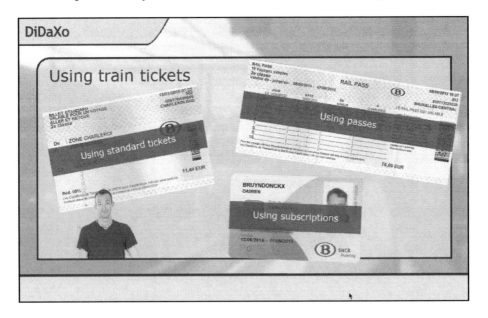

Your images are ready, but they are not yet clickable. To finish off with this section, you will draw an invisible button on top of each image using the following steps:

13. Use the **Interactions | Button** icon of the toolbar to create a new button.
14. In the **Properties** inspector, open the **Text Button** drop-down menu and select the **Transparent Button** option.
15. Change the **Fill Opacity** to 0% and the **Stroke Width** to 0.
16. Finally, clear the default Button **Caption** text.

You should now have a completely transparent button that you will place exactly on top of the ticket.png image.

17. Click the ticket.png image on the slide to select it with white selection handles.
18. Hold down the *Shift* key while clicking on the new transparent button to add it to the current selection.
19. Use the tools of the Align toolbar to resize and align the button. Give it the same size and position as the ticket.png image. Don't forget to also apply the same rotation to the transparent button.
20. Repeat the previous operations for the remaining two images, placing a transparent button exactly on top of each image.

In this section, you have created the buttons you will use for your branching system. To do it, you have used Images, Smart Shapes, and Buttons, as well as a bunch of other tools of Captivate to place and size your objects correctly. This is another example of multiple tools working together to produce the desired effect. Don't hesitate to go the extra mile by doing the following:

- Grouping the three objects that make up each button
- Animating the buttons by applying effects
- Arranging the objects on the timeline as you see fit, in order to achieve a strong visual appeal

Look at the Chapter05/final/takeTheTrain.cptx file to see what we have done with these objects and get inspired.

To pause or not to pause?

In this particular situation, you have three buttons on your slide and, by default, each of them pauses the playhead. This is unnecessary, as you want only one of these buttons to pause the playhead at the end of the slide. You can remove the pause behavior from a button, by deselecting the **Pause After** checkbox in the upper portion of the **Timing** panel.

Creating the Branching scenario

In this section, you will use your new buttons to create the branching scenario. To do it, you will change the action associated with each button. To make it easier, you will also give names to some of your slides using the following steps:

1. Use the **Filmstrip** to select slide 11 of the `Chapter05/takeTheTrain.cptx` project.
2. At the very top of the **Properties** inspector, name the slide `Ticket types navigation`.
3. Validate the new name of the slide with the *Enter* key.

Naming slides this way is not at all required for the branching to work. But it will make it much easier to work with these slides later in the process. It also has other benefits, such as increased accessibility (accessibility will be discussed in `Chapter 12`, *Creating Accessible eLearning*). Finally, note that you can give such names to any object of Captivate, including groups of objects:

Before continuing with this exercise, look at slide 11 in the **Filmstrip**. Note that the name you gave to the slide appears below the slide thumbnail.

4. Repeat the same operation to give these names to the following slides:
   - Slide 12: `Using standard tickets`
   - Slide 13: `Using passes`
   - Slide 14: `Using subscriptions`

5. Use the **Filmstrip** to return to slide 11.

6. Select the **Using standard tickets** button. Remember that if the button is part of a group, you need to click twice on the object: once to select the group, and a second time to sub-select the button within the group.

7. In the **Actions** tab of the **Properties** inspector, change the action of the button to **Jump to slide**.

8. Choose slide **12 Using standard tickets** in the **Slide** drop-down menu. Notice how the name you gave to the slide makes it easy to select it in the dropdown.

9. Repeat the preceding operation to make the **Using passes** button jump to slide **13 Using passes,** and the **Using subscriptions** button jump to slide **14 Using subscriptions**.

10. Use the **Preview | Next 5 slides** icon on the Toolbar to test your buttons. Make sure they all jump to the correct slide before continuing with the exercise.

The first part of the branching is now in place: you can go from the *Navigation* slide (Slide 11) to the other three slides of the sequence. Now, you will build the second part of the branching: going back to the *Navigation* slide from the other three slides of the sequence. To do it, you will change the action associated with the On Exit event of each slide:

11. Use the **Filmstrip** to select slide 12 of the current project.

12. With slide 12 selected, go to the **Actions** tab of the **Properties** inspector.

13. Open the **On Exit** drop-down menu and examine the available actions.

14. When ready, choose the **Jump to slide** option.

15. In the **Slide** dropdown, choose the **11 Tickets type navigation** item.

16. Repeat the same sequence of actions with slides 13 and 14.

This operation is illustrated in the following screenshot:

In Chapter 13, *Working with Variables and Advanced Actions,* you will add a *Continue* button at the bottom of slide 11 to take the user to slide 15. You will also make sure that this button only appears when the student has seen all three slides (Standard tickets, Passes, and Subscriptions) at least once. But now, let's make a quick summary of what has been covered in this section:

- The Button object is one of the interactive objects of Captivate.
- The Button object is able to pause the playhead and wait for the student to interact with the online course.
- When an interactive object is selected, the **Properties** inspector displays the **Actions** tab in addition to the usual **Style** and **Options** tabs.
- The **Actions** tab of the **Properties** inspector is used to define what happens when the Button is clicked.
- Captivate proposes three types of Buttons. These are the **Text Button**, the **Transparent Button,** and the **Image Button**.
- Image Buttons use three different images to create the _up, _over, and _down states of the Button.

- Because the Button stops the playhead, it is separated into two areas on the **Timeline** panel. The separator represents the exact moment when the playhead is stopped.

- It is possible to convert a Smart Shape into a Button. In such case, the **Properties** inspector displays the **Actions** tab when the Smart Shape is selected. Use it to define the action that occurs when the Smart Shape is clicked.

Before moving to the next section, take some time to add *Continue* buttons at the end of the slides of your projects, where you think it is appropriate to do so. Don't forget to arrange the buttons on the Timeline of each slide in order to determine when the button appears and when it pauses the playhead. Look at the `Chapter05/final/takeTheTrain.cptx` file to see where we have added buttons in our version of the project.

The Button object and the pedagogy

Two of the most important things to keep in mind while teaching are: to keep the students focused and to adapt your teaching to each student (the latter is known as **differentiated instruction**). Basically, it means that it is the course that has to adapt to the student and not the other way around (see `http://en.wikipedia.org/wiki/Differentiated_instruction` for more). The Button object helps you with both of these. While watching a longer sequence, your students' attention will inevitably drift away from the course. Each time you add a button, you make the students active, which helps refresh their attention. Another benefit of the button is that it lets each student manage the timing of the course. If you have a slide with a lot of text, it is a good idea to pause the playhead with a button and let each student read the slide at their own pace.

Working with Text Entry Boxes

The second interactive object in this chapter is the **Text Entry Box**. Just like the Button, the Text Entry Box is able to stop the playhead and wait for the user to interact. The difference lies in the nature of the interaction. Using a Text Entry Box, the student is expected to *type*.

You will now insert a Text Entry Box on slide 2 to capture the name of the student. Use the following steps to create a Text Entry Box:

1. Use the **Filmstrip** to go to slide 2 of the `Chapter05/takeTheTrain.cptx` file.

2. Use the **Text | Text Entry Box** icon on the toolbar to create a new Text Entry Box. Alternatively, you can use the *Cmd + Shift + T* (Mac) or the *Ctrl + Shift + T* (Windows) shortcut to perform the same action.

The Text Entry Box system adds up to five objects to the slide (it is okay if they don't all show on your slide):

- The Text Entry Box itself
- A Success Caption
- A Failure Caption
- A Hint Caption
- A **Submit** button (the **Submit** button is sometimes hidden below the Success Caption)

You will now set up the Text Entry Box so it looks the way you want:

3. Move and resize the Text Entry Box to place it under the **Your name :** title.
4. Move the **Submit** button and place it next to the Text Entry Box. Use the green dotted Smart Guides to align the objects correctly.
5. With the **Submit** button selected, use the **Style Name** drop-down menu of the **Properties** inspector to apply the **btn_quiz_submit** style to the button.

After this operation, your slide should look like the following screenshot:

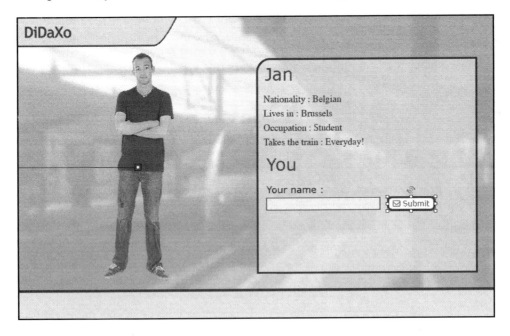

You will now inspect the available properties of the Text Entry Box object:

6. Select the Text Entry Box and look at the **Style** tab of the **Properties** inspector.
7. Inspect the available properties. Most of them should be self-explanatory.
8. When you are done, select the **Validate User Input** checkbox.

In Captivate, the Text Entry Box object serves two very different purposes. First, it can be used to gather data from the student. This is what you do in this example. In such cases, there is no correct or incorrect answer. What is typed in the Text Entry Box does not need to be validated. But sometimes, you'll use the Text Entry Box to capture a specific answer to a question or to mimic a typing action that requires a precise answer. In these situations, there are correct and incorrect answers. In these instances, what is typed into the Text Entry Box needs to be validated.

When the **Validate User Input** checkbox is selected, the Correct Entries box is displayed. You use this box to specify the list of correct answers. Captivate will compare whatever the student types in the Text Entry Box with this list of answers. If it finds a match, the answer is considered correct; otherwise, the answer is false.

9. Still in the **Properties** inspector, click the **More Options** button. Inspect the additional validation options. Click **Cancel** when done.
10. Switch to the **Actions** tab of the **Properties** inspector and inspect the available options.
11. Select the **Success** and the **Failure** checkboxes.

When the **Validate User Input** checkbox is selected, (in other words, when there are right and wrong answers) it is important to give feedback to the learner. This is the purpose of the Failure and Success captions you just turned on. The Failure Caption is shown to the user after an incorrect answer has been submitted. The Success Caption is displayed after the student submits a correct answer.

In this example, however, the Text Entry Box is used to capture the name of the student, so there are no right or wrong answers. Therefore, you will now deselect the **Validate User Input** checkbox:

12. Return to the **Style** tab of the **Properties** inspector.
13. Deselect the **Validate User Input** checkbox. Note that the Correct Entries window, as well as the Failure and Success captions, disappear from the slide.
14. Return to the **Actions** tab of the **Properties** inspector.
15. Notice that the **Success** and **Failure** checkboxes are grayed out. These two options are only relevant when the **Validate User Input** checkbox is selected.

16. Change the **On Success** action to **Go to the next slide**.

In the **Actions** tab, another important option is the **Shortcut** option. This option lets you choose the keyboard key (or combination) the student can use to submit the Text Entry Box. This **Shortcut** option can be used as an alternative or as a replacement to the **Submit** button when it is removed from the slide.

The next step is to arrange the Text Entry Box on the timeline:

17. If necessary click the **Timeline** button at the bottom of the screen to open the **Timeline** panel.

On the timeline, the Text Entry Box is represented just like a Button. It has a pause symbol that marks the exact moment when the playhead will be paused.

18. On the **Timeline**, move the Text Entry box so that the pause symbol corresponds more or less to the end of the narration.

After this operation, the **Timeline** of slide 2 should look like the following screenshot:

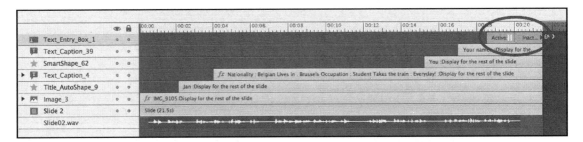

Use the **Preview** | **Next 5 slides** icon on the toolbar to test your slide. When the Text Entry Box appears, the playhead pauses to let you type your name. When you submit your name, the playhead jumps to the next slide and the course continues.

In Chapter 13, *Working with Variables and Advanced Actions*, you will learn how to store the value typed by the user in a variable and use that variable to display a custom welcome message. But for now, let's summarize what you have learned about the Text Entry Box:

- Just like a Button, a Text Entry Box is able to stop the playhead and wait for the student to interact.
- When using Text Entry Boxes, you can decide if the text entered by the student must be validated or not.

- If you decide to validate the text, you can define **Success** and/or **Failure** captions to give feedback to the student.
- If the **Validate User Input** checkbox is selected, you must also provide the correct answer(s) in the **Correct Entries** box.
- If the **Validate User Input** checkbox is not selected, the Text Entry Box is used to capture a piece of data. In that case, you want to store that data in a variable for later use.

Working with Click Boxes

There is one more interactive object that has the ability to stop the playhead and wait for the student to interact. This object is the **Click Box**. A Click Box is used to define an invisible sensitive area on the screen. If the learner clicks inside the Click Box, the correct action is performed. If the student clicks outside the box, the wrong action is performed and the appropriate feedback should be displayed.

The Click box object is very similar to the transparent button object that you used earlier in this chapter, with a few key differences:

- A Click Box can only be invisible. There are no Fill color, Opacity, or Stroke properties for a Click Box.
- Because a Click Box is always invisible, it does not support states (you will discuss Object States later in this chapter).

A Click Box is typically used in an interactive simulation. That is, a Captivate course based on screenshots. You will discuss this type of Captivate project in Chapter 8, *Capturing Onscreen Action*.

Discovering the Rollover objects

In this section, you will discover three more objects. These objects are known as the **Rollover Objects**. They are originally hidden and show only when the user *rolls over* a specific area of the slide with their mouse. This behavior makes the Rollover Objects impossible to use on touch devices such as tablets and smartphones. This is the reason why the Rollover Objects are not supported in HTML5 and will not be used in the project you are working on.

Nevertheless, these objects are an excellent addition to any flash-based project and are still an important part of Captivate's toolset.

Working with Rollover Captions

A **Rollover Caption** is a Text Caption that appears when the user places the mouse over a specific spot on the slide. Such a spot is known as a **Rollover Area**.

In the next exercise, you will experiment with Rollover Caption using the following steps:

1. Use the **Filmstrip** to return to slide 5 of the `Chapter05/takeTheTrain.cptx` project.
2. Make sure there is a *Continue* button at the bottom-right corner of the slide. If there is none, add one now. It is important that the playhead be stopped for the interaction to succeed. Use the **Timeline** panel to make sure the button stops the playhead at the end of the slide, when the narration ends.
3. Use the **Objects | Rollover Caption** icon on the toolbar to insert a new Rollover Caption. Alternatively, you can use the *Cmd + Shift + R* (Mac) or the *Ctrl + Shift + R* (Windows) shortcut to perform the same action.

A Rollover Caption inserts *two* objects on the slide. The first object is a Text Caption. The second object is the associated Rollover Area. The Text Caption is originally hidden and will show only *if* and *when* the student rolls the mouse over the associated Rollover Area.

4. Change the text in the Rollover Caption to `Brussels`.
5. In the **Properties** inspector, choose a **Caption Type** and a **Callout Type** of your liking.
6. Move the Text Caption so that the callout points to the blue dot are situated in the middle of the map.
7. Select the corresponding **Rollover Area**.
8. Move and resize so it is placed on top of the blue dot situated in the middle of the map of Belgium.
9. In the **Properties** inspector, change the fill **Opacity** of the Rollover Area to 0% and the stroke **Width** to 0. This makes the Rollover Area completely invisible.

Make sure your slide looks like the following screenshot before moving on with the exercise:

Use the **Preview** | **Next 5 slides** icon to test your Rollover Caption in the Preview pane. During the preview, wait for the *Continue* button to stop the playhead. The Text Caption is not displayed by default. It appears only *if* and *when* you roll your mouse over the invisible Rollover Area.

Working with Rollover Smart Shapes

In Chapter 2, *Working with Standard Objects*, you discovered the awesome Smart Shape object. You also typed text in Smart Shapes and used them as buttons earlier in this chapter. You will now discover another goodie of this type of object by performing the following steps:

1. Still on slide 5 of the takeTheTrain.cptx project, use the **Shapes** icon on the toolbar to draw an arrow shape pointing to the rightmost blue dot.
2. Depending on the chosen shape, you might need to adjust the size, the position, and/or the shape itself (using the yellow handles).
3. Double-click the arrow shape and type *Liege Guillemins*.

With the Smart Shape in place, you will now associate a corresponding Rollover Area. When the student takes the course, the Smart Shape will be hidden by default. It will become visible only *if* and *when* the student rolls the mouse over the Rollover Area.

4. Right-click the new Smart Shape and select the **Convert to rollover Smart Shape** menu item. This generates a corresponding Rollover Area.

5. Move and resize the new Rollover Area so it covers the rightmost blue dot.

6. With the Rollover Area still selected, use the **Properties** inspector to make it invisible (change the fill **Opacity** to 0% and the stroke **Width** to 0).

Your slide should now look as follows:

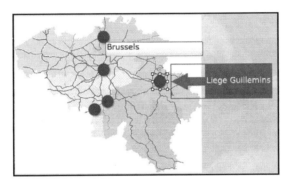

With the Rollover Smart Shape in place, use the **Preview** | **Next 5 slides** icon of the toolbar to test the interaction. Make sure that the Smart Shape only shows *if* and *when* you pass your mouse over the rightmost blue dot.

Working with Rollover Images

A **Rollover Image** is an image that shows only if and when the learner rolls the mouse over a corresponding Rollover Area. In this exercise, you will experiment with a Rollover Image using the following steps:

1. Still on slide 5 of the `takeTheTrain.cptx` project, use the **Objects** | **Rollover Image** icon on the toolbar to insert a new Rollover Image. Alternatively, you can use the *Cmd + Shift + O* (Mac) or the *Ctrl + Shift + O* (Windows) shortcut to perform the same action.

2. Browse the exercise folder to the `Chapter05/images/ruralTrain.jpg` image and click **open** to insert it onto the slide.

As with Rollover Captions and Rollover Smart Shapes, a Rollover Image inserts two objects on the slide: an Image and a corresponding Rollover Area. At runtime, the image will be displayed only *if* and *when* the learner rolls the mouse over the Rollover Area.

3. Move the image to an empty space on the right side of the slide.

4. Move and resize the Rollover Area so it sits on top of the bottommost blue dot.

5. With the Rollover Area selected, use the **Properties** inspector to make it invisible (change the fill **Opacity** to 0% and the stroke **Width** to 0).

6. Use the **Preview** | **Next 5 slides** icon on the toolbar to test the Rollover Image. Make sure the image appears only if and when you pass your mouse over the corresponding blue dot.

Working with Rollover Slidelets

The last Rollover Object of Captivate is the **Rollover Slidelet**. As with every other Rollover Object, the Rollover Slidelet adds *two* objects to the slide: the Slidelet itself and a corresponding Rollover Area. As you might have guessed, the Slidelet only shows *if* and *when* the student rolls over the corresponding Rollover Area.

Use the following steps to insert a Rollover Slidelet:

1. Still on slide 5 of the `takeTheTrain.cptx` project, use the **Objects** | **Rollover Slidelet** icon on the toolbar to create a new Rollover Slidelet. Alternatively, you can use the *Cmd + Shift + Z* (Mac) or the *Ctrl + Shift + Z* (Windows) shortcut to perform the same action.

2. Move the selected object anywhere on the slide, so that it does not overlap with the object with a thick blue border.

3. Click the object with the thick blue border to select it.

The selected object is called the **Rollover Slidelet Area**. It is the Rollover Area associated with Rollover Slidelet. You will position it on top of the topmost blue dot and make it completely transparent.

4. Move and resize the **Rollover Slidelet Area** to place it on top of the topmost blue dot on the map of Belgium.

5. In the **Properties** inspector, deselect the **Show Border** checkbox. Also set the **Opacity** to 0%. The combination of these two options is what makes the Rollover Slidelet Area invisible.

6. Look at the **Timeline** panel and take good note of the available objects.

7. Click on the other object of the Rollover Slidelet system to select it.

The selected object is the actual Slidelet. It is the object that appears only if and when the learner rolls the mouse over the topmost blue dot.

8. Take another look at the **Timeline** panel and notice that the objects of the slide are not listed anymore. This is because the timeline you are viewing at the moment is not the timeline of the slide, but the timeline of the Rollover Slidelet. This helps in understanding what a Rollover Slidelet is.

A Rollover Slidelet is a slide within a slide. Consequently, objects (such as Text Captions, Images, and so on) can be inserted *inside* the Rollover Slidelet and arranged on its timeline. At runtime, the Slidelet appears and plays its own timeline only if and when the student rolls the mouse over the corresponding **Rollover Slidelet Area**.

9. Move and resize the Rollover Slidelet so it covers the right half of the slide. It is OK if the Slidelet covers the other Rollover Objects already present.

 If you want to concentrate only on the Slidelet without viewing the other objects, remember that you can hide them using the eye tool of the **Timeline** panel.

10. Use the **Style Name** drop-down menu at the top of the **Properties** inspector to apply the **[Default Slidelet Style 2]** to the selected object.

With the Slidelet selected, open the icons of the toolbar one by one. Notice that some of the objects are grayed out. This means these objects cannot be inserted in a Slidelet. These objects are the interactive objects of Captivate, the Mouse and, of course, the Rollover Slidelet itself!

11. With the Slidelet still selected, use the **Text | Text caption** icon of the toolbar to insert a new Text Caption in the Slidelet.
12. Type Antwerpen Centraal in the **Text Caption** and move it to the upper area of the Slidelet.
13. Use the **Text | Text caption** icon on the toolbar again to insert a second Text Caption in the Slidelet.
14. Type One of the most beautiful train stations in the world! in the second Text Caption.
15. Place the second Text Caption below the first one inside the Slidelet.

The slide should now look like the following screenshot (note that the Rollover Smart Shape and the Rollover Image inserted previously have been hidden):

Before testing the new Rollover Slidelet, you will arrange the two Text Captions on the Slidelet's timeline:

16. With the Slidelet still selected, look at the **Timeline** panel. You should see the timeline of the Slidelet with only three objects: the two Text Captions and the Slidelet itself.

17. Use the **Timeline** or the **Timing** panel to extend the duration of the Slidelet to 7 seconds.

18. Select the **Antwerpen Centraal** Text Caption and make it **Appear After** 0 sec and **Display For** the **Rest of** the **Slidelet**.

19. Select the second Text Caption and make it **Appear After** 1 sec and **Display For** the **Rest of** the **Slidelet**.

20. Finally, use the **Preview** | **Next 5 slides** icon on the Toolbar to test your Slidelet.

The Slidelet is hidden by default. It appears and plays its own timeline when you pass your mouse over the topmost blue dot on the map of Belgium.

Removing the Rollover objects

The Rollover Objects that you have studied in this section are great tools to add interesting interactivity to the project. But remember that they have a major flaw. They are only available when publishing the project to Flash. Since you will publish this project in HTML5, you will remove these objects from your project using the following steps:

1. Make sure you are still on slide 5 of the `takeTheTrain.cptx` file.
2. If necessary, adjust the eye icons of the **Timeline** panel so that all the objects on the slide are visible.
3. Select the Rollover Slidelet Area that is on top of the topmost blue dot and delete it.

Note that both the Rollover Slidelet Area and the Slidelet itself have been deleted. This emphasizes the fact that these two objects are part of a single system. In other words, one cannot exist without the other. So, deleting one of them deletes both of them.

4. Select either the Rollover Area or the Rollover Caption that you added earlier in this chapter. Note that both the Rollover Area and the associated Text Captions are selected.
5. Delete the selected object. Once again, Captivate deletes the object and the associated Rollover Area.
6. Repeat the preceding operations to delete the remaining two Rollover Objects.

The slide should now be back as it was at the beginning of this section. Before moving to the next one, let's make a quick summary of what has been covered:

- There are four Rollover Objects available in Captivate: The Rollover Caption, the Rollover Smart Shape, the Rollover Image, and the Rollover Slidelet.
- Inserting a Rollover Object adds two objects to the slide: the object itself and a corresponding Rollover Area.
- At runtime, the Rollover Object appears if and when the learner rolls the mouse over the associated Rollover Area.
- When a Smart Shape is converted to a Rollover Smart Shape, a corresponding Rollover Area appears on the stage.

- A Rollover Slidelet is a slide within a slide. As such, it has its own timeline.
- Most of the standard objects of Captivate can be inserted in a Rollover Slidelet.
- Some objects, however, cannot be inserted in a Slidelet. These are the interactive objects (the Click Box, the Text Entry Box, and the Button), the Mouse, and of course, the Rollover Slidelet itself.
- The Rollover objects of Captivate are not supported in the HTML5 output.
- Deleting a Rollover Object also deletes the corresponding Rollover Area and vice versa.

Working with multistate objects

In Adobe Captivate, objects can have multiple states. This feature allows you to define some sophisticated interactivity and interface effects without any programming. In this section, you will explore some of the possibilities offered by multi-state objects and discuss a few typical use cases.

Working with the built-in states of buttons

The multi-states feature allows you to define the rollover, down, and visited states of your buttons. This is what you will explore using the following steps:

1. Use the **Filmstrip** to go to slide 4 of the `Chapter05/takeTheTrain.cptx` file.
2. Select the **Continue** button in the lower-right corner of the slide. Remember that this button is a rounded rectangle Smart Shape used as a button.
3. At the top of the **Properties** inspector, click the **State View** button.

This action takes you to the State View of the selected button. All the objects of the slide are dimmed, except the selected **Continue** button you are viewing the states of.

Also notice that the Filmstrip panel is now called the **Object State** panel. It displays the three built-in states of the selected button. This is shown in the following screenshot:

These three states are as follows:

- The **Normal** state is the default state. It defines the normal look of the Continue button when nothing is happening with it.
- The **RollOver** state defines the look of the button when the student rolls the mouse over the button. When the student removes the mouse from the button, it reverts back to the Normal state.
- The **Down** state defines the look of the button when the student has the mouse on top of the button and when the mouse button is held down. The button action occurs when the student releases the mouse button.

You will now slightly modify the RollOver and the Down states of the **Continue** button to create a nice effect.

4. In the **Object State** panel, click the **RollOver** state to select it.
5. Change the **Stroke** color to a lighter shade of blue.

When defining the RollOver state of a button, one subtle change like the one you just applied is usually more than enough to produce the desired effect.

Now, you will define the Down state. But you would like to start from the current look of the RollOver state to define it. So, you will delete the current Down state and recreate it based on the current Rollover state using the following steps:

6. In the **Object State** panel, right-click the **Down** state of the button.
7. Click the **Delete State** menu item (note the associated keyboard shortcut: *Alt + Cmd + Shift + D* on the Mac or *Ctrl +Alt + Shift + D* on Windows). Confirm your intention in the dialog box that appears.
8. Next, right-click the **RollOver** state and choose **Duplicate State** in the contextual menu. You can also use the *Alt + Cmd + Shift + Z* (Mac) or the *Ctrl +Alt + Shift + Z* (Windows) shortcut key.
9. In the box that appears, choose **Inbuilt State** in the first drop-down list and **Down** in the second, as shown in the following screenshot.
10. Click the **OK** button to create the new Down state:

You will now slightly modify the Down state of the button to make it unique:

11. In the **Object State** panel, select the **Down** state.
12. Use the **Properties** inspector to change the font **Color** to the same shade of blue you used for the Stroke on the RollOver state (the recently used colors are available at the bottom of the color picker).

Now that you have defined the three states of the Continue button, you can exit the State View and test your work in the Preview pane using the following steps:

13. On the Toolbar, click the **Exit State** button (the last one with the large Red X) to return to the regular Captivate interface.

14. Use the **Preview | Next 5 slides** icon to preview your changes in the **Preview** pane.

When the **Continue** button appears, notice that the Normal state of the button is displayed by default. When you pass your mouse on top of the button, the RollOver state is displayed. And when you press and hold the mouse button, the Down state is displayed. The *Go to the next slide* action occurs when you release your mouse button.

 Keep in mind that you always test your projects on a computer (desktop or laptop). The button states will not behave the same way on a touch device (Table or Smartphone). On such devices, the RollOver state is not visible. The Down state is briefly displayed whenever the student taps on the button

15. Close the **Preview** pane when you are done. Make sure the **Continue** button is still selected on the slide.

16. In the topmost section of the **Properties** inspector, open the **Normal (Default)** drop-down menu.

17. Choose the **RollOver** state in the list of available states.

This action displays the **RollOver** state on the slide. Use this drop-down menu to adjust the state using the tools of the **Properties** inspector without switching to the states view. Still in the **Properties** inspector, notice the + icon next to the state list. It allows you to create new states for the selected object. Also notice the trash icon, which allows you to delete the selected state.

18. In the topmost section of the **Properties** inspector, open the **RollOver** drop-down menu.

19. Choose **Normal (Default)** to return to the initial state of the button.

This exercise concludes your first approach to multi-state objects in Captivate.

Working with the Visited state

In this section, you will discover one additional built-in state available on buttons. This will help you apply the finishing touches to slide 11 using the following steps:

1. Use the **Filmstrip** to go to slide 11 of the `takeTheTrain.cptx` file. Remember that this is the slide you use as the navigation slide of the *Types of tickets* sequence.

2. Select the transparent button that is on top of the **Using Standard Ticket** image (remember that if the objects are grouped selecting the button required two clicks: one to select the group, and a second one to sub-select the button within the group).

3. At the top of the **Properties** inspector, click the **State View** button to switch to the state view.

Captivate has already created the default three states for this button. But, in this particular instance, the Rollover and Down states are irrelevant. You will now delete these two states. Then, you will add the Visited state using the following steps:

4. In the **Object State** panel, right-click the **RollOver** state and delete it. Repeat this operation with the **Down** state.

5. At the top of the **Object State** panel, click the **New State** button. This is one of the many ways to create a new state.

6. In the box that appears, choose **Inbuilt State** in the first dropdown and **Visited** in the second.

7. Click **OK** to validate and create the Visited state.

8. With the new **Visited** state selected in the **Object State** panel, use the **Media | Image** icon of the Toolbar to insert a new image.

9. Browse to the `Chapter05/images/check.png` image to insert it in the **Visited** state of the transparent button.

10. Move, resize, and rotate the `check.png` image to place it in the top-right corner of the **Using Standard Ticket** button.

Make sure the Visited state looks like the following screenshot before moving on with the exercise:

You will now exit the State View and test your work in the Preview pane using the following steps:

11. Click the **Exit State** icon on the Toolbar to return to the default Captivate interface.
12. Use the **Preview | Next 5 slides** icon on the Toolbar to test your sequence.

In the **Preview** pane, click the **Using Standard Tickets** button. This takes you to slide 12. At the end of slide 12, you are brought back to slide 11, but the visited state of the button is not showing!

This is because Captivate forgets about the button states when going to another slide, unless you complete the following steps:

13. Close the **Preview** pane and return to slide 11.
14. Make sure the **Using Standard Tickets** transparent button is selected.
15. In the topmost area of the **Properties** inspector, select the **Retain State on Slide Revisit** checkbox.
16. When you are done, use the **Preview | Next 5 slides** icon on the Toolbar again to test your sequence. Confirm it works as expected before moving on.

The **Visited** state of the button now produces the desired effect. It adds a green check when a particular slide has been viewed. Your next task is to repeat the same sequence of actions on the remaining two buttons.

Extra Credit - Creating the Visited state of the other buttons

In this extra credit section, you will repeat the actions of the previous exercise on the remaining two buttons. The general steps are as follows:

- First, you must select the transparent button you want to add a state to. Remember that you need two clicks if the objects are grouped.
- Switch to the states view and delete the unnecessary states.
- Create the Visited state and import the green check image (remember that this image is available in the Library. No need to import it a second time!).
- Return to the default Captivate interface and don't forget to select the **Retain State on Slide Revisit** checkbox.
- When this is done for both buttons, save your file and give it a try in the **Preview** pane.

Working with custom states

In the previous two sections, you discovered the built-in states of the Button object. In this section, you will go one huge step further and discover that you can add your own custom states to any object. This capability makes it incredibly easy to create complex interactions that are entirely compatible with any device, using either Flash or HTML 5.

In the next exercise, you will use the custom states to create a complex interaction with the map of Belgium on slide 5 of your project.

This slide contains five blue dots on top of the map of Belgium. When the student clicks a blue dot, more information about the selected train station should be displayed on the right side of the slide. To make it easier to know which blue dot to use, they will be numbered from one to five, as shown in the following screenshot:

Creating the custom states

Use the following steps to create the necessary custom states:

1. Use the **Filmstrip** to go to slide 5 of the `Chapter05/takeTheTrain.cptx` project.
2. Select the map of Belgium image.
3. At the top of the **Properties** inspector, give the selected image the following name: `img_belgium`. Don't forget to hit the *Enter* key to validate the new name.

Captivate allows you to name any object. Naming objects this way is not technically required. But it will make it much simpler later in the process.

4. With the map of Belgium image still selected, click the **State View** button in the upper section of the **Properties** inspector.

This action takes you to the State View of the selected image. Notice that Captivate has not created any default built-in states. Only a handful of objects (such as Buttons) have built-in states. You will now add five custom states to your image, one for each blue dot, using the following steps:

5. In the **Object State** panel, click the **New State** button.
6. In the box that appears, give your new state the following name: `Antwerpen`.
7. Click **OK** to validate and create the new custom state.
8. With the new **Antwerpen** state selected in the **Object State** panel, use the **Text | Text Caption** icon to insert a new Text Caption in the selected state.
9. Type `Antwerpen Centraal` in the Text Caption.
10. Hit the *Esc* key to exit the text edit mode and select the Text Caption as an object.
11. In the **Properties** inspector, increase the font size to `24` and make the text bold.
12. Move and resize the Text Caption to place it in the upper area of the right-hand side of the slide.
13. Still in the **Antwerpen** state, add a second Text Caption below the first one.
14. Write the following text in the new Text Caption: `This station has been nominated among the most beautiful train stations in the world.`

The **Antwerpen** state of your image is now ready. The state should look like the following screenshot:

You will now use the same procedure to create the remaining four custom states. Use the following table to add content to the states:

State name	Title	Description
Brussels	Brussels Centraal	This underground station was designed by world-famous architect Victor Horta.
Liege	Liege Guillemins	This brand-new station was designed by Spanish architect Santiago Calatrava. The grand opening took place on Dec 18, 2009.
Charleroi	Charleroi-sud	This 1847 building was entirely renovated in 2011. It now provides all the services of a modern station, while maintaining its historical character.
Thuin	Thuin	This rural station is unattended. Only local trains stop here. There is nothing special about it, except this is where I live!

After this process, you should have five custom states in addition to the **Normal (Default)** state on the map of Belgium image.

Aligning content across states

In order to place the title and the description Text Captions at exactly the same location on every state, here is a very simple trick. Instead of creating new states, right-click an existing state and duplicate it. Then, simply update the title and the description text. This will not only speed up your work, but also ensure proper alignment across the custom states you create.

Using buttons to change the state of an object

Now that the five custom states exist, you will use the five blue dots as buttons to change the state of the **img_belgium** image using the following steps:

1. If necessary, click the **Exit State** button on the Toolbar to return to the default interface.
2. Select the topmost blue dot (marked as 1 on the previous screenshot). Remember that this blue dot is a Smart Shape.
3. In the **Properties** inspector, notice that the **Use as Button** checkbox is selected and that an **Actions** tab is present.

4. Switch to the **Actions** tab of the **Properties** inspector.

5. Change the **On Success** action to **Change State Of**.

6. Select the **img_belgium** object in the next drop-down menu and the **Antwerpen** state in the last one.

7. If necessary, deselect the **Continue Playing the Project** checkbox.

The **Actions** tab of the **Properties** inspector should look like the following screenshot:

Now, the rest of the process is very simple. Just repeat the preceding sequence of actions to link each blue dot to the corresponding state of the image:

- Blue dot n° **2** goes to the **Brussels** state
- Blue dot n° **3** goes to the **Liege** state
- Blue dot n° **4** goes to the **Charleroi** state
- Blue dot n° **5** goes to the **Thuin** state

When you are done, use the **Preview** | **Next 5 slides** icon on the Toolbar to test your work. Make sure each button takes you to the correct state before moving to the next section.

Extra Credit - Customizing the Normal (Default) state

By default, each object of Captivate has a single state called the *Normal (Default)* state. Using the State View of Captivate, this *Normal (Default)* state can be customized as well. In this extra credit section, you will add a Character image and a callout Smart Shape to the *Normal (Default)* state of the *map_belgium* image. The general steps are as follows:

- Return to the **State View** of the **map_belgium** image and select the **Normal (Default)** state.
- Add a Character image of your liking to the right-hand side of the slide.
- Also add a callout Smart Shape. Write *Click the blue dots to see the corresponding station*. Arrange the callout so it points at the Character image.
- Exit the **State View** to return to the default Captivate interface.

Because you have added these two objects to the *Normal (Default)* state of your image, they will disappear and be replaced by the content of the other states whenever the student clicks on a blue dot. Consult the `Chapter05/final/takeTheTrain.cptx` file to see what we have done with the Normal (Default) state of this image.

Working with the Go to Next State action

In this section, you will explore another use case for multi-states objects. The goal is to show you how diverse and flexible this feature is. To illustrate this use case, you will work on slide 7. You will add an image, define multiple custom states, and use the Go to Next State action to create another interaction.

The steps are as follows:

1. Use the **Filmstrip** to go to slide 7 of the `Chapter05/takeTheTrain.cptx` file.
2. Use the **Media | Image** icon on the toolbar to insert the `Chapter05/images/scheduleDetail.png` image file.
3. Move and resize the image so it fits in the center of the slide. To speed up your work and make it easier, use the tools covered earlier (such as the Align toolbar, the Smart Guides, holding down the *Shift* key while resizing the images, and so on).
4. With the image selected, use the **Properties** inspector to give it the following name: `img_scheduleDetails`.
5. If there is no **Continue** button in the bottom-right corner of the slide, add one now (you can copy/paste the Continue button of another slide to go faster). Use the **Timeline** to make it pause the playhead when the narration finishes.

6. With the **Continue** button selected, use the *Cmd + D* (Mac) / *Ctrl + D* (Windows) shortcut key to duplicate it.

7. Place the second **Continue** button to the left of the first one and change the label to *Next*.

8. On the **Timeline**, arrange the timing of the objects as you see fit. Just make sure that the scheduleDetail.png image stays visible for the entire duration of the slide, and that the buttons pause the playhead after the narration is finished.

Make sure the slide looks like the following screenshot before continuing with the exercise:

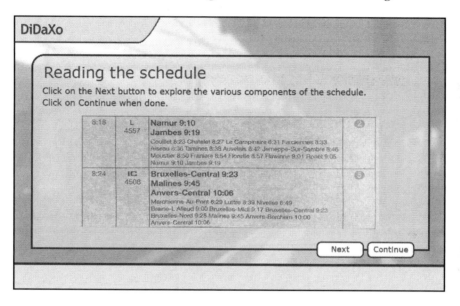

Now that the stage is set, you will define several custom states on the image and use the button to let the user circle through these states. Use the following steps to create the necessary states:

9. Select the **img_scheduleDetail** image. At the top of the **Properties** inspector, click the **State View** button to switch to the State view interface.

10. Right-click the **Normal (Default)** state and choose the **Add State** menu item. This is another way of creating a new state in the **State View** interface.

11. In the popup window, name the new state hour and click the **OK** button.

12. Use the **Shapes** icon of the toolbar to draw a rounded rectangle around the **8:18** text on top of the first column of the schedule image.

13. Use the **Style Name** drop-down menu to apply the **shape_As_HB** style to the rounded rectangle.

14. Use the **Shapes** icon of the toolbar again to draw a rounded rectangle callout shape on the image. Make it point to the rounded rectangle you drew in the previous step.

15. Apply the **alternate_Shape** style to that new shape.

16. Type `The departure time of the train` in the rounded rectangle callout.

17. Move and resize the shapes so the hour state looks like the following screenshot:

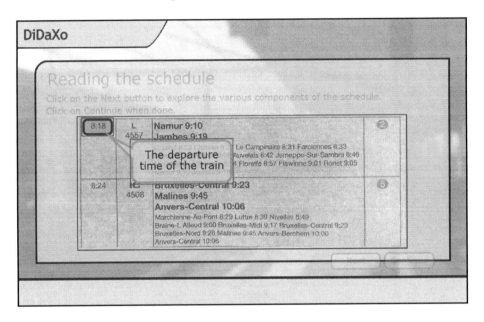

You will now repeat the preceding actions to create three additional states. Use the following table to add the proper content and shapes to the remaining states:

State name	Blue shape position	Callout text
typeNumber	Second column, on top of **L 4557**	Type and number of the train
destinations	Third column (on top of the list of destination)	Destinations Main destinations in bold Other destinations in regular
platform	Last column (on top of the number 2)	Departure platform

After this process, you should have four custom states in addition to the **Normal (Default)** state. You will now return to the default interface of Captivate and apply the required action to the **Next** button.

18. Click the **Exit State** button on the Toolbar to return to the standard Captivate interface.
19. Select the **Next** button in the bottom-right corner of the slide.
20. In the **Actions** tab of the **Properties** inspector, change the **On Success** action to **Go to Next State**. Make sure the `img_scheduleDetails` image is selected in the drop-down menu that appears just below.
21. Deselect the **Continue Playing the Project** checkbox to prevent the **Next** button from releasing the playhead.

A new interaction is now in place. It is time to test your work using the **Preview | Next 5 slides** icon on the Toolbar.

Before moving to the next section, here is a quick summary of what you have learned about multi-state objects in this section:

- Captivate allows you to define multiple states on (almost) any object.
- Some objects, such as Buttons, Smart Shapes used as buttons, and so on, have pre-defined built-in states. These define RollOver effects, Down effects, and more.
- The Visited state allows you to define a state for the buttons that have been clicked.
- Select the **Retain State on Slide Revisit** checkbox to maintain the visited state even if you jump to other slides and come back.
- Click the **State View** button of the **Properties** inspector, or use the state drop-down list to see the states on the stage and edit them.
- When in the State View, click the **Exit State** button on the Toolbar to return to the default interface.
- You can define any number of custom states and make them look the way you want.
- You can add extra objects (such as Shapes, Text Captions, images, and so on) to the states of an object.
- You can use the **Change State of**, the **Go to Next State**, or the **Go to previousState** actions with any button. This allows you to define interesting interactions involving states without any programming.
- To make defining these interactions easier, don't forget to give names to your objects and slides.

Working with the Drag and Drop interaction

In this section, you will explore some of the amazing possibilities of the **Drag and Drop** interaction. Drag and Drop requires at least two objects. One serves as the **Drag Source** and the second as the **Drop Target**:

- The Drag Source is the object that the student can drag
- The Drop Target is the object on which a Drag Source can be dropped

It does not matter what those objects are, as long as they are non-interactive. In the following example, you will use images as both the Drag Source and the Drop Target, but you could as well use Text Captions, Highlight Boxes, Smart Shapes, and so on.

To make things more interesting, a single slide can contain multiple Drag Sources and multiple Drop Targets. Thanks to this capability, you are able to create complex and fun interactions. Best of all, Drag and Drop is supported in both Flash and HTML 5.

Using the Drag and Drop Interaction wizard

For this first example, you will create a simple Drag and Drop. The goal is to ask your students which train car they can board with a second-class ticket. They have to drag the ticket on top of the car they can board. To create this Drag and Drop, you will use the Drag and Drop interaction wizard using the following steps:

1. Use the **Filmstrip** to navigate to slide 19 of the `Chapter05/takeTheTrain.cptx` project.
2. Use the **Interactions | Drag and Drop** icon on the Toolbar to start defining your Drag and Drop.

The Drag and Drop Interaction wizard is a three-step process that helps you define a simple Drag and Drop. In the first step, you have to select the Drag Source(s). In this case, there is only one Drag Source, which is the image of the train ticket.

3. Click the image of the train ticket to select it as a drag source. This adds a green outline around the image to indicate that it is selected as a Drag Source. If you made a mistake and selected the wrong object, use the red *minus* sign in the top-right corner of the object to remove the object from the selection.
4. Click the **Next** button at the top of the screen to go to the second step of the wizard.

In the second step of the wizard, you have to select the Drop Target(s). In this example, the two train car images are the Drop Targets:

5. Click the two train car images to mark them as Drop Targets. A blue outline is used to identify the Drop Targets.
6. Click the **Next** Button at the top of the screen to go to the last step of the wizard.

The last step of the wizard is used to associate the Drag Source(s) with the matching Drop Target(s). In this example, you want to associate the train ticket with the train car on the right (because it is a second-class train car).

7. Select the image of the train ticket and notice the arrow icon in the middle of the image.
8. Click and drag an arrow from that icon to the image of the train car in the top right corner of the slide.

 You can use the lock feature of the **Timeline** panel to ensure that you don't accidentally move the images themselves.

Make sure your slide looks like the following screenshot before you click the **Finish** button at the top of the screen:

And now, the finishing touches:

9. Type `Attention! You entered a first class coach with a second-class ticket!!!` in the red failure caption. When you are done, hit the *Esc* key to leave the text-editing mode and select the object (the red failure caption is hidden behind the green success caption).

10. Move and resize the failure Caption so it sits in the middle of the slide.

11. Use the same process to write `Great! You are ready to discover Belgium by train.` in the green success caption. Move and resize the success caption so it sits in the middle of the slide.

When moving and sizing the success and the failure captions, don't forget that these two messages will never be displayed together. The success caption is displayed when the student provides the correct answer and the failure caption, when the student provides the wrong answer. Therefore, it's perfectly fine if these two objects overlap on the slide.

12. Save the file and use the **Preview** | **Next 5 slides** icon to test your first Drag and Drop interaction.

In the **Preview** pane, drag the train ticket on one of the two train cars. Hit the **Submit** button in the bottom-right corner of the slide and make sure the right feedback is displayed.

Congratulations! You have created your first Drag and Drop interaction with Captivate! It is not yet perfect, but your students will certainly enjoy this high level of interactivity.

Using the Drag and Drop panel

The power of the Drag and Drop interaction goes way beyond this first example. In the next exercise, you will explore the **Drag and Drop** panel and use it to fine-tune the Drag and Drop you created in the previous section:

1. Make sure you are on slide 19 of the `Chapter05/taketheTrain.cptx` project.

2. Select the train ticket image.

3. Open the **Drag And Drop** panel. It is located on the right edge of the screen, next to the **Properties** inspector and **Timing** panel. It may be necessary to click the **Properties** icon on the Toolbar to toggle this panel group on.

If the **Drag and Drop** panel is not visible, use the **Window** | **Drag and Drop** to display it.

The **Drag and Drop** panel contains the options pertaining to the Drag and Drop interaction. The Drag and Drop Interaction wizard you used in the previous section only gives you access to a small subset of these options. The **Drag and Drop** panel is divided into three tabs. At the very top of the **Drag and Drop** panel, notice the trashcan icon that allows you to delete the Drag and Drop interaction if needed.

4. At the top of the **Drag And Drop** panel, click the eye icon. This removes the red line and displays the Drag and Drop on the stage.
5. In the **Actions** tab of the **Drag and Drop** panel, select the **Infinite Attempts** checkbox. This gives your students unlimited attempts to find the correct answer.
6. Select the **Reset All** radio button. This will move the Drag Sources back to their original location when a wrong answer is submitted.
7. Also select the **Auto Submit Correct Answers** checkbox.
8. Select one of the Drop Target images (identified by the blue outline).
9. Switch to the **Format** tab of the **Drag and Drop** panel.
10. Open the **Effects** drop-down menu and choose the **Zoom In** effect.
11. Repeat this action with the other Drop Target image.
12. Select the **Submit** button at the bottom-right corner of the slide.
13. In the **Properties** inspector, use the **Style Name** drop-down menu to apply the **btn_quiz_submit** style to the **Submit** button.
14. Move the **Submit** button in place, to a location that you like at the bottom right of the slide.
15. Take some time to examine the other options of the **Drag and Drop** panel before moving on.
16. Save the file and use the **Preview** | **Next 5 Slides** icon on the Toolbar to test your updated Drag and Drop.

When testing your interaction, pay close attention to the Zoom-in effects you applied to the Drop targets. Also notice that when you submit a wrong answer, the Drag Source automatically goes back to its original position. When submitting the right answer, you don't need to click the **Submit** button anymore!

Drag and Drop extravaganza

The exercise you just performed shows you the typical use case of a simple Drag and Drop interaction, but the true power of Drag and Drop goes way beyond this sole example. *Drag and Drop extravaganza* is the title of an excellent webinar by Dr Allen Partridge, Adobe eLearning evangelist. This webinar gives you a much deeper look at the possibilities of the Drag and Drop interaction. You can access the Drag and Drop extravaganza recording by following this link: `https://2252372.meetus.adobeevents.com/`. Note that you need a free Adobe ID to access this content. Lynda.com also offers a full online course on the Drag and Drop interaction at the following URL: `https://www.lynda.com/Captivate-tutorials/Captivate-Projects-Drag-Drop-Interactions/187496-2.html`.

Customizing the feedback messages

There are two feedback messages associated with the Drag and Drop interaction: The Success Caption and the Failure Caption. These types of messages can also be associated with other interactive objects such as Buttons, Click Boxes, Text Entry Boxes, and Quiz slides. Sometimes, a third feedback message (called the Hint Caption) can be added, though this is not the case for the Drag and Drop interaction you are currently working with:

- The **Success Caption** shows only if the student submits the correct answer or performs the correct action.
- The **Failure Caption** shows only if the student submits the wrong answer or performs the wrong action.
- The **Hint Caption** shows when the student rolls the mouse over an interactive object (such as a Click Box, a Text Entry Box, or a Button). It acts like a Rollover Caption, using the interactive object as its Rollover Area.

In Captivate 2017, these feedback messages are based on the Smart Shape object. It means that they have the same formatting capabilities as a regular Smart Shape. But in the past, these feedback messages were based on the Text Caption objects and had the same capabilities, options, and limitations as standard Text Captions.

You will now experiment with these feedback messages to discover their capabilities and limitations using the following steps:

1. Still on slide 19 of the `Chapter05/takeTheTrain.cptx` file, select the green Success Caption.
2. Look at the **Properties** inspector and take good note of the available properties. These are the same as for a Smart Shape.
3. Right-click the green Success Caption and choose the **Revert to Text Caption** menu item.
4. Take another look at the **Properties** inspector. The available properties are not the same as before. They are those of a Text Caption object.

This means that your Success Caption is now based on the Text Caption object. In other words, you can no longer control the opacity, you have fewer options for the fill and the stroke, and you are limited to a handful of shapes listed in the **Caption Type** dropdown.

5. Right-click the green Success Caption again and choose the **Convert to Smart Shape** menu item.
6. In the list of available shapes, choose the rounded rectangle shape.

Your Success Caption is now based on the Smart Shape object again. The **Properties** inspector gives you access to all the properties, including the Fill, Opacity, Stroke Style, and so on. You can also choose the shape to use, which gives you huge control over your feedback message.

7. With the green feedback message still selected, click the **State View** button at the top of the **Properties** inspector.

This action takes you to the State View of the Success Caption. Notice that the usual **Normal (Default)** state is already available. But if you try to click the **New State** button at the top of the **Object State** panel, nothing happens! This is because you cannot add additional states to those feedback messages. But you can customize the **Normal (Default)** state!

8. Click the **Library** icon at the far right of the Toolbar to open the project library.
9. In the **Images** section of the **Library**, locate the **check.png** image.
10. Drag the **check.png** image from the **Library** panel to the **Normal (Default)** state of your Success Caption.

11. Move and resize the green checkmark so it sits on the top-right corner of the Success Caption, as shown in the following screenshot:

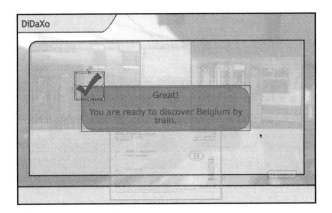

You will now change the shape used for the red Failure Caption using the following steps:

12. Click the **Exit State** button on the Toolbar to return to the default interface.

13. Select the red Failure Caption (you may have to move the green Success Caption to access it).

14. In the **Properties** inspector, notice that the same properties as for a Smart Shape are available. This means that your red Failure Caption is currently based on the Smart Shape object.

15. Right-click the Failure Caption and choose the **Replace Smart Shape** menu item.

16. In the list of shapes, choose the Rounded Rectangle (or any other shape of your choice).

17. With the red Failure Caption selected, click the **State View** button at the top of the **Properties** panel.

18. Once in the **Normal (Default)** state of the selected object, use the **Media | Image** icon on the Toolbar to import the Chapter05/images/cross.png image to the stage.

19. Move and resize the red cross so it sits on the top-right corner of the red Failure Caption.

20. Click the **Exit State** button on the Toolbar to return to the default interface.

21. Finally, use the tools of the Align toolbar to place the two feedback messages exactly in the center of the slide.

In this section, you have customized the green Success Caption and the red Failure Caption associated with the Drag and Drop defined in the previous section. Here is a summary of what you have learned:

- Captivate provides automatic feedback messages for a lot of interactive objects and features. This includes Buttons, Click Boxes, Text Entry Boxes, Drag and Drops, and Quiz slides.
- These feedback messages can be Success Captions, Failure Captions, Hint Captions, and so on. Note that the available messages depend on the interactive object being used.
- These feedback messages can be based on the Smart Shape object (this is the default) or on the Text Caption object.
- If based on the Smart Shape object, right-click a feedback message and choose the **Replace Smart Shape** menu item to choose which shape to use.
- Only the **Normal (Default)** state is available on those messages.
- You can use the **State View** button of the **Properties** inspector to access the **Normal (Default)** state and further customize the feedback messages.

Working with Learning Interactions

Learning Interactions are complex interactive objects with built-in logic and behavior. As such, they represent the easiest way to add interactivity to your courses. Captivate contains a selection of Learning Interactions by default. You will explore them in this section. When inserted on a slide, Learning Interactions can be used as is or customized in various ways. The best part is that Learning Interactions are entirely compatible with both Flash and HTML5.

Working with the Accordion interaction

One of the available Learning Interactions is the Accordion Widget. In this exercise, you will add one more slide to the *takeTheTrain* project and insert the **Accordion** Learning Interaction using the following steps:

1. If necessary, return to the `Chapter05/takeTheTrain.cptx` file.
2. Use the **Filmstrip** panel to go to the first slide of the project.
3. Use the **Slides | Blank Slide** icon on the Toolbar to insert a new slide based on the **Blank** Master Slide of the Theme. The new slide is inserted as slide 2.
4. Use the **Filmstrip** to go to slide 4 of the project.
5. Select the **Continue** button in the bottom-right corner of the slide.
6. Use the *Crtl+C* (Windows) or the *Cmd+C* (Mac) shortcut to copy the selected button.
7. Use the **Filmstrip** to return to slide 2.
8. Use the *Crtl+V* (Windows) or the *Cmd+V* (Mac) shortcut to paste the **Continue** button in the bottom-right corner of slide 2.

The stage is set! You now have a new slide with a **Continue** button whose job is to stop the playhead in order to let the student interact with the Accordion Widget. It is now time to insert the Learning Interaction, using the following steps:

9. Use the **Interactions | Learning Interaction** icon on the Toolbar to open the **Select Interaction** dialog.
10. Review the available interactions. When you are done, select the **Accordion** interaction (the first one on the list).

11. Click the **Insert** button to insert it onto slide 2. This is shown in the following screenshot:

This inserts the Accordion interaction into slide 2 and opens the **Widget Properties** dialog box. You will use it to customize the content and the look and feel of the Accordion.

12. Use the column on the left of the **Widget Properties** dialog to choose a Theme that you like (in the example of the Chapter05/final folder, we chose Theme 4).

13. Double-click the interaction title in the header area and type Objectives of this course module as the title of the Accordion interaction.

14. Repeat the same operation to customize the subtitle of the interaction.

You will now customize the content of the panels of the Accordion widget.

15. In the main area of the **Widget Properties** dialog, double-click the first button of the Accordion. Change its title to `Moving around in Belgium`.

16. Double-click the content area of the first Accordion, and type a short text such as `Belgium is a small country with a lot of people, so roads and highways tend to be over crowded. However, Belgium has an extensive train network that makes it easy and cheap to travel the country`.

17. Change the **Button Label 2** title to `Finding your way in a Belgian train station` and the **Button Label 3** title to `Travel cheap and relaxed`.

18. Double-click the **Button Label 4** title. Click the *Minus* button that appears on the left side of the label to delete it from the Accordion.

You should now have three panels left in the Accordion Interaction, as shown in the following screenshot:

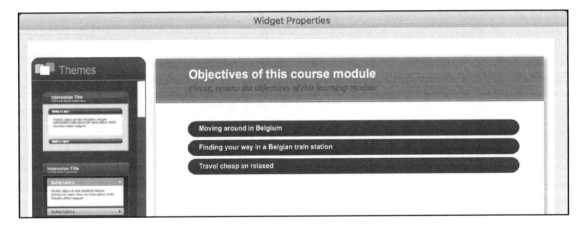

19. Add an appropriate descriptive text in each of the three panels.

20. Explore the other options available to further customize your Accordion interaction. When you are done, click the **OK** button.

21. Move and resize the Accordion so it integrates nicely into the slide.

22. Use the **Preview** | **Next 5 slides** icon on the Toolbar to test your interaction.

Your exploration of the Accordion interaction is now finished. If you want to further customize your interaction, double-click it to reopen the **Widget Properties** dialog.

The Accordion Widget is just one of the available interactions. Take some time to review the other available interactions. You will find great ideas to pimp up your next Captivate project. The basic principle is always the same and it goes as follows:

- A Learning Interaction is a self-contained complex behavior that encapsulates its own built-in logic.
- Inserting a Learning Interaction into the slide does not stop the playhead. Make sure you also add a button to give the student a chance to interact with the widget.
- Learning Interactions can be customized in many ways. But the extent of this customization is up to each interaction. This is both the strength and the weakness of these objects. They are simple to use and customize, but only go that far in what they allow you to do.
- To modify an interaction, double-click it on the slide to reopen the **Widget Properties** dialog.
- Learning Interactions are supported in both Flash and HTML 5.

Summary

At the end of this chapter, your project is very different from what it was at the beginning. By adding interactive elements to your slides, you have come a long way in making your online course engaging and fun to use. From a pedagogical standpoint, this interactivity is paramount in maintaining the student's attention and in improving retention.

In this chapter, you studied the Button, the Text Entry Box, and the Click Box objects. These objects have the ability to stop the playhead and wait for the learner to interact with the course. You used the Button object to provide content that is driven by your student's input in your course, a concept known as Branching.

You also experienced with the Rollover objects. You explored the Rollover Caption, Rollover Images, Rollover Slidelet, and Rollover Smart Shapes. But you decided not to use them because of their incompatibility with HTML5.

You discovered the awesome power of Multi-State objects, which allow you to define sophisticated interaction without the need of any programming skills. You have worked with the Drag and Drop interaction and with the associated feedback messages. Finally, you have discovered how Learning Interactions work.

In the next chapter, you will focus on the aesthetics of your project. You will learn how to create and apply a consistent look and feel that will further help your learner get the most out of your teaching.

Meet the community

In this section, we want to introduce you to Joe Ganci. He is a veteran eLearning developer and instructional designer. Joe is almost always presenting at all the major eLearning-related events around the world. Chances are that you will meet him sooner than later!

Damien

Joe has reviewed two of my previous Captivate books. The first time I contacted him via email, he was kind enough to include a small quote in French (my native language) in his reply. We finally met in October 2014, during the Adobe Learning Summit in Las Vegas.

Pooja

I first met Joe at the Training 2012 conference in Atlanta, and since then, we've been close friends. I always look forward to seeing him at the conferences, breaking bread with him, co-presenting sessions with him (if I get lucky), and spending time with him. He has a great sense of humor and is always keen to learn new things and to share what he knows with others.

Joe Ganci

Joe Ganci is an eLearning consultant with a long track record. His design approaches and his innovative use of tools, such as Adobe Captivate, Articulate Storyline, Trivantis Lectora, and many others, has caused many to improve how they design and develop their eLearning content and to implement newer and better methods. His personal and hands-on style of consulting keeps his services constantly in demand, and he is privileged to have visited many clients from all over the world.

He has been involved in every aspect of learning development since 1983. He holds a degree in computer science and is a published author, having written several books, research papers, and articles about eLearning. He is widely considered a guru for his expertise in eLearning development and conducts classes and seminars at commercial companies, government facilities, leading universities, and at many industry conferences, where he often serves as the keynote speaker. He is on a mission to improve the quality of eLearning with practical approaches that work. Call Joe for your training needs and to have Joe help with your eLearning projects.

Joe is certain that he is privileged to call both Damien Bruyndonckx and Dr. Pooja Jaisingh his friends!

Contact details:

- **Web:** http://elearningjoe.com/
- **Twitter:** @elearningjoe
- **Email:** joe@elearningjoe.com
- **Joe's Tool Reviews:** http://bit.ly/GanciReviews
- **Joe's Newsletter Sign Up:** http://bit.ly/eLearningJoeNewsletter

6
Crafting the Graphical Experience with Styles and Themes

In this chapter, you will focus on the aesthetic aspect of the project using Styles, Master Slides, Themes, and Templates. Your primary goal is to reach a high level of consistency in the look and feel of your eLearning content.

When developing eLearning, always keep in mind that your students will most likely experience your content while alone in front of their computer or mobile device with no one around to guide them. In this chapter, you will discover that a consistent look and feel is an efficient way to get your students on task. The idea is to free them from learning how eLearning works and looks so that they can be fully available for the actual teaching.

Captivate offers five features to help you achieve this high level of consistency. The first feature that will be discussed in this chapter is the **Swatch Manager**. You will also learn about **Styles**, **Master Slides**, **Themes**, and **Templates**.

In addition to serving your pedagogical efficiency, the proper use of Master Slides, Templates, Styles, Swatches, and Themes will dramatically speed up the development of your eLearning content.

In this chapter, you will do the following:

- Explore the Swatch Manager and the color management features of Captivate
- Experiment with Styles and with the Object Styles Manager
- Learn about different types of font available in Captivate

- Experiment with predefined Themes
- Create a Theme containing Styles and Master Slides
- Create and use a Template

There's a lot to cover, so let's dive into the first discussion of this chapter.

Preparing your work

To get the most out of this chapter, it is important to reset your workspace. If you are using the default interface mode, restart Captivate to reset your workspace to default. If you are using the advanced interface mode, use the **Window | Workspace | Reset 'Classic'** menu item.

In this chapter, you will use the exercise files in the `Chapter06` folder. If you get confused by any of the step-by-step instructions, take a look at the `Chapter06/final` folder, which contains a copy of the exercises as they should look at the end of this chapter.

Working with the Swatch Manager

When working on an eLearning project, it is very important to precisely format the objects present in your course. Never forget that you are teaching! In such situations, most students will try to make sense out of every single formatting anomaly. Inconsistent formatting will most likely mislead and confuse your learners.

Consistent formatting in eLearning

In my first eLearning project with Captivate, I used blue Text Captions to *explain* things to the learners and black Text Captions when I wanted them to *do* something. After a short while, the learners knew that when seeing a blue Text Caption, they just had to read through the text, and when seeing a black Text Caption, they made themselves ready to do something. Learners have reported that this formatting consistency helped them structure their learning.

When it comes to color, it is important to define a good-looking color scheme at the beginning of the project and to stick to it throughout the development. Sometimes this color scheme is enforced by company regulations. At other times, you must respect a strict color scheme defined by a graphic designer. In some situations, you are the only person involved and you can define your own color scheme.

The Swatch Manager allows you to customize the set of colors available in your project. In this exercise, you will take a look at the Swatch Manager using the following steps:

1. Open Captivate.
2. Use the **File | New | Blank Project** menu item to create a new Captivate project.
3. Choose **1024 x 627** as the new project size.
4. Save the new project as `Chapter06/styles.cptx`.
5. Use the **Window | Swatch Manager** menu item to open the floating **Swatch Manager** panel.

The **Swatch Manager** panel should look similar to the following screenshot:

The main area of the **Swatch Manager** is covered by a grid of colored squares. Each of these squares is called a **Swatch** and can be used to apply colors to the selected Captivate object. The five buttons in the upper portion of the **Swatch Manager** panel (**Append, Load, Save, Reset**, and **Clear)** are used to modify the collection of Swatches available.

Importing custom Swatches to the Swatch Manager

One of the main features of the Swatch Manager is the ability to import and export Swatches. You can use another Adobe application (such as Photoshop, Illustrator, or InDesign) to export Swatches and import them into Captivate.

In the next exercise, you will import the official brand colors of the DiDaXo company into the project using the following steps:

1. Click the **Append** button on the **Swatch Manager**.
2. Navigate to the `Chapter06/DiDaXo.ase` file and double-click it.

Five color swatches are added at the end of the **Swatch Manager**. The imported colors are the official corporate colors of the DiDaXo Company. You must use these colors in your projects in order to comply with the company policy.

Note that you can also use the **Load** button of the Swatch Manager. In that case, the imported swatches replace the default ones (as opposed to being added to the existing ones).

Creating the ASE file

An **Adobe Swatch Exchange** (**ASE**) file is used to export color swatches from an Adobe application and import them into other Adobe applications. Most Adobe applications can be used to create `.ase` files. In Captivate, use the **Save** button of the **Swatches** panel to save the current set of swatches as an `.ase` file. For this exercise, we have used an online service named **Adobe Color CC** to create the color scheme. Then we used the CC libraries to sync our color scheme with Photoshop. Finally, we used the Swatches panel of Photoshop to export the `.ase` file. You can find more about Adobe Color CC and create your own color schemes at `http://color.adobe.com`.

Using the custom colors

Now that the corporate colors of DiDaXo have been added to the **Swatch Manager**, you will use them to format the standard objects of Captivate:

1. Still in the `Chapter06/styles.cptx` project, select the title placeholder in the center of the only slide of your new project.
2. Open the **Properties** inspector if necessary.
3. In the **Character** section, open the **Color** picker by clicking the downward arrow in the color swatch.
4. At the top of the color picker, click the second icon to see the color swatches (see the arrow in the following screenshot).
5. Use the first custom swatch imported by the `.ase` file (purple) as the font color of the title placeholder.

As shown on the following screenshot, the color swatches available in the color chooser are the same as the swatches available in the **Swatch Manager**. This includes the five custom swatches that you have imported previously. Move or close the **Swatch Manager** if you feel it is in the way:

In the remaining exercises of this chapter, we will refer to the imported colors as custom color 1 to 5.

What is true for the font color is true for any other color properties. In other words, each time you have a color picker, you have access to your five custom color swatches. Let's experiment with this using the following steps:

6. With the title placeholder still selected, open the color picker associated with the **Fill** color property in the **Properties** inspector.
7. At the top of the Color Picker, click the second icon to switch to the color swatches if necessary. Then choose custom color 2 (light blue) as the fill color of the title.
8. Use the same process to change the **Stroke** color to Custom Color 3 (dark blue).
9. Increase the stroke **Width** to 4 pixels. (Notice that *pixels* is the default unit, so 4 means 4px.)

Thanks to the **Swatch Manager**, you have been able to import the custom colors of the DiDaXo brand into the project and to use them to format the Title placeholder of the first slide. Using the same techniques, you can use the same set of five colors throughout the entire project. This is your first step toward consistent formatting. Your learner will certainly appreciate this high level of professionalism when taking the course.

Custom swatches persistence

The custom swatches you have imported will remain available in Captivate for all the projects as long as Captivate stays open. If you close and reopen Captivate, the Swatch Manager panel will revert to default. Don't forget to reimport your custom swatches each time you open Captivate.

Before moving to the next section, let's quickly summarize what has been covered in this one:

- The **Swatch Manager** lets you customize the set of colors available in Captivate.
- One of the most interesting aspects of the **Swatch Manager** is the ability to import and export .ase file.
- The Adobe Swatch Exchange (.ase) files are used to export color swatches from one Adobe application and import them into another Adobe application.
- Adobe color (http://color.adobe.com) is an online service that allows you to create custom color schemes and to sync them with Adobe applications using CC libraries. From there, they can be exported as .ase files and reimported into Captivate using the **Swatch Manager**.
- Adobe Color is a free online service that requires an Adobe ID.

- Unfortunately, Captivate does not support CC libraries as of this writing, which makes the use of an intermediary Adobe application (such as Photoshop or Illustrator) mandatory to create the .ase files you want to import in Captivate.

Working with Styles

In Captivate, the formatting properties of an object can be saved in a style. This allows you to reapply the same properties on other objects of the same type. Captivate comes with predefined styles, but you can modify these default styles and even create your own custom styles.

Managing styles with the Properties inspector

In this section, you will explore how the **Properties** inspector can be used to apply and create styles:

1. Select the title placeholder on the first slide of the Chapter06/styles.cptx project.
2. If needed, click the **Properties** icon on the Toolbar to open the **Properties** inspector.

The **Style Name** drop-down list (shown as (**1**) in the following screenshot) tells you that the style currently applied to the selected object is the **+[Default Title Smart Shape Style]** style. The + sign in front of the style name means that the formatting has been manually changed on top of the original style. Technically, this is called a style override. There is no way of knowing which formatting changes have been made:

In the top-right corner of the **Properties** inspector is another icon (marked as 2 on the preceding screenshot). This icon gives you access to additional options pertaining to the selected object. In this chapter, we will refer to this icon as the *Style Options* icon.

3. Click the Style Options icon and inspect the available items.

The menu items available in the Style Options icon are used to manage the styles in different ways. In the upcoming sections, you will explore these options one by one.

Resetting a style

Resetting a style is one of the operations available in the Style Options icon:

1. With the formatted placeholder still selected, open the Style Options icon.
2. Click the **Reset Style** menu item.

The original **[Default Title Smart Shape Style]** style is reapplied to the selected object and the + sign disappears from the **Style Name** in the drop-down list.

3. Use the **Edit** | **Undo** menu item or the *Ctrl + Z* (Windows) or *Cmd + Z* (Mac) shortcut to undo the last action.

Resetting a style is very practical when you want to reset the format of the selected object back to default.

Creating new styles

Creating new styles is another operation that can be done with the Style Options icon. In this section, you will save the current formatting of the placeholder object as a new style using the following steps:

1. Make sure the formatted title placeholder is selected.
2. Look at the **Style Name** drop-down list of the **Properties** inspector. Confirm that the applied style is the **+[Default Title Smart Shape Style]** style.
3. Open the Style Options icon and click the **Create New Style** item.
4. In the **Save New Object Style** dialog box, name the new style `DiDaXo-MainTitle` and click **OK**.

Take another look at the **Style Name** drop-down menu on the **Properties** inspector. It tells you that the new **DiDaXo-MainTitle** style is applied to the selected object. This style can now be applied to any other Smart Shape in the project.

Applying styles

Applying styles to existing objects is yet another operation that can be done from the **Properties** inspector. In the next exercise, you will apply your new **DiDaXo-MainTitle** style to another Smart Shape of the project:

1. Use the **Slide | Content Slide** icon on the Toolbar to add a second slide to the `Chapter06/styles.cptx` file.
2. Use the topmost section of the **Properties** inspector to apply the **Objectives** Master Slide to the new slide.
3. Select the title placeholder in the topmost area of the slide.
4. At the top of the **Properties** inspector, open the **Style Name** drop-down menu.
5. Select the **DiDaXo-MainTitle** style.

Two title placeholders on two different slides now share the same look and feel thanks to your own custom style! You will now try to apply this same style to yet another object:

6. Select one of the Text Caption placeholders of slide 2.
7. At the top of the **Properties** inspector, open the **Style Name** drop-down menu.

Notice that your custom **DiDaXo-MainTitle** style is *not* available in the drop-down menu. This is because the selected object is not a Smart Shape, but a Text Caption.

In Captivate each object type has its own set of styles. So, a style defined for a Smart Shape can only be applied to Smart Shapes, and a style defined for a Text Caption can only be applied to Text Captions. In this case, your custom **DiDaXo-MainTitle** style can only be applied to Smart Shapes. This can be tricky, as, in some cases, a Smart Shape containing text and a Text Caption can be formatted to look the very same way. But since they are not of the same object type, they will never share the same style.

Modifying a style

Modifying a style is the next action that you will perform. In this exercise, you will modify the formatting of one of the Smart Shapes that has the **DiDaXo-MainTitle** style applied. You will then update your custom style to the new formatting and see how the other object reacts:

1. Make sure the title placeholder in the topmost area of slide 2 is selected.
2. Look at the top of the **Properties** inspector. Confirm the **DiDaXo-MainTitle** style is currently applied to the selected object.
3. In the **Style** tab of the **Properties** inspector, change the font size to `48`.

Because you have made a formatting change, the **+** sign appears in the **Style Name** drop-down menu. The style currently applied to the selected Text Caption is **+ DiDaXo-MainTitle**.

4. Open the Style Options icon and click the **Save changes to Existing Style** item.

5. This action updates the **DiDaXo-MainTitle** style after the current look of the selected object. The **+** sign disappears from the **Style Name** drop-down list.

6. Use the **Filmstrip** to return to the first slide of the project.

7. Select the main title placeholder. In the **Characters** section of the **Style** tab of the **Properties** inspector, confirm that the new font size is also applied to the selected title placeholder.

By updating the **DiDaXo-MainTitle** style, you have updated the formatting of every object this style is applied to, throughout the entire project.

Applying styles automatically

Imagine the style currently applied to the title placeholders of slide 1 and slide 2 is the one you want to apply to *every* slide title throughout the project. You could browse each slide one by one and manually apply the new style to each and every title. But there is another, more automated, way:

1. Make sure you are on slide 2 of the `Chapter06/styles.cptx` file.

2. Use the **Slide | Content Slide** icon on the Toolbar to add a third slide to the project.

3. Repeat the preceding operation three more times.

You should now have six slides in your project. The first slide uses the *Title* Master Slide. The remaining five are using the *Objectives* Master Slide. Your goal is to apply the **DiDaXo-MainTitle** style to every slide title throughout the project. But so far, only the first two slides are correctly using this style.

4. Use the **Filmstrip** to navigate to slide 3 and select the title slide placeholder.

5. Look at the **Style Name** drop-down menu on the **Properties** inspector. Notice that that the **[Default Title Smart Shape Style]** style is currently applied to the selected object.

6. Use the **Properties** inspector to change one of the formatting properties of the selected object. For example, change the font size to `36`. After this operation, the style applied is **+[Default Title Smart Shape Style]**.

You will now apply your custom **DiDaXo-MainTitle** style to all the slide titles of the project using the following steps:

7. Use the **Filmstrip** to return to slide 2. Select the slide title placeholder.
8. Open the Style Options icon and click the **Apply this style to...** item.
9. In the **Apply Object Style** box, select the **[Default Title Smart Shape Style]** style in the drop-down list and click **OK**. This operation is illustrated in the following screenshot.

By doing this, you apply the **DiDaXo-MainTitle** style to every title placeholder of the project currently using the **[Default Title Smart Shape Style]** style:

10. Use the **Filmstrip** to browse slide 4, slide 5, and slide 6 of the project. Confirm that your custom **DiDaXo-MainTitle** style is correctly applied to the title placeholder of each slide.
11. Use the **Filmstrip** to navigate to slide 3 of the project. Notice that the **DiDaXo-MainTitle** style is correctly applied, but the font size should be smaller than on the other slides of the project.
12. Select the title placeholder of slide 3 and look at the **Properties** inspector.

The **DiDaXo-MainTitle** style has been properly applied to the title placeholder, but the manual style override is still active. So, the actual style is **+DiDaXo-MainTitle**.

13. Open the Style Options icon and click the **Reset Style** item.

This action removes the style overrides, which properly applies the genuine **DiDaXo-MainTitle** style.

Automatically replacing the overrides

Before moving on to the next section, take note of the **Replace modified styles** checkbox. When this checkbox is selected, the style overrides are automatically cleared when a new style is applied to the selected object. This may sound very tempting, but it may lead to unwanted changes throughout the project, so use it with great care.

This concludes your first exploration of styles in Captivate. Using styles, it has been easy and quick to format every Title Placeholder of the project. This helps you achieve the high degree of formatting consistency that assists your students in the learning process and creates a more professional-looking project.

Before moving to the next topic, let's summarize what you have learned:

- Styles help create and maintain consistent formatting throughout the entire project.
- In the topmost section of the **Properties** inspector, use the **Style Name** dropdown to apply a style to the selected object.
- When additional formatting is applied, a + sign appears in front of the style name. This indicates that the style has been overridden by some manual adjustments.
- Use the **Reset Style** feature to clear the overrides and reapply the original style.
- When you modify a style, you change the formatting of all the objects using that particular style, throughout the entire project.
- The Style Options icon in the top-right corner of the **Properties** inspector contains the necessary options to create, update, reset, and apply styles.

Working with the Object Style manager

So far, you have used the Style Options icon of the **Properties** inspector to apply and manage styles. This icon provides a quick and easy access to the main styling features. However, behind the scenes, a much more sophisticated engine is at work!

This engine is the **Object Style Manager**. The items of the Styles Options icon are just shortcuts to the actual Object Style Manager. Everything these icons made possible is also possible through the Object Style Manager. But the Object Style Manager has much more to offer.

Renaming styles

One of the extra features offered by the Object Style Manager is the ability to rename an existing style. In this section, you will experiment with this ability hands-on, using the following steps:

1. Make sure you are in the `Chapter06/styles.cptx` project.
2. Use the **Edit** | **Object Style Manager** menu item to open the Object Style Manager. You can also use the *Shift + F7* (Windows) or the *Shift + fn + F7* (Mac) shortcut to do the same thing.

The Object Style Manager opens as shown in the following screenshot:

The left side of the Object Style Manager (shown as (**1**) in the preceding screenshot) lists the object types of Captivate.

3. In the left column of the Object Style Manager, expand the **Standard Objects** section.
4. In the **Standard Objects** section, expand the **Smart Shape** subsection and select the **Title** object.

The middle column (shown as (**2**) in the preceding screenshot) shows a list of styles that can be applied to the object type selected in the first column. In this case, the styles listed in the middle column can be applied to the Smart Shape object. Among them is your custom **DiDaXo-MainTitle** style. You will now use the Object Style Manager to rename it.

5. In the middle column, select the **DiDaXo-MainTitle** style.

When a style is selected in the second column of the Object Style Manager, its properties are displayed in the third column. One of these properties is the name of the style that appears at the very top of the third column (see (**3**) in the preceding screenshot).

6. Change the name of the selected style to **DiDaXo-SlideTitle.**
7. Click the **OK** button in the bottom-right corner of the Object Styles Manager to validate the change and close the dialog box.
8. Select the title placeholder of the slide you are on.
9. Look at the **Style Name** drop-down menu of the **Properties** inspector and confirm that the selected object now uses the **DiDaXo-SlideTitle** style.

Renaming existing styles is one of the many capabilities of the Object Style Manager. In the next two sections, you will experiment with exporting and importing styles.

Exporting a style

Exporting styles is another feature offered by the Object Style Manager. Let's experiment with this capability using the following steps:

1. Still in the `Chapter06/styles.cptx` file, use the **Edit | Object Style Manager** or the *Shift + F7* (Win) or the *Shift + fn + F7* (Mac) shortcut to reopen the Object Style Manager.
2. In the left column, select the **Standard Objects | Smart Shape | Title** object.
3. In the middle column, select the **DiDaXo-SlideTitle** style.

4. At the bottom of the **Object Style Manager**, click the **Export** button.
5. Save the style as `Chapter06/DiDaXo-SlideTitle.cps`.
6. Click the **OK** button to acknowledge the successful export.
7. Click **OK** to close the **Object Style Manager**.
8. Save the `Chapter06/styles.cptx` file.

Exporting a style creates a `.cps` file. This file will be used to import the style in another project.

Exporting multiple styles
Clicking on the drop-down arrow next to the **Export** button in the Object Style Manager gives you the ability to export all the Styles of a specific object type, or all the Styles of all the objects.

Importing a style

In order to use your custom **DiDaXo-SlideTitle** style in another project, you will now use the Object Style Manager to import the `.cps` file, created in the previous section, in the `takeTheTrain.cptx` project using the following steps:

1. Open the `Chapter06/takeTheTrain.cptx` file.
2. Use the **Edit | Object Style Manager** menu item to open the Object Style Manager.
3. In the **Object Style Manager**, expand the **Standard Objects** section, then the **Smart Shape** subsection.
4. Select the **Title** object.

Notice that your **DiDaXo-SlideTitle** style is *not* listed in the middle column. This is because the styles listed in the Object Style Manager are specific to the active file only. In Captivate, each project has its own list of styles.

5. At the bottom of the **Object Style Manager** dialog, click the **Import** button.
6. Browse to the `Chapter06/DiDaXo-SlideTitle.cps` file and click **Open**.
7. Read the message and click **Yes** to discard it.
8. Close the **Object Style Manager** dialog by clicking the **OK** button.

After this operation, the **DiDaXo-SlideTitle** style has been transferred to the `takeTheTrain.cptx` project. You are now able to apply it to the Smart Shapes of this project as well.

9. In the **Filmstrip**, select slide 1.
10. Select the main title of the project that reads **Take the train!**
11. Use the **Style Name** dropdown in the topmost area of the **Properties** inspector to apply the **DiDaXo-SlideTitle** style to the selected Smart Shape.

This confirms that your custom style has been correctly transferred from one project to the other and that it is now available in both projects.

12. Use the **Edit** | **Undo** menu item or the *Cmd + Z* (Mac) / *Ctrl + Z* (Windows) shortcut to undo your last action.
13. Save and close the `Chapter06/takeTheTrain.cptx` file when done.

Thanks to the Object Style Manager, you have been able to transfer a style from one project to another. This workflow helps you achieve formatting consistency not only within each project but also across different projects.

Adding styles globally

If you want to add styles to the Object Style Manager and make them available to every (future) projects of your Captivate installation, close all open files and go to the **Edit** | **Object Style Manager** menu item of Captivate when no file is open. This allows you to open the Object Style Manager of your Captivate installation rather than the Object Style Manager of a specific project.

Creating a style in the Object Style Manager

To create the **DiDaXo-SlideTitle** style, you used the **Create New Style** item of the Style Options icon in the **Properties** inspector. You will now create another style using the Object Style Manager:

1. Return to the `Chapter06/styles.cptx` file.
2. Use the **Edit** | **Object Style Manager** menu item or the *Shift + F7* (Win) or the *Shift + fn + F7* shortcut (Mac) to reopen the Object Style Manager.
3. In the leftmost column, select the **Standard Objects** | **Smart Shapes** category.
4. In the middle column, select the **DiDaXo-SlideTitle** style.
5. Just below the middle column, click the **Clone** button.

Captivate duplicates the **DiDaXo-SlideTitle** style and saves the clone as **DiDaXo-SlideTitle1**.

6. In the rightmost column of the **Object Style Manager** dialog, rename the new style `DiDaXo-ProjectTitle`.

7. In the **Text Format** section, change the font **Family** to **Verdana** and the font **Size** to `56`.

8. In the **Fill & Stroke** section, change the fill **Opacity** to `0%` and the stroke **Width** to `0` to make the Smart Shape transparent.

Make sure the Object Style Manager looks similar to what is shown in the following screenshot:

9. Leave the other options at their current settings and click **OK** to close the Object Style Manager.

10. Use the **Filmstrip** to go to slide 1.

11. Select the Title Placeholder.

12. Use the **Style** drop-down list of the **Properties** inspector to apply the new **DiDaXo-ProjectTitle** style to the selected object.

13. Save the `Chapter06/styles.cptx` file when done.

This exercise concludes your overview of the Object Style Manager. Before moving on, let's summarize what you have learned:

- The items in the Style Options icon of the **Properties** inspector act as shortcuts to the Object Style Manager
- The Object Style Manager provides extra tools compared to the Object Options icon
- The leftmost column of the Object Style Manager lists all the object types of Captivate
- Using the Object Style Manager, styles can be exported from a project and imported into another
- The Object Style Manager also provides the ability to rename existing custom styles
- It is possible to create styles entirely in the Object Style Manager

Working with fonts

In this section, you will learn how to properly use fonts in Adobe Captivate. This may sound a bit surprising. After all, when an object is selected, there is a **Font** property in the **Properties** inspector that works the exact same way as in most applications you commonly use. Just open the **Fonts** dropdown and pick the Font you want to use. This is very simple. But there is one thing you should keep in mind.

When working with Adobe Captivate, the last step of the process is to publish your work in Flash or in HTML5. When publishing in HTML5, your course is exported as a self-contained mini website that is viewed in a web browser by the learner. Well, here is the thing: on the internet, a website uses the fonts installed on the client machine to render text. This means that if you use a font in Captivate when designing your course, that very same font must be installed on the computer of all your learners for the text to render correctly on their side.

This problem is not limited to producing courses with Captivate. This is something the whole web-design industry has struggled with for years! But the web-design industry has come up with various solutions that you can use in Captivate.

Using web safe fonts

The first solution is to use fonts that are known to be available on most, if not all, computers around the world, regardless of the system (Windows, Mac or Linux) or version used by the learner. Using one of these fonts is therefore considered safe, hence the name *Web Safe fonts*. Let's now discover the list of Web Safe fonts available in Captivate using the following steps:

1. Make sure you are in the Chapter06/styles.cptx file.
2. Use the **Filmstrip** to go to slide 2 of the project.
3. Select one of the Text Caption placeholders.
4. Open the Fonts drop-down menu situated in the **Character** section on the **Style** tab of the **Properties** inspector.

Notice that the list of available fonts is divided into categories. One of these categories is **Web Safe Fonts**, and another one is **System Fonts**, as shown in the following screenshot:

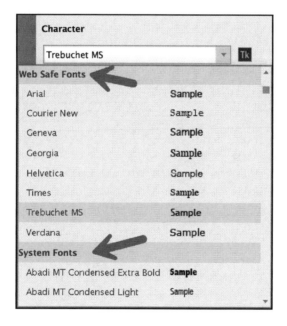

If you use one of the fonts listed under the **Web Safe Fonts** category, make sure that the font used to render text on the learner's computer is the exact same font you used when you designed the course on your computer. This is because the Web Safe fonts are known to be available on every computer in the world. The trade-off is that the list of available fonts is quite limited and very widely used.

Working with System Fonts

The second category of fonts available in the **Properties** inspector is **System Fonts**. The System Fonts category is a list of all the fonts installed on your computer that are not in the Web Safe fonts category. Using these fonts when developing a website (and remember that your Captivate courses are exported as mini-websites) is dangerous, because there is no guarantee that the fonts available on your computer are also available on the computer used to view your content.

When using a System Font, Captivate exports the Text Captions and Smart Shapes with text as images. This is the only way to make sure your text content is rendered exactly as you designed it.

 When creating a Responsive Project, text is never exported as images because it is difficult to make an image truly responsive. This stresses the danger of System Fonts even more. When developing eLearning content, you definitely don't want to use System Fonts. You will learn more about Responsive Projects in Chapter 10, *Creating a Responsive Project*.

Using images for text is really not the optimal solution:

- First, image file sizes are larger than text. So, the use of System Fonts dramatically increases the size of your published content.
- Another problem is the accessibility of the content. Text written on images is not visible to the assistive technologies used by students with disabilities (you will learn more about accessibility in Chapter 12, *Creating Accessible eLearning*).
- Finally, an image has a fixed size, which makes it very difficult to use in a responsive situation. For example, reflowing the text based on the available screen dimension is barely possible when using an image (you will learn more about responsive projects in Chapter 10, *Creating a Responsive Project*).

For all these reasons (plus the ones not listed here) you want to avoid using System Fonts in your projects.

Working with web fonts

A third solution is to use web fonts. The idea is very simple to understand. Instead of relying on fonts installed on your student's computer, you can use fonts hosted on the internet. The chosen font is downloaded before it is used to render text, which makes it available to all your students. Sure enough, this impairs performance, as an extra file (the font) must be downloaded from the server before the content is made available to the viewer. But, on the other hand, you have a much wider range of fonts to choose from. (Not mentioning that the caching technologies used by web browsers make the performance issue a very minor annoyance.)

Adobe has developed an online font library called Typekit. One of the new features of Adobe Captivate 2017 is the ability to use Typekit fonts in your projects. Let's explore this new feature using the following steps:

1. If needed, return to `Chapter06/takeTheTrain.cptx` and use the **Filmstrip** to navigate to slide 8.
2. Select the slide title Smart Shape that reads **Reading the schedule**.
3. In the **Properties** inspector, notice that this text uses the **Verdana** font family.

Verdana is one of the Web Safe fonts, because it is available on every single system. This is the main reason why it is used in this project. Using a Web Safe font ensures that the text is rendered correctly on every system without adding any extra file size to the project, without impairing accessibility, and with the ability to resize and reflow the text on smaller screens if necessary.

The trade-off is that Verdana is so widely used that it does not convey any graphical uniqueness anymore. To make this project stand out, you will now replace the Verdana font with another one from the Typekit online font library.

Typekit and the Adobe ID

Typekit is a commercial online service from Adobe. Access to the Typekit Library requires a free Adobe ID. Syncing the fonts with your computer also requires the installation of the Creative Cloud desktop app available at `http://www.adobe.com/creativecloud/desktop-app.html`.

4. With the slide title still selected, click the **Tk** icon just next to the Font drop-down menu in the **Properties** inspector. This action takes you to the Typekit website.
5. If needed, log in with your Adobe ID using the **Sign In** button in the top-right corner of the Typekit website.

The Typekit website allows you to browse the entire online font library. The dark column on the right side of the screen provides an easy-to-use search interface. Feel free to explore the capabilities of the site at your own pace before resuming this exercise:

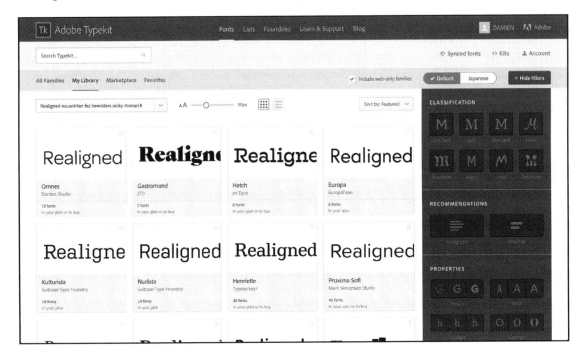

Before choosing the font you want to use, there are a few things you need to be aware of:

- Typekit is a commercial online service from Adobe that requires an Adobe ID and an extra subscription that is *not* included in the Captivate license. You can find more information on the available Typekit plans at https://typekit.com/plans.
- A small subset of the Typekit library is available for free.
- This exercise uses fonts that are available for free at the time of the writing. If the font is no longer available for free by the time you read the book, don't hesitate to choose another free font to your liking from the library.
- Some of the fonts of the Typekit library are available for desktop syncing only. This means that you can download those fonts and install them on your computer to use in your Adobe applications. Other fonts are only available for the Web. They can be used online, but cannot be downloaded on your computer. Adobe Captivate can only use fonts that are available both for desktop syncing and online browsing at the same time.

- More information on the integration of Typekit in Captivate can be found at `https://helpx.adobe.com/captivate/using/typekit-plan-captivate.html`.

You will now select a font from the Typekit library, sync it with your computer, and use it in your Captivate project:

6. Use the search field in the top-left corner of the Typekit website to search for the *Cooper Black* font.
7. Click the font name to reach the font page on the Typekit site (available at `https://typekit.com/fonts/cooper-black`). Notice that, at the time of writing, this font is available in the free plan for both sync and web.
8. Click the **Sync** icon associated with the **Cooper Black Std** font.
9. After a few moments, you will receive a notification from the Adobe Creative Cloud Desktop app that the font has been synced successfully.
10. Return to slide 8 of the `Chapter06/takeTheTrain.cptx` file. Make sure the slide title is still selected.
11. In the **Style** tab of the **Properties** inspector, open Font list.

At the top of the list, you should see a third category called **Typekit Fonts**. This category lists the Typekit fonts that you have synced with your computer. Among them, you find the **Cooper Std** font, which is now available on your system:

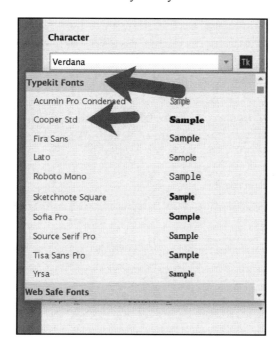

You can now use this new font in the same way as any other font installed on your system.

12. Select the new **Cooper Std** font to apply it to the selected slide title. Notice that the style applied to this object is now **+SlideTitle**.
13. Click the Style Options icon and choose the **Save Changes to Existing Style** item.
14. Browse the other slides of your project and confirm that every slide title now uses the new Typekit font.
15. If necessary, resize, move, and reset styles so that the font applies to all slide titles throughout the project.

This concludes your first exploration of the Typekit Library. Typekit and the Web Fonts technology give you access to a tremendous amount of creative flexibility and opportunities. Thanks to this technology, your online course will shine like never before, providing an even better training experience to your learners.

Extra credit - syncing a second Typekit web font

Now that you have used a Typekit web font for the slide titles, why not sync a second web font that you can use for regular text? In this extra credit section, you will return to the Typekit site, find a great font for the body text, sync it, and use it in your project. The general steps go as follows:

- Go to the Typekit website and search for a suitable font (in the project in the `Chapter06/final` folder, we have used the *Lato* font)
- Sync the chosen font with your computer using the Typekit website and the Creative Cloud desktop application
- Use the new synced font in Captivate for Text Captions and Smart Shapes containing body text
- Don't forget to save your changes in existing styles to quickly update the font used by the objects throughout the project
- Save and close the `Chapter06/takeTheTrain.cptx` file when done

At the end of this extra credit section, your project should convey a completely updated look and feel, thanks to the use of two Typekit web fonts.

Before moving to the next section, let's quickly summarize what you have learned about fonts in this section:

- When published in HTML5, your Captivate course is exported as a self-contained mini-website. As such, the technical possibilities and limitations of your published course are similar to those of a regular website.

- On the internet, web browsers use the fonts installed on the computer of the learner to render text. To see the course as you designed it, each learner must have the same fonts as the ones you used when creating the course.
- The *Web Safe Fonts* is a short list of fonts known to be installed on most (if not all) computers in the world, regardless of the system or version. Using these fonts on the internet is therefore considered safe.
- The System Fonts are the fonts available on your local computer that are not in the Web Safe fonts list. Using these fonts for designing sites is dangerous, as they might not be available on the learner's computer.
- When using System Fonts in non-responsive projects, Captivate exports the text as images. This is the only way to ensure that the text looks as intended. But it comes with many undesirable side effects, such as increased file size, limited accessibility, and limited responsiveness.
- When creating a Responsive Project, the text is never exported as images.
- Web Fonts are fonts hosted on the internet. They can be downloaded to the viewer's computer when visiting a site/course.
- Typekit is a Web Fonts library maintained by Adobe. Typekit is available in Captivate 2017, so you can use the Typekit fonts to design your courses. This ensures that the font you used to design a course is also available to your learners.
- Access to the Typekit library requires an Adobe ID, the Creative Cloud desktop application, and a subscription that is not included in the Captivate license. However, a small subset of the Typekit library can be used for free, without any extra subscription.

Working with Themes

A **Theme** is a file that collects all the formatting properties of a project, including (but not limited to) the Styles. Captivate installs with a handful of ready-to-use themes. In order to have a better idea of what a Theme is, you will start with some simple experiments using the predefined Themes of Captivate:

1. Save and close every open file.
2. Use the **File | New Project | Blank Project** menu item to create a new blank project.
3. In the **New Blank Project** dialog, use the **Select** drop-down menu to choose a size of **1024 x 627**. When you are done, click the **OK** button.

Captivate creates a new blank project of the chosen size. When a new project is created that way, a single slide is automatically added to the **Filmstrip**. This new slide is already formatted and contains several styled objects.

Creating a Blank project from the Welcome screen
To create a new blank project, you can also use the **New** tab of the Welcome screen. In such cases, you must choose the size of the new project in the bottom left corner of the Welcome screen and the **New Blank Project** dialog does not open.

Applying a theme to an existing project

When you install Captivate, predefined themes are installed along with the application. You will now apply one of these themes to your new project and explore what a Theme is made of:

1. Still in your new blank project, click the **Themes** icon on the Toolbar.

As shown in the following screenshot, the **Themes** icon lists the available themes. Looking at this list, you also learn that the theme currently applied is the **White** theme, as indicated by the frame around its thumbnail (see the arrow in the following screenshot):

Choosing the default theme

In the preceding screenshot, also notice the checkmark in the bottom-left corner of the **White** theme. This checkmark indicates that the **White** theme is the default theme applied to every new project. To choose another theme as the default, right-click a Theme and choose the **Set as Default Theme** menu item.

2. Click any thumbnail to apply the corresponding theme to the current project.
3. Read the warning message about the style overrides. Click **Yes** to acknowledge and clear the message.

The new theme is applied to the project. Take some time to look at what has changed. You should notice that not only has the background of the slide changed, but also the formatting of the placeholder objects.

Before moving on to the next section, you will reapply the original *White* theme to the project using the following steps:

4. Click the **Themes** icon on the Toolbar to reopen the list of available themes.
5. Click the **White** theme thumbnail to reapply it to the current project.
6. Click **Yes** to acknowledge and clear the warning message.

Now that you know how to apply themes, you will further explore this feature and discover what Themes are made of.

The elements of a Theme

A Captivate Theme is a collection of graphical elements and assets. In the next few pages, you will discover what Themes are made of by manipulating different Themes and exploring how they affect the slides and objects of the project.

The Master Slides

The first element that makes up a Captivate Theme is a set of **Master Slides**. To better understand what they are, your first stop is the **Master Slide** panel:

1. Make sure your new project is still open. If you closed it, just recreate a new one.
2. Use the **Window | Master Slide** menu item to switch to the **Master Slide** view.
3. Enlarge the **Master Slide** panel by dragging the vertical separator between the **Master Slide** panel and the stage to the right.

The **Master Slide** panel now replaces the **Filmstrip** panel on the Captivate interface. In this view, the **Filmstrip** is therefore not visible.

The White theme that is currently applied to the project contains an entire set of predefined Master Slides. Each of these Master Slides defines a layout that you can apply as is to any slide of the project. To ensure visual consistency across the Master Slides of a theme, the first Master Slide of the panel is known as the **Main Master Slide** (shown as (**1**) in the following screenshot). The Main Master Slide contains the visual elements that are common to most (if not all) slides of the project:

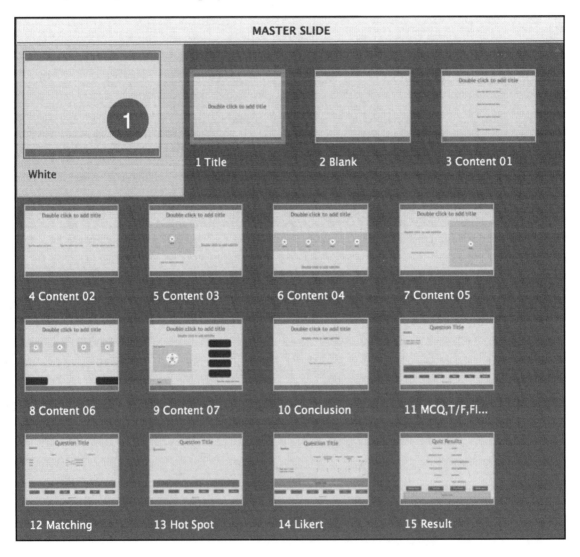

Creating slides based on Master Slides

Master Slides are used as templates for the individual slides of a Captivate project. In this section, you will create slides in your new project and explore how to apply Master Slides using the following steps:

1. Use the **Exit Master** icon on the Toolbar to switch back to the **Filmstrip** view. You can also use the **Window** menu and deselect the **Master Slide** item.
2. If needed, reduce the width of the **Filmstrip** panel by dragging the vertical separator between the **Filmstrip** and the stage to the left.
3. Use the **Insert** | **New Slide From** | **Content 07** menu item to insert a new slide based on the Content 07 Master Slide of the Theme.

The new slide already contains several Smart Shapes and Text Captions. To be exact, the elements contained on the slides are not actual Text Captions and Smart Shapes yet. These elements are Text Caption and Smart Shapes **Placeholders**. They are used to predefine the location, size, and other formatting options of a future object.

4. Double-click the **Double click to add title** Placeholder.
5. Type some text into the object and hit the *Esc* key.

Now that some text has been typed into the object, it is no longer a placeholder. It is an actual Smart Shape with text. The size, position, font family, font size, color, and so on, of this object are inherited from the placeholder, while the content has just been typed in.

Changing the Master Slide of an existing slide

Sometimes, you want to change the Master Slide applied to an existing slide. This is what you will learn in this section:

1. Use the **Slide** | **Content Slide** icon on the Toolbar to insert a third slide in the project.
2. With the new slide selected, look at the **Properties** inspector.

Remember that new slides are always inserted after the selected slide. When it comes to the Master Slide, Captivate uses whatever Master Slide is applied to the selected slide when inserting a new one.

3. In the topmost section of the **Properties** inspector, open the **Master Slide** drop-down menu and apply the **Content 01** Master Slide of the theme to the selected slide. This operation is illustrated in the following screenshot:

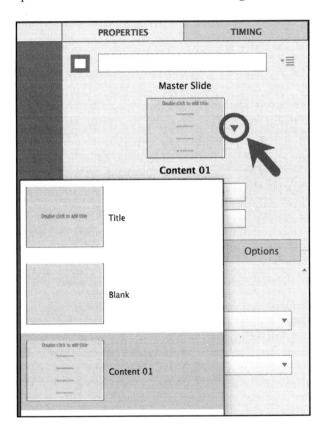

4. Use the **Filmstrip** to return to the second slide of the project.
5. On the left side of slide 2, notice the presence of a special placeholder. This type of placeholder is known as a **Content Placeholder**.
6. Roll your mouse over the icons of the Content Placeholder. Note that each icon corresponds to a Captivate object.

7. Double-click the **Image** icon on the Content Placeholder (see the arrow in the following screenshot):

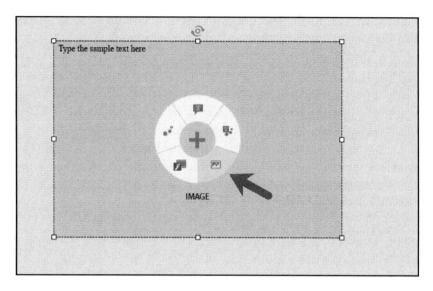

When double-clicking this icon, Captivate immediately opens the **Select Image from Library** dialog. From this dialog, you can choose the image to insert into the Placeholder.

8. Click **Cancel** to close the dialog without inserting an image.
9. Take some time to experiment with the other icons of the Placeholder.

Each of these icons acts as a shortcut to insert different types of content in the Placeholder. This illustrates the basic idea of Themes and Placeholders. By providing ready-made slide layouts and shortcut icons, the Themes and Placeholders are tremendous time savers. They enable you to rapidly develop your course, while maintaining a high degree of consistency throughout the project.

Inserting a blank slide in a themed project

In this section, you will insert a new blank slide into your project and see which Master Slide is applied by default:

1. Use the **Filmstrip** to select the third slide of the current project.
2. Use the **Slide | Blank Slide** icon on the toolbar to insert a new blank slide.
3. With the new slide selected, look at to the topmost section of the **Properties** inspector.

Notice that the **Blank** Master Slide has been automatically applied to this new slide.

4. Open the **Background** menu situated in the **Style** tab of the **Properties** inspector.
5. Select the **Master Slide Background** item. You should notice a slight change in the slide background (it is a little darker than before).

The background picture of the **Blank** Master Slide is now used as the background of the newly inserted slide.

5. Open the same **Background** menu again.
6. Select the **Custom** option. Extra icons appear in the **Properties** inspector.

Inspect the available options. Take good note of how you can change the background color of a slide, create a gradient, or use a picture as the slide background.

This exercise concludes your first exploration of Master Slides in Captivate. Now, you will explore the second element of a Theme.

The Styles

The second element of a Theme is a set of object Styles. You will now experiment with Styles in Themes using the following steps:

1. Use the **Filmstrip** panel to return to the second slide of the project.
2. Select the title (a Smart Shape with text) that you created in the previous section.
3. Inspect the **Properties** inspector of the selected object. Note the **Font**, **Color**, **Font Size**, and other formatting properties that are currently in use.

You will now apply another Theme to the project and see how this change affects the slides and the objects:

4. Open the **Themes** icon on the Toolbar.
5. Click the **Clean** theme to apply it to the project.
6. Read the warning message and click **Yes** to continue.

The new Theme is applied to the project.

7. Use the **Filmstrip** panel to go through the slides of the project one by one.

Note how the new Theme affects the look and feel of the project. The most obvious change is the new background picture, but a Theme is far more than that.

8. When on the second slide, select the Title Smart Shape.
9. In the **Properties** inspector, note how the formatting properties of the selected object have changed.

This illustrates that, in addition to Master Slides, a Theme also contains Object Styles. So, by applying another theme to a project, you update the Master Slides *and* the styles applied to the objects.

The third element of a Theme
In addition to Master Slides and Object Styles, a Theme affects a third element, called the **Skin**. The Skin of the project is covered in `Chapter 14, Finishing Touches and Publishing`.

You now have a much better understanding of what a Theme is. In the next section, you will take a look at how we created the `takeTheTrain_Theme.cptm` theme you applied to the `TakeTheTrain.cptx` file back in `Chapter 02 - working with standard objects`:

- A Theme is a collection of graphical assets and Styles. It is used to quickly define the look and feel of an entire project.
- Captivate contains predefined Themes. These are available in the **Themes** icon on the Toolbar.
- A Theme is composed of three basic elements: a collection of Master Slides, the Styles applied to the objects of the project, and the Skin of the project.
- When inserting a new slide, Captivate tries to determine the best Master Slide to apply.
- The **Properties** inspector makes it easy to change the Master Slide applied to any slide at any time.

Creating a custom Theme

In this section, you will recreate (part of) the theme you applied to the `takeTheTrain.cptx` file at the beginning of the book. While doing so, keep in mind that creating a theme should come much earlier in the production process of your Captivate courses. As a matter of fact, it should probably be one of the first things you do when starting a new project. In this book, it comes after you have a sufficient knowledge of the basic objects and concepts of Captivate, for pedagogical purposes only.

To create a custom theme, you first apply one of the predefined Themes of Captivate to a new project. You then modify the Master Slides and the Styles of this theme to slowly build your own theme:

1. Close every open file in Captivate.
2. Use the **File | New Project | Blank Project** menu item to create a new blank project.
3. In the **New Blank Project** dialog, use the **Select** drop-down menu to choose a size of **1024 x 627** for the project. When you are done, click the **OK** button.
4. Save the new project as `Chapter06/themeMaker.cptx`.
5. Use the **Themes** icon on the Toolbar to apply the **Blank** theme to the project.
6. Click **Yes** to acknowledge and clear the warning message.

By applying the **Blank** theme to the project, you modify the overall look and feel as well as the styles already present in the project. The **Blank** theme is an excellent starting point for creating your own themes.

7. Use the **Themes | Save Theme As** menu item to create a new Theme.
8. Save the new Theme as `Chapter06/DiDaXo-Theme.cptm`.
9. Acknowledge the successful creation of the new Theme by clicking the **OK** button.

With your new Theme saved, you can move to the next step, in which you will customize the Master Slides of the Theme.

Making the Blank theme the Default theme

Lots of Captivate developers decide to use the Blank theme as the default theme applied to new projects. This saves a step in the preceding procedure. To do so, open the **Themes** icon on the toolbar, right-click the **Blank** theme, and choose **Set as Default Theme**.

Customizing the Master Slides of the Theme

You create Master Slides with visual elements (backgrounds, logos, headers, and so on), so you can apply them to the standard slides of your project that need to share the same basic layout. If you are a PowerPoint or Keynote user, this process probably sounds very familiar:

1. Still in the `Chapter06/themeMaker.cptx` file, use the **Window | Master Slide** menu item to switch to the Master Slide view.

As shown in the following screenshot, the **Blank** theme that you applied to the project contains seven Master Slides (shown as **1** in the following screenshot) in addition to the Main Master Slide (shown as **2** in the following screenshot). Note that the **Master Slide** panel has been enlarged to capture the screenshot. Also notice that the name of the applied theme (here **DiDaXo-Theme**) appears below the Main Master Slide thumbnail:

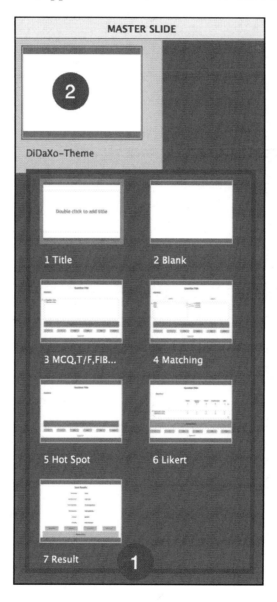

You will now try to delete one of these Master Slides and see what happens using the following steps:

2. Right-click any of the Master Slides (just make sure you don't right-click the Main Master Slide at the very top of the **Master Slides** panel).

3. Click the **Delete** menu item and confirm your intention to delete the selected Master Slide.

A second message appears indicating that the selected Master Slide cannot be deleted. This is because at least one Master Slide for each type of slide must be present in the Theme. In other words, the seven Master Slides of the current theme represent the minimal set of Master Slides each Theme must contain.

Customizing the Main Master Slide

The Main Master Slide is the first one in the **Master Slide** panel. You use it to insert the main graphical elements shared by most (if not all) of the other Master Slides of the project:

1. In the **Master Slide** panel, click the Main Master Slide to select it.

2. If needed, open the **Properties** inspector. Make sure it shows the properties of the Main Master Slide.

3. Use the **Media | Image** icon on the Toolbar to insert the `Chapter06/images/mainBackground.png` image on the main Master Slide.

4. With the image selected, look at the **Options** tab of the **Properties** inspector.

5. Make sure both the **X** and the **Y** properties are set to 0, so the image is positioned exactly in the top-left corner of the slide.

6. Open the **Timeline** panel and completely lock the image using the corresponding lock icon.

With the addition of this single image, your project already looks far different than it did a few minutes ago. If you take a look at the **Master Slide** panel, you notice that all the Master Slides of the Theme (except the Blank one) are now using the background image defined on the Main Master Slide.

The Main Master slide is also the perfect place to add legal mentions such as a copyright notice. This is what you will achieve using the following steps.

7. Still on the Main Master Slide, use the **Text | Text Caption** icon on the Toolbar to create a new Text Caption.

8. Double-click the new Text Caption to enter the text edit mode.

9. Delete the default text.

10. In the **Character** section of the **Style** tab of the **Properties** inspector, click the **Insert Symbol** icon. This operation is illustrated in the following screenshot:

11. Double-click the copyright symbol to insert it into the Text Caption.

12. Type `copyright - DiDaXo - 2017` after the copyright symbol.

13. When you are done, hit the *Esc* key to leave the text edit mode and select the Text Caption.

14. In the **Style** tab of the **Properties** inspector, change the font to **Lato** (or whatever other Typekit font you chose to use earlier in this chapter) and the font size to 8 points (it is possible to type it if it is not in the list).

15. Change the **Caption Type** to **Transparent**.

16. Switch to the **Options** tab of the **Properties** inspector and set the **Angle** to 270°.

17. Move and resize the Text Caption so it fits along the left edge of the slide, just above the footer area.

18. In the **Timing** panel, make sure the **Transition** is set to **No Transition**.

19. Switch back to the **Properties** inspector and use the Style Options icon to create a new style after the current formatting of the copyright notice. Give that new style the name of `DiDaXo-Copyright`.
20. Finally, use the lock icon on the **Timeline** panel to completely lock this object.
21. Save the file when you are done.

Browse the other Master Slides of the project and note that the copyright notice appears on (almost) every one of them.

Changing the background of a Master Slide

You will now customize the **Title** Master Slide of the theme. This Master Slide should use a different background than the one inherited from the Main Master Slide. You also want to remove the copyright notice so it does not appear on Title slides. Use the following steps to apply a different background image to the title Master Slide:

1. Still in the Master Slide view of the `Chapter06/themeMaker.cptx` file, use the **Master Slide** panel to select the **Title** Master Slide.
2. In the **Properties** inspector, deselect the **Show Main Master Slide Objects** checkbox.

This action removes the objects inherited from the Main Master Slide. This leaves you with a blank slide containing one placeholder.

3. Use the **Media | Image** icon on the Toolbar to insert the `Chapter06/images/titleBackground.png` image on the slide.
4. Use the **Timeline** panel to lock the image so it cannot be accidentally modified.

In this section, you have used the **Show Main Master Slide Objects** checkbox of the **Properties** inspector to import a slightly different background image on the Title Master Slide. Note that this checkbox hides all the objects defined on the Main Master Slide. This explains why the copyright notice does not show on the Title Master Slide.

5. In the **Master Slide** panel, select the **Blank** Master Slide.
6. Look at the **Properties** inspector and notice that the **Show Main Master Slide Objects** checkbox is already deselected for this particular Master Slide.

Now, you know why the Blank Master slide is ... blank!

Adding a Master Slide to the Theme

You will now add a new Master Slide to the theme. You will name it `Content` and insert another image onto it:

1. Still in the Master Slide view of the `Chapter06/themeMaker.cptx` file, use the **Master Slide** panel to select the **Title** Master Slide.
2. Use the **Insert | Content Master Slide** menu item to insert a new Master Slide in the project.

The new Master Slide is inserted as Master Slide number 2. Note that this new slide inherits the elements of the Main Master Slide by default. You will now give a name to this Master Slide and import another image:

3. Select the newly inserted Master Slide in the **Master Slide** panel and look at the **Properties** inspector.
4. At the very top of the **Properties** inspector, enter `Content` in the **Name** field and hit the *Enter* key to validate.

Note that the new name also appears below the Master Slide thumbnail in the **Master Slide** panel.

5. Use the **Media | Image** icon on the Toolbar to insert the `images/chapter06/contentBkg.png` image.
6. Use the Lock icon on the **Timeline** panel to completely lock the new image, preventing any accidental edits.

The project contains eight Master Slides in addition to the Main Master Slide, as illustrated in the following screenshot (The **Master Slide** panel has been enlarged to capture the screenshot):

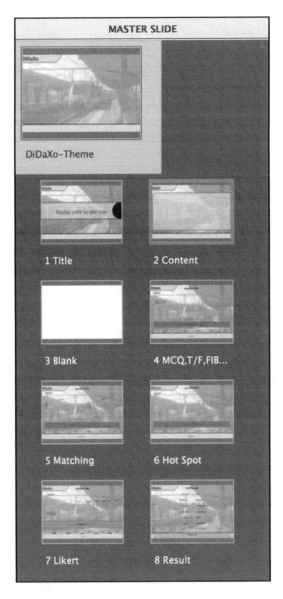

Extra credit - adding more Master Slides to the theme

In this extra credit section, you will add three more Master Slides to the theme using the same procedure as the one you used in the previous section. The general steps are as follows:

- Use the **Insert** | **Content Master Slide** menu item to insert new Master Slides in the Theme.
- Use the **Properties** inspector to change the name of the **Master Slides**.
- Insert the required images onto each new Master Slide.
- Lock the imported images using the lock icon of the **Timeline** panel.

Use the following table to name the new master slides and add the correct image:

Master Slide name	Image to import
Content 2 Cols	`Chapter06/images/2colsBkg.png`
Content Left Col	`Chapter06/images/leftColBkg.png`
Content Right Col	`Chapter06/images/rightColBkg.png`

At the end of this extra credit section, you should have eleven Master Slides in your Theme.

This extra credit section concludes your first exploration of the Master Slides in a Theme. Of course, you can add more Master Slides, import additional background images and objects, and so on. Feel free to further experiment with these concepts before moving to the next section. But before that, let's quickly summarize the key concepts you have learned in this section:

- To create a new Theme, apply one of the predefined Themes to your project and use the **Themes** | **Save Theme As** menu item
- A Theme is saved as a `.cptm` file, and it will appear in the list of themes in the **Theme** icon on the toolbar
- The first element contained in a Theme is a set of Master Slides
- The Main Master slide is used to quickly define the general look and feel of the whole project
- By default, all the Master Slides of the project inherit the elements defined on the Main Master Slide

- Deselect the **Show Main Master Slide objects** checkbox to prevent the elements of the Main Master Slide from showing on another Master Slide
- Use the **Insert | Content Master Slide** menu item to insert new Master Slides into the project

In the next section, you will define new Styles and save them in your custom Theme.

Adding Styles to the Theme

To create new styles, you will return to the Styles Options icon of the **Properties** inspector. You will save these new styles in the Theme at the end of the exercise.

Let's start by giving the proper look and feel to the standard objects of the project.

Styling the titles

In this section, you will return to the Title Master Slide of the Theme and modify the formatting of the Title Smart Shape using the following steps:

1. Still in the Master Slide view of the `Chapter06/themeMaker.cptx` file, use the **Master Slide** panel to select the **Title** Master Slide.
2. Select the **Double click to add title** placeholder.

A placeholder object, such as the one you just selected, is a special object used to predefine the size, location, and styling properties of a future Captivate object. You will now use this placeholder to predefine the look and feel of the future titles of your future Captivate projects that will use this particular theme.

The **Properties** inspector of the selected Title Placeholder shows the same properties as a Smart Shape. This is because the Title Placeholder is based on a Smart Shape object. It means that all the features and flexibility offered by Smart Shapes are available to the Title Placeholder.

3. Move and resize the selected placeholder so it fits on top of the central area of the **Title** Master Slide.
4. In the **Character** section of the **Style** tab of the **Properties** inspector, increase the font size to 60 points.
5. Change the Font to **Cooper Std** (or whatever Typekit Web Font you chose to use earlier in this chapter).

6. Also change the color of the text. Use Custom color 1 (purple) for the color of the slide Title.

Remember that if you closed and restarted Captivate during the course of this chapter, you need to reimport the custom color swatches defined in the `Chapter06/DiDaXo.ase` file to have access to your custom colors.

7. Use the Style Options icon to save the current formatting of the selected placeholder in a new style, named `DiDaXo-ProjectTitle`.

After the preceding actions, the title placeholder on the Title Master Slide has the proper look and feel, as shown in the following screenshot:

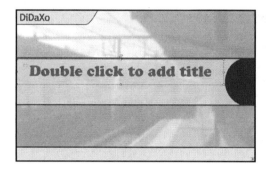

In the next section, you will learn how to add extra placeholders to your Master Slides.

Adding Placeholders to the Master Slides

The power of Master Slides goes way beyond defining common backgrounds and objects. By adding Placeholder objects, you can predefine the location and styling of future objects (such as Images, Text Captions, Smart Shapes, and so on). In this exercise, you will add a slide title placeholder to the Content Master Slide created in the previous section:

1. In the **Master Slide** panel, select the **Content** Master Slide.
2. Use the **Insert | Placeholder Object | Title** menu item to add a Title Placeholder on the Master Slide.
3. Move and resize the Placeholder object so it fits along the top edge of the content background image.
4. With the Title Placeholder selected, look at the **Style** tab of the **Properties** inspector.

5. In the **Style** tab of the **Properties** inspector, change the font to **Cooper Std** (or any other Typekit font).

6. Change the alignment to **Align Left**.

7. Also change the color of the text. Use Custom color 1 (purple) for the color of the slide Title.

8. Switch to the **Timing** panel and apply a **Fade In Only** transition to the Title Placeholder.

9. Switch back to the **Properties** inspector and use the Style Options icon to create a new style after the current formatting of the placeholder. Give this new style the name `DiDaXo-SlideTitle`.

When developing a project that uses this theme, the eLearning developer will simply double-click the placeholder and type the title of the slide. The size, location, and formatting properties of this title will be inherited from the placeholder. This will ensure visual consistency and will considerably speed up the development process. The Content Master Slide should look like the following screenshot:

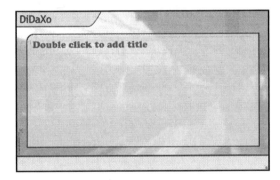

Note that Placeholder objects can only be inserted into Master Slides. In other words, it is not possible to insert a Placeholder object into regular slides.

Extra credit - adding Title Placeholders to the other Master Slides

In this extra credit section, you will repeat the preceding sequence of actions to add a Title Placeholder into the **Content 2 Cols**, **Left Content**, and **Right Content** Master Slides. The general steps are as follows:

- Select the desired Master Slide in the **Master Slide** panel and use the **Insert** | **Placeholder Object** | **Title** menu item to insert a new Title Placeholder on the selected Master Slide.
- Apply the **DiDaXo-SlideTitle** style to the newly inserted placeholder object.
- Resize the placeholder so it fits in the upper area of the slide.

At the end of this extra credit section, you should have added one Title placeholder to each new Master Slide.

 Don't forget that you can use the Align toolbar, the **Options** tab on the **Properties** inspector, and the Guides to make sure the objects are placed the same way on each Master Slide.

Saving the Styles in the Theme

You now have been exposed to (pretty much) all the tools, techniques, and features we used to create the `takeTheTrain_Theme.cptm` theme that you applied to your project at the beginning of the second chapter of this book. Of course, we have defined additional Master Slides, inserted more placeholder objects of different types, and defined additional styles. For the sake of time, we will not go any further in defining the theme.

Feel free to open to the `final/chapter06/takeTheTrain.cptx` file, and use the **Window** | **Master Slide** menu item to examine the Master Slides, Placeholders, and Styles that we have defined in the theme.

However, there is one additional step that we want to emphasize before moving to the next topic. In order to save the newly created styles and Master Slides into the theme, you need to save the theme file itself. By saving the Theme, you update the `DiDaXo-Theme.cptm` file so you can apply this theme to other projects as well:

Use the **Themes** | **Save Theme** menu item to update the current Theme with the new styles and Master Slides.

In the next section, you will discover the Captivate templates, but first, let's summarize what you have learned about Themes in this section:

- It is possible to create a custom theme in Captivate. Just use the **Themes** | **Save Theme As...** menu item to create a `.cptm` file on your computer.
- Always start by applying one of the predefined themes of Captivate, which you customize to create your own theme.
- The **Blank** theme is one of the predefined themes. It is an excellent starting point when creating your custom themes from scratch.
- Use the **Window** | **Master Slide** menu item to switch to the Master Slide view. Alternatively, there is a **Master slide view** button at the top of the **Properties** inspector when a slide is selected.
- When in the Master Slide view, use the **Filmstrip view** button on the **Properties** inspector (when a Master slide is selected), the **Exit Master** icon on the Toolbar, or deselect the **Window** | **Master Slide** menu item to return to the regular Filmstrip view.
- The Main Master Slide is used to define the general look and feel of all the Master Slides of the theme.
- A theme must contain at least seven Master Slides, in addition to the Main Master Slide. This is to ensure that every possible type of slide is covered by at least one Master Slide.
- It is possible to add additional Master Slides to a theme by using the **Insert** | **Content Master Slide** menu item.
- When a Master Slide is selected, deselect the **Show Main Master Slide Objects** on the **Properties** inspector to define a custom background for that Master Slide.
- You can add different types of Placeholders into Master Slides. A Placeholder is a template object used to define the size, location, and formatting properties of a future object.
- The styles you create and modify are saved in the Theme along with the Master Slides.
- Don't forget to use the **Themes** | **Save Theme** menu item to update the `.cptm` file. You will see your theme in the Themes icon on the toolbar, so you can apply it to other projects.

Working with Templates

The basic idea of a Template is to create a project that can be used as a blueprint for future projects. When creating a project from a Template, a duplicate of the Template is created, which serves as the starting point of a new project. In the new project, the teacher can edit, remove, and add objects, with no restrictions.

A Template can contain the same slides and objects as a regular project. The preferences applied to the Template become the default preferences of future projects based on that Template. The Theme applied to a Template becomes the default Theme of future projects based on that Template.

In the next exercise, you will create a Template that will be used for all the Captivate files of the `Take the train` project. To do so, let's pretend that the instructional and graphic designers at DiDaXo decided the following:

- All files should have a resolution of 1024 x 627 pixels (so they fit on an iPad screen in landscape mode).
- All files should use your custom `DiDaXo-Theme.cptm` theme.
- All files should begin with a title slide. The title should be written in a Smart Shape using the **DiDaXo-ProjectTitle** style.
- The second slide of each project should state the objectives of the project.
- The actual course begins on the third slide.
- When the main course is finished, a summary slide should emphasize the key points of what has been covered in the project.
- The project should end with a quiz containing at least three question slides.
- The final slide should be similar to the first one, but with closing text.

Creating a Template

To help the company enforce these rules, you will create a Template that the eLearning developers will use to create future courses. This Template will help in producing consistent content and design across projects. It will also speed up the development of the eLearning courses by reusing common designs, properties, and content:

1. Save and close every open project.

2. Use the **File** | **New Project** | **Project Template** menu item to start the creation of a new template. (Make sure to use the **Project Template** item not the **Project From Template** item.) Alternatively, you can use the *Cmd + T* (Mac) or the *Ctrl + T* (Windows) menu item.

3. In the **New Project Template** box, select the **1024 x 627** resolution, and click **OK**.

The first rule is already enforced! All the files that will be based on this Template will be of the same **1024 x 627** size by default.

4. Open the **Themes** icon on the Toolbar.

5. Click the **Browse** link in the bottom-left corner of the Themes panel.

6. Navigate to the `Chapter06/DiDaXo-Theme.cptm` file you created earlier in this chapter to apply that theme to the new Template.

 If you did not succeed in creating the theme file following the instructions of the previous sections, you can use the `Chapter06/final/DiDaXo-Theme.cptm` file.

Second rule enforced! All future projects based on this Template will use your custom `DiDaXo-Theme.cptm` theme.

7. Make sure that the **Properties** inspector shows the properties of the first slide of the project.

8. At the top of the **Properties** inspector, use the **Master Slide** drop-down menu to apply the **Title** Master Slide of the Theme to the selected slide if necessary.

9. At the top of the **Properties** inspector, change the slide name to `Intro Slide` and press *Enter* to validate.

Third rule enforced! The first slide of the Template is based on the Title Master Slide of the Theme and contains a Title Smart Shape placeholder with the **DiDaXo-ProjectTitle** style already applied.

10. Use the **Slide** | **Content Slide** icon on the Toolbar to insert a new slide in the template.

11. Use the **Properties** inspector to change the name of this slide to `Objectives`.

12. Also make sure that the **Content** Master Slide of the Theme is applied to the new slide.

13. Double-click the slide title placeholder and write `Objective of this module` in the placeholder.

14. Hit the *Esc* key to exit the Text Edit mode and select your slide title as an object.

The second slide of your template should now look like the following screenshot:

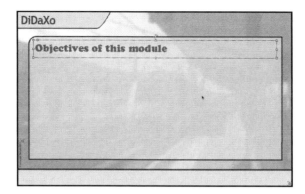

Fourth rule enforced! The second slide of the Template is ready to receive the objectives of the project. The layout and styling of that content is already predefined in the Theme and in the Master Slides.

15. Use the **Slide | Content** icon on the Toolbar to insert a third slide based on the **Content** Master Slide of your Theme.
16. Use the **Text | Text Caption** icon on the Toolbar to add a Text Caption in the center of this new slide.
17. Type `Your project begins here` in the Text Caption and hit the *Esc* key.

Fifth rule enforced! The third slide of the Template is where the course module actually begins. When using the template, eLearning developers will be able to add extra slides, change the Master Slides, add more objects, and so on.

18. Use the **Slide | Content Slide** icon of the Toolbar to insert a new slide in the project.
19. Use the **Properties** inspector to change the name of this slide to `Summary`.
20. Still in the **Properties** inspector, make sure the **Content** Master Slide of the Theme is applied to the new slide.
21. Double-click the slide title placeholder and write `Summary of this course module` in the placeholder.
22. Hit the *Esc* key to exit the Text Edit mode and select your slide title as an object.

Sixth rule enforced! After the main course, a summary slide should list the key takeaways of this course module

Adding Placeholder Slides

The next slide of the Template is where the three question slides of the project should be placed. When developing the template, you do not know what question types will be used, and what the actual questions will be. You only know that the quiz begins on that slide and should contain at least three questions. To enforce this rule, you will add **Placeholder Slides** to the Template.

There are two types of Placeholder Slide available:

- A **Recording Slide Placeholder** is meant to be replaced by a screenshot-based recording using the techniques you will learn in Chapter 8, *Capturing Onscreen Action*.
- A **Question Slide Placeholder** is meant to be replaced by a Question Slide. Quizzes and Question Slides will be covered in Chapter 7, *Working with Quizzes*.

In this case, you need three Question Slide Placeholders. Use the following steps to insert them into the Template:

1. If needed, use the **Filmstrip** panel to go to the last slide (slide 4) of the Template.
2. Use the **Insert | Placeholder Slides | Question Slide Placeholder** menu item to add a first Question Slide Placeholder at the end of the Template.
3. Repeat the preceding operation twice more to add two additional Question Slide Placeholders to the Template.

Seventh rule enforced! Three Question Slide Placeholders have been added at the end of the Template.

Just like Placeholder objects can only be added to Master Slides, Placeholder slides can only be added to Captivate templates. Also note that the options of the **Properties** inspector, as well as most icons on the Toolbar, are grayed out when a placeholder slide is selected. This is because this Placeholder is not an actual slide. Therefore, there are no properties to show in the **Properties** inspector and no objects can be added onto it.

Adding the last slide

You will now create the last slide of the Template. Because it is very similar to the first slide, you will duplicate the first slide, move the duplicated slide to the end of the Template, and change the text content of the title Smart Shape using the following steps:

1. In the **Filmstrip** panel, select the first slide of the Template.
2. Use the *Ctrl + D* (Windows) or *Cmd + D* (Mac) shortcut to duplicate the selected slide.
3. In the **Filmstrip** panel drag the duplicated **Intro Slide** to the very end of the project. After this action, the duplicated slide is the eighth and last slide of the Template.
4. Use the **Properties** inspector to change the name of that last slide to *Ending slide*.
5. Double-click the Title placeholder and type Thank you for taking this online course with us.
6. Resize the title Smart shape so the text fits on the slide.

Eighth rule enforced! The last slide of the Template is very similar to the first one, with a nice closing comment.

Saving the Template

For the sake of time, you will consider this Template as finished. Keep in mind, though, that you could go much further in the development of a Captivate Template. For example, you could use the **Preferences** dialog to define project properties directly in the Template. These would become the default preferences used by future projects based on that Template:

1. Save the Template as Chapter06/DiDaXo-Train.cptl.

Note that the file extension used for a Captivate Template is .cptl and not .cptx as for a regular project. Next, you'll create a new project from this template.

Creating a new Captivate project from a Template

In this section, you will play the role of an eLearning developer who has to use the new Template to develop a new course module for the DiDaXo Company:

1. Close every open file so that you can see the Captivate Welcome screen.
2. Use the **File | New Project | Project From Template** menu item to start creating a new Captivate project based on an existing template.
3. Navigate to the Chapter06/DiDaXo-Train.cptl Template file created in the previous section to choose it as the base of a new project.

The new project that opens in Captivate is a copy of the Template you created in the previous section. Note that the new project uses the standard .cptx file extension.

Before moving on, you will quickly preview the project:

4. Use the **Preview | Project** icon on the Toolbar to preview the entire project.

When the project appears in the **Preview** pane, note that the Smart Shape Placeholder of the first slide does not appear in the final output. Also, note that the three Question Slide Placeholders are also not part of the final output. Actually, the slide count (shown at the top left corner of the **Preview** pane) is **5** and not **8**.

As long as actual objects and slides have not replaced the Placeholder objects and slides, they do not appear in the published version of the project.

5. Close the **Preview** pane to return to Captivate.
6. Use the **Filmstrip** panel to go to the first slide of the project.
7. Double-click the Title Placeholder and type Take the train in Belgium. Hit *Esc* when done to quit the text edit mode and leave the shape selected.

This action turns the Title Placeholder into an actual Smart Shape object. Note how quick it was to insert the project tile on the first slide. Rapid development is one of the key advantages of using Themes, Templates, Styles, and Placeholders.

8. With the title selected, look at the **Style** tab of the **Properties** inspector.
9. Try to change the font to another one of your choice.

No warning messages appear to tell you that this property is locked by the Template and cannot be changed. In other words, the developer has the freedom to override the choices made on the Template. Remember that the Template sets the *default* properties of slides and objects, but it does not force the teacher/developer to use them in the final version of the project.

10. Use the **Filmstrip** panel to go to slide 5 of the project.

Slide 5 is the first **Question Slide Placeholder**. Remember that it did not show in the **Preview** pane when testing the project earlier in this section.

11. Double-click the **Question Slide Placeholder** slide.
12. In the box that appears, select the **Multiple choice** checkbox and click the **OK** button

Captivate replaces the Question Slide Placeholder with a Multiple Choice question slide. You will learn more about Quizzes and Question Slides in the next chapter, Chapter 7, *Working with Quizzes*.

13. Keep experimenting with this file. Try to turn the remaining two Question Slide Placeholders into question slides of different types. Try to add more slides, change the applied Master Slides, modify the content of Placeholders, and so on. Notice that you have full freedom to do so.
14. When you are done, close the project without saving it.

This exercise concludes your overview of Templates. Before moving on to the next chapter, let's quickly summarize what has been covered in this section:

- A Captivate Template is a blueprint used as a starting point for standard Captivate projects.
- A Template contains the same objects and slides as a standard project.
- The Theme applied to a Template serves as the default Theme for all future projects based on that Template.
- Placeholder Slides are used to mark the location of a screen recording or the location of Question Slides in the Template.
- A Template sets the default properties and objects, but it does not strictly enforce them. In other words, a teacher/developer can override the choices made on a Template when designing the project.
- A Template file has a .cptl file extension. When you create a course using a template, remember to save it as a .cptx file.

Summary

In this chapter, you concentrated on the graphic design aspect of the project. You discovered that it is important to create a consistent learning environment in which your learners feel comfortable enough to concentrate on learning the content, and not on how the online course works.

In the first part of this chapter, you learned about the Swatch Manager, the Styles, and the Object Style Manager. You focused on the different types of font that you can use and discovered the Typekit collection of Web Fonts available in Captivate 2017. You then used the predefined Themes to better understand what Themes are and how they work. Next, you moved on to creating your own Theme, and finally, you created a Template and used that Template to create a new project.

By using the Styles, Master Slides, Themes, Swatches, and Templates, you created a consistent and professional look and feel that can be used across multiple projects. You have also made the life of your eLearning developers much easier by giving them a tremendous amount of assets they can use and reuse in their projects. This will dramatically speed up their work.

With the completion of this chapter, an important part of the book comes to an end. The project you have been working on is pretty much ready to be published.

In the next few chapters, you will learn about the more advanced features of Captivate, such as Quizzes, Capturing on-screen actions, and Advanced Actions. If all you need is to create simple projects such as the one you just completed, feel free to jump directly to Chapter 14, *Finishing Touches and Publishing*, to learn about the publishing phase, which is the last of the Captivate Production processes.

In the next chapter, you will jump into Quizzes, one of the most powerful and popular features of Captivate.

Meet the community

In this section, we will introduce you to two individuals. James and Adam both work for a company called eLearning Brothers. It is the company that provides the assets you find under the Assets icon on the Toolbar of Captivate.

James Kingsley

James Kingsley has worked in the eLearning industry since 2001. James enjoys making tools, desktop applications, and web applications do things they were not meant to do. He keeps an eye on the latest web and mobile technologies and looks for ways to combine them with eLearning to create new solutions. James is a regular speaker at conferences and has won several awards for combining technologies to produce better eLearning.

During his time in the military, James was the course supervisor for Instructor Training and Curriculum Design. When he joined the civilian workforce, he combined his love for programming and software development with his military experience.

As an entrepreneur, James has founded several software, web, and mobile development companies, primarily in the eLearning arena, including ReviewMyElearning.com, which is the most feature-packed solution for collecting feedback from SMEs, team members, clients, and so on.

Currently, James is the senior technology architect for eLearning Brothers, where he shapes the direction of mobile and HTML5 eLearning development. James regularly blogs and hosts webinars on the eLearning Brothers site as well.

Contact details

- **LinkedIn**: https://www.linkedin.com/in/jameskingsley/
- **Twitter**: @onEnterFrame
- **Blog**: http://elearningbrothers.com/author/jkingsley/

Adam Cannon

Adam Cannon has worked in the eLearning and training industry for over 15 years. He's done everything, from instructor-led training to instructional design and LMS implementation. He has presented at several conferences, including FocusOn Learning 2017 and Training 2017. Currently, he works as an eLearning Evangelist for eLearning Brothers. His areas of specialization include Articulate's suite of products, Adobe Captivate, Captivate Prime, and Instructional Design.

Contact details

- **Twitter**: @aqcannon
- **LinkedIn**: https://www.linkedin.com/in/aqcannon/
- **Facebook**: https://www.facebook.com/aqcannon
- **Blog**: http://elearningbrothers.com/elearning-blog/

7
Working with Quizzes

Assessing students' knowledge has always been one of the primary concerns of anyone involved in some kind of teaching activity. When it comes to eLearning, addressing the assessment issue is both a pedagogical and a technical challenge.

On the pedagogical side, one of the factors that characterize the eLearning experience is the fact that learners sit alone in front of their computers or mobile devices with no one around to assist them. As teachers, we have to leave lanterns along the learner's path to make sure that the lonely learner does not get lost and confused. Constant assessment helps in keeping the learners on track. By giving them many opportunities to test and validate their new knowledge, the learners can immediately identify the areas of the course that deserve more attention and can build new knowledge on solid grounds.

On the technical side, Captivate contains a powerful quizzing engine that lets you insert different kinds of **Question Slides** in your projects. At the end of the quiz, Captivate is able to send a detailed report to a **Learning Management System** (**LMS**). It is a server that is used to host eLearning content and track the learner's progression into your online courses.

In this chapter, you will perform the following:

- Insert various kinds of Question Slides in your Captivate projects using several different techniques.
- Explore how some of the objects of Captivate can be added to the quiz.
- Create knowledge check questions throughout the course.
- Create a Question Pool and insert random Question Slides in the project.
- Explore and set Quiz Preferences.
- Provide feedback to the students by using the branching capabilities of the Question Slides and the quiz.

- Set up the reporting to an LMS.
- Discuss the SCORM, AICC, and xAPI standards used to communicate the quiz results to the LMS.

Preparing your work
To get the most out of this chapter, reset the Captivate interface to default. If you are using the default interface mode, just close and restart Captivate. If you use the advanced interface mode, use the **Window | Workspace | Reset 'Classic'** menu item to reset Captivate to default. In this chapter, you will use the exercises stored in the Chapter07 folder. If you get confused by any of the step-by-step instructions, take a look at the Chapter07/final folder, which contains a copy of the files, as they will be at the end of this chapter.

Introducing the quiz

During the first part of this chapter, you will insert a quiz at the end of the takeTheTrain.cptx project. For obvious pedagogical reasons, it is very important to introduce the quiz to the students. You should explicitly state what is going to happen. You will now insert one more slide in the project using the following steps:

1. Open Captivate.
2. Open the Chapter07/takeTheTrain.cptx.
3. Use the **Filmstrip** to go to slide 21.

Slide 21 is the last slide of the actual course. You want your quiz to be inserted in between slide 21 and the final slide of the project.

4. Use the **Slides | Content Slide** icon on the Toolbar to insert a new slide in the project. Remember that a new slide is always inserted *after* the currently selected slide.
5. In the **Properties** inspector, apply the **Title&Text** Master Slide to the new slide.
6. Double click the Title placeholder and type Time for the Quiz.
7. Double click the Caption placeholder and type the following text Answer the following questions the best you can.[Enter] Your answers will be reported to the LMS. [Enter] You must score 50 % to pass.
8. Draw a Rounded Rectangle Smart Shape in the bottom area of the slide.
9. With the Rounded Rectangle selected, look at the **Properties** inspector.

10. Select the **Use as Button** checkbox and apply the **shape_As_Button** style.

11. Change the text of the button to `Start the Quiz`.

12. Adjust the size and the position of the button to your taste.

13. Don't hesitate to add additional decorative elements, (such as a character image) and to further modify the properties of the existing objects.

14. Arrange the **Timeline** of the new slide, making sure that the **Start the Quiz** button stops the playhead at the end of the slide and jumps to the next slide when being clicked.

See how easy and fast it is to insert new slides when a Theme is applied to the project. Because the visual aspect is, for the most part, taken care of by the Master Slides, you can concentrate on the content to deliver.

Your new slide should look similar to the following screenshot:

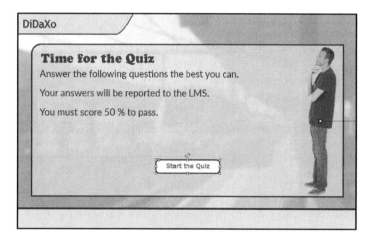

Creating Question Slides

In Captivate, a Question Slide is a very special type of slide. When inserting the first Question Slide in a project, you automatically create a Quiz. There are many options that you can set either for each individual Question Slide or for the entire quiz.

Although very powerful, the quiz engine of Captivate has some limitations. While it is possible to insert regular slides in between the Question Slides, all the Question Slides of a project (excluding the Knowledge Check questions) always belong to the same Quiz. In other words, each project can only contain a single Quiz.

Captivate supports eight types of Question Slides. In the upcoming sections, you will explore each of these question types, one by one.

Inserting the first Question Slide

To get started, you will now insert the first Question Slide in your project by performing the following steps:

1. Return to the `Chapter07/takeTheTrain.cptx` project.
2. Use the **Filmstrip** panel to go to slide 22. Notice that the project currently contains 23 slides.
3. Click the **Slides | Question Slide** icon on the Toolbar. You can also use the **Quiz | Question Slide** menu item to perform the same action. The **Insert Questions** dialog box opens.

The **Insert Questions** dialog box lists the types of Question Slides available in Captivate. For this first example, you will add a single **Multiple Choice** question to the project.

4. In the **Insert Questions** dialog, select the **Multiple Choice** checkbox.
5. Open the **Graded** drop-down list associated with the **Multiple Choice** question.

The dropdown provides three options: **Graded**, **Survey**, and **Pretest**:

- **Graded**: This type of question has correct and incorrect answers. For example, *Does Belgium have an extensive train network? (True/False)* is a question that has a correct and an incorrect answer, so it is a graded question (by the way, the answer is *True*!).
- **Survey**: This type of question is used to gather the learner's opinion. As such, it has no correct or incorrect answer. For example, *Would you recommend this eLearning course to your friends? (Yes/No)* is a survey question.
- **Pretest**: This type of question is graded, but is not a part of the Quiz. In other words, the answer to a Pretest question is not considered when calculating the score of a Quiz. Also, these answers are never reported to the server. A pretest is used to assess the student's knowledge before taking the course. It is possible to add branching based on the outcome of the pretest. For example, the students passing the pretest can skip the course if they want to. But the students failing the pretest have to take the course to gain the required knowledge.

There is a fourth type of Question Slide available in Captivate 2017 called the Knowledge Check Slides. These will be covered at the end of this chapter.

In this example, you will add a single *Graded* Multiple Choice question.

> 6. Select **Graded** in the drop-down list.

Make sure the **Insert Questions** dialog looks like the following screenshot:

> 7. Click the **OK** button to generate the Question Slide and to close the **Insert Questions** dialog.

Take a look at the **Filmstrip**. It now contains *25* slides. This means that the operation you just completed has added *two* slides to the project;

- As expected, the Multiple Choice question has been inserted after the active slide. In this case, the Multiple Choice question is slide 23.
- Because the new slide is the first Question Slide of the project, Captivate has also generated the **Quiz Results** slide as slide 24.

The **Quiz Results** slide contains a lot of automatically generated elements.

8. Use the **Filmstrip** to go to slide 23.
9. Inspect the various elements that have been automatically added to the Multiple Choice question slide.

Most of these elements are self-explanatory. The only element that probably requires an explanation is the **Review Area**. This area is used to display feedback messages to the student at the end of the quiz. The content of these messages depend on how the students answered this particular question.

10. Use the **Filmstrip** to go to slide 24.
11. Inspect the elements on the **Quiz Result** slide.

The **Quiz Results** slide is generated by default when a new quiz is created (or in other words, when the first Question Slide is added to the project). It is possible to turn this slide off if you want to.

12. Use the **Quiz | Quiz Preferences** menu item to open the Quiz Preferences dialog.
13. On the left side of the **Preferences** dialog, click the **Settings** category of the **Quiz** section.

 Watch out! There is another **Settings** category in the **Recording** section. Make sure you use the one in the **Quiz** section, as shown in the following screenshot:

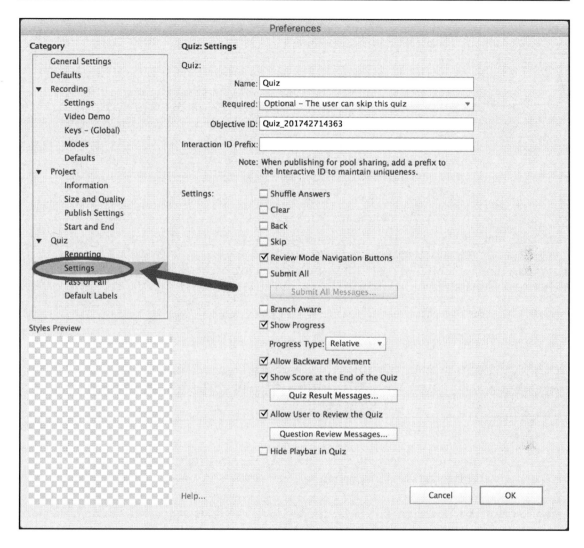

14. Deselect the **Show Score at the End of the Quiz** checkbox.

15. Click the **OK** button to apply the changes and close the **Preferences** dialog.

When this operation is complete, look at the **Filmstrip**. Note that slide 24 is grayed out and that an eye icon appears under its thumbnail. This means that the slide is hidden. In other words, it is still in the project, but it won't be displayed to the students.

15. On the **Filmstrip**, click the eye icon below slide 24.

This action turns the visibility of slide 24 back on. It is equivalent to returning to the **Preferences** dialog to select the **Show Score at the End of Quiz** checkbox again.

Turning the visibility of slides on and off

Turning the visibility of slides on and off is not limited to the **Quiz Results** slide. You can use this handy feature on any slide of the project. Simply right click a slide in the **Filmstrip** and choose **Hide Slide** in the contextual menu. This might be useful when a slide has been updated, but you want to retain a record of the original slide. It can also be used on multilingual projects to hide or show the slides pertaining to a particular language version.

Completely removing the Quiz Results slide is only possible when there is no more Question Slides in the project. But if you have a Quiz in the project (in other words, if you have at least one Question Slide), the Quiz Results slide is mandatory. This is because, behind the scenes, most of the variables and internal logic associated with a Quiz refer to these particular slides.

Using the Multiple Choice question

The basic principle of a Multiple Choice question is to provide multiple answers to a given question. The student has to choose the correct answer from a predefined list.

In the following exercise, you will configure the Multiple Choice question you added in the previous section by performing the following steps:

1. Return to the `Chapter07/takeTheTrain.cptx` project.
2. Use the **Filmstrip** to go to slide 23.

Slide 23 is the first Question Slide of the project. Lots of objects have been automatically generated on this slide.

Watch out! It is possible that some objects sit on top of other objects. For example, move the yellowish *Incomplete Caption* to reveal the *Incorrect Caption* and the *Correct Caption*!

The purpose of most of the generated objects should be obvious, but some of them require more explanation:

- The **Review Area** is related to the **Review Quiz** button on the **Quiz Results** slide (currently, slide 24). If the learner clicks that button at the end of the quiz, they will be allowed to review the quiz. In such case, the **Review Area** is used to display an appropriate feedback message to the student.
- The student uses the buttons at the bottom of the slide to interact with the quiz. It is possible to control the visibility of each of those buttons either for the entire quiz or for each individual Question Slide.
- The **Progress Indicator** in the top right corner of the slide can also be customized in the **Preferences** dialog.
- During the quiz, the feedback messages in the middle of the slide are hidden by default. They are automatically revealed depending on the student's answer to the question. It is therefore not a problem if they overlap.

Every element of the Question Slide can be customized. If needed, you can even insert extra objects (such as Images, Animations, or additional Text Captions) using the same techniques as those used for a standard slide. Note that extra buttons and other interactive objects cannot be added on a Question Slide.

Understanding the basic question properties

Text Captions and Smart Shapes are used to display the question and the list of possible answers. Your next task is to customize these objects by performing the following steps:

1. Double click the placeholder that reads **Type the question here** to select it in text edit mode. When done, triple click the same object to select its content.
2. Type `What type of ticket would you choose if you use the train every day to go to work or school?` and hit the *Esc* key.
3. Click the thin blue line that wraps the answers. This selects the Answer Area on the slide.
4. Use the *Shift* + down arrow shortcut several times to move the Answer Area down 10 pixels at a time.

 Remember that when using the arrow keys, you move the selected objects *one pixel* at a time. But when combining the arrow keys with the *Shift* key, you move the objects *10 pixels* at a time. This is one of the shortcuts we use the most in Adobe applications, because yes.... it also works in other applications such as Photoshop, Illustrator, InDesign, and more!

5. Now, you can increase the height of the Question Smart Shape, so the text fits in the object.

6. Double click the first possible answer to select it in the edit mode. Then triple click the same object to select its content. Type `A standard one-way ticket.` as the first answer.

7. Don't hesitate to move the feedback messages out of the way before continuing with this procedure

8. Use the same technique to write `A standard round trip ticket.` as the second answer.

To make this question more interesting, you need to add more possible answers to the list.

9. Open the **Quiz** inspector next to the **Properties** inspector in the panel group on the right edge of the screen. You may need to click the **Properties** icon of the Toolbar to open the panel group.

10. In the top most section of the **Quiz** inspector, change the number of **Answers** to 4. Captivate generates two more answers on the Question Slide.

11. Type `A 10 trips pass in first class.` and `A renewable three months subscription.` in the newly generated answers.

12. Click the radio button associated with the last answer (**A renewable three month subscription.**) to mark it as the correct answer.

Your multiple choice Question Slide should now look as follows (note that the success, failure, and incomplete feedback messages have been moved to the scrap area before taking the screenshot):

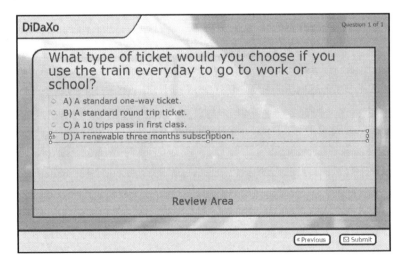

Working with Partial Scoring

In this particular example, the first question is complete. But sometimes, you'll need a more sophisticated Multiple Choice with multiple correct answers. Fortunately, Captivate has an option that allows the Multiple Choice question to accept multiple correct answers. You will now experiment with this feature by performing the following steps:

1. Return to the `Chapter07/takeTheTrain.cptx` project.
2. Use the **Filmstrip** to go to slide 23.
3. Select the **Multiple Answers** checkbox in the topmost section of the **Quiz** inspector.

On the Question Slide, this action changes the radio buttons associated with each possible answer to checkboxes. You can now tell Captivate what are the right answers.

4. On the Question Slide, select any three answers out of the four available. (Remember that in this example, what you need is a single correct answer, so this exercise is made for demonstration purposes only. The actual answers you select are therefore not important).

At this moment, the question is either entirely correct (if the user selects all three correct answers) or entirely wrong (in every other case). **Partial Scoring** allows you to make this question partially correct if the student selects some of the right answers but not all. This advanced option is currently available on Multiple Choice questions only. You will now turn Partial Scoring on using the following steps:

5. Select the **Partial Score** checkbox in the topmost section of the **Quiz** inspector.

Note that by selecting the **Partial Score** checkbox, the **Points** and **Penalty** options of the **Quiz** inspector are disabled. When Partial Scoring is turned on, each possible answer of the Multiple Choice question is assigned a specific score.

6. Select the first answer you marked as correct.
7. Switch to the **Properties** inspector and go to the **Options** tab. Change the **Points** of this answer to 5.
8. Repeat the same procedure with the other two answers you marked as correct.
9. Finally, select the only answer not marked as correct and make sure the **Points** property is set at 0 (note that you can also assign a negative score to the incorrect answer).

In this configuration, the student can be awarded, 5, 10, 15, or 0 points for this question depending on the answers provided. You will now return to the initial situation by performing the following steps:

10. Return to the **Quiz** inspector and deselect the **Multiple Answers** checkbox. On the Question Slide, the checkboxes associated with each answer revert to radio buttons.
11. Also deselect the **Partial Score** checkbox.
12. On the slide itself, make sure to mark the last answer (**A renewable three months subscription**) as the only correct answer.

Even though you don't need the *Multiple Answers* and *Partial Scoring* options in this example, you now have the required knowledge about these features if you ever need to use them.

Branching with Question Slides

The last thing to do with this Question Slide is to decide how Captivate should react when the learner submits an answer. Remember that Captivate can react differently when the correct or the incorrect answer is submitted. This concept is known as Branching. Perform the following steps to implement branching on this Question Slide:

1. Make sure you are still on slide 23 of the `Chapter07/takeTheTrain.cptx` file.
2. Scroll down the **Quiz** inspector until you see the **Actions** section.
3. Make sure the **On Success** action is set to **Continue.**
4. Also confirm that the **Attempts** option is set to **1**.
5. Open the **Last Attempt** dropdown and inspect the available options.
6. Select the **Jump to slide** action and choose **11 Slide 11** in the **Slide** dropdown that appears just below.

Slide 11 explains the main types of train tickets available in Belgium. If the student does not answer the Multiple Choice question correctly, you want to redirect them to that slide in order to re explain this particular topic.

7. Use the **Filmstrip** to return to slide 11 of the project.
8. Select the **Continue** button in the bottom center of the slide.
9. In the **Action** tab of the **Properties** inspector, change the **On Success** action to **Return To Quiz**.

If a quiz is in progress, this action redirects the student to the current Question Slide in the quiz. If no quiz is in progress, this action has no special effect and the **Continue** action is assumed.

10. When you are done, use the **Filmstrip** to return to slide 23 of the project.

Discovering the other options of the Quiz inspector

In this section, you will explore the other options of the **Quiz** inspector. While doing so, keep in mind that the features and properties that you are about to discover are available regardless of the question type (Multiple choice, True/False, Matching, and so on). Perform the following steps to experiment with the options of the **Quiz** inspector:

1. In the **Quiz** inspector, locate the **Buttons** section.
2. Select the **Clear, Back,** and **Skip** checkboxes.

This adds the corresponding buttons to the question slide (note that the **Clear** button appears just above the **Previous** button; therefore, you might want to move the **Clear** button a little bit to reveal the **Previous** button that is underneath).

 These buttons have been customized using the Theme that is applied to the project.

3. Return to the previous situation by deselecting the **Clear, Back,** and **Skip** checkboxes.
4. Still in the **Quiz** inspector, locate the **Actions** section.
5. Change the number of attempts to 2.
6. Select the **Retry Message** checkbox to see the corresponding **Try Again** Smart Shape appearing on the stage.

You can, of course, customize the content and the styling of this feedback message. But for this example, you will disable it.

7. Deselect the **Retry Message** checkbox to discard the **Try Again** message.
8. Open the **Failure Messages** dropdown. Notice that it allows you to choose between **None, 1,** or **2.**
9. Close the **Failure Messages** dropdown and change the number of **Attempts** to 3.
10. Reopen the **Failure Messages** dropdown. Notice that this time it allows you to choose between **None, 1, 2,** or **3.**

The options visible in the Failure Messages dropdown depend on the **No. of Attempts** property. The highest number available in the **Failure Message** dropdown always matches the defined number of attempts.

11. Change the **Failure Messages** to **3**.

This inserts three failure messages (in red) on the stage. Be aware that some of them might overlap, so it is possible that you don't see three distinct failure messages until you move them around. You can now customize the failure message displayed to the user for each failed attempt.

> There is no visible difference in the failure messages. All three of them look identical. To identify which one is which, you can hover over the caption, and it will show the incorrect shape number.

12. Open the **Failure Messages** dropdown and choose **None**.

In this configuration, there is no failure message displayed to the student when a wrong answer is submitted.

13. Change the **No. of Attempts** back to 1 (notice that this, logically, disables the **Retry Message** checkbox).
14. Open the **Failure Messages** drop-down menu and choose **1**. This generates a single red failure caption at the bottom of the slide, which is the default configuration.
15. In the **Captions** section, deselect the **Incomplete** checkbox to discard the corresponding caption on the stage.
16. Take some time to inspect the remaining options available in the **Quiz** inspector, but do not change any of them at this time.

Pay particular attention to the following:

- You can still change the question **Type** (**Graded** or **Survey**).
- You can set a **Time Limit** to answer this particular question.

Customizing the feedback messages

Providing quality feedback to the students is paramount in any pedagogical situation, eLearning, or classroom. In this section, you will look into the basic ways of creating feedback messages on question slides. Keep in mind though, that more sophisticated feedback strategies can also be implemented. For example, you can use the Branching capabilities of the Question Slides to redirect the student to a specific slide or sequence of slides. But for now, let's start with the basics by performing the following steps:

1. Still on slide 23 of the `Chapter07/takeTheTrain.cptx` project, select the red failure caption.
2. Double click the object and change the text of the red failure message to `Sorry, this is not the correct answer - Click anywhere or press 'y' to continue..`
3. Change the text of the green feedback message to `Great answer! - Click anywhere or press 'y' to continue..`
4. Hit the *Esc* key to leave the text edit mode and select the green success message as an object.
5. Turn your attention to the **Properties** inspector.

Notice that the properties available in the **Properties** inspector are the same as those available when a Smart Shape is selected. This is because the feedback messages of a Question Slide are Smart Shapes with text. Therefore, all the capabilities of standard Smart Shapes are available on those feedback messages, including the ability to change the shape of the messages.

6. Select the red rectangular failure message.
7. If needed, move and resize it so the text fits in the shape.
8. Right click the rectangular failure message and choose the **Replace Smart Shape** menu item.
9. In the list of available shapes, select the rounded rectangle. This changes the shape of the underlying object to a rounded rectangle.

Keep this capability in mind when working with feedback messages as the shape used to provide the feedback message might reinforce the message itself.

Now, remember that in Chapter 2, *Working with Standard Objects*, you have used another object to display text to the learner. This object is the Text Caption. If you prefer to use Text Captions instead of Smart Shapes for your feedback messages, you can do so by performing the following steps:

10. Right click the red failure caption and choose the **Revert to Text Caption** menu item.
11. With the red Text Caption selected, turn your attention to the **Properties** inspector.

Notice that the available properties are those of a Text Caption. Personally, we tend to prefer using Smart Shapes over Text Captions, as Smart Shapes give me much more creative and pedagogical capabilities. This includes a wealth of shapes to choose from, the ability to control opacity, or to use image backgrounds. Therefore, you will now revert to using a Smart Shape for your red failure message before finalizing your first question slide.

12. Right click the red failure caption and choose the **Convert To Smart-shape** menu item.
13. Choose the Rounded Rectangle in the Smart Shape gallery.
14. Move and resize the red Failure Caption and the green Success Caption to taste.

While resizing and moving your feedback messages, don't hesitate to use the Align toolbar (remember to use the **Window | Align** menu item to display it) and the Smart Guides to easily align and size the objects. When you are done, your Question Slide should look as follows:

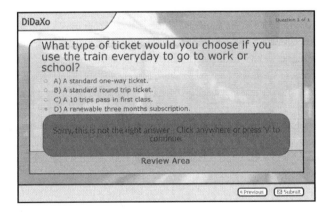

Notice that we've used the Align toolbar to give both feedback messages the same size and the same position, so they overlap on the screenshot. This is not a problem since Captivate only displays one message *or* the other depending on the submitted answer.

This concludes your exploration of the Multiple Choice question. As you can see, there is a multitude of options available to help you fine-tune your assessments.

Importing Question Slides from a GIFT file

GIFT stands for **General Import Format Technology**. A GIFT file is a text file that allows you to use a simple text editor to write various types of questions. Such a text file can then be imported into any GIFT compliant eLearning application and system, making it easy to share question banks across these systems.

Captivate offers the ability to import GIFT files into your projects. Thanks to this feature, you can import into Captivate questions that were originally created in another GIFT compliant application. Note that Captivate can only import GIFT files created in other systems, but it cannot export the Question Slides of a quiz into a GIFT file.

 The GIFT format was invented by Moodle, a popular open source LMS. To learn more about the GIFT format, see the following page on the official Moodle website: `https://docs.moodle.org/33/en/GIFT_format`.

In the following exercise, you will take a look at a GIFT file and import it in the `takeTheTrain.cptx` project by performing the following steps:

1. Open the `Chapter07/takeTheTrain-questions.txt` file in a text editor such as Text Edit (Mac) or Notepad (Windows).
2. Read through this text file, making sure you don't change any of its content.

A GIFT file is a specially formatted text file, with a `.txt` file extension. Even without knowing anything about the GIFT format, reading it is easy. This particular file contains three questions. The first one is a **Matching** question, the second a **Short Answer** question, and the last one is a **True/False** question. Notice that the feedback messages for those questions are also included in the GIFT file.

3. Return to the `Chapter07/takeTheTrain.cptx` project and use the **Filmstrip** to return to slide 23.
4. Use the **Quiz | Import GIFT Format File** menu item.
5. Navigate to the `Chapter07/takeTheTrain.cptx` file and click **Open** to begin importing the file.
6. Read the message stating that the feedback captions will, unfortunately, not be imported. Click the **OK** button to continue.

Captivate parses the GIFT file and creates three additional Question Slides in the project. These new slides are added after the selected one as slides 24, 25, and 26.

The GIFT file you just imported is a Moodle question bank that has been exported with the built-in export feature of Moodle. To learn more on creating question banks with Moodle, see `https://docs.moodle.org/33/en/Question_bank`. To learn more on exporting Moodle questions to a GIFT file, see `https://docs.moodle.org/33/en/Export_questions`.

After this simple process, you should have four Question Slides and a total of 28 slides in your project.

Our good friend Paul Wilson published a video tutorial on this feature. Don't hesitate to take a look at it (and the other videos on his YouTube channel) to have yet another perspective on creating GIFT files and inserting them in Captivate. `https://www.youtube.com/watch?v=tkXM2d8lcag`

Working with Matching Questions

The first question that has been imported from the GIFT file is a **Matching question**. The basic idea is to provide two columns of elements. The student has to match an element of the first column with one or more element(s) of the second column. In this exercise, you will take a look at the imported Matching question and modify some of its properties by performing the following steps:

1. Still in the `Chapter07/takeTheTrain.cptx` project, use the **Filmstrip** to go to slide 24.
2. Move the feedback messages out of the way if necessary.
3. Take some time to inspect this slide and to compare it with the content of the GIFT file.
4. When ready, select the **Column 1** and the **Column 2** captions (remember to hold the *Shift* key while selecting the second object to add it to the selection).
5. Move the two captions down using the *Shift* + down arrow key of the keyboard.
6. When done, you should have enough room to increase the size of the Question Smart Shape to see the whole text.
7. Double click in the **Column 1** text area and change the text to `Type of train`.
8. Use the same process to change the text of the **Column 2** object to `Description`.

To make the question more interesting (and the answer more difficult to find), you will provide a different number of items in both columns.

9. In the topmost area of the **Quiz** inspector, increase the number of items of **Column 2** to 4.

10. Select the **Shuffle Column 1** checkbox.

The **Shuffle Column 1** checkbox instructs Captivate to display the options of the first column in a random order each time a student takes the quiz.

You will now change the text of the new item you just added to the **Description** column.

11. Type T trains are for tourists only in the extra item of the **Description** column.
12. Move and resize the four items of the **Description** column so the text fits in each one of them. You can use the tools of the Align toolbar to make it easier.
13. Return to the **Quiz** inspector.
14. In the topmost section, change the **Points** to 15.
15. Select the **L Train** item in the first column of the Matching question.
16. Open the dropdown that appears in front of the **L Train** item.

This dropdown is used to tell Captivate the right answer. In this case, this operation is useless as the right answer is part of the information that has been imported from the GIFT file. Note that many items of the first column can match a single item of the second column. This can be used to create very interesting and complex Matching questions.

17. Click an empty area of the slide to deselect the currently selected object and close the associated dropdown.
18. In the **Captions** section of the **Quiz** inspector, deselect the **Incomplete** Caption to remove the yellow feedback message.
19. In the **Buttons** section, make sure that only the **Clear** button is selected.
20. Leave all the other options of the **Quiz** inspector at their current values.
21. Customize the green correct message and the red failure message to taste.

Before moving on to the next question type, feel free to move and resize the objects of this slide so they look good to you. Remember that when it comes to aligning and resizing objects, great tools are available on the Align toolbar. Your slide should look similar to the following screenshot when done:

Connecting the lines

In the following screenshot, notice how the lines are connected to the elements of the **Type of train** column. To achieve this result, we have manually reduced the width of each elements of the first column to better fit the actual length of the text.

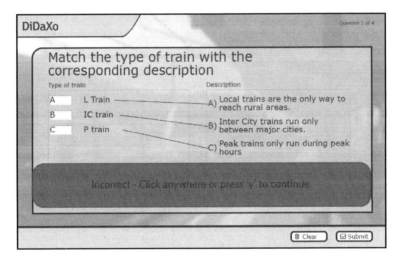

Working with Short Answer questions

The second question inserted from the GIFT file is a Short Answer question. In a Short Answer question, the student must type in a few words or a short sentence as the answer. Captivate then matches the supplied answer against a predefined list of correct answers. Let's take a look at the Short Answer question by performing the following steps:

1. Still in the Chapter07/takeTheTrain.cptx, use the **Filmstrip** to go to slide 25.
2. Inspect this slide and to compare it with the content of the GIFT file.
3. Move the feedback messages out of the way.
4. Move the answer area down using the *Shift* + down arrow shortcut and increase the height of the question text object.

5. Select the big Answer Area in the middle of the slide. When selected, the **Correct Entries** box is displayed.

6. Compare the content of the **Correct Entries** box to the content of the GIFT file.

The **Correct Entries** box contains the list of entries that the answer provided by the student will be matched against. You can add more correct answers by clicking the **+** icon in the top right corner of the **Correct Entries** box. You can also make the correct entries case sensitive if needed.

Coming up with the right question

As a teacher, coming up with the right question is always a challenge. This is especially true with the Short Answer question type. You need to find a question whose answer is obvious enough for a computer to correct, complicated enough to have some pedagogical value, and flexible enough to allow the students to type the same answer in different versions. All in all, I must admit that I don't use the Short Answer type very often for graded questions. That being said, it is a great survey question. Something like *"Do you have any comment to make regarding this online course?"* is easily done using a Short Answer survey question.

The main properties of this question are now in place. It's time for some fine-tuning.

7. In the topmost section of the **Quiz** inspector, change the **Points** value to 5 and the **Penalty** value to 1.

The **Penalty** value removes one point from the student's score if the incorrect answer is submitted.

8. In the **Captions** section of the **Quiz** inspector, deselect the **Incomplete** Caption. This removes the yellow feedback message.

9. In the **Buttons** section of the **Quiz** inspector, make sure **Clear** is the only selected checkbox.

10. Leave the other options of the **Quiz** inspector at their current settings.

11. Don't hesitate to rearrange the elements of the slide, keeping in mind that the success and failure captions will never be displayed at the same time. Therefore, it is not a problem if they overlap.

That's it for the Short Answer question. Make sure your slide looks similar to the following screenshot and save the file before moving on:

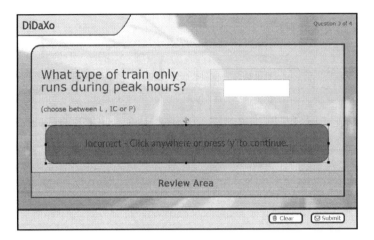

Working with True/False questions

The third question imported from the GIFT file is a **True/False** question. A True/False question is a Multiple Choice question with only two possible answers. By default, these two answers are *True* and *False*, but you can change these defaults to anything you like (such as Yes/No, Man/Woman, and so on) as long as there are no more than two different answers. Perform the following steps to explore and modify the imported True/False question:

1. Still in the `takeTheTrain.cptx` file, use the **Filmstrip** to go to slide 25.
2. Move the feedback messages out of the way if needed.
3. Move the answer area a few pixels down to allow for a higher question text.
4. Double click the **True** answer and try to change the text.

You should be able to change the text without any problems. This illustrates that the possible answers of a True/False question can actually be something else than *True* and *False*. The important point here is to ask a question that has no more than two possible answers, whatever these answers are. Make sure to undo your changes so the text actually reads **True** before continuing with this exercise.

5. Make sure that **False** is marked as the correct answer (this should have been imported from the GIFT file, but a double check is always a good thing!).
6. In the **Quiz** inspector, change the **Points** to 5.

As usual, you will now fine-tune the other properties of this question slide.

7. In the **Quiz** inspector, deselect the **Incomplete** Caption to remove the yellow feedback message.

8. Make sure the **Clear** button is the only one selected in the **Buttons** section.

9. Leave all the other options of the **Quiz** inspector at their current value.

10. Rearrange the elements of the slide however you want and customize the success and failure feedback messages too.

When you are done, your slide should look like the following screenshot:

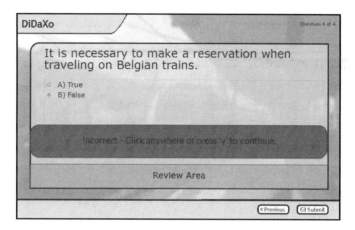

Adding the remaining Question Slides

To speed you up and let you focus on the Question Slides specifics, the remaining Question Slides of this project have already been created for you. They are stored in the `Chapter07/additionalQuestions.cptx` file. In this section, you will copy and paste the questions of the `additionalQuestions.cptx` file into the `takeTheTrain.cptx` file:

1. Open the `Chapter07/additionalQuestions.cptx` project.

2. Use the **Filmstrip** of the `additionalQuestions.cptx` file to select the first slide.

3. Hold the *Shift* key down and select slide 3 in the **Filmstrip** panel.

This action selects from slide 1 to slide 3. In other words, you have selected all but the last slide of the `additionalQuestions.cptx` file. The last slide of this project is the automatic **Quiz Result** slide of the quiz, which cannot be copied and pasted to another project

4. Use the *Ctrl + C* (Windows) or the *Cmd + C* (Mac) shortcut to copy the selected slides to the clipboard.

5. Return to slide 26 of the `takeTheTrain.cptx` file.

6. Use the *Ctrl + V* (Windows) or the *Cmd + V* (Mac) shortcut to paste the slides.

Three Question Slides are added to the project after slide 26. At the end of this section, there should be 31 slides in the `takeTheTrain.cptx` file.

7. Save the `TakeTheTrain.cptx` file.

8. Close the `additionalQuestions.cptx` file.

The stage is set for you to explore the remaining Question Types available in Captivate.

Working with the Fill-in-The-Blank question

The next question type is the **Fill-in-The-Blank** question. The idea is to take one or more words out of a given sentence. The student has to *fill in the blank(s)* either by typing the missing words or by choosing them from a drop-down list. Perform the following steps to explore the Fill-in-The-Blank question:

1. Use the **Filmstrip** panel to go to slide 27 of the `Chapter07/takeTheTrain.cptx` project.

2. Click an empty area of the slide.

3. In the **Properties** inspector, click the **Reset Master Slide** button.

This action reapplies the Master Slide to the imported question slide. This ensures that the styles defined in the theme and the elements defined in the Master Slide are properly applied.

4. As usual, move the feedback messages out of the way, move the answer area, and increase the height of the question text.

5. Inside the answer area, select the sentence that begins with **Belgium is so small...**

6. Increase the height of the selected element to reveal the whole sentence.

This sentence is the one from which some words will be taken out. In this case, you will delete three words and replace them by three drop-down lists of possible answers.

7. Select the word **Small**.

8. At the top of the **Quiz** inspector, click the **Mark Blank** button.

Note that a dashed line now underlines the selected word. This is how Captivate marks the words that are taken out of the original sentence. You will now tell Captivate that you want to replace this word with a drop-down list.

9. Click the underlined word until the **Correct Entries** box appears on the screen.

10. In the bottom left corner of the box, change **User Input** to **Dropdown List** (see **1** in the following screenshot).

11. Click the + icon (see **2** in the following screenshot) three times to add three additional entries in the list. There are now four possible answers in the list.

12. Type big, wide, and strange as possible entries.

13. Show Captivate the right answer by selecting the checkbox associated with the **small** option (note that you can mark multiple entries as correct).

14. Select the **Shuffle Answers** checkbox.

The **Shuffle Answers** checkbox instructs Captivate to display the options of the drop-down list in a random order each time a student takes the quiz. Make sure your list looks like the following screenshot before moving on:

15. Repeat the same procedure to mark the **..not very long..** part of the sentence and the **...two hours.** part at the end of the sentence as blanks.

16. Replace those two additional blanks with drop-down lists of answers. Don't forget to select the correct answer in order to let Captivate know how to grade this question.

17. In the **Quiz** inspector, deselect the **Incomplete** Caption and make sure the **Clear** button is the only one selected.

18. Customize the feedback messages and arrange them on the slide as you see fit.

The other properties of this Question Slide have already been taken care of for you. Feel free to arrange the object contained on the slide to taste.

Spacing the answer

Make sure you place the longest answer at the top of the list since Captivate uses the width of the first item of the drop-down menu to determine the width of the blank and of the dropdown.

When it comes to grading a sentence with multiple blanks, Captivate awards points only if the whole sentence is correct. This question type does not support partial scoring and is, therefore, completely correct or completely incorrect!

That's it for the Fill-in-The-Blank question. Make sure it looks like the following screenshot before moving on with the next question type:

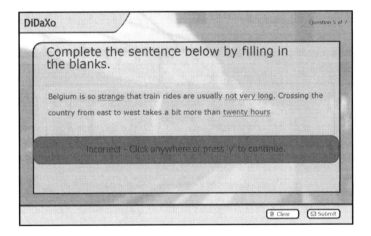

Working with Hotspot Questions

The idea of the **Hotspot** question is to display an image on the slide and let the student choose the right spot(s) on this image. In this example, you will display an extract of the train schedule and ask the student to click the departure platform information of a specific train:

1. Return to the `takeTheTrain.cptx` file and use the **Filmstrip** to go to slide 28.
2. Click the **Reset Master Slide** button in the topmost section of the **Properties** inspector to reapply the Master Slide.
3. Move the feedback messages out of the way and increase the height of the question text.

Slide 25 has been imported from the additionalQuestions.cptx file. A picture of an extract of the train schedule is visible in the middle of the slide. There is also a single rectangular Hotspot on top of the image. The students will be asked to click the image. The goal is to click inside the area defined by the hotspot.

4. In the topmost section of the **Quiz** inspector, notice the **Answers** property.

This property allows you to create additional hotspots that you can place on top of the image. This allows you to define multiple areas of the picture as the correct answer. Note that this question type does not support partial scoring, so if you have multiple hotspots on your image, the students have to mark all the hotspots for the answer to correct.

5. Select the only hotspot of the slide in the bottom right corner of the image.
6. In the **Style** tab of the **Properties** inspector, change the stroke **Width** to 0 and set the **Opacity** to 0%. This makes the hotspot completely transparent.
7. At the top of the **Properties** inspector, click the Style Options icon and choose the **Create New Style** item in the list.
8. Save the current formatting of the selected hotspot as a new style called transparentHotspot.

The next time you need the same type of hotspot, you'll be able to reapply this style, which will save you some steps.

9. In the **Quiz** inspector, deselect the **Incomplete** Caption and make sure the **Clear** button is the only one selected.
10. Customize the feedback messages and arrange them on the slide as you see fit.

At the end of this section, the Hotspot Question Slide should look similar to the following screenshot:

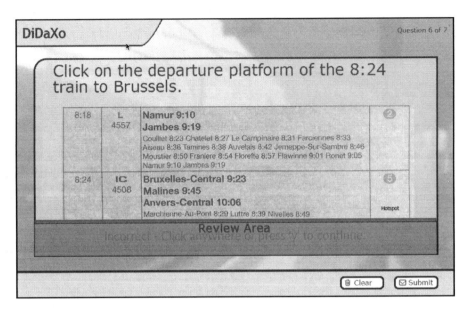

That's it for the Hotspot question! This question type is particularly well suited when assessing computer-related skills. You can, for example, display the screenshot of a toolbar and ask the student to click the correct icon. As you can see, there is nothing really difficult about this question type, just another great assessment tool in your teacher's toolset.

Working with Sequence questions

The idea of the **Sequence** question is to provide the student with a set of steps that have to be arranged in the correct order. Perform the following steps to use the Sequence question:

1. Still in the `Chapter07/takeTheTrain.cptx` project, use the **Filmstrip** to go to slide 29.
2. In the upper section of the **Properties** inspector, click the **Reset Master Slide** button to reapply the Master Slide to the currently selected question.
3. Move the feedback messages out of the way and increase the height of the question text.
4. In the top section of the **Quiz** inspector, notice the **Answers** property.

This property controls the number of steps that students will have to put in order. In this case, it has been set to **5** and the five steps have already been filled in for you.

With the Sequence question, there is no need to show Captivate the correct answer. Captivate displays these steps in a random order each time a student takes the quiz. The correct answer is the order in which you typed the sentences on the slide.

> 5. In the **Quiz** inspector, make sure the **Points** option is set to **10**. Also, add a **Penalty** value of **2** points.

These options instruct Captivate to add *10* points to the student's score in case the answer is correct and to subtract two points from the score when the answer is wrong. Note that the answer is considered correct only when all the steps are in order. This type of question does not support partial scoring.

> 6. In the **Quiz** inspector, make sure the **Clear** button is the only one selected.

Notice that the **Incomplete** option is grayed out. This makes sense since the answer will always include the five displayed steps. Technically, this question type can therefore never be incomplete.

> 7. To get rid of the yellowish incomplete caption, just select and delete it as if it was a regular object.
> 8. Customize the feedback messages and arrange them on the slide however you want.
> 9. As usual, feel free to further arrange the objects of this Question Slide so it looks good to you.

This concludes your overview of the Sequence question. Make sure it looks like the following screenshot before continuing:

There is one last question type to go through before you can give your quiz a first test run in the **Preview** pane.

Creating surveys with Likert questions

This one is a bit special. It is the only question type that cannot be graded. The **Rating Scale (Likert)** question is used to gather feedback and opinions, so there is no right or wrong answer for this type of question. The idea is to display statements on the screen and have students express their level of agreement with these statements using a rating scale.

Reporting Likert questions to an LMS

It is the LMS that determines what kind of information may be extracted from the course. Some LMSes support a very detailed set of information, while other LMSes only support basic information about the course and the quiz. Although Captivate sends a comprehensive report to the LMS, all the items of the Likert question might not be available for data analysis on your server. Check the documentation of your LMS to find out what exactly is supported. There will be more on LMS and reporting in the *Reporting scores to an LMS* section later in this chapter.

In the following exercise, you will configure a Likert question by performing the following steps:

1. Go to slide 29 of the `Chapter07/takeTheTrain.cptx` project.
2. Use the **Slides | Question Slide** icon on the Toolbar to open the **Insert Questions** dialog.
3. Choose to insert a single **Rating Scale (Likert)** question.

The **Insert Questions** dialog should now look like the following screenshot. Note that the **Survey** dropdown associated with this type of question is grayed out, which means that it cannot be used as a graded question.

4. Click the **OK** button to proceed with the insertion of the new Question Slide.
5. Move the Incomplete Caption out of the way. Notice that, since the question cannot be graded, there are no success or failure captions on survey questions.
6. Double click the question text placeholder and type `Please, fill this quick survey`.
7. In the **Quiz** inspector, change the number of **Answers** to 3. Notice that Captivate generates two additional items in the answer area.
8. Open the **Rating Scale** drop-down list to reduce the scale to **3** items. This property controls the number of radio buttons associated with each statement.

9. Before leaving the **Quiz** inspector, make sure the **Clear** button is the only one selected.

10. Change the text of the three statements to `I learned interesting things in this online course.`, `eLearning is a great learning solution.`, and `I would recommend this course to a friend.`

11. Change the label of the three columns to `Disagree`, `Neutral`, and `Agree`.

12. Customize the Incomplete message and move it back to the stage where you see fit.

13. Feel free to move and resize the other objects of this slide as per your taste.

14. It is a good idea to save the file when done.

At the end of this section, your survey question should look as follows::

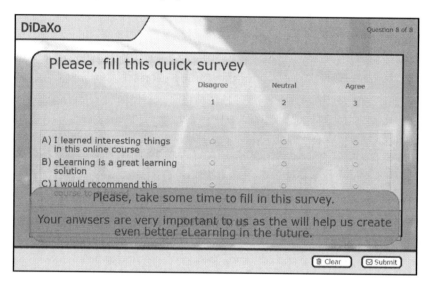

In this exercise, you have created a **Rating Scale (Likert)** question. Remember that this question can only be used as a survey question. However, keep in mind that you can use any type of question as survey questions. You could, for example, decide to use Multiple Choice, True/False, or Short Answer questions as additional survey questions as well.

Previewing the quiz

You now have one example of each possible question type in the project. It is now time to experience the quiz hands-on! Since you have not changed any of the quiz preferences yet, you will go through the default quiz experience. Perform the following steps to preview the quiz:

1. Use the **Filmstrip** to return to slide 22 of the `Chapter07/takeTheTrain.cptx` file.
2. Use the **Preview | From this slide** icon on the Toolbar to preview the project from slide 22 to the end.
3. Go through the entire quiz as a learner would.
4. When you reach the **Quiz Results** slide, click the **Review** button.

The **Review Quiz** button takes you back to the first slide of the quiz. Use the **Previous** and the **Next** buttons to go through each Question Slide. Note how Captivate shows the correct, incorrect, incomplete, and expected answers.

When you get back to the **Quiz Results** slide, inspect the information it contains. Pay particular attention to the message at the end of the slide (**Sorry you failed** or **Congratulations, you passed**). It is a general feedback message that depends on the outcome of the whole quiz. Obviously, you have to set a passing score to let Captivate know when to display one or the other message.

5. Click the **Continue** button to move on to the last slide of the project.
6. When you are done, close the **Preview** pane to return to Captivate and save the file.

Remember that you have not changed any of the quiz preferences yet. In the *The Quiz Preferences* section later in this chapter, you will review the options that allow you to customize the quiz. But before that, you will take a deeper look at the quiz modes.

Understanding the Quiz modes

When previewing the quiz in the previous section, you noticed that, by default, you are presented with a button allowing you to review the quiz. This button is, logically, located on the Quiz Result slide. To make it work, Captivate defines two different viewing modes for the quiz:

- The **Quiz Mode** is the initial viewing mode. It is used when you take the quiz, which means when all the questions of the quiz have not yet been answered. The Quiz Mode begins when the playhead enters the first question slide of the Quiz and ends at the Quiz Result slide.
- The **Quiz Review Mode** is used when all the questions of the quiz have been answered and when the student has clicked the **Review Quiz** button on the Quiz Result slide.

Captivate allows you to define navigation buttons that are specific to each of these viewing modes. In other words, some buttons are displayed in the regular Quiz Mode, while other buttons only appear in Quiz Review Mode. Let's experiment with this feature by performing the following steps:

1. Still in the `Chapter07/takeTheTrain.cptx` file, use the **Filmstrip** to return to slide 23, which is the first Question Slide of the quiz.
2. In the **Quiz** inspector, select the **Back** and the **Skip** buttons.

This adds two more buttons at the bottom of the Question Slide. You should now have four buttons labeled **Previous**, **Next**, **Clear,** and **Submit** displayed at the bottom of the slide.

3. Select the **Clear** button and move it towards the top of the slide to reveal the **Previous** button that was hidden underneath.
4. Do the same with the **Submit** button to reveal a **Next** button that was hidden underneath the **Submit** button.

You now have six buttons on your question slide. Two of these are labeled **Next**, two others are labeled **Previous,** and the remaining two are labeled **Clear** and **Submit**. This is illustrated in the following screenshot:

The **Clear** and the **Submit** buttons are only displayed when in the regular Quiz Mode (that is, when taking the quiz). When in the Quiz Review Mode, these buttons are hidden, which explains why they can be placed on top of other buttons that only appear in the Quiz Review Mode.

Regarding the **Previous** and **Next** buttons, two of these are displayed in the regular Quiz View Mode, and the other two only appear when in the Quiz Review Mode. Perform the following steps to determine which one is which:

5. Select the leftmost **Previous** button (based on the preceding screenshot).
6. At the very top of the **Properties** inspector (see the following screenshot), notice that this object is called **Back Button**. It means that it is the back button of the normal Quiz Mode.
7. Now, select the leftmost **Next** button (based on the preceding screenshot). At the very top of the **Properties** inspector, this button is the **Next Button**. It means that it is the Next button of the normal Quiz Mode.
8. Select the rightmost **Previous** button (the one that was hidden beneath the **Clear** button).
9. At the top of the **Properties** inspector, this object is called the **Review Mode Back Button**. This is the Back button that only shows when in the Quiz Review Mode.
10. Finally, select the rightmost **Next** button (that used to be hidden beneath the **Submit** button). At the top of the **Properties** inspector, this button is called the **Review Mode Next Button**. This is the Next button of the Quiz Review Mode.

Having all these buttons at your disposal allows you to very precisely define the user experience when taking and when reviewing the Quiz. Just remember to take a look at the top of the **Properties** inspector to make sure you are working with the right button.

You will now revert to the initial project using the following steps:

11. In the **Quiz** inspector, deselect the **Back** and **Skip** buttons. This turns off the **Previous** and the **Next** buttons of the normal Quiz Mode.
12. If needed, use the **Window | Align** menu item to display the Align toolbar.

13. Select the remaining **Previous** button (which is the Previous button of the Quiz Review Mode).

14. Hold down the *Shift* key while selecting the **Clear** button. This adds the **Clear** button to the current selection.

Note that white selection handles surround the **Previous** button, while the **Clear** button is surrounded by black selection handles. As you remember from Chapter 4, *Working with the Timeline and Other Useful Tools*, it means that the tools of the Align toolbar are currently calibrated based on the **Previous** button.

15. Click the last available icon of the Align toolbar. This action places both buttons exactly on top of one other.

16. Repeat the same sequence of actions to place the **Submit** button exactly on top of the **Next** button.

In this section, you have seen the normal Quiz Mode and to the Quiz Review Mode. You have discovered that each mode has an associated set of navigation buttons, which gives you a high level of control over the user experience of your Quiz.

Understanding Pretests

So far, you have created Graded and Survey questions. But the **Insert Questions** dialog allows a third type of question slide. Pretest questions are exactly the same as the Survey or Graded questions. What makes them special is the following:

- First, the Pretest questions are not part of the quiz. Their result is not considered when generating the **Quiz Results** slide.
- Second, the Pretest questions are not part of the interaction report that is sent to your LMS (more on reporting to an LMS in the *Reporting scores to an LMS* section later in this chapter).

The idea of a pretest is to assess the student's knowledge prior to taking the course. The decision to take the course module or to skip it can be made based on the outcome of the pretest. However, in practice, we often use other techniques to do this. For example, you can develop a dedicated course module (a regular Captivate Quiz for instance) as a pretest and use the branching capabilities of your LMS to display or not display the next module depending on the outcome of that pretest. Check with your LMS administrator to see what are the branching capabilities of your particular LMS.

In other words, Pretest is a feature of Captivate that not many people use, so it has not been inserted in the sample files associated with this book and will not be further explored in this chapter. If you want more information about this feature, please refer to the following page of the Adobe Captivate help site:

`https://helpx.adobe.com/captivate/using/insert-pretests.html`.

You have now inserted one question of each type and explored the two quiz viewing modes of Captivate. It is time to make a summary of what has been covered:

- There are eight types of Question Slides available in Captivate.
- Each question can either be a Graded, a Survey, or a Pretest question. The only exception to this is the Rating Scale (Likert) question that can only be a Survey question.
- A Graded question has correct and incorrect answers. A Survey question is used to gather feedback and opinions from the students. It does not have correct or incorrect answers. A Pretest question is not part of the quiz and is used to assess the student's knowledge before taking the online course or as a method of keeping the student engaged.
- Use the **Slides** | **Question Slide** icon on the Toolbar to insert Question Slides into the project.
- The GIFT file format can be used to import questions created in third-party systems. Captivate is not able to export the questions of a Quiz in a GIFT file. It can only import a GIFT file created externally.
- When inserting the first Question Slide, Captivate automatically generates the **Quiz Results** slide. This slide can be hidden in the Quiz Preferences or in the **Filmstrip**, but it cannot be deleted from the project.
- The **Quiz** inspector is used to control the options specific to each type of Question Slide.
- Each Graded question can be weighted by using varying **Points** when the student answers the question correctly. If the answer is incorrect, it is possible to remove points from the student's score by applying a **Penalty**.

- Partial Scoring is available for Multiple Choice questions only.
- By default, the feedback messages contained on a question slide are based on a customizable Smart Shape object. You have the ability to convert these messages to Text Captions if needed.
- When the playhead enters the first Question Slide of the project for the first time, Captivate switches to Quiz Mode behind the scenes. The Clear, Submit, Back, and Skip buttons are specific to this mode.
- By default, the students may be allowed to review the Quiz, which gives them access to some more extensive feedback. The **Review Quiz** button is located on the Quiz Results slide.
- When the student is reviewing the Quiz, Captivate switches to Quiz Review Mode behind the scenes. Special Previous and Next buttons are available to enable navigation when reviewing the Quiz.

In the next section, you will concentrate on the Quiz Preferences.

Exploring the Quiz Preferences

Now that you have a better idea of how a quiz works by default, you will return to the **Preferences** dialog to take a deeper look at the available Quiz options by performing the following steps:

1. Return to the `Chapter07/takeTheTrain.cptx` file.
2. Make sure you are on one of the Question Slides you inserted in the previous section.
3. Use the **Quiz | Quiz Preferences** menu item to open the **Preferences** dialog.

By default, the **Preferences** dialog opens on the **Reporting** section. This section will be discussed later in this chapter.

4. On the left side of the **Preferences** dialog, click the **Settings** category of the **Quiz** section, as shown in the following screenshot:

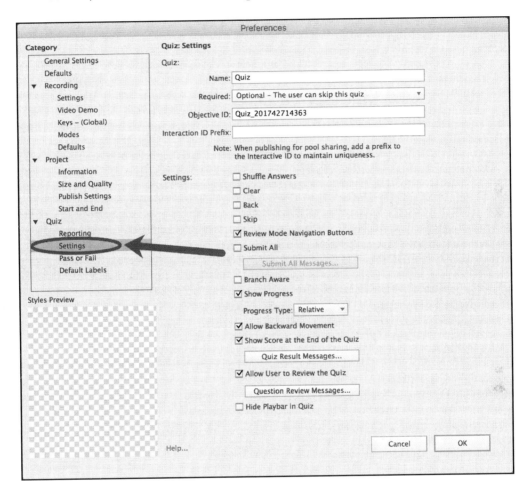

Take some time to review the options of this page.

5. Deselect the **Show Progress** checkbox. This removes the progress indicator in the top right corner of the Question Slides.

The progress indicator is used to provide the students with an indication of their progress in the quiz. The default progress indicator of Captivate can show the relative progress (**Question 1 of 3**) or the absolute progress (**Question 1**) to the student.

A customized progress indicator

Lieve Weymeis, also known as *Lilybiri*, is the queen of Advanced Actions. She has found a way to create a customized progress indicator using Advanced Actions and Variables. See her blog post at `http://blog.lilybiri.com/customized-progress-indicator`. Advanced Actions and Variables will be covered in `Chapter 13`, *Working with Variables and Advanced Actions*.

6. Select the **Skip** checkbox and read the message that appears.
7. Click **Yes** to discard the message and turn the Skip button on throughout the entire quiz.
8. Click **OK** to apply the changes.

Use the **Filmstrip** to browse through the Question Slides of the Quiz and confirm that a **Next** button is now displayed at the bottom of each Question Slide. Also notice that the progress indicator that used to be displayed in the top right corner of each Question Slide is now gone.

9. Return to the Quiz Preferences by using the **Quiz | Quiz Preferences** menu item and return to the **Settings** category.
10. Deselect the **Skip** checkbox and click **Yes** to remove all the **Next** buttons from the Question Slides of the Quiz.
11. Select the **Clear** checkbox, and then click **Yes** to display a **Clear** button on each Question Slide.

This should not change much in your project, as you should have enabled the **Clear** button on each Question Slide individually during the previous section. This tells you a bit more about those options of the Quiz Preferences dialog. They represent the *default* settings of new Question Slides, but you can always override those preferences in the **Quiz** inspector of each individual Question Slide.

12. Deselect the **Allow Backward Movement** checkbox.

By doing this, you remove all the **Previous** buttons (of the Normal Quiz Mode) present on the Question Slides. Notice that it also grays out the **Back** checkbox.

13. Make sure the **Show Score at the End of Quiz** checkbox is selected.
14. Click the **Quiz Results Messages...** button. The **Quiz Results Messages** dialog opens.

The **Quiz Results Messages** dialog is where you can customize the information that appears on the **Quiz Results** slide.

15. Deselect the **Correct Questions** and **Total Questions** checkboxes.
16. Also, deselect the **Quiz Attempts** checkbox.

This removes the corresponding messages from the **Quiz Results** slide.

17. If needed, customize the **Pass Message** and **Fail Message**.

These are the messages displayed in the **Review Area** of the **Quiz Results** slide at the end of the quiz.

18. Click the **OK** button to validate your changes and close the box.
19. Deselect the **Allow User to Review the Quiz** checkbox.

This action removes the **Review Quiz** button from the **Quiz Results** slide and the **Review Area** from each Question Slide. It also grays out the **Review Mode Navigation Buttons** option. This option lets you choose whether or not to display the special Previous and Next navigation buttons of the Quiz Review Mode. But since you just turned off the ability for the students to review the quiz, this option doesn't make sense anymore.

19. Select the **Hide Playbar in Quiz** checkbox.

This option hides the Playback Controls during the quiz. This is made to ensure students cannot use the Playback Controls to go back and forth in the quiz or to skip the quiz.

Note the **Submit All** checkbox. When selected, the answers to the questions are all submitted together at the end of the quiz. This allows the students to travel back and forth into the quiz and change their answers before submitting them all at once at the end.

20. Click the **OK** button to validate the changes and close the **Preferences** dialog.
21. Use the **Filmstrip** to go to slide 31.

Slide 31 is the **Quiz Results** slide. Note that it contains less information than before and that the **Review Quiz** button has been removed. This matches the checkboxes configuration you created in the **Preferences** dialog.

21. While on the **Quiz Results** slide, look at the **Quiz** inspector.

Notice that you can choose the information you want to be displayed on the slide from the **Quiz** inspector as well.

Setting the passing score of a quiz

When the student reaches the **Quiz Results** slide, Captivate displays a Pass/Fail message that depends on the quiz score. To display this message, Captivate must be informed of what the passing score of the quiz is. If the student reaches that passing score, Captivate displays the **Pass Message**; otherwise, the **Fail Message** is displayed.

In this section, you will set the passing score of the quiz and add some branching. First, you will import an additional slide in the project and place it after the quiz. This slide should be displayed only to the students that passed the quiz. Perform the following steps to import the new slide:

1. Open the `Chapter07/quizFeedback.cptx` file.
2. In the **Filmstrip**, select the one and only slide of that project.
3. Use the *Ctrl+C* (Windows) or the *Cmd+C* (Mac) shortcut to copy the selected slide.
4. Return to slide 31 of the `takeTheTrain.cptx` file and paste the slide using the *Ctrl+V* (Windows) or the *Cmd+V* (Mac) shortcut.
5. Use the **Filmstrip** to go to slide 32 and take some time to review the objects of that slide. Feel free to rearrange them however you like.

After this procedure, the `takeTheTrain.cptx` file should contain 33 slides.

The stage is set! You will now return to the **Preferences** dialog to set the passing score of the quiz and arrange the branching.

6. Use the **Quiz | Quiz Preferences** menu item to return to the **Preferences** dialog.
7. Click the **Pass or Fail** category in the **Quiz** section of the **Preferences** dialog.

The main **Pass or Fail** option is at the top of the dialog box. Note that there are two ways to set the passing score for a quiz: as a *percentage* or a certain amount of *points*. The total number of points is the sum of the points set for all the Question Slides of the quiz (excluding the points of the Pretest slides, if any).

8. In the **Pass/Fail Options** section, set the passing score to 50 percent (make sure the % radio button is selected).
9. In the **If Passing Grade** section, set the **Action** dropdown to **Jump to slide**. Then, select the **32 Quiz Passed** slidefrom the **Slide** drop-down list.
10. In the **If Failing Grade** section, allow the user one attempt and set the **Action** dropdown to **Jump to slide**. Then, select the last slide (labeled **33 slide33**) from the **Slide** drop-down list.

Setting the Pass and Fail options and adding some branching to the quiz is that easy! Before moving on to the next step, take a quick look at the **Default Labels** preferences pane.

11. Click the **Default Labels** category situated on the left side of the **Preferences** dialog.

The **Default Labels** preferences are used to change the default text and the default styles applied to the various elements of a Question Slide. It is best to define these options as part of your preparatory work or in a Template. In this case, it is too late!

12. Click the **OK** button to validate the changes and close the **Preferences** dialog.

13. Use the **Preview | Project** icon on the Toolbar to test the entire project. When you are done, close the **Preview** pane and save the file.

Your quiz is now up and running. In the next section, you will add some spice to the mix by creating a Question Pool. Before that, let's summarize what you have just learned:

- By default, Captivate generates a **Quiz Results** slide and displays it at the end of the quiz.
- By default, the **Quiz Results** slide contains the **Review Quiz** button that allows the student to return to each Question Slide and get feedback on the submitted answer.
- The **Clear, Back,** and **Skip** options of the Quiz Preferences are used to define which buttons should be displayed by default on the Question Slides. It is possible to override these defaults using the **Quiz** inspector of each individual Question Slide.
- You can allow students to go backward in the quiz, but once a question has been submitted, the student cannot change the answer.
- The **Submit All** checkbox allows the students to change their answers until they click the **Submit All** button at the end of the quiz.
- The **Preferences** dialog contains many options to let you fine tune the student experience. Some of these options are used to universally turn the objects of the Question Slides on or off.
- You can use the **Preferences** dialog to set the passing score of the quiz and to add branching that is dependent on the quiz score.

Working with Question Pools

A **Question Pool** is a repository of Question Slides. The idea is to let Captivate randomly choose questions from the pool in order to create a unique quiz for each student. You can have as many Question Pools as needed, and each pool can contain an unlimited number of Question Slides.

Perform the following steps to create a Question Pool:

1. Make sure you are in the `Chapter07/takeTheTrain.cptx` project.
2. Use the **Quiz | Question Pool Manager** menu item to open the **Question Pool Manager** dialog.

As described in the following screenshot, **The Question Pool Manager** dialog is divided into two main areas:

- On the upper left side of the box is a list of all the Question Pools of the current project. Just above the list of pools, the **+** and **-** icons (see **1** in the following screenshot) are used to add or remove Question Pools.
- The right side of the box shows the list of the Question Slides associated with the pool selected on the right side. The **+** and **-** icons (see **2** in the following screenshot) are used to add Questions into the selected pool or to remove existing Questions from the selected pool.

Also notice the ability to import a GIFT file directly into the selected Question Pool.

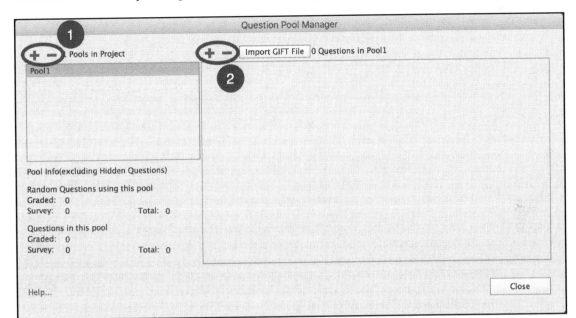

A first Question Pool named **Pool1** has been automatically created by Captivate when you opened the **Question Pool Manager**. You will now rename this Question Pool by performing the following steps:

3. On the left side of the **Question Pool Manager** dialog, double click the **Pool1** entry of the list of pools.

4. Name the pool `takeTheTrain_Questions` and press the *Enter* key. The name of a Question Pool cannot exceed 100 characters and cannot contain any spaces or special characters.

5. Click the **Close** button to close the **Question Pool Manager** dialog.

Now that you have a Question Pool available, you will add questions into it.

Inserting questions in a Question Pool

You could have used the **Question Pool Manager** dialog to create new Question Slides directly into the pool. But you will use another technique. Instead of creating new Question Slides to fill the Question Pool, you will move the existing Question Slides of the quiz into the new pool by performing the following steps:

1. Use the **Filmstrip** to go to slide 23 (which is the first Question Slide of the Quiz).
2. Hold down the *Shift* key and click slide 29. This operation selects seven slides from slide 23 to slide 29.
3. In the **Filmstrip** panel, right click one of the selected slides.
4. In the contextual menu, click the **Move Questions to | takeTheTrain_Questions** item.

This operation removes the selected slides from the **Filmstrip** and moves them into the Question Pool. The **Filmstrip** now contains 26 slides.

5. Open the **Question Pool** panel that appears next to the **Timeline** panel at the bottom of the screen (if the **Question Pool** panel is not visible, use the **Window | Question Pool** menu item to turn it on).

Seven Question Slides are displayed in the **Question Pool** panel indicating that they have been moved into the **takeTheTrain_Questions** Question Pool correctly. Another way of accessing the same information is using the **Question Pool Manager** dialog.

6. Use the **Quiz | Question Pool Manager** to open the **Question Pool Manager** dialog.
7. Make sure that the **takeTheTrain_Questions** Question Pool is selected on the left side of the dialog and look at the right side.

When the **takeTheTrain_Questions** is selected, the right side of the **Question Pool Manager** lists the Question Slides included in the pool.

8. Click the **Close** button to close the **Question Pool Manager** dialog.

The Question Pool is now ready for action! The next step is to randomly pick questions from the pool and add them to the main quiz.

Sharing Question Pools with other projects
You may have noticed the **Quiz | Import Question Pools** menu item. Using this feature, you can import a Question Pool from another project into this project.

Inserting random Question Slides in the main project

Remember that the idea of a Question Pool is to have a repository of questions available to generate random quizzes. In this section, you will randomly pick three questions from the **takeTheTrain_Questions** Question Pool and insert them into the quiz by performing the following steps:

1. Use the **Filmstrip** to go to slide 22 of the `takeTheTrain.cptx` file. Slide 22 is the introduction slide of the Quiz that you created earlier in this chapter.

2. Use the **Quiz | Random Question Slide** menu item to insert the first random question into the main project.

Another way of inserting Random Question Slides in the project is to use the **Insert Questions** dialog.

3. Use the **Slides | Question Slides** icon on the Toolbar to open the **Insert Questions** dialog.

4. At the bottom of the dialog, select the **Random Question** checkbox.

5. Set the number of questions to insert to 2.

The **Insert Questions** dialog should now look like the following screenshot. Notice the **Linked Question Pool** dropdown that you can use to choose the Question Pool to pick questions from:

6. Click **OK** to validate and insert two additional Random Question Slides in the project.

The quiz currently contains three Random Question Slides, as well as the Survey slide (slide 26), which is the same for every student. This illustrates the capability to mix standard Question Slides and Random Question Slides in the same Captivate Quiz.

7. Use the **Filmstrip** to go to slide 23, which is the first Random Question Slide of the Quiz.
8. Take a look at the **Quiz** inspector.

The **Quiz** inspector of a **Random Question** Slide only contains a fraction of the options available in the **Quiz** inspector of a regular Question Slide. Two of the available options are: the **Points** and **Penalty** properties.

9. If needed, open the **Question Pool** panel next to the **Timeline** panel at the bottom of the screen.
10. Select any Question Slide in the **takeTheTrain_Questions** Question Pool.
11. When the selected question appears in the main area of the Captivate interface, take a look at the **Quiz** inspector.

Notice that, here again, the **Quiz** inspector contains fewer options than the **Quiz** inspector of a regular Question Slide. Two of the missing options are the **Points** and **Penalty** properties.

When combining the options of the **Quiz** inspector of the Random Question Slide in the main project with the options of the **Quiz** inspector of a Question Slide within a Question Pool, you more or less obtain the **Quiz** inspector of a regular Question Slide.

12. Return to slide 23 of the main **Filmstrip**. In the topmost section of the **Quiz** inspector, make sure the **Points** property is set to 10 and the **Penalty** property is set to *1*.
13. Set the same **Points** and **Penalty** values for the other two Random Question Slides.

Now that you have random questions in the quiz, you can give your random quiz a try.

14. Use the **Preview | Project** icon on the Toolbar to test the project in the **Preview** pane.

When you reach the quiz, pay close attention to the questions asked. Try to provide the correct answers so that the **Quiz Passed** slide is displayed when the quiz is finished.

15. When you are done, close the **Preview** pane.
16. Use the **Preview | Project** icon to test the entire project a second time.

When you reach the quiz for the second time, the questions should not be the same as compared to your first attempt (if they are, close this book and get a Lottery ticket right away! This is your lucky day!).

17. Provide wrong answers so that you fail the quiz.
18. Make sure the **Quiz Passed** slide is *not* displayed at the end of the quiz.

Your random quiz is now up and running. It is time to summarize what you have just learned:

- A Question Pool is a repository of Question Slides from which Captivate randomly picks questions at runtime.
- A Captivate project can include as many Question Pools as needed. A Question Pool can contain as many Question Slides as needed. It's a good idea to use the **Question Pool Manager**, which gives your Question Pools unique names so you know where to pull the questions from.
- The **Quiz | Import Question Pool** menu item can be used to import a Question Pool of another project into the current project.
- Use the **Quiz | Question Pool Manager** menu item to create new Question Pools and to add Question Slides in the available pools.
- GIFT files can be imported directly into a Question Pool.
- If the project already contains Question Slides, they can be moved to a Question Pool at any time. Questions in a Question Pool can also be moved back to the main project using the same technique.
- A Quiz can be made up of a mix of standard Questions Slides and random questions from different Question Pools.
- The **Quiz** inspector of a Random Question slide contains only a fraction of the options available for a regular Question Slide. The remaining options are associated with each Question Slide in the **Question Pool**.

Great! You now have a pretty good idea of what a Captivate quiz is and of the myriad of options available.

Styling the elements of the Question Slides

In this section, you will return to the Master Slide view and take a quick look at the Master Slides that define the look and feel of the Quiz by performing the following steps:

1. Make sure you are in the `Chapter07/takeTheTrain.cptx` file.
2. Use the **Window | Master Slide** menu item to return to the Master Slide view.

On the left side of the screen, the **Master Slide** panel contains 14 Master Slides in addition to the Main Master Slide. Some of them control the look and feel of the Question Slides and of the **Quiz Results** slide.

3. In the **Master Slide** panel, right click the **MCQ, T/F, FIB, Sequence** Master Slide (slide 10) and try to delete it.

Captivate informs you that at least one quiz Master Slide of each type must be present in the project. The selected Master Slide can therefore not be deleted. This particular Master Slide is used to control the look and feel of the Multiple Choice, True/False, Fill-in-The-Blank, and Sequence Question Slides.

4. Take a quick look at the other Master Slides present in the **Master Slides** panel.

The **Matching** Master Slide is used by the Matching questions, the **Hot Spot** Master Slide is used by the Hot Spot questions, and the **Likert** Master Slide is used by the Likert questions. Finally, the **Result** Master Slide controls the look and feel of the Quiz Results slide.

5. While in the Master Slide view, open the **Insert | Quiz Master Slide** menu item.

From this menu item, you can insert additional Question Master Slides and define alternative layouts for the various question types.

6. Use the **Window | Question Pool** menu item to return to the Question Pool panel.
7. Within the **Question Pool** panel, select the Multiple Choice question.
8. With the Multiple Choice question selected, look at the **Properties** inspector.

As shown in the following screenshot, Captivate has automatically applied the **MCQ, T/F, FIB, Sequence** Master Slide to the Multiple Choice Question. When inserting a Question Slide into the project, Captivate automatically applies the proper Master Slide to the new question depending on the type of question.

You will now try to apply a different Master Slide to this question slide.

9. In the **Properties** inspector, click the arrow next to the **Master Slide** thumbnail.

Even though there are 15 Master Slides in the Theme, only that one Master Slide can be applied to the selected question. If you insert additional Master Slides for that particular question type, the **Properties** inspector will filter the list of available Master Slides to those that can be applied to the selected question.

Before moving on to the next section, let's quickly summarize what has been covered in this section:

- When a Question Slide is added to the project, Captivate automatically applies the proper Master Slide based on the type of question being inserted.
- In the Theme, there are five Master Slides that are used to control the look and feel of the Question Slides and of the Quiz Results slide.
- You can insert additional Question Master Slides in the Theme using the **Insert | Question Master Slide** menu item when in the Master Slide view.
- There must be at least one Master Slide for each question type in the Theme.
- The position and formatting of the object as defined on these Master Slides are inherited by the Question Slides of the main project.

Reporting scores to an LMS

LMS stands for **Learning Management System**. The help files of Captivate give the following definition for an LMS:

> *"You can use a learning management system (LMS) to distribute a computer-based tutorial created using Adobe Captivate over the Internet. A learning management system is used to provide, track, and manage web-based training."*

An LMS offers many services to both teachers and students involved in eLearning activities. The following list states some of them:

- An LMS is a website that is able to host your eLearning courses.
- An LMS maintains a list of teachers and students. Thanks to this listing, an LMS can be used to enroll students in online courses and to define one or more teacher(s) for each course.
- An LMS is able to enforce the pedagogical decisions of the teacher. For example, the LMS can be programmed to give access to the next activity of the course only if the current activity has been completed. Some LMSes can also enforce branching by automatically providing an additional activity for students who have failed a quiz, and so on.
- An LMS is able to communicate with your Captivate content (and vice versa). This gives you access to many pieces of information, such as the number of students that have taken the course, the time it took to complete an activity, the results of the quizzes, and even a detailed report of every interaction performed by each student while taking the course.
- There are many other services that an LMS has to offer.

There are many LMSes available, and there are a myriad of companies, schools, and universities that have deployed some kind of LMS to deliver, track, and manage their web-based trainings. Some LMSes are commercially licensed and can be quite expensive, but there are also several open source LMS platforms that are free to use and easy to deploy on a web server.

Moodle

Moodle is one of the most popular and powerful open source LMS solution. Personally, I have used Moodle for many eLearning projects, and it has never let me down. However, Moodle has a fairly steep learning curve. Packt Publishing has published an impressive array of titles on Moodle, providing the necessary documentation to get you started. More information on Moodle is available at `http://www.moodle.org`. More information about Packt books on Moodle is available at `https://www.packtpub.com/all/?search=moodle`.

Captivate Prime

Captivate Prime is the LMS solution developed by the Captivate team itself! It is a paid solution available in SAAS (Software as a Service) mode. The course modules that you create with Adobe Captivate can be published and uploaded to your Adobe Captivate Prime account right from within Captivate. More information about Captivate Prime can be found at `http://www.adobe.com/products/captivateprime.html`. The co-author of this book, Dr. Pooja Jaisingh, also has a dedicated course on this topic on Lynda.com. It can be found at `https://www.lynda.com/Captivate-tutorials/Adobe-Captivate-Prime-2016-Essential-Training/550717-2.html`.

For a list of the most popular LMSes, see the following web page on Wikipedia:

`http://en.wikipedia.org/wiki/List_of_learning_management_systems`.

Rod Ward from Infosemantics has done some work with LMSes and Captivate. One interesting example can be found at: `http://www.infosemantics.com.au/adobe-captivate/reduce-load-on-your-learning-management-system`.

Understanding SCORM, AICC, and xAPI

Each LMS has its pros and cons, and each contains a unique set of features. However, every LMS must be able to host eLearning content created by a myriad of different authoring tools (Adobe Captivate being one of the many eLearning authoring tools available).

To make web-based learning possible, it is important to ensure that the course modules can communicate with the underlying LMS platform. This communication should be possible regardless of the Authoring tool/LMS combination. This is where SCORM, AICC, and xAPI come into play.

These are three internationally accepted standards used to make the communication between your eLearning content and your LMS possible. When choosing an LMS for your organization, make sure that the chosen solution is either SCORM, AICC, or xAPI compliant. Captivate is SCORM, AICC, and xAPI compliant. So Captivate courses can be integrated in virtually every LMS available in the market. Let's now discuss these three standards in more details:

- **SCORM** stands for **Sharable Content Object Reference Model**. SCORM is maintained by the **Advanced Distributed Learning (ADL)** (`http://www.adlnet.org/`) project of the US Department of Defense. SCORM is a **reference model**. It means that it aggregates standards created by other organizations. The goal is to build a single standard based on the work done by other organizations that are active in the eLearning field. See the Wikipedia page on SCORM at `http://en.wikipedia.org/wiki/SCORM`.

- **AICC** stands for **Aviation Industry Computer-based Training Committee**. The initial idea was to provide a unique training and testing environment for the aviation industry in order to ensure the same training and testing standard for all airline companies in the world. For more information, see the AICC page on Wikipedia at `http://en.wikipedia.org/wiki/Aviation_Industry_Computer-Based_Training_Committee`. On December 11, 2014, the AICC committee announced that AICC would be dissolved and the AICC standard would no longer be maintained. All the work of AICC has been transferred to ADL, which oversees both the SCORM and the xAPI standards. Captivate still maintains an AICC option for backward compatibility with older LMSes.

- **xAPI** is the newest standard, launched in April 2013. During its development phase, this standard was known as the **Tin Can API**, and many people still refer to it as *Tin Can*, even though its official name is now the **Experience API** (xAPI). This new specification allows eLearning content and Learning Management Systems to speak to each other in a manner that records and tracks all types of learning experiences. Learning experiences are recorded in a **Learning Record Store (LRS)**. LRSes can exist within traditional LMSes or on their own. You can find out more about the xAPI at `http://experienceapi.com/`.

Now that you have a better idea of what an LMS is, and of the standards used, you will enable reporting in your Captivate project.

Enabling reporting in Captivate

To have Captivate publish an LMS-ready package, you have to set options at different locations throughout the project.

In the next exercise, you will make your quiz ready to be integrated in a SCORM-compliant LMS. You will first inspect the options available at the interaction level before moving on to project level reporting options.

Reporting options at the Question Slide level

Each of the scorable objects of Captivate are automatically assigned with a unique **Interaction ID**. This Interaction ID is what makes data tracking by the LMS possible. Perform the following steps to view and change the Interaction IDs:

1. Use the **Filmstrip** to go to slide 23 of the `Chapter07/takeTheTrain.cptx` file.
2. At the end of the **Quiz** inspector, notice the **Report Answer** checkbox.

This checkbox allows you to choose which interactions are reported to the LMS. For Question Slides, this checkbox is checked by default, because it is assumed that you want to report these interactions to the LMS. It means you must explicitly deselect this option if you don't want to report a particular question of the Quiz.

3. If needed, use the **Window | Question Pool** menu item to open the Question Pool panel.
4. Select any Question Slide within the Question Pool.
5. At the end of the **Quiz** inspector, notice the **Interaction ID** in the **Reporting** section.

Captivate automatically assigns a random **Interaction ID** to each Question Slide. Most of the time, this default random **Interaction ID** is fine. But you can assign a unique **Interaction ID** on your own if you want to. Note that there can be no spaces or special characters in the **Interaction ID**. If you type your own **Interaction ID** with a prohibited character, Captivate turns the spaces and special characters into underscores. You may also have to check with your LMS vendor for specific naming conventions that will work smoothly.

Finally, when working with regular Question Slides (versus Question slides within a Question Pool), these two options are grouped in a single **Reporting** section at the end of the **Quiz** inspector, as shown in the following screenshot:

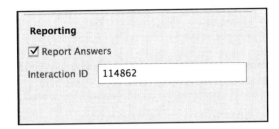

Reporting other types of interactions

The Question Slides that make up a quiz are not the only interactions that can be reported to an LMS. Other objects also have this capability.

For example, the Drag and Drop interaction has built-in reporting capabilities that are very similar to those of a regular Question Slide, as you will see by following these simple steps:

1. Use the **Filmstrip** to return to slide 21 of the `Chapter07/takeTheTrain.cptx` file. This is the slide where you defined a Drag and Drop interaction earlier in this book.
2. Select one of the objects of the Drag and Drop (for example, select one of the two images).
3. Look at the **Drag And Drop** panel on the right side of the screen. It may be necessary to use the **Window | Drag And Drop** menu item to make this panel visible.
4. Open the **Actions** tab of the **Drag And Drop** panel and notice the **Reporting** section at the very end of the panel.
5. Select the **Include In Quiz** checkbox.

This last action reveals more options. These are very similar to the **Reporting** options found in the **Quiz** inspector when a standard Question Slide is selected. It is therefore very easy to include Drag and Drop interactions into the quiz, and to report the results to the LMS. Note, however, that those interactions are not included in the Quiz by default. You must explicitly include them by selecting the **Include In Quiz** checkbox. This is very different from the behavior of a regular Question Slide, which is reported by default.

6. If needed, also select the **Report Answer** checkbox to have this interaction reported to the LMS.
7. In this example, however, you don't need to include this Drag and Drop interaction in the Quiz, so you can safely deselect the **Include In Quiz** checkbox.
8. Save the file when done.

If you ever need to grade a Drag and Drop interaction and to report it to the LMS, you now have the required knowledge to do so.

When selecting the **Include In Quiz** checkbox, and not the **Report Answer** checkbox, you include an interactive object in the quiz without reporting the interaction to the LMS. Captivate then uses these objects to calculate the score displayed on the **Quiz Results** slide, but does not report these interactions to the LMS.

In addition to regular Question Slides and the Drag and Drop interaction, other Captivate objects can also be scored and tracked by an LMS. These are the three interactive objects that have the ability to stop the playhead. These objects have been covered in Chapter 5, *Working with Interactive Objects*. They are the Click Boxes, the Buttons, and Text Entry Boxes. Let's take another look at these objects by performing the following steps:

9. Use the **Filmstrip** to return to slide 3 of the Chapter07/takeTheTrain.cptx file.
10. Select the Text Entry Box object and look at the **Properties** inspector.
11. At the end of the **Actions** tab, notice the **Include in Quiz** checkbox in the **Reporting** section.

In this case, the **Include in Quiz** checkbox is grayed out. This is because you have deselected the **Validate User Input** option on the **Style** tab of the **Properties** inspector when creating this object back in Chapter 5, *Working with Interactive Objects*. However, if you decide to validate the user input, it is easy to add this Text Entry Box interaction to the Quiz and to report the answer to the LMS.

12. Use the **Filmstrip** to go to slide 4 of the Chapter07/takeTheTrain.cptx file.
13. Select the **Continue** button in the bottom right corner of the slide and look at the **Properties** inspector.
14. At the end of the **Actions** tab, select the **Include in Quiz** checkbox.

As for the Drag and Drop interaction, this action reveals the options used to assign points when clicking that button and to report this interaction to the LMS. In this case, however, reporting a **Continue** button makes little sense. You will now deselect this checkbox before wrapping up this section.

15. At the end of the **Actions** tab, deselect the **Include in Quiz** checkbox of the selected button.

In this section, you have explored the scorable objects of Captivate and learned that the reporting capabilities are not limited to Question Slides.

The Advanced Interaction dialog
Use the **Project | Advanced Interaction** menu item or the *F9* shortcut key
to open the **Advanced Interaction** dialog. This floating panel provides a
list of all the scorable objects of the project in addition to a summary view
of their current settings.

In the next section, you will explore project level reporting options.

Setting up the project level reporting options

Now that you have decided which interactions will be included in the quiz and reported to
the LMS, it's time to focus on project level reporting options. This is where you configure
the global settings used to report the data to the LMS.

Before putting in all this effort, it is important to check with your LMS vendor what level of
information your LMS can receive and what is the standard (SCORM, AICC, or xAPI) that
your LMS supports. In this exercise, you will report the data to a Moodle LMS. A quick look
at the Moodle documentation
(`https://docs.moodle.org/33/en/SCORM_FAQ#Supported_Versions`) tells you that Moodle
is SCORM 1.2 compliant.

Perform the following steps to create a SCORM 1.2 package that can be integrated into
Moodle:

1. If needed, return to the `Chapter07/takeTheTrain.cptx` file.
2. Use the **Quiz | Quiz Preferences** menu item to open the **Preferences** dialog.
3. In the left side of the **Preferences** dialog, make sure you are on the **Reporting**
   category.
4. At the top of the page, select the **Enable reporting for this project** checkbox.

When I teach a Captivate class, I often refer to this checkbox as being the *main circuit breaker*
of the reporting system.

5. Open the **LMS** drop-down menu.

The LMS dropdown lists some of the most popular LMSes and lets you quickly apply
specific settings that are optimized for each LMS.

6. Choose **Moodle** as the LMS.

This action automatically adjusts most of the options of **Reporting Preferences** to the values that a Moodle LMS expects. If your LMS is not listed, you would use the **Other Standard LMSs** item and complete the form manually. Check with your LMS vendor which settings are expected by your LMS.

7. Open the **Standard** drop-down list.

The **Standard** drop-down menu probably is the single most important option of this **Preferences** page. It allows you to choose the reporting standard used to communicate with the LMS. By choosing **Moodle** as the LMS in the previous step, this option has been automatically set to **SCORM 1.2**.

8. Make sure you choose the **SCORM 1.2** option in the drop-down list.

You will now decide how Captivate should report the status of the course. If there is a quiz in the project, you probably want the status to be either *Pass* or *Fail*. If the project does not contain a quiz and you just want to track the completion status of the project, choose *Complete/Incomplete*. Knowing your LMS and how it receives and deals with the information is important for making these decisions. In this case, Moodle can accept both representations of the status, but it might not be true for every LMS.

9. In the **Status Representation** section, select the **Incomplete --> Passed/Failed** option.

You will now instruct Captivate that you want to consider this eLearning module complete when the student has passed the quiz.

10. In the **Success/Completion Criteria** section, choose the **Slide views and/or quiz** option.
11. If needed, deselect the **Slide Views** checkbox, but leave the **Quiz is Passed** checkbox selected.

Finally, you need to decide what data you want to report to the LMS. You can choose to report only the final score of the student or to report the final score plus some details about each interaction. In this case, you want to report the score of the student as a percentage as well as the interaction data.

12. In the **Data To Report** section, choose to report **Quiz Score** as **Percentage**.
13. Make sure the **Interaction Data** checkbox is selected.

At the end of these steps, make sure your **Preferences** dialog looks like the following screenshot:

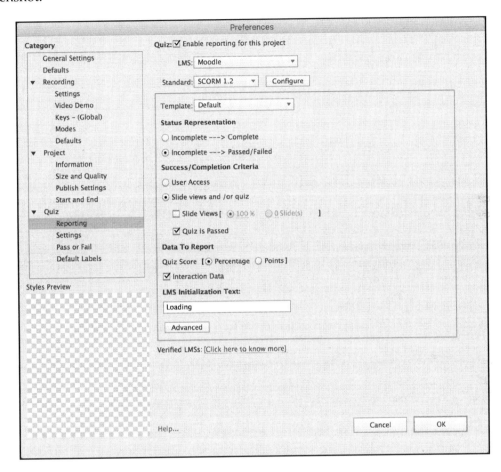

Because you are using the SCORM standard, there is one extra step to go through. This extra step is the creation of the SCORM manifest file. Note that a manifest is also required when using the xAPI standard. When using AICC, a Manifest file is not required.

Enabling reporting in a project with no quiz

These reporting options are not limited to projects containing a quiz. Reporting can be used to track only the completion status of a project. Some LMSes are able to reveal the next activity of a course when and only when they receive the *complete* status report from the current activity.

Creating a SCORM manifest file

A SCORM manifest is a `.xml` file named `imsmanifest.xml`. This manifest file is an essential component of any SCORM package. It is used to describe the course to the SCORM compliant LMS. Without this file, the LMS is unable to integrate SCORM enabled content in a course or to gather the tracking data sent by the course module.

If this sounds too technical for you, don't worry! Captivate has you covered and can generate that manifest file for you by using the very simple procedure described here:

1. Still in the **Reporting** category of the **Preferences** dialog, click the **Configure** button next to the **SCORM 1.2** standard at the top of the box.

The first section of the **Manifest** dialog is the **Course** section. The **Course** section is used to enter the metadata of the project. This metadata is used by the LMS to display the course information to the student and to enhance the integration of the project into the LMS.

2. In the **Course** section of the **Manifest** dialog, enter the following information:
   - **Identifier**: `takeTheTrain101`
   - **Title**: `Take the train in Belgium`
   - **Description**: Enter any meaningful description here

The second part of the **Manifest** dialog is named **SCO**.

For the techies, **SCO** stands for **Shareable Content Object**. This concept is at the heart of the SCORM standard. In the SCORM specification, a course can be composed of many activities. Each of these activities must have a unique SCO identifier. Using a SCORM Packager application (such as the *Multi SCO Packager* or *Reload*), it is possible to integrate a Captivate project in a larger SCORM compliant course containing lots of other content made by lots of other SCORM compliant authoring tools. This is why it is important to specify the SCO identity of your Captivate project.

3. Enter `takeTheTrain101` in the SCO **Identifier** field (no spaces allowed).
4. Enter `Take the train in Belgium` in the SCO **Title** field.

The **Manifest** dialog should now look like the following screenshot:

5. Click **OK** to validate the changes and close the dialog box.
6. Also click the **OK** button of the **Preferences** dialog.
7. Make sure you save the file when you are done.

The project is now ready to be published as a SCORM package. This step will be covered in Chapter 14, *Finishing Touches and Publishing*.

Testing your SCORM enabled projects with SCORM Cloud

Now that you have enabled the reporting capabilities of your course module, you can take advantage of another Captivate feature that helps you test the communication between your course module and the LMS.

To do so, Adobe has teamed up with SCORM Cloud. SCORM Cloud is an eLearning hosting service developed by a company called Rustici Software.

 Rustici Software is a well-known company in the eLearning industry. It helped develop both the SCORM and the xAPI standards. SCORM Cloud is just one of the services it provides. You can find more info about Rustici Software at https://rusticisoftware.com/ and more info about SCORM Cloud at https://scorm.com/cloud.

You will now upload your course module to SCORM Cloud and test the communication between your Captivate module and the LMS by performing the following steps:

Even though SCORM Cloud is a commercial service from Rustici Software, testing your eLearning content with SCORM Cloud is included in your Captivate license. You don't need to sign up for a SCORM Cloud account or subscribe to an extra service.

1. Still in the Chapter07/takeTheTrain.cptx file, use **the Preview | Preview in SCORM Cloud** icon on the Toolbar.
2. Captivate generates a temporary preview of the entire project. When this operation is finished, Captivate displays a message on the screen. Read the message and click the **Accept** button.
3. Captivate uploads the generated preview to SCORM Cloud.
4. When the upload is complete, the preview appears in a special Preview pane. At the bottom of the Preview pane, you will find a log of all communications between the course content and the LMS.

This is shown in the following screenshot:

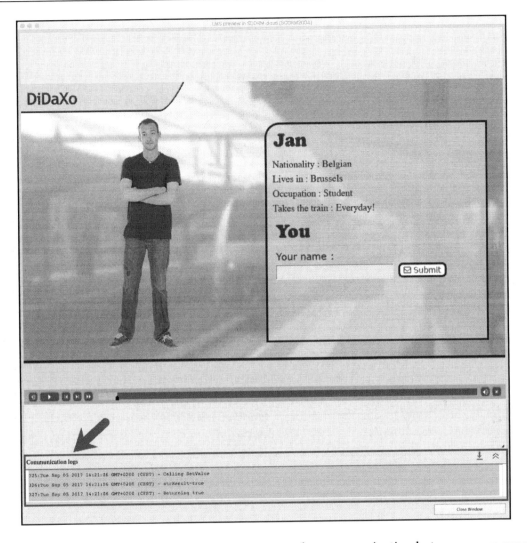

Thanks to this special preview option, you can test the communication between your course module and the LMS. If an error occurs, an error message will appear in the **Communication Log** window. This allows you to diagnose and fix the errors before releasing your course module to the students.

5. When you are done, click the **Close Window** button in the bottom right corner of the Preview pane.
6. Click the **Get Results** button in the message that appears.

This action opens your web browser with a page showing a digest of the data available to the LMS. This gives you a pretty good idea of what SCORM is capable of. Note that the actual data gathered by your LMS and the way it is presented to you depends on the LMS you use. Check with your LMS vendor for more details.

7. Return to Captivate.
8. Click the **Close** button in the **Relaunch the Preview** message.

Captivate deletes the course you uploaded to SCORM Cloud and closes the **Relaunch the Preview** message.

Thanks to this handy feature, you have been able to test the SCORM communication between your course content and the LMS.

Note that, despite the name, SCORM Cloud is also able to test your xAPI and AICC content.

Working with Knowledge Check Slides

The typical use case of a Quiz is to assess the student's knowledge either at the end of a learning process or at the very beginning.

But you can use Question Slides for other purposes as well. Sometimes, all you need to do is to check and reinforce what the student has just learned right in the middle of a learning module. In such cases, you don't need to grade the questions or to track these interactions using your LMS. All you need is an informal question that challenges the learners and helps them identify the topics needing more attention. This is precisely what Knowledge Check Slides are for.

Knowledge Check Slides work exactly like regular Question Slides. The differences are that:

- Knowledge Check Slides are never graded, though they do have correct and incorrect answers.
- Knowledge Check Slides are never reported to the LMS. Therefore, they cannot be tracked or otherwise used in any kind of formal assessment activity.

In this section, you will experiment with Knowledge Check Slides by performing the following steps:

1. Use the **Filmstrip** to go to slide 8 of the `takeTheTrain.cptx` file.

2. Use the **Slides | Knowledge Check Slide** icon on the Toolbar to open the **Insert Questions** dialog.

3. Choose to insert a single **Hotpot** question. Notice that the **Graded** drop-down menu is completely disabled when inserting a Knowledge Check Slide.

Make sure the **Insert Questions** dialog looks like the following screenshot before clicking the **OK** button:

Your new Knowledge Check Slide is inserted as slide 9 of your project. It should look exactly like a standard Hotspot Question, with a few differences in the **Quiz** inspector.

4. Turn your attention to the **Quiz** inspector of your newly inserted Knowledge Check Slide.

Notice that, even though you can turn the **Correct** and the **Failure** captions on (indicating that correct and incorrect answers are indeed supported), there are no properties to set a number of *Points* or a *Penalty* value. Also, there is no *Reporting* section at the end of the **Quiz** inspector.

5. Write `Click the yellow poster to use when traveling by train on a Saturday.` in the Question Text placeholder.

6. Increase the height of the Question Text so the question is entirely visible on the slide.

7. In the **Quiz** inspector, deselect the **Incomplete** and the **Infinite Attempts** checkboxes. The corresponding captions disappear from the stage.

8. Use the **Media | Image** icon on the Toolbar to add the `Chapter07/images/ScheduleWeek.png` file.

9. Place the image on the left side of the slide.

10. Use the **Media | Image** icon on the Toolbar a second time to add the `Chapter07/images/ScheduleWeekEnds.png` file.

11. Place this image on the right side of the slide.

12. Don't hesitate to use the tools of the Align toolbar and other tools (such as the Smart Guides, the ability to group objects, and so on) to properly place and align those two pictures on the slide.

13. At the top of the **Quiz** inspector, set the number of **Answers** to 2. This adds a second hotspot on the slide.

14. Move and resize the Hotspots to place one Hotspot on top of each image.

15. At the top of the **Quiz** inspector, select the **Allow Clicks Only on Hotspots** checkbox.

With this checkbox selected, the students will only be able to click on the Hotspots when answering the question. Obviously, you should now tell Captivate which one of the two Hotspots is the correct answer.

16. Select the Hotspot on top of the `ScheduleWeek.png` image (the one on the left side, with a blue strip at the top).

17. In the **Style** tab of the **Properties** inspector, deselect the **Correct Answer** checkbox.

In this configuration, the students can only click on the Hotspots when answering the question. Captivate knows that the Hotspot on the right is the correct answer. Notice that the Hotspot representing the correct answer has a blue checkmark, as shown in the following screenshot:

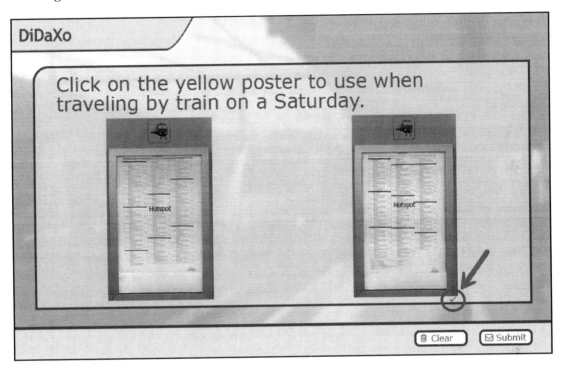

The main properties of this Knowledge Check question are now in place. You should now provide some meaningful and engaging feedback to the students. This is what you will do in the next section.

Using the Object States to customize the feedback messages

In this section, you will create the feedback messages of your Knowledge Check Slide. You need to create a Correct Caption and a Failure Message. You could use the exact same techniques as those already discussed earlier in this chapter. However, this time, you want to go a little further, using the Object States feature of Captivate 2017.

Perform the following steps to create a meaningful failure message:

1. Still on slide 9 of the `Chapter07/takeTheTrain.cptx` file, look at the **Quiz** inspector.

2. Open the **Failure Messages** drop-down menu and choose 1 in the list of options. A single red failure message appears on the stage.

3. Write `Nope! Click anywhere or press 'y' to continue.` into the failure message.

4. Right click the failure message and choose the **Replace Smart Shape** menu item.

5. In the list of available shapes, choose the **Oval Callout** (or any other callout of your liking).

6. Move and resize the callout Smart Shape so the text fits in the object.

You will now add a character image to your failure callout. Inserting a character image is very easy and has been covered in `Chapter 2`, *Working with Standard Objects*. But in this case, the red failure callout and the character image you are about to insert are both part of the failure feedback. In other words, both those objects are initially hidden from the slide and should appear together only if and when the student provides an incorrect answer. Creating a multi-object feedback message is possible using the Object States, as shown in the following steps:

7. Make sure the red failure message is selected and click the **State View** button at the top of the **Properties** inspector.

8. Once in the State View, use the **Media | Characters** icon on the Toolbar to open the **My Assets** dialog box.

9. In the top left corner of the box, open the **Category** drop-down menu and select the **Casual** option.

10. In the left column, select the last character of the **Casual** category.

11. In the central section of the box, choose the most appropriate image.

12. In the rightmost column, choose the most appropriate shot (**CloseUp**, **Half**, or **Full**).

13. Arrange the objects so they look good to you.

14. Click the **Exit State** icon on the Toolbar to return to the normal view.

Your Knowledge Check Slide should now look similar to the following screenshot:

Because you have inserted the Character image to the Normal state of the failure message, both the message and the associated image are part of the failure feedback. This is how you can use the Object States (covered in more detail in Chapter 5, *Working with Interactive Objects*) to create sophisticated, fun, and engaging feedback messages for your students.

Extra credit - creating the Correct feedback message

In this Extra Credit section, you will create the correct feedback message and associate a character image using the same procedure.

As a reminder, the general steps are as follows:

- Select the **Correct** caption checkbox in the **Quiz** inspector to generate the green Correct caption on the stage.
- Customize the message and replace the Smart Shape with a callout of your liking.
- Switch to the **State View** of the green Correct caption and add the most appropriate character image.

In this section, you have added a Knowledge Check Slide in your project. You have also used the Object States to provide much more sophisticated and engaging feedback messages to your students. It is time to summarize what has been covered in this section:

- Knowledge Check Slides work just like regular Question Slides with two important exceptions: they cannot be graded and they cannot be reported to your LMS.
- Because of these two exceptions, Knowledge Check Slides are not included in the quiz that is in the project.
- Knowledge Check Slides are an invaluable pedagogical tool allowing you to help students reinforce their knowledge and identify areas needing attention. This is done without interfering with the formal assessment (and thus with the scores) of the students.
- These slides are used as informal challenges to check and reinforce the knowledge of the student throughout the learning module.
- You can use the Object State view of the feedback messages to further customize those messages and create even more engaging eLearning modules.

Allowing the students to fail

Failure is a normal step of any learning process and every teacher should allow students to fail while learning something new. By using the Knowledge Check Slides, you allow students to test themselves, and potentially to fail, but without any consequences on the final outcome (in other words, on their score) of the course. This makes the Knowledge Check Slides an invaluable pedagogical tool. Don't hesitate to use them in your own teaching.

Summary

With the addition of Question Slides and quizzes, your project has reached an important milestone. It is now a highly interactive eLearning package that is able to integrate nicely in virtually every LMS on the market. On the pedagogical side, you have discovered the eLearning answer to the assessment challenge, which is one of the primary concerns of any teacher. On the technical side, you have discovered the SCORM, AICC, and xAPI standards that make communication between the eLearning content and the LMS possible.

In this chapter, you have learned about each of the eight question types of Captivate. You created a Question Pool before exploring the **Quiz Preferences** and the myriad of options available. In the second part of this chapter, you learned how the quiz results and other interactions can be reported to an LMS, before discovering the pedagogical power of the Knowledge Check Slides.

In the next chapter, you will learn how to capture onscreen action using Captivate. Be ready to discover a completely different and exciting type of project.

Meet the community

In this section, we will introduce you to two individuals from the same family. Together with two other family members, they own and manage *Infosemantics*, an Australian-based company specialized in eLearning development and Captivate widgets.

Rod Ward

Rod, Director of Infosemantics, is a technical author, information designer, and eLearning developer with over a decade of industry experience. Based in Perth since 1986, he has worked for companies, large and small, across Australia. Rod's specialties are the design and development of eLearning courses using sound instructional design principles and Adobe's suite of eLearning software tools. Rod is also the author of four e-books about Adobe Captivate, three about troubleshooting issues in various versions of Captivate, and one about using Advanced Actions and Variables to create custom interactivity.

Tristan Ward

Tristan is a Flash, ActionScript, and HTML5 expert. He builds some of the Flash Animations and interactivity add-ins included in Infosemantics' Captivate eLearning courses. Tristan is deservedly famous throughout the Adobe Captivate world for his *Widget King* blog, which contains many articles about creating AS3 and HTML5 widgets using his WidgetFactory API, now the leading platform for creating AS3 Widgets for Captivate. He's also our go-to guy for video editing. In addition, he is the creator of the CpExtra HTML5 widget, which has quickly become the most popular widget for creating powerful HTML5 and Responsive Design content in Adobe Captivate. CpExtra is now widely regarded as an essential part of any serious Captivate developer's toolkit.

Contact details

- **Website** : http://www.infosemantics.com.au/
- **Twitter**: Rod @Infosemantics and Tristan @WidgetFactory
- **Tristan's blog**: http://www.infosemantics.com.au/widgetking/
- **CpExtra:**
  http://www.infosemantics.com.au/adobe-captivate-widgets/cpextra

8
Capturing Onscreen Action

Now that you have learned how to create an eLearning course with text, shapes, audio, video, interactions, and quiz questions, it is time to explore how to create simulations in Adobe Captivate 2017. You will create this type of eLearning course/module, when you need to teach software-related skills, such as performing some steps in an application, or demonstrating how a website works.

This step can be compared to the filming of a movie. When filming a movie, the director wants to capture all the images, sequences, and shots he needs. In the movie industry, this raw footage is called the **rushes**. When the filming is complete, the director goes back to the studio to start the post-production process. It is during the post-production step of the process that the final movie takes shape. Only the best rushes make their way to the movie theater while the others are discarded along the way. That being said, the post-production phase can only be successful if the filming provides enough good-quality material to create a great movie.

This same basic idea applies to Captivate. When capturing the screen content, you should always keep in mind that the post-production phase will follow. Therefore, the goal of the capture phase is to create enough quality slides to ensure the success of the next phase of the process.

At the end of this chapter, you will have recorded and edited your first simulation project.

In this chapter, you will:

- Choose the right size/resolution for the project
- Tour the recording preferences and the recording modes
- Record demonstrations and simulations
- Record System Audio
- Discuss and use the Full Motion Recording

- Discuss and experience the Video Demo recording mode
- Use Manual Panning
- Resize a project
- Modify the object properties

If you are ready, it's almost time to turn the camera on and start the real action!

Choosing the right resolution for the project

Choosing the right resolution for capturing the slides is the first critical decision you have to make. You have to make it right because the size of the captured slides will play a critical role in the quality of the final movie.

Describing the problem

A typical Captivate project, such as the Encoder demonstration you experienced in Chapter 1, *Getting Started with Adobe Captivate 2017*, involves taking screenshots of an actual piece of software. At the end of the process, the project typically will be published in HTML5 or Flash and placed on a web page. Most of the time, that web page displays many other page elements (such as logos, headers, footers, navigation bars, and so on) in addition to incorporating your Captivate movie. This can lead to a very crowded situation, as shown in the following screenshots:

The preceding screenshots show the application you need to capture on the left. Let's pretend this application requires a minimal width of 1024-pixels to be displayed without horizontal scrollbars. On the right hand screenshot is the wireframe of the web page you must put your finished movie on. The page has been designed to fit a 1024-pixel-wide screen and has to display lots of elements in addition to the Captivate content. To cope with the design requirement of the web page, your project should not be wider than 800 pixels.

So here is your problem: you have to find a way to fit 1024-pixels in 800-pixels! Several approaches are available to address this situation. Each of these approaches has its pros and cons, and we will go through a brief review of each.

Resizing the project after the initial shooting

The first approach is a two-step process. The first step is to record the project with a width of 1024-pixels, and the second step is to use the Rescale Project feature of Captivate to downsize the project to 800-pixels.

By recording with a screen width of 1024-pixels, the application is captured in its intended size, matching the student's experience of the application.

The main disadvantage of this approach is that it requires resizing the Captivate project. In Captivate, the resize operation is an irreversible operation. It always has a cost in terms of image quality. Surprisingly, the resize operation can result in a larger file size, even if the new resolution is smaller than the original one. Also, in case the new resolution is smaller, the screenshots will be smaller as well and the information they contain might become somewhat difficult to read.

Here are a few things you need to keep in mind when resizing a project:

- It is always better to downsize a project than to make it bigger.
- Always keep a backup copy of the project in its original resolution. Remember that the resize operation is an irreversible operation. Your backup copy is the only way to rollback the resize operation, in case something goes wrong!

Downsizing the application during shooting

The second approach is to downsize the application to record during the capture in order to fit the requirements of the project. In this example, it means the application would be 800-pixels wide instead of 1024-pixels during the capture.

As far as Captivate is concerned, this is the easiest solution, as no irreversible or complex resize operation is needed. But for the captured application, this situation is quite crowded. Remember that the application you capture requires a minimal width of 1024 pixels. So, by downsizing it to a width of 800-pixels, it does not have enough room to display all its components and generates horizontal scrollbars. These scrollbars and their associated scrolling actions (if any) will be captured and will appear in the resulting Captivate animation. Also, scrollbars sometimes hide important information from the screen, and therefore, from your students.

Using the panning feature of Captivate

In the movie industry, panning refers to moving the camera while filming. In Captivate, it means that you can move the recording area while capturing the slides.

This approach tries to cope with both the requirements of the application to record, and the requirements of the movie to be produced.

The idea is to leave the application at its intended width of 1024-pixels, and at the same time define a capture area that is 800-pixels wide. During the recording, the smaller capture area can be overlaid on the bigger application, as shown in the following screenshot:

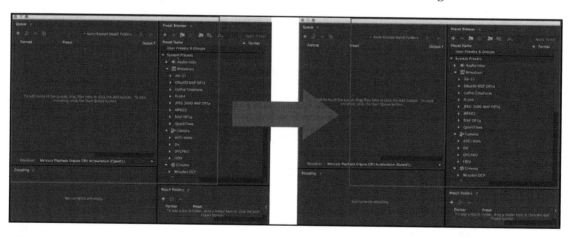

In the preceding screenshot, the capture area is the red rectangle. In other words, Captivate only captures what is inside the red rectangle. As you can see, the capture area does not always cover the same part of the application during the recording.

This approach is a good compromise, but it has two major disadvantages. Moving the recording area while filming increases the file size of your final movie. But more importantly, using this approach, your learner never sees the application entirely, which could compromise the quality of the learning process.

Using the Scalable HTML Content feature

The Scalable HTML Content feature makes the published movie fluid, so it fits the screen it is viewed on (even as the screen is resized!).

For example, say you shoot and publish your movie at a size of 1024-pixels, but the movie is viewed on a website where the maximal resolution can only be 800-pixels. In such a case, the Scalable HTML Content feature scales the movie down to 800-pixels so it fits in the available space.

This approach is quick and easy to implement, but it has a major flaw: you lose control over how your content will actually be experienced. Only a small percentage of your learners (those who have the exact same screen as yours) will see the course as you designed it. The other learners will see the course either bigger (which means possibly pixelated) or smaller (which probably means too small to be comfortable).

This option will be covered in `Chapter 14`, *Finishing Touches and Publishing*.

Using a responsive project

Creating a responsive simulation also helps you solve this problem. By using a responsive project, you can rearrange the layout and the content of your course to make it fit various screen sizes.

The main advantage of this approach is that you can control almost every aspect of your project on virtually any screen size. On the other hand, the projects built using this solution can only be published in HTML5, so only objects supported in HTML5 can be used in such projects. Also, creating a responsive project takes a bit more time and requires using special tools and features of Captivate, like the Fluid Boxes.

Building a responsive project will be covered in `Chapter 10`, *Creating a Responsive Project*.

Conclusion

None of these approaches are perfect, but you'll have to choose one anyway. The best approach depends on the project, on your learners, and on your personal taste. Here are some general guidelines to help you make the best choice:

- The size of the capture area should match the size of the application to capture whenever possible.
- If you need to resize the project, take a bigger project and make it smaller to help maintain the best possible image quality. Also, make sure you keep a backup copy of the project at its original size.
- Use panning only if you really need it.
- When panning, move the camera (the red capture area) only when necessary, and move it slowly enough to help the students build a mental picture of the entire application.
- If you use the Scalable HTML Content feature, make sure you test your work on an array of different screens and devices to ensure the best possible student experience in the majority scenarios.
- Responsive projects can only be published in HTML5. They also require some more work and the use of special tools.

Finally, never forget that you are teaching. Your learners don't care about your sizing concerns; they just want to learn something. If the chosen approach compromises the quality of the learning process, then it is the wrong approach!

About screen sizes
For more information about the screen sizes in use today, visit
`http://www.websitedimensions.com/`.

Recording the first project

It is time to have a first hands-on experience of an actual recording session. Recording a Captivate project is a five-step process:

1. Preparing the application to record.
2. Rehearsing the scenario.
3. Resetting the application.
4. Recording the project.
5. Previewing the rushes.

Let's review these five steps one by one.

Preparing the application to record

For this exercise, the application you will record is Adobe Media Encoder CC 2015. This application is used to convert video and audio files in a wide range of formats. **Adobe Media Encoder (AME)** is included in the standard Captivate package; if you have Captivate (even the trial version), you also have AME.

First, you will reset the Captivate workspace and open AME by performing the following steps:

1. Open Captivate. If Captivate is already open, close all the open files.
2. If needed, reset the Classic workspace using the **Window** | **Workspace** | **Reset 'Classic'** menu item.
3. Open AME. On Mac, it is in the `/Applications/Adobe Media Encoder CC 2015` folder. On Windows, a shortcut to AME should be available in the **Start** menu.

When AME opens, make sure it looks like the following screenshot:

 This exercise and the screenshots are based on Adobe Media Encoder CC 2015, which is the version installed with Adobe Captivate 2017, but it also works with Adobe Media Encoder CC 2017, which is a part of Creative Cloud.

Rehearsing the scenario

The goal of this Captivate project is to teach students how to use AME to convert a QuickTime movie (with a `.mov` extension) to a `400x300` pixels dimension video (with a `.mp4` extension). This scenario follows the exact same steps as those used in the demonstration and simulation of the first chapter. Make sure the audio system of your computer is turned on before rehearsing the following scenario. Here are the steps:

1. Go to the Adobe Media Encoder application.
2. On the top left corner of the application, click the + icon.
3. Browse to the `Chapter08\video\MOV` folder of the exercise files. Select the `demo_en.mov` QuickTime movie and click **Open**.
4. Open the **Format** drop-down list and choose the `H.264` format. You may have this option already selected.
5. Open the **Preset** drop-down list and apply the `Android Phone & Tablet – 480p 25` preset.
6. Click the preset name to open the **Export Settings** dialog.
7. If the size of the Export Settings dialog does not fit the red rectangle, resize the dialog so that it is well inside the red rectangle.
8. Go to the **Video** tab in the lower right area of the **Export Settings** dialog.
9. Make sure the Maintain Aspect Ratio icon (the chain icon) is active, and change the width of the video to 400-pixels. The new height of the video will automatically set to 300-pixels.
10. Click the **OK** button to validate the new export settings.
11. Click the **Start Queue** button (the green play icon) to start the actual encoding.

The encoding process begins. In the Encoding panel at the bottom of the screen, you will see a progress bar for this operation. When the operation is complete, the system plays a brief chime sound effect and shows a green check mark.

 If you don't hear the chimes sound effect at the end of the encoding process, go to AME **Preferences** and select **Play chime when finished encoding**.

Make sure you master these steps, and make sure AME behaves as expected before continuing. If you need more practice, feel free to rehearse this scenario a few more times before the recording. After all, on a real movie set, even the most famous actors rehearse their scenes many times before the director finally decides to turn the camera on.

Resetting the application

When you are ready to record the sequence, don't forget to reset AME to its original state. The best way to do this is to perform the following steps:

1. Close and restart AME.
2. When the application reopens, make sure it looks like the previous screenshot again.

Also, delete the .mp4 file(s) generated during the rehearsal(s) by performing the following steps:

3. Open the **Finder** (Mac) or the **Windows Explorer** (Windows) and browse to the Chapter08\video\MOV folder of the exercises.
4. Delete every .mp4 file present in this folder.

On a real movie set, this is the job of the script supervisor!

Recording the movie

You know the scenario and Adobe Media Encoder is ready to be captured. Let's head back to Captivate and start the actual recording process.

Enabling access to assistive devices (Mac users only)

If you work on Mac, there is one system option to change before Captivate can record the project. Use the following steps to make your Mac ready to record:

1. The first time you create a new software simulation with Captivate, a warning message appears to turn on Adobe Captivate in System Preferences to allow Captivate to control your computer.
2. Click **OK** to dismiss the message, and then click **Cancel**.
3. Open the **System Preferences** application.
4. In the **System Preferences** dialog, click **Security & Privacy**.
5. If needed, click the lock icon at the bottom left corner of the **System Preference** application and authenticate as an administrator.
6. Select the **Captivate** option to grant Captivate access to the assistive devices.

Without this step, macOS does not broadcast the events that Captivate uses to capture user interactivity (clicking a button, typing into a text entry, and so on).

Preparing Captivate to record the sequence

For this first practice recording, you will use the default options of Captivate to record the sequence using the following steps:

1. Close every open file so that the Captivate Welcome screen is displayed.
2. On the **New** tab of the Welcome screen, double click the **Software Simulation** thumbnail. You can also use the **File | Record new Software Simulation** menu item to achieve the same result.

The Captivate interface disappears and you should see a red rectangle on the screen. This red rectangle is the recording area.

3. In the recording window, choose **Application** to record an application.
4. In the **Select the window to record** drop-down list, choose to record the **Adobe Media Encoder CC 2015** application.

The **Adobe Media Encoder** application opens and the red recording area snaps to the application window.

5. In the **Snap to** section of the box, choose to record at **Custom Size**.
6. Choose the **1024 x 768** size from the drop-down list. The red recording area and AME are both resized to the chosen size.

If you are using scaled display settings for your computer, Adobe Media Encoder application might not resize to exactly **1024 x 768** pixels. In such a case, use the smallest display resolution allowed for the Adobe Media Encoder application as the size for your Captivate project.

7. Leave the remaining options at their default settings.

8. The recording window should look like the following screenshot:

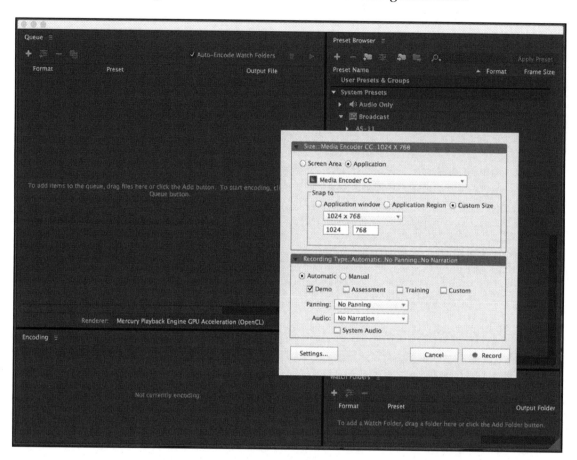

In the preceding screenshot, notice the **Demo** checkbox in the lower part of the window. Make sure this checkbox is the only one selected.

 Mac users, the **System Audio** checkbox might be unavailable on your system. This problem will be addressed later in this chapter.

The stage is set and the actors are in place. Everyone is waiting for the director's signal to get started!

And action!

The signal is the red **Record** button at the bottom of the recording window. Once you click it, all your actions are recorded by Captivate until you stop the capture:

If you have a problem while doing this exercise, refer to the `Chapter08/final/encoderDemo_1_1024.cptx` file of your exercises folder.

1. Click the red **Record** button at the bottom of the recording window. After a short countdown, you'll be in the recording mode.
2. In the **Adobe Media Encoder** window, perform the actions as written in the scenario you rehearsed earlier in this chapter.

During the recording, pay close attention to the following things:

- Each time you click, you should hear a camera shutter sound.
- When you type in the **Width** field, you should hear keystrokes.
- After clicking the **Start Queue** button, AME displays a progress bar in the bottom left panel.
- When the encoding process is finished, the application plays a brief chimes sound effect and shows a green check mark.

Also, make sure you perform the actions slowly to allow Captivate enough time to capture all the needed images and actions. Don't worry about being too slow. The captured slides will still be three seconds long.

3. After completing all the steps, hit the *End* key (Windows) or use the *cmd + Enter* shortcut (Mac) to stop the recording and generate the slides in Captivate.

Shortcuts on the Mac
On some Mac models, it is necessary to add the *fn* key to the mix. In this instance, some Mac models require the *cmd + fn + Enter* shortcut to stop the recording.

4. When the project has finished loading in Captivate, save it as `Chapter08/encoderDemo_1_1024.cptx`.
5. Close the **Adobe Media Encoder** application.

The recording phase of the project is now finished. If you don't get it right the first time, don't worry, you can simply discard your sequence and start over. On a real movie set, even the most famous actors are granted many chances to do it right.

Previewing the rushes

The project should be open in Captivate. To launch the preview, you will use the same icon as in Chapter 1, *Getting Started with Adobe Captivate 2017*, as explained in the following steps:

6. Click the Preview icon on the Toolbar. From the drop-down list, choose **Project** to preview the entire project (you can also use the *F4* shortcut key to do the same thing).
7. Captivate generates the slides in a temporary Flash file and opens the Preview pane.

Captivate has already generated lots of objects on the slides. Remember that in the recording window, the **Demo** mode was selected by default. The **Demo** mode automatically adds Text Captions, Highlight Boxes, and Mouse movements to the slides.

Of course, some of the content of the Text Captions must be corrected; the size and position of the Highlight Boxes and Text Captions must be fine-tuned; and the overall rhythm of the project is probably too fast, but this is an acceptable start point.

The main problem with these rushes is how the movie ends. While previewing the project, you probably noticed that the progress bar has not been captured by Captivate.

In order to understand why Captivate did not capture this progress bar, it is necessary to further dive into the inner working of the Captivate capture engine.

8. Close the Preview pane when done.

The inner working of the Captivate capture engine

For you techies, the Captivate capture engine is based on static screenshots. Going back to the Adobe Media Encoder project, let's review what exactly happened when you clicked on your mouse during the capture using the following steps:

1. Return to the `Chapter08/encoderDemo_1_1024.cptx` file.
2. Make sure that the first slide is selected in the **Filmstrip** panel.

The first slide shows the initial state of the application. When recording, you used your mouse to click the Add Source icon of AME. When you clicked on this icon, Captivate launched a sequence of actions behind the scenes:

- Captivate recorded the position of the mouse at the time of the click (using x and y coordinates).
- Adobe Media Encoder executed the action.
- When Adobe Media Encoder completed its action, Captivate took a second static screenshot to capture the new state of the application. This second screenshot is used as the background image of slide 2.

You then used your mouse a second time to select the `demo_en.mov` file. When this second click occurred, Captivate launched the same sequence of actions and took a third static screenshot to use as the background image of slide 3.

When the movie plays, the static screenshot of the first slide (a `.bmp` image) is displayed. When the mouse has to move, Captivate recreates a movement from the top left corner of the slide to the position of the click as recorded during the filming. Just after the click, Captivate displays the static (`.bmp`) screenshot of the second slide.

When it is time to move the mouse on the second slide, Captivate recreates a movement from where the click occurred on the first slide to the location of the click on the second slide as recorded during the filming. Right after the second click, Captivate displays the third static screenshot. This process repeats itself until the end of the movie.

It may sound very simple and logical, but the way this process works has lots of implications as mentioned in the following list:

- Only the start and the end points of the mouse movements are recorded by Captivate. During the playback, a movement is recreated between these points.
- The actual mouse movements made during the recording between two clicks are therefore not recorded.
- The animations displayed by the Captured application (in this case, the progress bar) are not captured.
- The Timeline of the generated movie is independent of the time that has passed during filming.

This system creates a very lightweight animation: a bunch of images and a few coordinates are enough to reproduce an entire movie.

However, this system is limited. Some mouse actions, such as drag and drop and scrolling actions, cannot be reproduced that way. These actions require an actual frame-by-frame video recording to be played back correctly. In Captivate, such a frame-by-frame sequence is known as **Full Motion Recording (FMR)**.

Understanding the FMR mode

To make sure you understand this concept, let's take a look at some of the preferences of Captivate:

1. In Captivate, use the **Edit | Preferences** (Windows) or **Adobe Captivate | Preferences** (Mac) menu item to open the **Preferences** window.
2. Once the **Preferences** window opens, click **Settings** under the **Recording** group, as shown in the following screenshot:

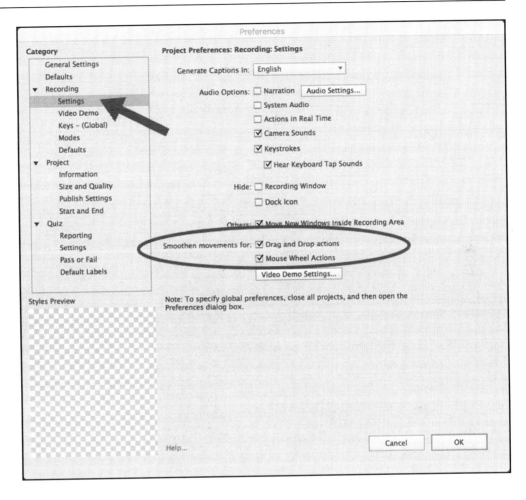

At the end of the **Preferences** window, there are two options that help you control the FMR behavior of Captivate: **Smoothen movements for Drag and Drop actions** and **Smoothen movements for Mouse Wheel Actions**. These two options should be selected by default.

3. Make sure these two options are selected and close the **Preferences** window.
4. In the **Filmstrip** panel, take a close look at the icons beneath each of the slide's thumbnails.

While most of the slides display the icon of a mouse, one slide should display the icon of a video camera. This is shown in the following screenshot:

As shown in the preceding screenshot, slide 9 is where the scrolling movement in the preset list of AME occurs.

 The actual slide number may vary depending on how your particular recording session went.

Because the **Smoothen movements for Drag and Drop actions** and **Smoothen movements for Mouse Wheel Actions** options were turned on, Captivate has detected this scrolling movement and has automatically switched to the FMR mode when capturing that particular slide.

One of the limitations of FMR is that it does not allow any kind of interaction. During the playback, the learners cannot perform such scrolling movement themselves. Another limitation of FMR is that it increases the file size of the simulation.

The FMR mode will also help you capture the progress bar at the end of the project. The only problem is that the progress bar is not linked to any scrolling or drag-and-drop action. Fortunately, there is another way to control the FMR mode.

Controlling Captivate during the shooting session

Controlling Captivate during the recording session is quite a challenge for your operating system (Mac or Windows). Even though both Windows and Mac OS are multitasking operating systems (it means they can handle multiple applications running at the same time), there can only be one active application at any given time. The active application is the one you currently interact with and therefore is the one that currently listens to the keyboard, the mouse, and other input devices.

When recording with Captivate, there are two active applications: the application you capture and Captivate itself. You should be able to interact with both these applications, so they both share the same mouse and the same keyboard at the same time. That is a very unusual situation to deal with for an operating system.

By default, the mouse and the keyboard send their data to the application you record, except for a few keys and shortcuts that are wired to Captivate. Let's take a deeper look at this system using the following steps:

1. Use the **Adobe Captivate** | **Preferences** (Mac) or **Edit** | **Preferences** (Windows) menu item to open the **Preferences** window of Captivate.

2. In the left column of the **Preferences** window, open the **Keys - (Global)** category.

This part of the **Preferences** dialog lists all the keys and shortcuts that allow you to interact with Captivate during the recording, as shown in the following screenshot:

The preceding screenshot has been taken on a Mac. If you work on Windows, the dialog box will be exactly the same with the exception of the shortcuts that are a bit different on Windows.

Remember that all the other keys as well as the mouse are wired to the application you capture.

3. Take some time to review the available keys and shortcuts.

Of special interest are the keyboard shortcuts you can use to manually start and stop a FMR. Also, notice that you can use a keyboard shortcut (*Print Screen* on Windows or *cmd + F6* on Mac) to manually take extra screenshots if needed. Finally, the *End* (Windows) or *cmd + Enter* (Mac) shortcut is used to stop the recording.

In some situations, you may need to change these recording keys. For example, if the software you are recording uses the same shortcut key that is defined for Captivate recording functions, you will need to change the key combinations. Here are the steps you can follow to modify the shortcut keys assigned for each task:

4. Click the field where the key used to stop recording is defined (*End* on Windows or *cmd + Enter* on the Mac).
5. Type the *Ctrl + E* shortcut on your keyboard. The *Ctrl + E* shortcut is now assigned to the stop recording action.
6. At the bottom of the window, click the **Restore Defaults** button to return to the default settings.
7. Leave the **Preferences** window open.

Now take some time to inspect the remaining preferences of Captivate.

Exploring the preferences

In this section, you will explore the remaining recording preferences of Captivate. You will start by exploring the automatic recording modes.

Exploring the automatic recording modes

In the previous section, your first recording experience was based on the default preferences of Captivate. In order to take full control of the situation, you will explore and fine-tune the automatic recording modes before having a second try. Perform the following steps to explore the automatic recording modes:

1. To the left of the **Preferences** window, click the **Modes** category under the **Recording** section.
2. At the top of the **Preferences** window, make sure the **Mode** drop down list is set to **Demonstration**, as shown in the following screenshot:

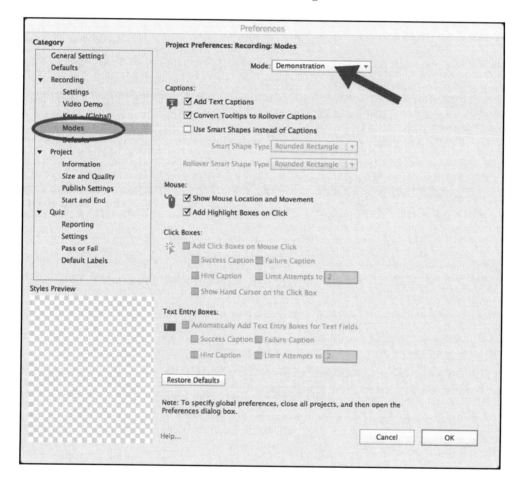

The **Preferences** window currently displays the settings of the **Demonstration** recording mode you used during your first capture session. As expected, this recording mode adds Text Captions to the slides.

If you wish to use Smart Shapes instead of Text Captions to have more flexibility to style the text, select **Use Smart Shapes instead of Captions**.

It also shows the mouse and adds a Highlight Box each time the mouse is clicked during the capture.

3. These settings reflect what you have seen when previewing the rushes of the first movie. At the top of the **Preferences** window, open the **Modes** drop down list.
4. Choose the **Assessment Simulation** option.

The **Assessment Simulation** mode is the second automatic recording mode of Captivate. As discussed earlier, a simulation is a project in which the user is active, so the **Show Mouse Location and Movement** option is, logically, not selected. Instead, each time a mouse click occurs during the filming, a **Click Box** is automatically added to the slide.

The Click Box is one of the interactive objects of Captivate. It can pause the course and wait for the learner to click the same location as where you clicked during the capture. Because the **Failure Caption** option is selected, a failure notice will be displayed if the learner does not click the right spot.

If you use the keyboard during the recording process, Captivate generates a Text Entry Box. The Text Entry Box is another interactive object of Captivate that stops the playhead and waits for the student to interact with the course.

5. Open the **Modes** drop-down list again.
6. In the list, choose the **Training Simulation** mode.

The **Training Simulation** mode is very similar to the **Assessment Simulation** mode. The only difference is the **Hint Caption** option that is selected for both the Click Box object and the Text Entry Box object. A Hint Caption is a Text Caption or a Smart Shape that is displayed when the student passes the mouse over the hit area of the Click Box / Text Entry Box.

7. Open the **Modes** drop-down list one last time.
8. In the drop-down list, choose the **Custom** mode.

Surprise! When choosing the **Custom** mode, no option is selected by default. In fact, the Custom mode is yours to create, so let's go!

9. In the **Caption** section, select the **Add Text Captions** box.
10. In the **Click Boxes** section, select the **Add Click Boxes on Mouse Click** option. Also, select the **Failure Caption** and **Hint Caption** boxes.
11. Finally, in the **Text Entry Boxes** section, select the **Automatically Add Text Entry Boxes for Text Fields** option with a **Failure Caption** and a **Hint Caption**.

Depending on the recording mode, Text Captions, Failure Captions, and/or Hint Captions will be added to the slides.

Exploring the recording settings

Let's now focus on the **Recording Settings** category of the **Preferences** window:

1. Open the **Recording Settings** category by clicking **Settings** under the **Recording** category in the left column of the **Preferences** window.

The first available option at the top of the recording settings preference pane is the **Generate Captions In** drop-down list. Use it to choose the language used by Captivate to generate the various types of captions.

Other options available on this pane include the following:

- When the **Actions in Real Time** checkbox is selected, the recording is played back at the same speed as the actions performed during the recording.
- The **Camera Sounds** click box is used to turn the camera shutter sound on or off during the recording. Make sure this option is selected.
- The **Keystrokes** and **Hear Keyboard Tap Sounds** options are responsible for recording the keystrokes and for the keystrokes sound during the filming. It is best to leave these options selected.
- The **Move New Windows Inside Recording Area** option is used during the capture when the application you record opens a new window or a dialog box. It prevents the new window from opening outside or partially outside of the recording area. This option should be selected at all times.
- The **Hide Recording Window** option turns off the display of red border around the recording area.

- (For Windows only) The **Hide System Tray Icon** and **Hide Task Icon** checkboxes are great when you record fullscreen. When turned on, they hide the **Captivate** button from the Windows taskbar and the Captivate icon from the notification area.
- (For Mac only) The **Hide Dock Icon** checkbox is used to remove the Captivate icon from Dock during the filming. This option is very useful when recording fullscreen.

The Video Demo preferences pane

To finish off with the **Recording** preferences, you will now explore one last **Preferences** pane:

1. Click the **Video Demo** category to open the **Video Demo** preferences pane.

The **Video Demo** preferences pane shows options to control and optimize the conversion of an FMR into a HTML5 or Flash video. Normally, the default options should work fine in almost every situation, so there is no need to change anything on this page right now.

2. Click **OK** to close the **Preferences** window and save the changes.

Now that you have a better idea of the available preferences, it is time to have a second try at recording your project.

Recording the other versions of the project

It is now time to start another recording session. For this second experience, you will pursue the following objectives:

- You will generate both the demonstration and simulation versions of the project in a single recording session.
- At the end of the project, you will use an FMR to capture the progress bar of the encoding process.

Before turning on the camera for the second time, here are some additional tips and tricks for successful capture:

- Use the automatic recording modes whenever possible.
- If you have to record fullscreen, reset your desktop to its default appearance, that is, remove your custom wallpaper, and turn off any custom color scheme, or mouse pointer sets. Your computer should look like any computer.
- Turn off your screensaver.
- Turn off the instant messaging apps or make yourself unavailable.
- Turn on the sound so that you can hear the camera shutter and the keystrokes. This will help you have better control over the recording process.
- If you are not sure whether or not Captivate took a given screenshot, don't hesitate to take one manually using the *Print Screen* key (Windows) or the *cmd + F6* shortcut (Mac). During the editing phase that follows, it is much easier to delete an extra slide than to generate a missing slide.
- Perform the actions slowly, especially the text typing actions and the actions that require an FMR. You'll be able to set up the timing of each slide with great precision during the editing phase.
- Rehearse your scripts before recording.

With these tips and tricks in mind, let's concentrate on the actual recording. Your first concern is to reset the stage by performing the following steps:

1. Reopen AME. When the application appears, make sure it looks like the screenshot in the *Preparing the application to record* section earlier in this chapter.
2. Delete all the `.mp4` files in the `videos/MOV` folder of the exercise files.
3. Return to Captivate and close every open file, if needed.
4. Use the **File | Record new Software Simulation** menu item or the Software Simulation thumbnail on the **New** tab of the welcome screen to create a new project. The main Captivate interface disappears and the red recording area is displayed.
5. In the recording window, choose **Application** to record **Adobe Media Encoder CC 2015**. The red recording area snaps to the **Adobe Media Encoder** window.
6. Use **Custom Size** of **1024 x 768** pixels to record your application.
7. In the recording modes section of the recording window, select all four automatic recording modes (**Demo**, **Assessment**, **Training**, and **Custom**).
8. Leave the other options at their current value.

9. Make sure your recording window looks like the following screenshot:

10. When you are ready, click the red **Record** button. After a short countdown, you'll be back in the recording mode.

11. In Adobe Media Encoder, perform the actions as rehearsed earlier in this chapter. Behind the scenes, Captivate is recording!

You should hear a camera shutter sound each time you click and a keystroke sound each time you use the keyboard. Notice that, even though two applications are currently active, the mouse and the keyboard are interacting with AME, not with Captivate.

12. Just before clicking on the Start Queue button (the Play icon), press the *Print Screen* (Windows) or *cmd + F6* (Mac) keys to take an extra screenshot manually.

This extra screenshot is necessary to correctly capture the progress bar with an FMR. A camera shutter sound lets you know that an extra screenshot has indeed been captured.

Mac users, if you don't hear the camera shutter sound, remember that some Mac models require that you add the *fn* key to the mix. The shortcut to take an extra screenshot might therefore be *cmd + fn + F6*.

You will now turn FMR on and click the **Start Queue** button.

13. Use either the *F9* (Windows) or *cmd + F9* (Mac) shortcut to turn FMR on.

14. Click the Start Queue button of AME to start the actual encoding of the video.

15. When the encoding is finished, use either the *F10* (Windows) or *cmd + F10* (Mac) shortcut to stop FMR.

16. Finally, use the *End* key (Windows) or the *cmd + Enter* shortcut (Mac) to stop the recording.

Captivate generates the slides. When that process is over, Captivate has a nice surprise for you!

Alternate way to stop a Captivate recording
In addition to the keyboard shortcuts discussed previously, you can also use your mouse to stop a Captivate recording. On Windows systems, click the Captivate taskbar icon at the bottom of the screen. On Mac, the same icon is in the notification area at the top right corner of the screen.

Previewing the second rushes

The nice surprise is that Captivate has generated four versions of the same project. This is due to the four checkboxes that you selected at the end of the recording window just before pressing the **Record** button:

- The untitled_demo1.cptx file was generated based on the **Demo** mode. Save it in your exercises folder as Chapter08/encoderDemo_1024.cptx.

- The untiteld_assessment1.cptx file was generated based on the **Assessment Simulation** mode. Save it in your exercises folder as Chapter08/encoderAssessment_1024.cptx.

- The untiteld_training1.cptx file was generated based on the **Training Simulation** mode. Save it in your exercises folder as Chapter08/encoderTraining_1024.cptx.

- The untiteld_custom.cptx file was generated with the settings of your very own **Custom** mode. Save it in your exercises folder as Chapter08/encoderCustom_1024.cptx.

Now that these files are saved, you will preview them one by one:

1. Select the `Chapter08/encoderDemo_1024.cptx` file.
2. Use the **Preview | Project** icon on the Toolbar to preview the entire project.

Captivate generates the slides and opens the **Preview** pane.

 If you did not succeed in producing great recordings, you can use the files in the `Chapter08/final` folder of the exercises.

The **Demo** version of the project is very similar to the one you shot earlier in this chapter. The only major difference is the progress bar that has been correctly captured by FMR.

3. When the preview is finished, close the **Preview** pane.
4. Select the `Chapter08/encoderAssessment_1024.cptx` file.
5. Use the **Preview | Project** icon to preview the entire project.

As described in the **Assessment Simulation** recording mode, the mouse pointer and the Text Captions have not been added to this version of the project. After a short while, the project pauses. If you don't do anything, nothing happens as Captivate is waiting for you to click the right spot. If you click the right icon, the project moves on to the next slide and pauses again waiting for your second action. If you do not perform the right action, a Failure Caption is displayed.

6. When you complete the entire project, close the **Preview** pane.
7. Return to the `Chapter08/encoderTraining_1024.cptx` file.
8. Once again, use the **Preview | Project** icon on the Toolbar to preview the entire project.

As expected, this version of the project is very similar to the previous one. The only difference is the Hint Caption that is displayed when the mouse is over the hit area of the Click Boxes or Text Entry Boxes. This Hint Caption can provide some useful information on the action to be performed by the student.

9. When you are through the entire project, close the **Preview** pane.
10. Go to the `Chapter08/encoderCustom_1024.cptx` file.
11. Use the Preview icon one more time to preview the entire project.

Your **Custom** recording mode has added Text Captions, Click Boxes, and Text Entry Boxes to the slides, effectively providing an entirely new customized experience.

Of course, none of these four versions of the project are final in any way. There is a lot of work to be done before these projects can be published. That being said, the automatic recording modes of Captivate have successfully provided enough raw material of good quality to get you started. Remember, this is exactly what you should expect from the capture step of the process.

Recording with System Audio

System Audio is the audio that is generated from the application you capture or from your operating system. In the AME example, it is the chimes sound effect that is played when the encoding is finished. In this exercise, you will once again capture the sequence of actions described in the scenario. This time, Captivate will record the System Audio in addition to screenshots and mouse movements.

First, you should reset your applications to their original state:

1. Close AME if it is still open.
2. Reopen AME.

By restarting AME, you effectively reset the application to its default state.

3. Delete every `.mp4` file that is in the `video/MOV` folder of the exercise.

The second step is to get Captivate ready for the capture session.

4. Return to Captivate, and use the **File** | **Close All** menu item to close all open files (if any).
5. Use the **File** | **Record New Software Simulation** menu item or the Software Simulation thumbnail on the **New** tab of the welcome screen to create a new project.
6. In the recording window, choose **Application** to record the Adobe Media Encoder application. The red recording area snaps to the AME window.
7. Use a **Custom Size** of **1024 x 768** pixels to shoot your application.
8. In the recording modes section of the recording window, make sure the **Demo** mode is the only one selected.
9. Also, select the **System Audio** checkbox.

System Audio on Mac

If you are on a Mac, the **System Audio** checkbox is not available. You will need to install the Soundflower system extension and configure your audio system accordingly before being able to use the System Audio feature of Captivate. The procedure is explained in the knowledge base article at

`http://helpx.adobe.com/captivate/kb/system-audio-disabled.html.`

On Windows, System Audio should work right out of the box!

Once System Audio has been correctly set up, the recording window should look like the following screenshot:

10. When you are ready, click the red **Record** button. After a short countdown, you'll be back in the recording mode.

11. In Adobe Media Encoder, perform the actions as rehearsed earlier in this chapter. Behind the scenes, Captivate is recording!

Notice that you do not hear the camera shutter sounds and the keystrokes sounds anymore. When System Audio is activated, these sounds are automatically disabled, because-obviously-they don't need to be recorded.

12. Just before clicking on the Start Queue button (the Play icon), press the *Print Screen* (Windows) or *cmd + F6* (Mac) shortcut to take an extra screenshot manually.

13. Use the *F9* (Windows) or *cmd + F9* (Mac) shortcut to turn FMR on.

14. Click the Start Queue button of AME to start the actual encoding of the video.

15. When the encoding is finished, use the *F10* (Windows) or *cmd + F10* (Mac) shortcut to stop FMR.

16. Finally, use the *End* key (Windows) or the *cmd + Enter* shortcut (Mac) to stop the recording.

17. When Captivate has finished generating all the slides, save this file in the exercises folder as `Chapter08/encoderDemo_sysAudio_1024.cptx`.

As usual, let's now preview the rushes of this new recording session.

18. Use the **Preview | Project** icon on the Toolbar to preview the entire project.

This version of the project is, again, very similar to the demonstrations you have seen earlier. However, you should notice one significant difference. At the end of the project, when the encoding process is completely finished, you should hear the chimes sound of AME that has been captured, thanks to the System Audio feature of Captivate!

The Video Demo recording mode

The Video Demo recording mode was introduced in Captivate 6. It allows you to create a video file by shooting the onscreen actions. A Video Demo recording project actually is a big Full Motion Recording.

A Video Demo project is very different from the other projects you have worked on so far. Because a Video Demo project can only be published as an .mp4 video file, no interactive objects can be included in such projects. In other words, it can only be a demonstration. Because a Video Demo project is based on a single big video file, there is no slide and no **Filmstrip** panel in a Video Demo project. This makes Video Demo projects particularly suitable for upload to an online video hosting service such as YouTube, Vimeo, or Dailymotion.

In the next exercise, you will create a Video Demo version of Encoder Demonstration. The first operation to do is to reset your system.

 If you have a problem while doing this exercise, refer to the Chapter08/final/encoderVideo.cpvc file of your exercises folder.

1. Restart the Adobe Media Encoder application.
2. Delete all the .mp4 files present in the videos/MOV folder of the exercise files.

Now that your system is ready, let's create a Video Demo project.

3. Use the **File | Record new Video Demo** menu item to start a new Video Demo project.

This option is also available on the **New** tab of the welcome screen of Captivate when no file is open.

4. In the drop down list at the top of the recording window, choose to record the Adobe Media Encoder application.
5. In the **Snap to** section, choose to record at **Custom Size** of **1024 x 768** pixels.

Most of the time, a narration is added to such projects. If you have a microphone available, you'll record your voice in addition to the onscreen action. If you don't have a microphone available, just read through these steps. Audio can also be added later in the process if needed.

6. If a microphone is available, open the **Audio** drop-down list and choose your microphone (or the audio interface the microphone is plugged in to) in the list of entries.

7. Make sure the other options are at their default settings. The recording window should now look like the following screenshot:

As demonstrated in the preceding screenshot, it is possible to record both the narration and the System Audio simultaneously.

8. Click the red **Record** button to start the recording.

If it is the first time you are recording sound with your Captivate installation, you'll have to calibrate the sensitivity of your microphone.

In the **Calibrate Audio Input** dialog, click the **Auto Calibrate** button. Speak normally into the microphone until the **Input level OK** message appears on the screen. Click **OK** to validate the sensitivity settings and to discard the box.

9. After a short countdown, the recording begins.
10. In Adobe Media Encoder, perform the actions as rehearsed earlier in this chapter. If you have a microphone, speak as you go through the steps of the scenario.
11. When done, hit the *End* key (Windows) or the *cmd + Enter* shortcut (Mac).

Captivate finalizes the video capture. When the finalization process is finished, your entire video is played back. Enjoy the show!

12. When the video has finished playing, click the **Edit** button in the bottom right corner of the screen.

By clicking on the **Edit** button, you leave the preview mode of the Video Demo project and enter the editing mode. Note how the interface of a Video Demo project is different from the interface of a standard Captivate project.

13. Save your file as `Chapter08/encoderVideo.cpvc`.

Notice that a Video Demo project does not use the standard `.cptx` file extension, but uses the `.cpvc` file extension instead. The **Video Demo** recording mode will be covered in more details in `Chapter 9`, *Producing a Video Demo*.

Automatic and manual panning

In the movie industry, panning refers to moving the camera during filming. In Captivate, the camera is the red recording area. When panning is turned on in Captivate, it simply means that the red recording area can be moved during the recording. This enables you to capture a bigger application with a smaller recording area.

Earlier in this chapter, we had a discussion on how to solve the project-sizing problem. Panning was one of the possible approaches. Let's take a closer look at it:

If you have a problem while doing this exercise, refer to the Chapter08/final/encoderDemo_panning.cptx file of your exercises folder.

1. Restart AME to reset the user interface.
2. Delete all the .mp4 files present in the videos/MOV folder of the exercise.
3. Return to Captivate and use to the **File | Record New Software Simulation** menu item or the corresponding thumbnail of the **New** tab of the Welcome screen to start a new project.

The Captivate interface disappears, and the red recording area shows up.

4. In the recording window, choose to record a **Screen Area** (and not an **Application** as before). Give the area a **Custom Size** of **800 x 600** pixels.

Normally, the size of the **Adobe Media Encoder** application should still be **1024 x 768** pixels from the previous filming sessions.

5. Move the red recording area such that its top left corner corresponds to the top left corner of the **Adobe Media Encoder** application window.

In this configuration, the size of AME does not match the size of the red recording area. The recording area should be smaller than AME.

6. In the bottom part of the recording window, make sure the **Demo** mode is the only one selected.
7. In the **Panning** drop-down list, choose **Manual Panning**.
8. If necessary, set the **Audio** dropdown to **No Narration** and deselect the **System Audio** checkbox.

Your computer screen should look like the following screenshot:

9. When ready, click the red **Record** button to switch to the recording mode.

10. After the countdown, perform the first few steps of the scenario in the **Adobe Media Encoder** application.

11. When the **Export Settings** window opens, place your mouse above the red line of the recording area until the mouse turns into a grabbing hand. Then, slowly move the red recording area until it covers more or less the lower right section of the **Export Settings** window.

12. In AME, modify the size of the video as defined in the scenario.

13. When the **Export Settings** dialog closes after you clicked on the **OK** button, move the red recording area back to its original position.

14. Just before clicking on the Start Queue button (the Play icon), press the *Print Screen* (Windows) or *cmd + F6* (Mac) shortcut to take an extra screenshot manually.

15. Use the *F9* (Windows) or *cmd + F9* (Mac) shortcut to turn FMR on.

16. Click the Start Queue button of AME to start the actual encoding of the video.

17. When the encoding is finished, use the *F10* (Windows) or *cmd + F10* (Mac) shortcut to stop the FMR.

18. Finally, use the *End* key (Windows) or the *cmd + Enter* shortcut (Mac) to stop the recording.

19. Use the **Preview | Project** icon on the Toolbar to preview the entire project.

20. When the movie is finished, close the *Preview* pane, and save the file as `Chapter08/encoderDemo_panning.cptx`.

Back in Captivate, take a look at the **Filmstrip** panel. Beneath some of the slide thumbnails, you should see the camera icon indicating that there are some FMR slides in the project. FMR is used to reproduce the panning movements made during the capture.

In this example, you have used manual panning. When using automatic panning, Captivate places the mouse at the center of the red recording area. During filming, the red recording area automatically follows any mouse movement. Automatic panning produces a lot of unnecessary movements, and, consequently, a lot of extra FMR slides.

Responsive capture

Responsive projects were first introduced in Adobe Captivate 8. It allows you to adapt the content and the layout of your Captivate project for different device sizes.

When it comes to screen capture, the responsive projects allow you to capture static screenshots and to pan to the relevant area which contains the highlight box or click box. The exact procedure is as follows:

1. Restart AME to reset the user interface.

2. Delete all the `.mp4` files present in the `videos/MOV` folder of the exercise.

3. Return to Captivate and close any open files, so that you see the Welcome screen.

4. Double click the Responsive Project thumbnail on the **New** tab of the Welcome screen. You can also use the **File | New Project | Responsive Project** menu item.

This action creates a new responsive project. For this first experiment with the responsive projects, you will use the default settings of Captivate. At the top of the stage, you should see the **Preview-in** drop down list and the **Preview Slider**, to see how the content will be displayed on different device sizes.

Notice that the desktop size is set to 1024 x 627. To record the AME window correctly, we will need to increase the height of the desktop view to 768-pixels.

5. To do so, click **Modify | Rescale Project.**
6. Change the height to **768** pixels and click **Finish.**
7. Click **OK** to close the alert box.
8. You will now see a Custom preset added to the preview preset dropdown, with the dimensions set to **1024 x 768**, which will allow us to capture the screen perfectly.
9. Optionally, click the **+** sign to add this custom size to the **Preview in** drop-down list.

Now it's time to start recording the responsive simulation. You can use the following steps to add slides into this responsive project using the capture engine of Captivate:

10. Click the **Slides** icon, which is the very first icon on the Toolbar.
11. Choose the **Software Simulation** option in the drop-down menu.
12. Click the **OK** button at the end of the **Record Additional Slides** dialog to insert the new slides after the first (and only) slide of the project.

The Captivate interface disappears and the red recording area shows up.

13. In the drop-down list at the top of the recording window, choose to record the **Adobe Media Encoder CC 2015** application.
14. Make sure the **Snap to window** checkbox is selected to have the red recording area snap to the AME window.
15. Make sure the **Demo** mode is selected on the **Mode** drop-down menu.
16. If needed, reset the **Panning** dropdown to **No Panning** and the **Audio** dropdown to **No Narration**.

Unlike your previous recording experiences, you cannot choose the recording size. This is because the project already exists and already has a size of 1024 x 768 pixels. Therefore, the red recording area already has the same size as the project. Your screen should now look like the following screenshot:

You are now ready for your first responsive capture!

17. Click the red **Record** button. After a short countdown, you'll be back in the recording mode.

18. In Adobe Media Encoder, perform the actions as rehearsed earlier in this chapter. Behind the scenes, Captivate is recording!

19. Click the Start Queue button of AME to start encoding the video.

20. Finally, use the *End* key (Windows) or the *cmd + Enter* shortcut (Mac) to stop the recording.

21. When Captivate has finished generating all the slides, save this file in the exercises folder as `Chapter08/encoderDemo_responsive.cptx`.

So far, so good! The story is almost exactly the same as before. But, this project is a bit special.

22. To see what's special, use the **Filmstrip** panel to select the second slide of the project.

23. Notice that there's a blue rectangle on the slide. This blue rectangle is the focus area of your simulation and will always appear on your slide. The size of this blue rectangle is the minimum supported device size for Captivate responsive projects.

24. You can reposition this blue rectangle to any other location. But while doing so, make sure you don't move the rectangle away from the click area.

25. To preview the simulation in different device sizes, select different device options from the **Preview-in** drop-down list. Notice that the visible area is always surrounding the blue rectangle.

26. Use the **Preview | Project** icon on the Toolbar to preview the entire project. Because you are in a responsive project, this option plays the demonstration in the default web browser.

27. When in the browser, feel free to use the slider at the top of the preview to test the responsiveness of the project.

28. When done, close the browser and return to Captivate.

 When you publish these simulations and view them on devices, you will be able to pan to the areas that are not shown in the simulation. And because of this special panning functionality for simulations, the default Swipe Right, Left, Up, or Down gestures are disabled for the responsive simulation.

While there is a lot more to learn about the new responsive projects of Captivate, you will now move on to the next section of the book. You will cover this topic in much more detail in Chapter 10, *Creating a Responsive Project*.

Rescaling a project

This chapter opened with a discussion on choosing the right size for the project. This discussion led to four possible approaches to manage the size difference between the application to capture and the course to produce.

The first approach was to shoot big and then downsize. The first step of this approach was done when you used a resolution of 1024 x 768 pixels to record your very first sequence. You will now take care of the second step: resizing the movie to 800 x 600 pixels.

Remember that resizing a project is a one-way operation that always results in data and quality loss. If another solution that does not require resizing the project is available, go for it! If a resize operation cannot be avoided, always keep a backup copy of your project at its original size.

1. In Captivate, open the `chapter08/encoderDemo_1024.cptx` file.

If you did not successfully save this file earlier in this chapter, you can use the one saved in the `chapter08/final` folder.
If you have a problem while doing this exercise, refer to the `Chapter08/final/encoderDemo_800.cptx` file of your exercises folder.

2. Use the **File | Save As** menu item to save the file as `Chapter08/encoderDemo_800.cptx`.

3. When the project is saved, use the **Modify | Rescale Project** menu item to open the **Rescale Project** dialog.

This window is divided into three parts. The top part allows you to define the new size of the project. It is the only part available at the moment.

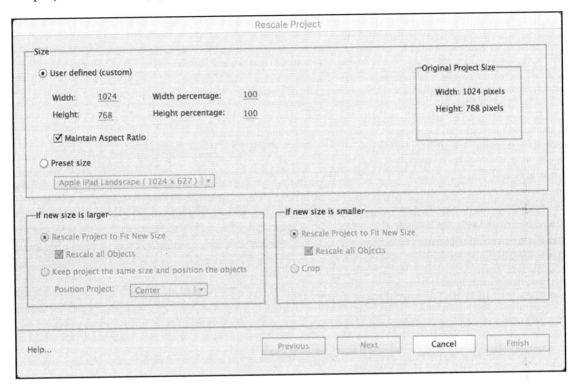

4. Make sure the **Maintain Aspect Ratio** box is selected.

5. Reduce the **Width** of the project from **1024** to **800** pixels. The new **Height** of **600** pixels should be calculated automatically.

Since the new size is smaller than the original size, the lower right part of the box becomes available. It is titled: **If new size is smaller**. The lower left part of the box is still inactive. It would activate if the new size of the project were larger than the original size.

6. Take some time to review the available options, but leave the default unchanged. When ready, click **Finish**.

7. A dialog box informs you that resizing a project cannot be undone. Click **OK** to confirm you want to resize the project anyway.

8. Captivate resizes each slide, one by one.

9. Save the file when the resize process is complete.

Although Captivate does a great job resizing all the objects on the slides, we still recommend going through each slide to ensure the size conversion was successful for every object on every slide.

Modifying the object properties

Now that you have finished recording a demonstration, assessment, simulation, and a custom project, let's talk about the objects that are automatically generated with these screen recordings. You will also learn how to modify the properties and styles of these objects to suit your project requirements and match your project style-guide.

The objects that are generated with screen recording projects are Text Captions, Text Entry Boxes, Mouse, Highlight Boxes, and Click Boxes. In Chapter 2, *Working with Standard Objects* you have already learned how to modify the properties of Text Captions, Text Entry Boxes, and Click Boxes. In this chapter, let's learn how to work with Highlight Boxes and Mouse in screen capture projects.

The Highlight Box object

Let's start with talking about the **Highlight Box**. As its name implies, a Highlight Box is used to highlight a specific area of the screen. A Highlight Box is a rectangle that appears and disappears from the screen according to its position on the **Timeline** panel.

When using the Demo recording mode during the capture, Captivate adds one Highlight Box for each mouse click:

1. In Captivate, open the chapter08/encoderDemo_800.cptx file.
2. Use the **Filmstrip** panel to go to the first slide.

On Slide 1, you will see three objects: A Text Captions, a Mouse, and a small blue Highlight Box below the mouse pointer.

This Highlight Box has been automatically added by Captivate during the filming.

   3. Click the Highlight Box to make it the active object.

Selecting the Highlight Box
Because the Highlight Box is so close to the Mouse object, you may end up selecting the Mouse instead of the Highlight Box. Remember that you can use the **Timeline** panel to select the desired object.

Selecting the Highlight Box updates the **Properties** inspector. At the top of the **Style** tab, notice the **Fill** and the **Stroke** sections that provide the main formatting options of the selected Highlight Box:

- **Fill** indicates the color *inside* of the object.
- When the **Opacity** parameter is set to **0%**, the object is completely transparent. When the **Opacity** is set to **100%**, the object is completely opaque.
- The **Stroke** is the border *around* the object. You can change both the stroke **Style** and the stroke color.
- The last option is **Width**. This option lets you choose the width of the stroke. Set this option at **0** to remove the stroke from the object.

Now that you have a better idea of the available options, you will change the formatting of the selected Highlight Box:

   4. Choose a dark orange as the **Fill** color.

   5. Leave the **Opacity** value at **20%**.

   6. Click **Stroke**. In the color picker, choose the same orange color as the one you chose for the fill. Notice that the recently selected colors are available at the bottom of the color swatches.

   7. Set the stroke **Width** to **2** pixels.

Make sure your **Fill** and **Stroke** sections look like the following screenshot:

Finally, you will use the **Options** tab of the **Properties** inspector to modify the size and the position of the Highlight Box.

8. Still on Slide 1 of the `encoderDemo_800.cptx` file, make sure the Highlight Box is the selected object.

9. Switch to the **Options** tab of the **Properties** inspector.

10. For the size, change the **Width** to **24** pixels and **Height** to **19** pixels (to be able to modify the **Height** independently from the **Width**, make sure the **Constrain proportions** checkbox is deselected).

11. For the position, give the Highlight Box an **X** coordinate of **9** pixels and a **Y** coordinate of **64** pixels.

The Highlight Box should precisely cover the **Add Files (+)** icon.

12. Use the **Preview | Next 5 Slides** icon on the Toolbar to test your sequence.

Captivate generates the slides and opens the **Preview** pane. Take a close look at the Highlight box of slide 1. The timing and the formatting of the objects are of no importance at this time.

When the preview is finished, close the **Preview** pane to return to Captivate. There is one last option to experiment with.

13. Return to Slide 1 of the encoderDemo_800.cptx file and select the orange Highlight Box.

14. In the **Style** tab of the **Properties** inspector, change the **Opacity** value to **70%**.

15. Select the **Fill Outer Area** checkbox just below the **Fill** color section.

With this option selected, the fill color of the Highlight Box will be applied to the area outside the object. The only part of the slide that will not be covered by the fill color will be the inside the Highlight Box. It is necessary to see the project in preview mode to see the **Fill Outer Area** option in action!

16. Still on slide 1 of the encoderDemo_800.cptx file, use the **Preview** | **Next 5 Slides** icon on the Toolbar.

When the project starts playing in the **Preview** pane, pay close attention to the way the Highlight Box behaves:

17. Return to slide 1 of the encoderDemo_800.cptx file and select the orange Highlight Box one last time.

18. In this particular case, you want the Highlight Box to behave normally. So, in the **Style** tab of the **Properties** inspector, deselect the **Fill Outer Area** checkbox and reduce the **Opacity** value back to **20%**.

19. Save the file when done.

This last experiment concludes this discussion on Highlight Boxes. Here is a summary of what you learned:

- A Highlight Box is a rectangle used to highlight a particular spot on the slide.
- **Fill** is the inside of the Highlight Box object. The **Style** tab of the **Properties** inspector lets you choose the color and the opacity of the fill.
- **Stroke** is the border around the Highlight Box object. You can choose the style, the color, and the width of the stroke in the **Properties** inspector.
- Select the **Fill Outer Area** option to apply the fill color to the outside of the Highlight Box rather than to the inside.

Working with the mouse

The second object to study is the **Mouse**. Remember that during the filming, only the coordinates of the mouse clicks were recorded and that the mouse movements are recreated during the playback.

Understanding the mouse movements

You will start your study of the mouse object by discovering how Captivate manages the mouse movements:

1. If needed, use the **Filmstrip** panel to return to Slide 1 of the encoderDemo_800.cptx file.

You should see four red dots in the top left corner of the slide. These four dots mark the starting point of the mouse.

2. Use your mouse to move the four red dots anywhere on the slide.

By moving the four red dots, you change the starting point of the mouse on slide 1 as illustrated in the following screenshot:

From the chosen spot, Captivate generates a curved blue line that represents the mouse movement. This curved line ends with the mouse pointer.

3. Click the mouse pointer at the end of the curved blue line to select the Mouse object. The **Properties** inspector updates.

When a Mouse object is selected, the **Properties** inspector does not contain any tabs.

4. Select the **Straight Pointer Path** checkbox.

By clicking on this box, Captivate generates a straight line between the start and the end points of the mouse movement.

5. Deselect the **Straight Pointer Path** checkbox.
6. Use the **Filmstrip** panel to select slide 2.

On the second slide, the four red dots visible on slide 1 are not visible. It means that you cannot move the starting point of the mouse on slide 2. This is because the starting point of the mouse on slide 2 corresponds to the end point of the mouse on slide 1.

7. Use the **Filmstrip** panel to browse the remaining slides of the project.

When browsing the slides of the project, you should notice that the first slide is the only one where the starting point of the mouse movement can be moved. No other slides display the four red dots at the beginning of the curved blue line.

8. When done, return to slide 1.
9. Take the mouse pointer and move it to a random location.
10. Use the **Filmstrip** panel to select slide 2.

On slide 2, you should notice that the starting point of the curved blue line has changed and corresponds to the random location you chose on slide 1.

11. On the **Filmstrip** panel, click slide 1 to make it the active slide.
12. Move the mouse pointer back to its original location.
13. Use the **Filmstrip** panel to go to the last slide of the project.

On the last slide, the mouse makes a long movement. As this is the last slide of the project, this movement is unnecessary and you can remove the Mouse object from this slide.

14. On the last slide, right click the mouse pointer at the end of the blue line.
15. In the contextual menu, deselect the **Show Mouse** item. You can also use the **Modify | Mouse | Show Mouse** menu item to achieve the same result.

Note that the coordinates of the Mouse object as recorded during the filming are still saved with the slide should you change your mind about the Mouse being hidden on the last slide.

16. Use the **Filmstrip** panel to go to slide 14 of the `encoderDemo_800.cptx` file.

This is the slide where you typed `400` in the **Width** field of AME. The next slide (slide 15) is where the Mouse moves to click the **OK** button of the **Export Settings** dialog. For this particular sequence, you want to have a single action per slide. So, slide 14 should only show the typing in the **Width** field with no mouse movement. Slide 15 should show the entire Mouse movement.

17. Still on slide 14, right click the mouse pointer to select the Mouse object.
18. In the contextual menu, click the **Align to Previous Slide** item.

By clicking on the **Align to Previous Slide** item, the mouse pointer on slide 14 is aligned to the mouse pointer on slide 13. Consequently, the start and end points of the Mouse object on slide 12 have the same coordinates and the mouse no longer moves on slide 12. Another consequence is that the starting point of the mouse on slide 13 has changed to match the location of the mouse on slide 12, effectively transporting the entire mouse movement to slide 13.

19. Go to the **Preview** icon on the Toolbar to preview the entire project.
20. In the Preview pane, pay close attention to the mouse movements. Make sure each click occurs at the right place.
21. When the preview is complete, close the **Preview** pane.

22. If needed, adjust the position of the Mouse on the slides where the click area is not well positioned.
23. Save the file when done.

Formatting the mouse object

During the preview, you would have seen a blue circle and heard a click sound on most mouse clicks. These two options, and a few others, can be managed in the **Properties** inspector. The steps are as follows:

24. Use the **Filmstrip** panel to return to slide 1.
25. Once on slide 1, select the mouse pointer to make it the active object.
26. Take some time to inspect the properties available in the **Properties** inspector, as shown in the following screenshot:

Notice the two drop-down lists that let you chose the click sound to use (single click or double-click) and the shape of the visual click. You can also change the color of the visual click, if necessary.

The topmost part of the **Properties** inspector lets you choose the most appropriate mouse pointer. In this example, the default pointer is perfect, so you will not change it in this project.

Choosing the right mouse pointer

My very first big eLearning project was to build an online course on SAP for a big multinational company. SAP uses custom mouse pointers that I wanted to reproduce in Captivate. A mouse pointer is a .cur file, so I clicked on the **Browse** button right below the collection of mouse pointers in the **Properties** inspector and searched for the appropriate .cur file in the C:\Program files folder of Windows. I eventually found the .cur file I was looking for, and I could import it in Captivate. If you work on a Mac, you can inspect the content of an .app file by right clicking on the file and choose **Show package content**. You might find the .cur file you are looking for in the package. The bottom line is, your Captivate project should reproduce the behavior of the actual application as close as possible.

27. Use the **Filmstrip** panel to go to slide 8 and select the Mouse object.

Slide 8 is used to move the mouse pointer to the scroll bar of the **Export Settings** window before slide 9 uses a Full Motion Recording to show the scrolling movement. In the **Properties** inspector, the **Mouse Click Sound** and the **Show Mouse Click** checkboxes are therefore not selected.

This concludes your first exploration of the Mouse object. Let's quickly summarize what you learned in this section:

- During the capture, only the position of the mouse at each click is recorded. A mouse movement is recreated between these positions at runtime.
- By default, the mouse movement uses a curved line, but you can make it a straight line in the **Properties** inspector.
- The first slide of the project is the only slide where you can move both the start and the end points of the mouse movement.

- To prevent the mouse from moving on a given slide, right click the mouse pointer and choose **Align to Previous Slide** in the contextual menu.
- Removing the Mouse from a slide does not remove its coordinates. This makes it easy to turn the Mouse back on should you change your mind.
- Moving the mouse pointer on a slide also moves the origin of the mouse movement on the next slide.
- You can add a visual click as well as a click sound in the **Properties** inspector.

The Text Caption object

As you learned in Chapter 2, *Working with Standard Objects*, the **Text Caption** is the most basic object in Captivate. It is typically used to display text to learners.

During the screen recording, text captions are automatically generated in the form of captions with instructions to perform the steps, success captions, failure captions, and hint captions. Some of these might be just right, but most of them--if not all of them--need some extra work.

Modifying the content of a Text Caption

You have already learned in Chapter 2, *Working with Standard Objects* how to modify the text captions to change the formatting and timing of the text caption, and change the text in these captions.

Now you can modify the Text Caption properties and replace the text in the captions with meaningful instructions for the learners. When you are ready, save the file in the chapter08 folder and name it as encoderDemo_800_final.cptx.

Summary

In this chapter, you have explored different options to capture the screen and edit the properties of the objects automatically generated in these projects. Throughout this chapter, your main concern was to manage the size of the project as compared to the size of the application to capture.

Several approaches are possible to address this size issue. While experiencing each of these approaches you uncovered three important features of Captivate: Full Motion Recording (FMR), Panning, and responsive capture.

You also discovered that Captivate has four automatic recording modes that are **Demonstration**, **Assessment Simulation**, **Training Simulation**, and a **Custom** mode that is yours to create. Each of these automatic recording modes adds Text Captions and other objects to the slides.

The **Video Demo** recording mode is entirely dedicated to producing linear, non-interactive `.mp4` video files. These can be easily uploaded to online video hosting services such as YouTube, Vimeo, and Dailymotion.

The System Audio feature allows you to capture sound effects originating from the applications or from the system, in addition to the screenshots and the onscreen action.

You also learned how to modify the properties and styles of the automatically generated objects in the recorded projects.

In the next chapter, you will quickly review the Video Demo you captured in this chapter and generate an .mp4 video file that can be uploaded to YouTube.

Meet the community

In this section, it is our pleasure to introduce you to Akshay Bharadwaj. Akshay leads the Adobe team that builds Adobe Captivate. (He is the one we try to steal information from during conferences, but it never works!) He is also active in the community portal, writing blog posts, helping Captivate users, and commenting on Captivate news.

Damien

When I asked Akshay to author the Foreword of my fourth Captivate book, he was very enthusiastic and he wrote a great foreword. Whenever I have a chance to meet with him, I'm always impressed by his simplicity and his great sense of humor.

Pooja

I've been working with Akshay since 2011, and there's never been a conversation where I've not learned anything new from him. He has missed no chance to impress me with the data and current trends about eLearning, and his fantastic ideas to take Captivate to the next level. I feel privileged to have him as a colleague and friend!

Akshay Bharadwaj

Akshay Bharadwaj is the Senior Product Manager for Adobe Captivate. Akshay has helped build products across the eLearning and internet domains. In his eight years at Adobe, Akshay has seen Captivate evolve from primarily the strengths of a simulation tool to a comprehensive and responsive authoring tool. Apart from authoring tools, Akshay is also interested in building learning communities, the psychology of learning, and building next-generation learning experiences. Some of our experiments in this space can be seen in Adobe Knowhow. Akshay also loves interacting with customers and eLearning folks. You can reach him on any of the following social accounts.

Contact details

- **Blog**: https://elearning.adobe.com/
- **Twitter**: https://twitter.com/akshay_bh
- **Facebook**: http://www.facebook.com/adobecaptivate
- **LinkedIn**: https://www.linkedin.com/in/akshaybharadwaj/
- **YouTube**: http://www.youtube.com/adobeelearning/
- **Email**: akshay@adobe.com

9
Producing a Video Demo

Sometimes, all you need is a good old video file that you can embed into your website or upload to YouTube. In such cases, all you need is a Video Demo project. Video demos are used to create .mp4 video files that the learner experiences from the beginning to the end in a linear fashion. Therefore, the interactivity features of Captivate are not supported in Video Demos.

In this chapter, you will experience the entire Captivate production process using a Video Demo file as an example. First, you will return to the Video Demo you created in Chapter 8, *Capturing Onscreen Action*. Second, you will turn it into a professional screencast using the features in Captivate. Finally, you will publish it as an .mp4 video file. If you happen to have a YouTube account, you will even upload the video file to YouTube from within Captivate.

In this chapter, you will do the following:

- Tour the Video Demo interface
- Trim unwanted portions of the Video Demo
- Add objects in a Video Demo project
- Remove unwanted popups
- Add transitions and Pan & Zoom effects
- Publish the Video Demo as an .mp4 file
- Publish the Video Demo to YouTube

Preparing your work

To get the most out of this chapter, it is a good idea to reset the Captivate interface to default. If you are using the default interface mode, just close and restart Captivate to reset it. If you are using the advanced interface mode, use the **Window | Workspace | Reset 'Classic'** menu item to reset Captivate to default. In this chapter, you will use the exercises stored in the Chapter09 folder of the download associated with this course. If you get confused by any of the step-by-step instructions, take a look at the Chapter09/final folder, which contains a copy of the files, as they will be at the end of this chapter.

The Video Demo interface

For this chapter, you will use the Video Demo file that you created in Chapter 8, *Capturing Onscreen Action*. First, let's open this file and take a closer look at this project:

1. Start Captivate and open the Chapter09/encoderVideo.cpvc file.
2. Use the **Preview | Project** icon on the Toolbar and take the necessary time to view the entire project.

As you click the **Preview** icon, note that most of the previewing options are grayed out. The only thing that you can actually do is preview the entire project. Remember that a Video Demo project is aimed at producing an .mp4 video file. Such content plays in one big chunk from the beginning to the end with no interactivity whatsoever. Technically, it is said that a video file offers a *linear* experience, versus the nonlinear interactive experience of a regular project. It is therefore not based on slides, so the previewing options involving slides (Preview From this Slide, Preview Next Five slides, and so on) are, logically, unavailable.

3. At the end of the preview, click the **Edit** button in the bottom right corner of the screen to return to Edit mode.
4. Take some time to inspect the interface of Captivate.

When working on a Video Demo project (with a .cpvc file extension), the Captivate interface is a bit different than what you've been used to when working on a regular project (with a .cptx file extension). All these interface changes come down to the simple fact that the published version of the project can only be an .mp4 video file.

First, note that there is no **Filmstrip** panel on the left side of the screen. Since the project is not based on slides, this makes perfect sense. Also note that the **Interactions** icon on the toolbar is greyed out. Since video files do not support any kind of interaction, this, again, makes perfect sense.

5. Browse the other icons on the Toolbar and take good note of the objects that are available in a Video Demo project.
6. Click the **Properties** icon at the right end of the Toolbar.

As expected, this action opens the **Properties** inspector. Just next to the **Properties** inspector is the **Video Effects** panel.

7. Switch to the **Video Effects** panel and take some time to examine the available properties.

The **Video Effects** panel contains options and tools that are specific to Video Demo projects.

8. Take some time to further explore the interface. Try to spot other differences between the standard Captivate interface and the one used for Video Demo projects.

This concludes your first overview of Video Demo projects and the associated Captivate interface. Before moving on, let's make a quick summary of what you have learned so far:

- Video Demos are used to generate linear video files in .mp4 format.
- Video Demos use their own .cpvc file extension that is different from the .cptx extension used by the standard projects of Captivate.
- When working on a .cpvc project, the Captivate interface is slightly different from the standard interface of .cptx projects. Some panels, such as the **Filmstrip** panel, are not relevant to video files and are therefore not present in the interface. Other panels, such as the **Video Effects** panel, are specific to Video Demos projects, and are not available in the standard Captivate projects.

The post-production phase of a Video Demo

Remember that the Captivate production process is made of three phases. When it comes to this particular project, the first phase (the Capture phase) has already been done in Chapter 8, *Capturing Onscreen Action*. You will now dig into the second phase of the process.

Deleting unwanted portions of the Video Demo

When you are recording videos, it's very difficult to get everything right in one take. Adobe Captivate understands that, and allows you to trim out the unwanted portions from your Video Demo. Let's trim these unwanted portions from the video using the following steps:

1. Go to the **Timeline** panel. If it is not open, click the **Timeline** button at the bottom of the screen.
2. Move the Playhead to around the **1:25** timestamp on the timeline.
3. Click the **Play** button at the bottom of the timeline to play the video. Note that I made a mistake there, and then, after a few seconds, rephrased the same sentence.
4. You need to trim the portion where I made the mistake. To do so, bring the red playhead back to the **1:25** timestamp on the timeline. You may have to change the zoom of your timeline to see the **1:25** timestamp.
5. Then click the **Trim** button at the bottom of the timeline.
6. You will get Trim *Start* and *End* markers around the playhead. Either move the Trim Start Marker so that it begins at the playhead position, or click the **Snap trim start marker to playhead** button at the bottom of the Timeline.
7. Listen to the audio and place the Trim End marker right before the sentence is rephrased. You can also position the playhead at the end position, and then click the **Snap trim end marker to playhead** button.
8. If required, listen to the audio multiple times and make sure the marking is correct. Once you follow the next step, you will not be able to recover the deleted video portion.

As a best practice, save a copy of the Video Demo before making any further changes so that if something goes wrong, you have a master recording to fall back on.

9. Now, click the **Trim** button again to remove the unwanted portion of the video:

The unwanted portion of the Video Demo is now removed. Play the video to confirm that it looks and sounds good.

Adding objects to a Video Demo

First, you will take a closer look at the objects that can be added in a Video Demo project and explore how they can be used in the context of a linear video file.

Inserting images in a Video Demo project

You will create the beginning and the ending of the video using an image that you will overlay on top of the video track. Use the following steps to insert an image in the Video Demo:

1. Go to the **Timeline** panel. If it is not open, click the **Timeline** button at the bottom of the screen.
2. In the **Timeline** panel, make sure that the playhead (the vertical red line) is at the very beginning of the project. If it is not at the beginning, click the **Move the playhead to the beginning** icon, as shown in the following screenshot:

3. Use the **Media | Image** icon on the Toolbar to insert the `Chapter09/images/mftc-titleBkg_VideoDemo.png` at the beginning of the project.

The imported image appears in the **Timeline** panel, at the position of the playhead, as an extra layer on top of the video file.

4. Use the **Timeline** or the **Timing** panel to extend the duration of the image to 7.5 seconds.

The **Properties** and **Timing** panels of the image are exactly the same as in a regular project. Inserting images in a Video Demo is very similar to inserting images in a standard Captivate project.

Extra Credit –inserting the end image of the Video Demo

In this Extra Credit section, you will insert the very same image at the end of the Video Demo. Because the image has already been inserted in the project, it is available in the project Library and does not need to be imported a second time. The general steps go as follows:

1. Move the Playhead to around the **2:03** timestamp on the timeline.
2. Drag the `mftc-titleBkg_VideoDemo.png` file from the **Library** panel and drop it on top of the video.
3. Place the image in the top left corner of the video (**X** = 0 and **Y** = 0).
4. Extend the duration of the image to the end of the Video Demo.

After this extra credit section, the `mftc-titleBkg_VideoDemo.png` should be displayed at the beginning and at the end of the project.

Inserting objects in a Video Demo project

A small subset of the Captivate objects is supported in a Video Demo project. Supported objects include Smart Shapes, Highlight boxes, and Text Captions, among others. Inserting and formatting these objects in a Video Demo happens the exact same way as in a standard Captivate project. That's why this section of the book will not contain any step-by-step instructions, as it usually would. Instead, you will apply the skills you learned in the previous chapters to insert objects in the Video Demo project.

Your assignment goes as follows:

- Insert a rounded rectangle Smart Shape at the beginning of the project, on top of the image you inserted in the previous section. Write a nice title for the Video Demo and format it to your liking.
- Repeat the preceding operation to add a closing comment at the end of the project.
- When you feel like an area of the screen should be further highlighted, insert a Smart Shape and format it as a Highlight Box. Don't forget to use the **Timeline** panel to sync these Highlight Boxes with the rest of the Video file.
- Feel free to add other objects or Text Labels as you see fit.

After this section, your project Video Demo should contain Images, Highlight Boxes, and other objects used to further enhance the screencast. As far as these objects are concerned, there is nothing new to learn in this section. Just take this as an opportunity to practice your new skills in a new situation. If you get confused by this assignment, don't hesitate to take a look at the `Chapter09/final/encoderDemo.cpvc` file for clarification and inspiration.

Themes in a Video Demo

You probably noticed that the **Themes** icon on the Toolbar is disabled in a Video Project. This is because Themes are, unfortunately, not supported in a Video Demo project. Styles, however, are fully supported, including importing and exporting slides to and from other Captivate projects regardless of these projects being Video Demos or regular Captivate files.

Removing unwanted popups

In your Video Demo projects, you have the ability to remove unwanted popups and tooltips that were captured during the recording. In this project, there is such a tooltip between the **00:59** and the **01:01** mark in the **Timeline** panel. You will now remove this unwanted tooltip using the following steps:

1. Still in the `Chapter09/encoderDemo.cpvc` file, use the **Timeline** panel to place the red playhead around the **00:59** mark.
2. Use the **Play/Pause** icon at the bottom left corner of the **Timeline** panel to spot the exact timing where the unwanted tooltip appears and disappears.
3. When done, place the playhead to the point on the timeline that the tooltip appears on the screen.
4. Turn your attention to the **Video Effects** panel.

Remember that the **Video Effects** panel is tied to the **Properties** inspector. It may therefore be necessary to open the **Properties** inspector to access the **Video Effects** panel. Also remember that the **Video Effects** panel contains options that are specific to Video Demo projects.

5. Switch to the **Popup** tab of the **Video Effects** panel.
6. Click the **Replace** button and draw a rectangle on top of the unwanted yellow tooltip.
7. In the **Timeline** panel, extend the duration of the **Popup_Freeze_Item** so it matches the duration of the unwanted tooltip of the video track.

At the end of this process, this portion of the timeline should look like the following screenshot:

Thanks to this awesome and yet easy-to-use feature of Captivate 2017, you are now able to clear your video captures of unwanted popups and tooltips!

Adding Pan and Zoom

Another very nice and easy-to-use feature of Video Demos is the **Pan & Zoom** animation. It allows you to zoom in on a specific area of the video and to move the camera during the movie. In the next exercise, you will add two **Pan & Zoom** animations into this particular project by performing the following steps:

1. In the **Timeline** panel, move the playhead to the **01:01** mark in the **Timeline** panel.
2. Turn your attention to the **Pan & Zoom** tab of the **Video Effects** panel.
3. In the **Pan & Zoom** panel, click the **Add Pan & Zoom** button.

The **Pan & Zoom** panel updates and shows the available pan and zoom controls, along with a thumbnail image of the current frame of the video. A blue bounding box with eight handles surrounds this thumbnail image.

4. Resize and move the blue bounding box so it covers only the **Video** tab part of the thumbnail (see **1** in the following screenshot).

5. Increase the **Speed** value of the **Pan & Zoom** animation to 1 . 0 sec **(2)**, as shown in the following screenshot:

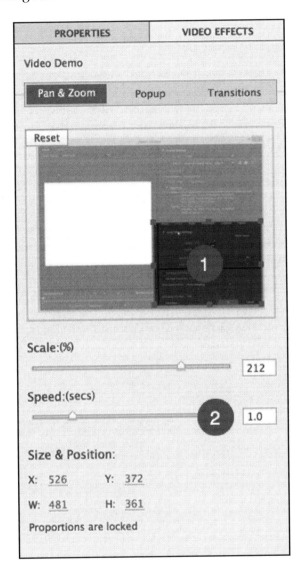

After this procedure, a Pan & Zoom icon appears in the **Timeline** panel. If you want to modify or delete the Pan & Zoom animation, just click this icon to load the properties of this **Pan & Zoom** animation in the **Pan & Zoom** panel.

6. Because of the **Pan & Zoom** effect, it may be necessary to move and resize some of the objects you added on top of the video in the previous section.

7. Earlier in this chapter, you trimmed an unwanted portion of the video. As a result of this trim, the video is split in two parts. Go ahead and add one more Pan & Zoom effect at the start of the second video portion. Make sure the size and position of the effect is the same as the previous **Pan & Zoom** effect.

8. Also decrease the **Speed** value of this Animation to 0.0 sec.

You will now move the playhead ahead on the **Timeline** panel and add the corresponding *Zoom Out* Animation.

9. In the **Timeline** panel, move the playhead more or less to the **1:30** mark.

10. Return to the **Pan & Zoom** tab of the **Video Effects** panel and click the **Zoom Out** button to restore the view.

11. Increase the **Speed** value of the Animation to 1.0 sec.

These actions add a second **Pan & Zoom** animation in the project, as indicated by the second Pan & Zoom icon in the **Timeline** panel around the **1:30** mark, as shown in the following screenshot:

Adding Transitions

Another way of adding a kind of animation to a Video Demo project is to add **Transitions**. A Transition defines how the project moves from one video clip to the next.

Because you trimmed the original video, you have two video clips in your project, so the only places you can add Transitions are at the very beginning of the project, the very end of the project, and the position where you trimmed the project. To add Transitions in any other portion of the video clip, you first have to *split* the video into smaller sequences. You will then be able to add transitions between these sequences. Let's check it out by performing the following steps:

1. In the **Timeline** panel, move the playhead to where the front title of the video finishes (see **1** in the following screenshot).

2. At the bottom of the **Timeline** panel, click the **Split** button, shown as **(2)** in the following screenshot:

This effectively splits the video file into two separate sequences, as indicated by the small diamond that appears in the **Timeline** panel at the exact location of the split. Because you have now split the video, it is possible to add a Transition between these two sequences.

3. Turn your attention to the **Transitions** tab of the **Video Effects** panel.

4. In the **Timeline** panel, click the diamond between the two sequences that you have split.

5. In the **Transitions** panel, choose a Transition of your liking. Note that as soon as you apply a transition effect, the color of the diamond on the timeline changes.

6. At the top of the **Transitions** tab, adjust the **Speed** of the Transition to your liking (Fast, Medium, or Slow).

7. Repeat the same sequence of actions at the end of the project (more or less at the **02:03** mark of the **Timeline** panel).

8. When done, use the **Preview | Project** icon on the Toolbar to take a look at the entire Video Demo.

During the preview, pay particular attention to the newly added **Pan & Zoom** and **Transitions**.

9. When the preview is finished, click the **Edit** button at the bottom right corner of the screen to return to edit mode.

10. Save the file when done.

This exercise concludes the post-production step of the process. Your Video Demo is now ready for publication, but before that, let's make a quick summary of what has been covered in this section:

- Unwanted portions of the video can be deleted using the Trim functionality in the Video Demo.
- Objects can be added on top of a Video Demo using the very same procedures and options as in a standard Captivate project.
- The only difference is that Video Demos only support a small subset of the objects available in Captivate. Interactive objects, such as Buttons and Rollover Objects, are, for example, not supported.
- Video Demos do not support Themes, but they fully support Styles, including importing and exporting styles to and from other projects.
- The **Video Effects** panel contains options that are exclusive to Video Demos.
- You can remove the unwanted popups and tooltips from the video.
- **Pan & Zoom** animations can be used to zoom in on a specific part of the screen and move the camera while playing the movie.
- **Transitions** can be added between two video clips. If your project is composed of a single big video track, you can split it into smaller sequences and add Transitions between these sequences.

Publishing a Video Demo

Due to its very nature, a Video Demo project can only be published as an `.mp4` video file. In the following exercise, you will explore the available publishing options and publish the `Chapter09/ecoderVideo.cpvc` project using the following steps:

1. Open or return to the `Chapter09/encoderVideo.cpvc` file.

2. Make sure the file opens in edit mode.

3. If you are not in edit mode, click the **Edit** button at the lower right corner of the screen (if the **Edit** button is not displayed on the screen, it simply means that you already are in edit mode).

4. Click the **Publish | Publish to Computer** icon or use the **File | Publish** menu item. In both cases, the **Publish Video Demo** dialog opens.

5. In the **Publish Video Demo** dialog, make sure the **Name** of the project is `encoderVideo`.

6. Click the **...** button and choose the `publish` folder of your exercises as the destination of the published video file.

7. Open the **Preset** dropdown. Take some time to inspect the available presets. When done, choose the **Video | Apple iPad** preset.

8. Make sure the **Publish Video Demo** dialog looks similar to what is shown in the following screenshot and click the **Publish** button:

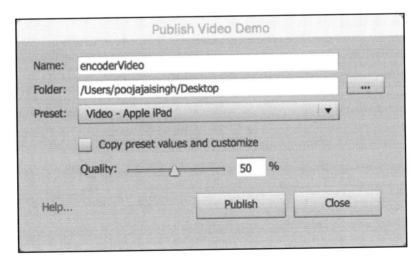

Publishing a Video Demo project can be quite a lengthy process, so be patient. When the process is complete, a message asks you what to do next. Note that one of the options enables you to upload your newly created video to YouTube directly.

9. Click the **Close** button to discard the message.
10. Use Windows Explorer (Windows) or the Finder (Mac) to go to the `publish` folder of your exercises.
11. Double click the `encoderDemo.mp4` file to open the video in the default video player of your system.

While enjoying the final product of your hard work, remember that a Video Demo project can only be published as a video file. Also remember that the published `.mp4` video file can only be experienced in a linear fashion, and does not support any kind of interactivity.

Publishing to YouTube

Captivate includes a workflow that allows you to upload the published video file to your YouTube account even without leaving Captivate. In the next exercise, you will experiment with this workflow using the following steps:

This exercise requires a working YouTube account. If you do not have a YouTube account, you can create one for free on the YouTube website (see `https://support.google.com/youtube/answer/161805?hl=en` for details) or read through the steps of the exercise.

1. Still in the `Chapter09/encoderVideo.cpvc` file, use the **File | Publish to YouTube** menu item to start the procedure.

Captivate directly converts your Video Demo into an `.mp4` video file without asking you to choose a preset. Since Captivate already knows that this video will be uploaded to YouTube, an appropriate preset is applied automatically.

2. When the publishing process is complete, click **Log in** in the **Publish to YouTube** window.
3. Sign in using your YouTube credentials.
4. You will get an alert that Adobe Captivate would like to manage your YouTube account and YouTube videos. Click **Allow** to confirm.

5. Once logged in, enter the relevant project information:

- Enter the title of the movie in the **Title** field.
- Enter a description in the **Description** field.
- Choose the level of **Privacy** (**Public**, **Private**, or **Unlisted**).
- Select the **I have read the terms & conditions** checkbox and click the **Upload** button.
- Enter a list of comma-separated tags. These tags will help YouTube reference your video so that other YouTube users can find it easily.
- Choose the best **Category** for your video.

Captivate will then upload the video to YouTube. When the process is complete, you can see a preview of the video in the same dialog. To go to the YouTube page and view the video, click the **YouTube** button in the bottom right corner of the video.

6. Now return to Captivate and click the **Close Window** button to close the **Publish to YouTube** window.

As you can see, Captivate makes it incredibly easy to publish a Video Demo to YouTube!

For more information on YouTube's privacy settings and the difference between a public and private video, visit
`https://support.google.com/youtube/answer/157177?hl=en`.

Inserting a Video Demo project in a regular project
When in a regular Captivate project based on slides (using the `.cptx` file extension), use the **Insert | CPVC Slide** menu item to create a new slide based on a Video Demo project. This is a great feature if you want to have your Video Demo file in the middle of a regular interactive project, or if you want to add quiz slides after your Video Demo.
To further edit the embedded Video Demo project, go to the Properties inspector, and click **Edit Video Demo**. This will open the Video Demo project for you. Here, you can make the changes and then click the **Exit** button on the top left corner to save the changes and return to the main project.

Summary

In this chapter, you have gone through the entire production process of a Video Demo project. Video Demos are a very special kind of project aimed at producing linear `.mp4` video files. They use their own file extension (`.cpvc`) and their own customized Captivate interface.

During the post-production phase, you have trimmed out the unwanted portions from your Video Demo. You have also learned how to place Captivate objects on top of the video file in order to enhance the screencast and provide the best possible experience to your learners. Inserting and formatting objects in a Video Demo works the exact same way as in a regular Captivate project. The only difference is the type of objects available. Since a Video Demo project can only be published as a linear video file, the interactive objects of Captivate are, logically, not supported.

On one hand, Video Demos only support a small subset of the Captivate tools and objects. But on the other hand, the **Video Effects** panel contains three tools (**Pan & Zoom**, **Popup**, and **Transitions**) that are only available in Video Demo projects. The Popup Removal tool allows you to remove unwanted popups and tooltips from your Captivate project.

Finally, you have performed the third and last step of the production process by publishing your project as an `.mp4` video file. You even uploaded that video directly to your YouTube channel without even leaving Captivate.

Video Demos are an excellent solution when all you need is to quickly create a short screencast. In the next chapter, you will explore responsive projects. These projects are yet another special type of project using a slightly customized interface. They allow you to optimize your eLearning course for multiscreen delivery, placing Captivate at the cutting edge of the multiscreen content production workflow.

Meet the community

In this section, we want to introduce you to Paul Wilson. Like all the nicest people in the world, Paul is based in Canada. Besides being a talented Adobe Captivate eLearning designer and developer, Paul is a YouTuber. He manages and creates YouTube video tutorials on his own YouTube channel dedicated to Adobe eLearning. You definitely want to bookmark his awesome YouTube channel, which had over 250 free video tutorials at the time of writing this book.

Damien

I first met Paul in Washington DC in April 2016 during the first annual east-coast Adobe eLearning conference. If you ever been to Washington, DC, you know that the international airport is very far away from the city. On our way back home, Paul and I shared the same taxi ride to get to the airport, which gave us 50 minutes of quality time chatting together.

Pooja

Paul is truly a hero in the Captivate community. The number of videos he has produced to teach the eLearning professionals how to use Captivate is mind blowing. I got to meet Paul in person during the last two Adobe conferences and really enjoyed talking to him.

Paul Wilson

Paul has been designing and developing Adobe Captivate for over 12 years. Getting into the training field by accident, Paul has worked as a senior instructional designer for companies such as Bell Canada and the Greater Toronto Airports Authority. When he decided to start his own eLearning development company, he began creating video tutorials on YouTube to share his knowledge of Adobe Captivate. As of summer 2017, his videos have been seen all over the world by hundreds of thousands of viewers, and his channel has over 5,000 regular subscribers. He works with companies all over the globe, consulting, designing, and teaching eLearning for a variety of organizations.

Contact details

- **Blog**: https://www.paulwilsonlearning.com/articles/
- **Twitter**: @paulwilsonLD
- **Facebook**: https://www.facebook.com/paulwilsonlearning/
- **LinkedIn**: https://www.linkedin.com/in/paul-wilson-ctdp-b096559/
- **YouTube**: http://www.youtube.com/PaulWilsonLearning

10
Creating a Responsive Project

In today's ultra-connected world, the majority of your students probably own multiple devices. And, of course, they want to be able to take your eLearning course on all of their devices. They might want to start the course on their desktop computer at work, continue it on their phone while commuting home, and finish it at night on their tablet. In other situations, students might only have a mobile phone available to take the course, and sometimes, the topic being taught only makes sense on a mobile device. To address these needs, you want to deliver your course on multiple screens, which is possible by creating a responsive project in Captivate.

A responsive project is a project that you can optimize for the desktop, the tablet, and the mobile phone. It is like providing several different versions of the course, based on the device size, in a single project.

In this chapter, you will be introduced to the key concepts and techniques required to create a responsive project in Captivate 2017. Keep in mind that everything you have learned so far can be applied to a Responsive Project.

In this chapter, you will:

- Create a new Responsive Project in Captivate 2017
- Explore the interface differences in Responsive Projects
- Use Fluid Boxes to create screen layouts
- Add objects to the Fluid Boxes and modify their properties
- Modify the flow, wrap, and alignment properties of the Fluid Boxes
- Use Optional and Static Fluid Boxes
- Modify the text properties in responsive projects
- Convert a non-responsive project to responsive
- Switch to the Breakpoint Mode

At the end of this chapter, your first responsive project will be ready for publishing and you will be at the cutting edge of the mobile learning revolution.

Preparing your work

To get the most out of this chapter, it is a good idea to reset the Captivate interface to default. If you are using the default interface mode, just close and restart Captivate to reset it. If you use the advanced interface mode, use the **Window | Workspace | Reset 'Classic'** menu item to reset Captivate to default. In this chapter, you will use the exercises stored in the Chapter10 folder of the download associated with this course. If you get confused by any of the step-by-step instructions, take a look at the Chapter10/final folder, which contains a copy of the files, as they will be at the end of this chapter.

Responsive projects

A responsive project is meant to be used on multiple devices, including tablets and smartphones that do not support Flash technology. Therefore, it can only be published in HTML5 format. This means that all the restrictions of a traditional HTML5 project also apply to a responsive project. For example, you will not be able to add Text Animations or Rollover Objects in a responsive project because these features are not supported in HTML5.

Creating a responsive project

It is now time to open Captivate and create your first responsive project using the following steps:

1. Open Captivate or close every open file.
2. On the Welcome screen, under the **New** tab, double click **Responsive Project**. Alternatively, you can also use the **File | New Project | Responsive Project** menu item.

This action creates a new responsive project. Note that the choice to create a responsive project or a regular Captivate project must be done upfront when creating the project. However, you can also convert an existing regular project created using Captivate 8 or 9 to a responsive project. You will learn about this workflow later in the chapter.

The workspace of Captivate should be very similar to what you are used to, with the exception of the **Preview in** device options and the **Preview Slider** spanning across the top of the stage.

These options will help you view how the content will be displayed on different device sizes, right inside the Captivate edit area.

3. Move the **Preview Slider** on the top right corner of the stage area to preview how the content will appear on different device sizes.

4. You can also open the **Preview in** dropdown list to view the content in specific device sizes.

Adding new Preview devices

If you wish to add more devices to the **Preview in** device list, first drag the **Preview Slider** to the position where it reflects the width of the new device, then click the + symbol, enter the new device name in the box, and finally click **OK**. If you are running Captivate in Admin Mode on Windows, any custom device added will show up for the project as well as any other project created in the future. However, when Captivate is running normally on Windows or Mac, any custom device added will be specific to that project. Also, if you save, close, and reopen the project, the custom devices will disappear from the list and you will need to add them again.

Resizing the Responsive Project

The default maximum width and height of responsive projects in Captivate 2017 is set to 1024 x 627. You can increase or decrease this by rescaling the project. Let's take a look at the steps required:

1. Make sure you have **Desktop** selected in the **Preview in** dropdown list. If not, open the dropdown and select **Desktop**. Notice that the width and height of the project is set to 1024 x 627.

2. To increase the width and/or height of the project, use the **Modify | Rescale Project** menu item.

3. In the **Rescale Project** dialog, deselect **Maintain Aspect Ratio**.

4. Enter the new width and height in pixels or as a percentage. Let's set the new width and height to 1280 x 768, which is a 16:10 ratio.

5. Click **Finish**.

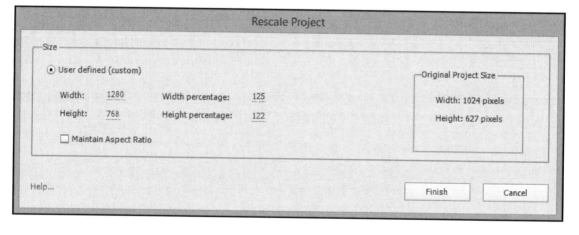

6. You will see an alert that the resize project operation cannot be undone. Click **OK** to confirm.

7. The maximum width and height of the project will now be changed to 1280 x 768. The new project height will automatically be reflected on the slide. You can move the Preview Slider to the right to view the slide contents in maximum width.

Fluid Boxes

Now that you have learned how to create a responsive project and resize it to the required size, it's time to design the responsive slides. The first step of designing responsive slides in Captivate 2017 is to add the Fluid Boxes.

Fluid Boxes are the containers which lay out your content intelligently as per the defined settings.

Adding Fluid Boxes

Let's take a deep dive into learning how to add Fluid Boxes, change their properties, and further add content to these Fluid Boxes.

1. If you still have the project open from the last exercise, close it. Then, open the `Chapter10/FluidBoxes.cptx` file.

2. Go to `Slide 3`. You can start adding Fluid Boxes to this blank slide.

3. On the Toolbar, click **FluidBox**. It gives you the option of selecting either a Horizontal or Vertical flow based on your screen layout requirements. Let's select **Vertical** in this example.

4. Now select the number of Fluid Boxes you wish to add. You can add up to 10 Fluid Boxes in each direction on the slide. Let's select 3 boxes here:

5. This creates one main Fluid Box on the screen, with three child Fluid Boxes. You can see the hierarchy of the Fluid Boxes anytime in the **Fluid Box Selector** section in the **Properties** inspector. Please note that the Fluid Box number you see on your computer might be different from the number you see here in the screenshot.

6. You can then resize the child Fluid Boxes by selecting the main Fluid Box, and then clicking and dragging the resize handles on the slide.

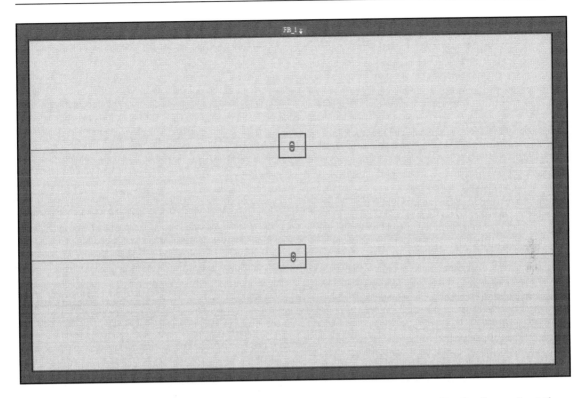

7. You can further add child Fluid Boxes to these Fluid Boxes. To do that, select the Fluid Box on the slide to which you wish to add child Fluid Boxes. Let's select the second Fluid Box here.

8. On the toolbar, click **Fluid Box | Horizontal** or **Vertical** based on your preferences and then select the number.

9. Resize the Fluid Boxes using the resize handles, if required.

10. Continue adding Fluid Boxes until you get the desired layout for the screen. Notice that the **Fluid Box Selector** in the **Properties** inspector starts showing all the Fluid Boxes in a nested view.

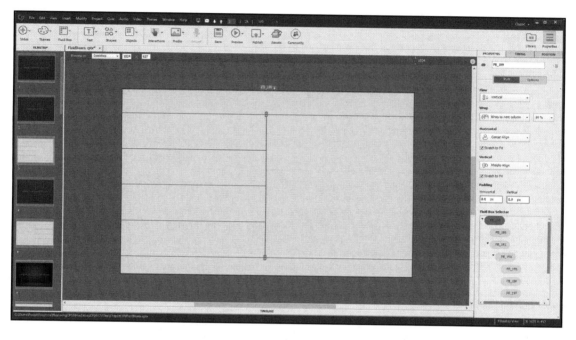

11. From the **Fluid Box Selector**, you can easily switch to any other Fluid Box and modify their properties, or you can directly select the Fluid Box on the slide by clicking on the Fluid Box.

12. To select the main Fluid Box on the slide, hover over the border of the slide. When you see a teal green boundary around the slide, click it to select the main Fluid Box.

13. You can also rename each of these Fluid Boxes by selecting the Fluid Box and changing the name in the **Properties** inspector from FB_<number> to something more meaningful.

You have now successfully created a slide layout using Fluid Boxes. In the next section, you will learn how to add objects to the Fluid Boxes. But before that, let's summarize the key points we've covered up to this point:

- A responsive project works well on any device size.
- Responsive projects can be published only in HTML5 format.
- You can preview how the content will be displayed on different device sizes in the Captivate edit area, using the Preview Slider and **Preview in** dropdown list.
- The default maximum dimension of responsive projects is 1024 x 627, and you can increase or decrease it by rescaling the project.
- Fluid Boxes are the containers which lay out your content intelligently as per the defined settings.
- The Fluid Boxes in Captivate can flow either vertically or horizontally.
- You can add up to 10 Fluid Boxes in each direction on the slide.
- The Fluid Boxes can be resized on the slide using the resize handles.
- You can add child Fluid Boxes to each Fluid Box on the slide.

Adding Objects to Fluid Boxes

Now let's learn how to add objects to the Fluid Boxes.

1. In the FluidBoxes.cptx file, go to Slide 5. Fluid Boxes are already added to this slide.
2. Select one of the Fluid Boxes and then go to the Toolbar, click **Media | Image** and open the Chapter10/Images/Image1.png file.

The image has now been added to the selected Fluid Box.

If you don't have a Fluid Box selected when adding objects to the slide, the object will be added to the center of the slide and not linked to any of the Fluid Boxes. You can then drag and move the object to the desired Fluid Box.

3. To move the image to another Fluid Box, click and drag the image to another Fluid Box. When you see a blue highlight in the desired Fluid Box, drop the image. The image will now move to the new Fluid Box.

You will notice that the size of the image changes when it is moved to a smaller or bigger Fluid Box, but the aspect ratio for the image is maintained. This happens because the Maintain Aspect Ratio option for images is selected by default.

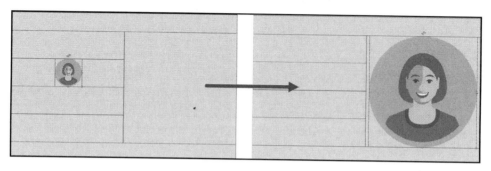

4. With the image still selected, go to the **Properties** inspector and you will notice that the **Maintain Aspect Ratio** option is selected. Deselect the option and the image will be resized to fill the entire Fluid Box.
5. Selecting the **Maintain Aspect Ratio** option again will bring it back to normal.

For objects like Images, Shapes, Buttons, etc., the **Maintain Aspect Ratio** option is selected by default. For Text Captions, it is disabled by default, so that the text is able to fill the entire Fluid Box and flows based on the device's width and height.

6. Now select an empty Fluid Box.
7. Go to the Toolbar and click **Text | Text Caption**.
8. Notice that the Text Caption takes up the entire Fluid Box space end-to-end.
9. Now select the Fluid Box to which you added the Image1.png image. Then, go to the Toolbar, click **Media | Image** and open the Chapter10/Images/Image2.png file.

Notice that the Image1.png image resizes to make space for Image2.png.

10. Similarly, add Image3.png and Image4.png in the same Fluid Box. The images will further resize to make space for new objects.

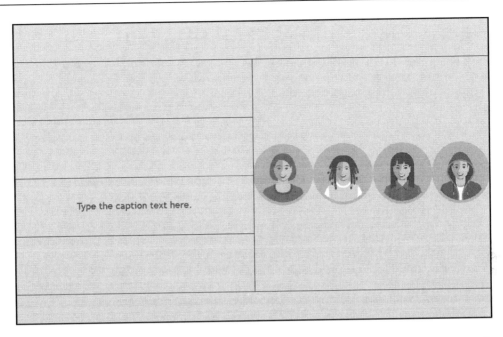

Type the caption text here.

11. You can also change the order of these objects by dragging and dropping the object at the desired location in the Fluid Box.

12. Drag the Preview Slider on the top right corner of the slide to see how these objects will realign on the slide based on the dimension of the device.

Another requirement when adding objects can be that you want to add the object, but don't want to associate it with any Fluid Box. You want this object to be present on the screen at the same position, regardless of the device size.

13. In such cases, you can select the object and select **Unlock from Fluid Box** in the **Properties** inspector.

14. Unlike the other objects, moving the unlocked object will not prompt you to add it to any of the Fluid Boxes. To add it back to one of the Fluid Boxes, uncheck **Unlock from Fluid Box** and move it to the desired Fluid Box.

This will give you an idea of how well the objects are sized and positioned automatically on the slide. If you don't like the way the objects are flowing, don't worry, you will learn how to change the properties of Fluid Boxes and objects so that you can make them look the way you like!

Using the Fill option for Fluid Boxes

The Fill option for Fluid Boxes is the best way to add a background color, gradient, or images to the slide or objects. The Fill option for Fluid Boxes works in exactly the same way as the Fill option for Smart Shapes, which was covered in Chapter 2, *Working with Standard Objects*.

1. In the FluidBoxes.cptx file, go to Slide 7. Fluid Boxes are already added to this slide.
2. Select the main Fluid Box. Remember that you can use the **Fluid Box Selector** in the **Properties** inspector to easily select the main Fluid Box.
3. In the **Properties** inspector, switch to the **Options** tab. Here, you will find the **Fill** option for Fluid Boxes. You can fill the Fluid Boxes with a solid color, gradient, or an image. Let's fill the main Fluid Box with an image.
4. Select the **Image Fill** option from the first dropdown under the Fill section.

5. Then, open the second dropdown and click the **Browse** icon (the icon of a folder).
6. In the **Select Image/Audio from Library** dialog, click **Import**.
7. Open the Chapter10/Images/Background.jpeg file.
8. Similarly, if you wish to apply background fill to any other Fluid Box on the slide, you can select that Fluid Box and apply the Fill.

Modifying the properties of Fluid Boxes

You've got a good headstart with creating responsive courses in Captivate 2017 using Fluid Boxes. You have learned how to add Fluid Boxes, resize the boxes on the slide, add objects to Fluid Boxes, and fill them with background color or images.

Captivate assigns some default properties to the Fluid Boxes, which automatically flows, aligns, and wraps the objects on smaller device sizes. Now, let's learn how to modify these default settings to get your desired result.

1. In the `FluidBoxes.cptx` file, go to `Slide 9`. Fluid Boxes and some images are already added to this slide.
2. Select the main Fluid Box and go to the **Properties** inspector.
3. Switch to the **Style** tab. Here you will find the **Flow**, **Wrap**, **Horizontal**, and **Vertical** alignments, as well as **Padding** properties for the Fluid Box.

Let's talk about these properties before making any modifications.

Flow: The Flow property denotes the direction in which the objects will be laid out. When this Fluid Box was added to the slide, the direction specified was **Vertical**. The same is shown in the Flow dropdown. If, after adding the Fluid Box, you wish to change the direction, you can change it from the **Properties** inspector by changing the **Vertical** flow to **Horizontal**, or the **Horizontal** flow to **Vertical**.

Wrap: With the Wrap property, you can control when and how the objects wrap to the next row on the smaller device sizes. There are four different wrapping options available for the horizontal flow:

- **Wrap to the next row**: Wrap to the next row is the default wrap property for Fluid Boxes. When the wrap point reaches its threshold and can no longer hold all of the objects in the same row, the last object in the Fluid Box is moved to the next row, and then when it hits the threshold again, the second to last object is moved to the next row. This happens in a sequence and the objects are moved to the next row one at a time.
- **Squeeze in a row**: If you don't want the images to wrap to the next row and want them all to appear in the same row, you can select the **Squeeze in a row** option. With this property, instead of the images moving to a new row, the image size will shrink to allow them all to fit when the screen size gets smaller.
- **One Row/Column**: This property will squeeze the objects in a single row or a single column. When the wrap point reaches the threshold, the objects move from being horizontally aligned to vertically aligned.

- **Symmetrical**: The last wrap property is symmetrical, which moves the objects to the next row in groups, instead of moving one object at a time. For example, if you have four objects in a Fluid Box, it will move two objects together to the next row on smaller device sizes so that the first and the second row have an equal number of objects.

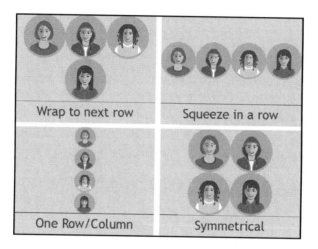

Similar to these options, there are four wrapping options available for the vertical flow: Wrap to next column, Squeeze in a column, One Row/Column, and Symmetrical.

Now let's modify these properties to see how the objects behave:

4. We are still on `Slide 9` in the `FluidBoxes.cptx` file. Select the Fluid Box on the right side of the screen, which has four images added to it. Notice that the **Flow** for the Fluid Box is set to **Horizontal**.

5. Change the **Wrap** property to **Squeeze in a row** and move the **Preview Slider** to see how the images wrap on smaller device sizes.

6. Similarly, switch to the other two **Wrap** properties and preview how the images wrap on smaller device sizes for those wrap properties.

7. Now change the **Flow** for the fluid box to **Vertical**, change the **Wrap** properties, and preview how the images wrap on smaller devices.

Align: As the name indicates, this option will allow you to decide how to align the objects in the Fluid Boxes.

- **Left align**: Use this option to left-align the objects. The first object will be placed at the left-hand side of the Fluid box and the others will follow.

- **Center align**: The objects will be center-aligned in the Fluid Box.
- **Right align:** The objects will be right-aligned in the fluid box. The last object will be placed at the right of the Fluid box and the others will be placed after it in a right-to-left direction.
- **Top align**: The objects will be top-aligned in the Fluid Box.
- **Middle align**: The objects will be middle-aligned in the Fluid Box.
- **Bottom align**: The objects will be bottom-aligned in the Fluid Box.
- **Space in Between**: The objects will be evenly distributed in the Fluid Box. The first object will be placed on the left and the last object on the right side of the Fluid Box.
- **Space Around**: The objects will be evenly distributed in the Fluid Box with equal space around the objects.

Now let's apply these alignment options one by one to the Fluid Box with images to see how it appears.

8. But before that, deselect the **Stretch to Fit** options for both the **Horizontal** and **Vertical** alignment properties.

9. Now select each option from the **Horizontal** and **Vertical** alignment dropdown list and see how the alignment changes based on your selection.

Padding: If you need some space around the objects in the Fluid Boxes, you can add padding from 0 to 50 pixels in both the horizontal and vertical direction. This option is especially useful for text inside the Fluid Boxes.

You have now covered all the basics for adding objects to Fluid Boxes and modifying the properties of the Fluid Boxes. Let's summarize what you have learned so far:

- You can add an object to a Fluid Box by selecting it and then adding the object. Alternately, you can first add the object to the slide and then move it to the required Fluid Box.

- Objects can be easily moved from one Fluid Box to another Fluid Box by dragging and dropping the objects on the stage.

- Use the **Maintain Aspect Ratio** option to avoid distorting the shape of the object added.

- You can add multiple objects to a single Fluid Box. The size and position of the existing objects are adjusted to accommodate the new objects added to the Fluid Box.

- The order of objects in the Fluid Box can be changed by dragging and dropping the object at the desired position.

- You can position the object outside the Fluid Box by selecting the **Unlock from Fluid Box** option.

- You can fill the Fluid Boxes with a background color, gradient, or image. The fill options are similar to those of the Smart Shape Fill option.

- You can change the flow of the objects in Fluid Boxes from horizontal to vertical, and vice versa.

- By default, the objects will be wrapped to the next row/column when it reaches the threshold, but you can change the wrapping behavior to squeeze in a row/column, one row/column, or be symmetrical.

- You can also align the objects in the Fluid Boxes. The options available are: Left align, Center align, Right align, Top align, Middle align, Bottom align, Space in Between, and Space Around.

Marking Fluid Boxes/objects as optional

In eLearning courses, some of the objects are critical for learning, while others are less important, and sometimes only decorative. These less important objects can take up a lot of space on smaller devices and may take away student's attention from the critical objects. In addition, these objects may simply contribute less to learning as the object gets smaller. For example, a map of a company property is helpful when it's large, but it's unreadable when viewed on smaller devices. In such cases, you can mark the less important fluid boxes or objects as optional. This will show all the objects on screens with a bigger dimension, but as the screen dimension decreases, the optional objects automatically disappear to make more space for critical objects.

Let's first look at the workflow for marking objects in a Fluid Box as optional:

1. In the `FluidBoxes.cptx` file, go to `Slide 11`. Fluid Boxes and some images are already added to this slide.
2. Select one of the images on the slide.
3. Go to the **Properties** inspector and select **Optional**.

4. Then select the Fluid Box and change the Wrap property to **Squeeze in a row**. This step is very important, as the **Optional** property works only with the **Squeeze in a row** wrap setting.

5. Notice that the **Wrap** threshold is set to 80%. You can increase or decrease it as per your requirement.

By default, the Wrap threshold property is available only for the main Fluid Box on the slide. If you need to set different threshold properties for the child Fluid Boxes as well, you can enable this property. Open the **Preferences** dialog and switch to the **Defaults** category. In the **General** section, select **Enable WrapPoint** and click **OK**. You will now be able to change the Wrap threshold points for all the Fluid Boxes.

6. Move the **Preview Slider**. You will notice that for smaller devices, the image marked as optional disappears from the screen and the others automatically adjust their size and position to cover the entire space.

Similarly, you can mark the entire Fluid Box as optional. Here are the steps required:

7. In the `FluidBoxes.cptx` file, go to `Slide 12`. On this slide, the images are placed in separate Fluid Boxes.
8. Select one of the Fluid Boxes with images.
9. Go to the **Properties** inspector and select **Optional**.

10. Then select the main Fluid Box and change the **Wrap** property to **Squeeze in a row**.

11. Move the **Preview Slider**. You will notice that for smaller devices, the Fluid Box marked as optional disappears from the screen and the other Fluid Boxes automatically adjust their size and position to cover the entire space.

Modifying the text properties

When you add text to Fluid Boxes in Captivate 2017, the text automatically scales down on the smaller devices, corresponding to the font size selected for the text caption. You also have the ability to define a minimum font size so that the text is readable on smaller devices.

1. In the `FluidBoxes.cptx` file, go to `Slide 14`. Notice that this slide has a lot of text.

2. Let's preview this slide to see how the text scales on smaller devices. For previewing text, you should not use the **Preview Slider** in the edit area, as it will not show you the true text scaling. Go to the Toolbar and click **Preview | Next 5 Slides** to preview the slide.

3. In the Browser, click the **Pause** button on the Course Playbar.

4. Now move the slider above the slide to see how the content appears on smaller device sizes. You will notice that as you move to the smaller device sizes, the text scales to fit the width and height of the viewing area.

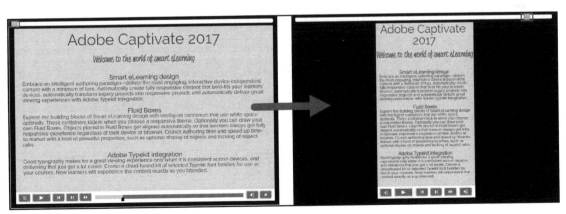

5. When the text is no longer able to fit on the slide, a **Read More** button appears. You can click the button to read the whole text, and then after reading you can click anywhere on the screen to dismiss it.

6. Now close the browser and get back to the Captivate project.
7. In the **Properties** inspector for the slide, under the **Style** tab, you can change the **Minimum Font Size**. The default size is set to 14 pixels. You can increase or decrease the minimum size based on your requirements.
8. Also, if you have text with different lengths in different Fluid Boxes, you can select the **Enable Uniform Text Scaling** option to make sure that all the text captions on the slide scale at the same time.

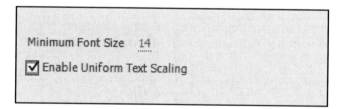

Marking Fluid Boxes as static

In eLearning courses, we often have content that is overlaid on top of each other or is positioned relative to each other. For example, a Highlight Box on top of a screenshot, an arrow around the Button indicating that it needs to be clicked, a Caption close to the Character image, a description on top of the image, and so on. In such situations, the regular Fluid Boxes will not work, as they will line up the objects next to each other and will not allow you to overlay them and change the position of the object to absolute.

Also, if you have to use a multi-state object on the slide and need to add additional objects to the states, it will not be supported by normal Fluid Boxes. In such cases, you will need to convert the normal Fluid Boxes to Static Fluid Boxes.

Here are the steps required:

1. In the `FluidBoxes.cptx` file, go to `Slide 16`.
2. Select the Fluid Box with the image.
3. Go to the **Properties** inspector and select the **Static** option.

Notice that as soon as you select the Static option, the other options related to Flow, Wrap, Alignment, and so on disappear. See the blank space under the Style tab.

4. Now you have the control to move and resize the image inside the Fluid Box.
5. Move the image to the bottom left corner of the Fluid Box, and make it a little smaller so that we have some space for the Text Caption.

6. Now drag the caption from the scrap area to the Static Fluid Box and position it on the top right corner of the Fluid Box, with the caption overlapping the image a bit.

7. Move the **Preview Slider** to see that even when the fluid boxes are realigned, the relative position of the image and caption remains the same.

Using Fluid Boxes with Master Slides

Fluid Boxes on Master Slides work in the same way as they work on the normal slides, apart from a few differences, as follows:

- Fluid Boxes on Master Slides cannot be named
- When a slide is associated with a Master Slide, the Fluid Boxes from the Master Slide are inherited by the slide
- These inherited Fluid Boxes cannot be deleted, but they can be resized
- Along with these inherited Fluid Boxes on the slide, new Fluid Boxes can be added or deleted on the slide

Exploring the possibilities

Now that you have covered all the basics of using Fluid Boxes in Captivate, you are ready to create responsive courses using Fluid Boxes. Like any new workflow, you might need to tweak your course design a bit in order that it lends itself well to the responsive layout. Don't shy away from reimagining how you would be presenting the content to your students.

To get some ideas on how to create responsive courses using Fluid Boxes, explore the example course included with Captivate 2017.

1. Start Captivate 2017. If you already have the Captivate application open, close all the open projects so that you have the Welcome screen visible.
2. On the Welcome screen, click the **Sample Projects/Tutorials** icon.
3. Select the **Adobe_Captivate_2017_Training** thumbnail and click **Open**.

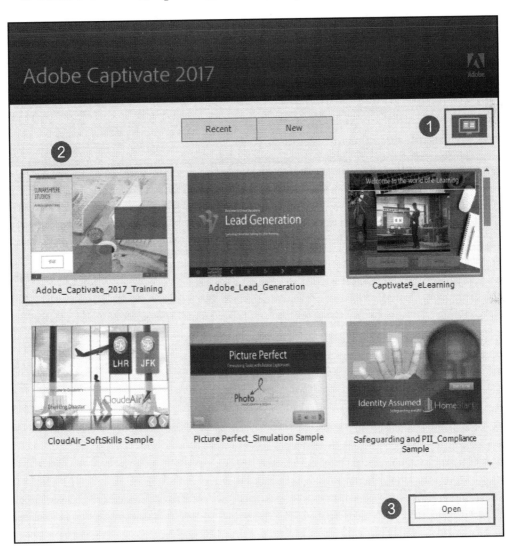

4. This opens the Adobe Captivate 2017 training course for you. Explore how the content is laid out on the slides and how different Fluid Box and object properties have been used to bring it all together. You can also learn about the new features of Captivate 2017 along the way.

Converting a Non-responsive project to Responsive

If you have an existing non-responsive course created using Captivate 8 or 9, you can convert it to a responsive course in Captivate 2017. This will allow you to repurpose the static courses into responsive ones, and this will save you from spending hours converting the course to responsive from scratch.

Let's see an example of converting a non-responsive course to a responsive one.

1. Start Captivate 2017. If you already have the Captivate application open, close all the open projects so that you have the Welcome screen visible.
2. On the Welcome screen, click the **Sample Projects/Tutorials**icon.
3. Select the **Captivate9_eLearning** thumbnail and click **Open**.

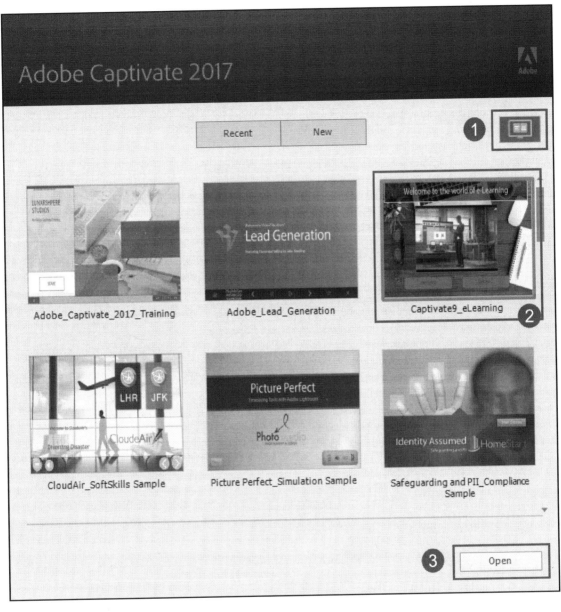

4. This opens **Captivate9_eLearning** course in Captivate. It is a non-responsive course built using Captivate 9.
5. To convert this course to responsive, click **File | Save as Responsive**.

6. You will get an alert that some of the items in non-responsive projects may not be supported after upgrade. Do you wish to proceed?

7. Click **Show Unsupported Items** to see the unsupported slides or objects in the HTML5 output, or click **Save** to proceed.

8. Rename the project as Responsive.cptx and save it in the Chapter10 folder.

9. Click **Save**. The project has now been converted to a responsive project, but the Fluid Boxes are not yet added to the project.

There are two options for adding Fluid Boxes to each slide. The first option is to manually add Fluid Boxes by using the options from the Toolbar, and then to drag the objects inside the Fluid Boxes. Alternately, you can click the **Suggest Fluid Boxes** button in the **Properties** inspector, and Captivate will automatically add Fluid Boxes and add all the slide objects to them.

10. Let's add Fluid Boxes to one of the slides in this project. Select the second slide.

11. Go to the **Properties** inspector and click **Suggest Fluid Boxes**.

12. The Fluid Boxes are automatically added to the slide and the objects are placed inside the Fluid Boxes. Click **Preview | Next 5 slides**.

By following these few simple steps, you can convert existing non-responsive courses to responsive. If you don't like the way content is flowing on your slide, change the properties of the Fluid Boxes to your liking, and you'll have a perfectly responsive course ready to be served to students!

Switching to Breakpoint Mode

Responsive eLearning was added to Captivate back in version 8, but Fluid Boxes are new to version 2017. In Captivate 8 and 9, Adobe used a completely different approach to create responsive eLearning. This approach, based on breakpoints and viewport sizes, is still available today in Captivate 2017.

- **Breakpoints** are the different layouts that are designed based on the viewport size of the devices your students use.
- **Viewport size** is the visible area (excluding the area covered by the address bar and other menu options) in the device browser.

You can use the older Breakpoints approach if you have an older responsive project to maintain, or if you feel more at ease with the Breakpoint approach rather than with the new Fluid Boxes approach.

Follow these steps to switch to the Breakpoint Mode in Captivate 2017:

1. Create a new responsive project in Captivate 2017.
2. Click **File | Save**, navigate to the `Chapter 10` folder, and save the file as `Breakpoints.cptx`.
3. Click the **Project** menu and select **Switch to Breakpoint Mode**.
4. You will get an alert that all your Fluid Box layouts will be lost. Click **Yes** to confirm.
5. This will give you another opportunity to save the file with a new name so that you don't lose your work. We have created a brand new project, so let's click **Save** to continue using the same name.
6. Click **Yes** to replace the existing project.
7. This creates the project in Breakpoint Mode and you can continue from here to create responsive projects in a similar fashion as in Captivate 9.

Responsive eLearning with Breakpoints:
Here are a few handy resources for learning how to create responsive projects in the Breakpoint Mode:

How do I create my first responsive project?: `http://bit.ly/ Cp9FirstResponsive`

Tips and Tricks for Creating Responsive Courses: `http:// poojajaisingh.com/pooja/cp9/responsive.pdf`

Create responsive eLearning with Adobe Captivate 8: `https://www. adobeknowhow.com/courselanding/create-responsive-elearning- adobe-captivate-8`

Summary

After reading this chapter, you will have been exposed to the tools and techniques used to create a responsive eLearning project.

Remember that the basic idea of a responsive project is to let you optimize the way the project looks on mobile devices. To do this, Captivate uses Fluid Boxes to automatically lay out the content on the screen so that it looks good on all device sizes. The default properties of Fluid Boxes give you a nice result, but you can modify these defaults to make the content look better for smaller devices.

If you are more comfortable creating your responsive eLearning courses using the legacy breakpoints mode, or if you have to maintain responsive projects created with Captivate 8 or 9, you can still switch to the legacy breakpoint mode.

Another new feature of Captivate 2017 is the ability to save a regular (non-responsive) Captivate project as a responsive project. However, as a responsive project can only be published in HTML5, keep in mind that some objects cannot be carried over in a responsive project, and you might need to adjust a few things manually after the conversion.

With a bit of practice and a lot of testing throughout your development, you'll soon be an expert at creating responsive eLearning content that your students will be able to use across all their devices.

In the next chapter, you will learn how Captivate integrates with other applications like Microsoft PowerPoint, Microsoft Word, Adobe Audition, and Adobe Photoshop.

Meet the community

In this section, it is our pleasure to introduce you to Michael Lund, also known as CpGuru. Michael is an eLearning designer and a Captivate expert located in Denmark. He is one of the key members of the worldwide Captivate community and specializes in the development of Captivate Widgets. Make sure you take a look at his blog and at his awesome collection of Widgets.

Michael Lund

Michael, also known as CpGuru, has been a part of the Adobe Captivate community since Version 2 and started experimenting early on with pushing Captivate to the limit and expanding its functionality with custom Flash components. He is an active participant on the Adobe Captivate forums and a community champion on `http://captivate.adobe.com/`.

He runs the website `www.cpguru.com` where he provides tips and tricks on common issues and problems with Adobe Captivate and tutorials on how to achieve more advanced things with Adobe Captivate.

The site also has a number of free and commercial Widgets for Adobe Captivate that can help you achieve more with your Adobe Captivate projects. Michael also provides freelance support and troubleshooting and develops custom Adobe Captivate Widgets if you need to achieve something special in your projects.

Contact details

- Twitter: `@cpguru_com`
- E-mail: `support@cpguru.com`
- Website: `www.cpguru.com`

11
Using Captivate with Other Applications

In this chapter, you will explore how Captivate can be used with other applications. These external applications include Adobe products such as Audition, Illustrator, and Photoshop. However, Captivate can also integrate with third-party applications such as Microsoft Word and Microsoft PowerPoint.

There are many benefits to using Captivate with these external applications. If your company already has a significant amount of training material made with PowerPoint, you'll be able to use this existing material and build on what already exists. If you are localizing your content, you can export your Text Captions and Slide Notes to Microsoft Word for your translators to use, where the translators won't need any knowledge of Captivate to help you localize your eLearning content.

In this chapter, you will:

- Create a new Captivate project from a PowerPoint presentation
- Add a PowerPoint slide in the middle of an existing Captivate project
- Explore the round trip editing workflow between Captivate and PowerPoint
- Localize a Captivate project by exporting the Text Captions and Slide Notes to Microsoft Word, and reimporting them back into Captivate once translated
- Import a Photoshop document into Captivate
- Explore the round tripping operations with Adobe Audition
- Edit SVGs in Captivate projects with Adobe Illustrator
- Export the project to an XML file

Preparing your work

At the beginning of this chapter, it is a good idea to take some time and reset the Captivate interface to default. If you are using the default interface mode, just close and restart Captivate and you're good to go. If you use the advanced interface mode, use the **Window | Workspace | Reset 'Classic'** menu item to reset Captivate to default. In this chapter, you will use the exercises stored in the Chapter11 folder. If you get confused by any of the step-by-step instructions, take a look at the Chapter11/final folder, which contains a copy of the files, as they will be at the end of this chapter.

Integrating Captivate with PowerPoint

In this section, you will discover the integration that unites Microsoft **PowerPoint**and Adobe Captivate. This integration includes many features such as creating a new Captivate project from a Microsoft PowerPoint presentation or including some slides of a presentation in an existing Captivate project.

Captivate shares these features with another software product from Adobe called **Adobe Presenter 11**. Adobe Presenter 11 is a Microsoft PowerPoint plug-in. In PowerPoint 2007 and later versions, Presenter installs an extra ribbon at the top of the PowerPoint interface. Presenter can be used to publish a PowerPoint presentation to HTML5 and/or SWF using a technique that is similar to what is used in Captivate. Presenter also includes the ability to add narration and subtitles to a PowerPoint presentation and includes pretty much the same quiz engine as the one used in Captivate. One of the best features of Presenter is the Adobe Presenter Video Express, which allows you to create stunning professional screencasts. The Adobe Presenter PowerPoint plug-in is only available on Windows. Adobe Presenter Video Express is available on both Mac and Windows. More info can be found at
http://www.adobe.com/products/presenter.html.

Converting an existing presentation to Captivate

In the first exercise of this chapter, you will convert an existing PowerPoint presentation into a new Captivate project. You will use a simple workflow that allows you to open a PowerPoint file from the Welcome Screen of Captivate. But first, let's take a look at the original PowerPoint presentation.

Viewing the presentation in PowerPoint

If PowerPoint is available on your system, take a look at the presentation before converting it into a Captivate project. Perform the following steps to view the presentation in PowerPoint:

1. Open Microsoft PowerPoint.
2. When in PowerPoint, open the `Chapter11/Presentation.pptx` presentation in the exercises files.
3. Use the **Slide Show** | **From Beginning** menu item or hit the *F5* shortcut key to start the slideshow.

While viewing the presentation, focus your attention on the following:

- The presentation has 11 slides.
- There is a transition between all the slides of the presentation.
- The presentation is mainly composed of text and images. Most of it is animated.
- The presentation also contains smart art, shapes, and a table.
- Some of the effects used to animate the objects of PowerPoint have an equivalent in Captivate, but some do not.
- Sometimes a mouse click is needed to go to the next step of the presentation, but sometimes not.
- Slide 2 of the presentation includes Slide Notes.
- The last slide of the presentation has a hyperlink to a blog article on the internet.

Grammatical errors and typos have been intentionally left over in the presentation. Don't correct them; they will be used to demonstrate the round tripping workflow between Captivate and PowerPoint.

4. Close PowerPoint without saving the changes made to the presentation.

You will now convert this presentation into a Captivate Project and see how the PowerPoint features listed previously are carried over (or not) into Captivate.

Creating a Captivate Project from a PowerPoint presentation

In this section, you will convert the file you have viewed in PowerPoint, into a Captivate project.

Should you use .ppt or .pptx?

Captivate can import both .ppt and .pptx files. However, when importing a .pptx file, it must first be converted to .ppt before being imported into Captivate. The conversion from .pptx to .ppt requires opening the file in PowerPoint. Consequently, PowerPoint must be installed on your computer when importing a .pptx file into Captivate. When importing a .ppt file, the conversion is not needed, and therefore PowerPoint is not mandatory.

Before starting with this exercise, make sure the PowerPoint presentation is closed. Perform the following steps to convert the Power Point presentation into a Captivate project:

1. Return to Captivate and close any open file. The exercise begins on the Welcome Screen of Captivate.
2. Switch to the **New** tab of the Welcome Screen, if needed.
3. Double-click the **From PowerPoint** Thumbnail, as shown in the following screenshot (alternately, you can use the **File | New Project | Project From MS PowerPoint** menu item to do the same operation).

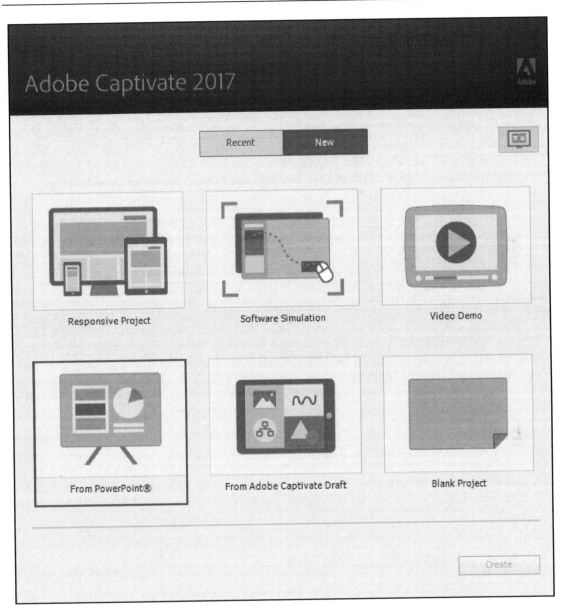

4. Navigate to the Chapter11/Presentation.pptx file in the exercises folder and click **Open**. If you don't have PowerPoint installed on your system, open the Chapter11/Presentation.ppt file.

Captivate converts the PowerPoint slides into Captivate slides. Depending on the presentation to convert, and on the capabilities of your computer, this operation can be quite lengthy, so be patient. When the conversion is finished, Captivate opens the **Convert Microsoft® PowerPoint Presentations** dialog box.

5. There are two sections in this dialog, **Project Properties** and **Slide Preview**. In the **Project Properties** section, change the **Name** of the project to Introduction to Fluid Boxes.

6. Notice the **Width** and **Height** of the project is set to 1280 and 720 pixels respectively. This is a direct conversion of the dimension of the PowerPoint presentation from inches to pixels.

7. Open the **Preset Sizes** dropdown and review the available preview sizes. You can pick one of the presets or you can input the custom values in the **Width** and **Height** fields.

8. If you have made any changes to the values for **Width** and **Height**, change them back to 1280 and 720.

9. In the Slide Preview section, there are thumbnails for all the slides in the PPT with a small checkbox allowing you to include or exclude the slide from the Captivate project.

10. You can also use the **Clear All** and **Select All** buttons to quickly select or deselect the entire set of slides. In this case, you want to import the entire PowerPoint presentation into Captivate, so make sure all the PowerPoint slides are selected before moving on.

11. At the end of the dialog box, set the **Advance Slide** option to **On mouse click**.

12. Make sure the **Linked** checkbox is selected.

It is very important to get these last two options right! The **Advance Slide** option lets you decide how Captivate advances from one slide to the next one:

- By choosing **On mouse click**, Captivate will generate a Click Box on top of every imported slide. This Click Box stops the Playhead and waits for the student to click anywhere on the slide to continue to the next step of the project.
- The **Automatically** option moves to the next slide automatically after the defined duration. You can also select **Automatically**, if you wish to use our own navigation buttons in the Captivate project.

The **Linked** checkbox is even more important. Captivate proposes two ways to insert a PowerPoint presentation in a project. They are as follows:

- When **Linked** is not selected, you create an **Embedded** presentation. It means that a copy of the original PowerPoint presentation is entirely integrated into the .cptx file. This copy is completely independent from the original .pptx (or .ppt) file.
- When the **Linked** checkbox is selected, the PowerPoint presentation is also embedded into Captivate, but Captivate maintains a link between the copy of the PowerPoint file that is embedded in the .cptx file and the original PowerPoint file. This link can be used to update the Captivate file when a change is made to the PowerPoint presentation.

13. If you are on the Windows platform, make sure you select the **High Fidelity** option. This will ensure that all the PowerPoint objects such as animations, Smart Art, effects, tables, triggers, and so on are imported correctly in your Captivate project. This option is not available on Mac.

Make sure the **Convert Microsoft® PowerPoint Presentations** dialog looks like the following screenshot before moving on. It might look different when you see it on Mac. Also, if you are importing a `.ppt` file instead of `.pptx`, you will not see the High Fidelity option, on either the Windows or Mac platform.

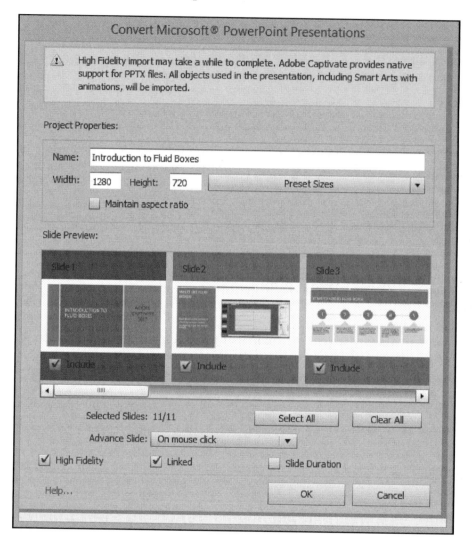

14. Click the **OK** button.

Captivate creates a new project from the original PowerPoint presentation. Depending on the presentation to convert and on the capabilities of your computer, this process can be quite lengthy, so be patient. When the import process is finished, an 11 slides project is loaded into Captivate. In the **Filmstrip** panel, notice that each slide has a name that is derived from the slide title as entered in PowerPoint.

You will now test the entire project to see how well (or how badly) Captivate handles the conversion from PowerPoint.

15. Save the file as `Chapter11/Introduction to Fluid Boxes.cptx`.

16. Use the **Preview | Project** icon on the Toolbar to test the entire project in the Preview pane.

Now test the entire project noticing that:

- Captivate does a pretty good job in of converting a PowerPoint presentation into a Captivate project.
- Most animations are carried over from PowerPoint, even if a corresponding effect does not exist in Captivate.
- The slide transitions are NOT carried over from the PowerPoint presentation. If you need to apply slide transitions, you will have to apply them again inside Captivate using the **Timing** inspector.
- On slide 11, the link is NOT functional. You will make it functional in the following exercise.

The conversion of the PowerPoint presentation to a Captivate project is now complete.

17. Close the **Preview** pane when done.

What you just experienced in the **Preview** pane is close to how the students will experience the project. You will now take a closer look at the Captivate editing environment to discover other properties from the original presentation that are carried over in Captivate.

18. Now let's make the link work on slide 11. Use the **Filmstrip** to return to the last slide of the project.

19. Select the Click Box covering the slide and press the *Delete* key on the keyboard. This big Click Box was hindering the functionality of the hyperlink on the slide. Removing it will make the hyperlink functional.

20. Use the **Preview | From this slide** icon on the Toolbar to test the slide in the Preview pane.

21. Click the hyperlink text at the bottom left corner of the slide. It will open the **Getting started on Fluid Boxes - Adobe Captivate 2017 release** article on the eLearning Community site.

22. Go back to Captivate and close the **Preview** pane.

23. Use the **Filmstrip** to go to slide 2 of the project.

24. Use the **Window | Slide Notes** menu item to open the **Slide Notes** panel. Remember that, by default, this panel appears at the bottom of the screen, next to the **Timeline**.

The Slide Notes typed in Microsoft PowerPoint have been imported into the **Slide Notes** panel of Captivate. Remember that these Slide Notes can be converted to Speech and to Closed Captions. The fact that Captivates imports this data from PowerPoint is a great productivity feature and a huge timesaver.

 Warning: The Slides Notes added to the original PowerPoint file after it has been converted into a Captivate project will not be synced with the Captivate file.

25. Use the **Filmstrip** to go to slide 3.

26. At the bottom of the screen, open the **Timeline** panel.

In PowerPoint, this slide is made up of quite a few pieces of text and objects. You would expect the Captivate version of that slide to contain a lot of objects. Unfortunately, the PowerPoint to Captivate conversion does not go that far. In Captivate, each PowerPoint slide is considered as a single animated object. The individual components of this animation do not show in the **Timeline** panel.

Consequently, modifying the content or the layout of the project must be done in PowerPoint, not in Captivate. In the next section, you will learn how you can modify the project in Power Point and import the edits in Captivate through a process called Round Tripping.

Round Tripping between Captivate and PowerPoint

Round Tripping is the process by which you can invoke PowerPoint from within Captivate, edit the presentation in PowerPoint, and import the modifications back into Captivate. If you are working on Windows, PowerPoint can even be displayed right within the Captivate interface, so you won't even have to leave the Captivate environment. If you are working on a Mac, you'll be redirected to the actual PowerPoint application.

The following exercise requires both PowerPoint and Captivate to be installed on your computer. On Windows, Office 2003 (SP3) or higher is required. On Mac, Office 2004 and up will do.

In the next exercise, you will modify a slide in PowerPoint and return to Captivate using the following steps:

1. Still in the `Chapter11/Introduction to Fluid Boxes.cptx` file, use the **Filmstrip** to go to slide 3.

2. Right-click anywhere on the slide and choose **Edit With Microsoft PowerPoint |
Edit Presentation**, as shown in the following screenshot:

If you get a message saying that Captivate is unable to open the
PowerPoint presentation because of a permission problem, return to
PowerPoint to make sure the presentation is closed before starting this
procedure in Captivate.

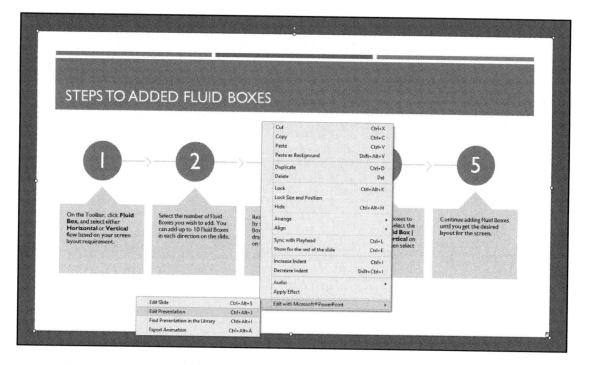

What follows depends on the operating system you are working on. On **Windows**,
PowerPoint opens within the Captivate Interface, allowing you to edit the presentation
using all the tools and features of PowerPoint without even leaving Captivate. On the **Mac**,
PowerPoint automatically opens in its own separate window and loads the presentation
you want to edit.

Pay close attention to the remaining steps of this exercise. The round tripping experience on
Windows is very different from the one on the Mac.

3. [**Mac Only**]: When PowerPoint is open; go to slide 3 of the PowerPoint
presentation.
4. [**Everyone**]: On slide 3, change **ADDED** to ADD in the title.

5. [**Mac Only**]: Use the **File | Save** menu item of PowerPoint to save the presentation.

6. [**Mac Only**]: Return to Captivate. A message asks if you want to import the updated presentation. Click **Yes** and let Captivate make the necessary changes in the project.

7. [**Mac Only**]: Close the PowerPoint application manually.

8. [**Windows Only**]: Click the **Save** button in the upper left corner of the interface. PowerPoint closes and the Captivate project is automatically updated.

9. [**Everyone**]: Save the Captivate file when done.

10. [**Everyone**]: Use the **Preview | Project** icon on the Toolbar to preview the entire project in the preview pane.

When the preview reaches slide 3, pay close attention to the text in the title. The modification done in PowerPoint should be reflected in the Captivate project.

Updating a linked PowerPoint presentation

In the next exercise, you will open PowerPoint and modify the presentation in the PowerPoint application. This is very different from what you did in the previous exercise where the workflow was triggered from Captivate. You will then return to Captivate and update the project accordingly. The steps are as follows:

1. Return to PowerPoint and open the `Chapter11/Presentation.pptx`.

2. Go to slide 6 of the presentation and change **WRAPP** to `WRAP` in the title.

3. **Save** the presentation and close PowerPoint.

4. Return to Captivate.

Because you selected the **Linked** checkbox when converting the PowerPoint presentation, Captivate is able to pick up the change made in the PowerPoint file and should display the same message asking if you want to import the updated presentation. If the message is not displayed automatically, the **Library** panel offers a way to manually update the Captivate Project so it reflects the changes made in the PowerPoint presentation.

5. If the message is displayed on your screen, click **No** to close the message without updating the Captivate project.

6. Open the **Library** panel next to the **Properties** inspector on the right side of the screen.

7. In the **Presentations** section of the **Library**, locate the **Presentation** object.

Notice the red dot in the **Status** column as shown in the following screenshot. It indicates that the linked PowerPoint presentation and the Captivate project are out of sync:

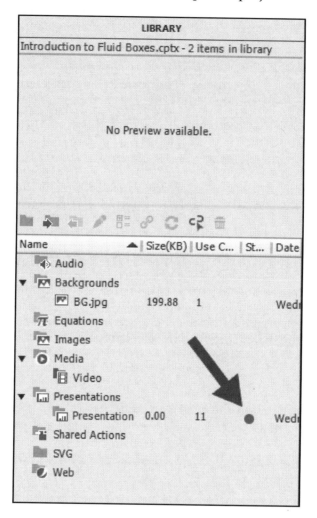

8. In the **Library** panel, click the red dot associated with the presentation.

This refreshes the linked presentation and puts the Captivate project and the PowerPoint presentation back in sync. At the end of the process, the **Status** color should turn back to green.

Using the **Library** panel, there are a few more operations that can be done on a PowerPoint presentation.

9. In the **Library** panel of Captivate, right click the **Presentation** object.
10. In the contextual menu, click the **Change To "Embedded"** menu item.
11. Click **OK** to clear the acknowledgement message.

After this operation, the link between the copy of the PowerPoint file that is embedded in Captivate and the external PowerPoint presentation is broken. The changes made to the external PowerPoint file will no longer be picked up by Captivate.

12. Still in the **Presentations** folder of the **Library**, right click the **Presentation** object again.
13. In the contextual menu, click the **Change To "Linked"** menu item.
14. Browse to the /Chapter11 folder of the exercises files and save the PowerPoint file as Chapter11/Presentation_linked.ppt.
15. Again, click the **OK** button to clear the message.
16. Save the Captivate project when done.

This operation saves a new copy of the embedded PowerPoint presentation as a new PowerPoint file and creates a link between this new file and the Captivate Project. It is not possible to actually recreate the link to the original PowerPoint file. Instead, you create a new PowerPoint file, and link that new file to the Captivate project.

Inserting a PowerPoint slide in a Captivate Project

In the previous two sections, you learned how to convert an entire PowerPoint presentation into a new Captivate project. But sometimes, only a few PowerPoint slides must be inserted in the middle of an existing Captivate project.

In the next exercise, you will insert a single PowerPoint slide in the middle of the Introduction to the Fluid Boxes project you created in the previous exercise, using the following steps:

1. Open the chapter11/Additional PPT Slides.cptx file in the exercises folder.
2. In the **Filmstrip**, make sure Slide 1 is selected. You need to add a new slide with course objectives after this slide.

3. Click the **Slides | PowerPoint Slide** icon on the Toolbar.

4. In the dialog box, make sure that **Slide 1** is selected as shown in the following screenshot:

The imported PowerPoint slide(s) will be inserted after the slide selected in this dialog box.

5. Click the **OK** button and browse to the chapter11/Objectives.pptx PowerPoint file in the exercises folder. Click the **Open** button.

6. In the **Convert PowerPoint Presentations** dialog, open the **Advance Slide** dropdown and select the **Automatically** option.

This time, you do not want Captivate to generate an extra Click Box on top of the slide, as you did when converting a PowerPoint file earlier in this chapter.

7. Select the **High Fidelity** option, if you are on Windows and have imported a .pptx file.
8. Leave the other options at their current value and click the **OK** button.

The PowerPoint slide is inserted as slide 2 of the *Additional PPT Slides* project. You will now insert a native Captivate object on top of the imported PowerPoint slide. Note that adding a Power Point slide to a Captivate project can be done with any Captivate project, including the projects that do not originate from a converted PowerPoint presentation.

9. With the new Objectives slide selected, use the **Shapes** icon on the Toolbar to draw a rounded rectangle on the bottom right corner of the slide.
10. Double click in the rounded rectangle and write Continue into the shape.
11. Hit the *Esc* key to quit the text edit mode and leave the shape selected.
12. In the **Properties** inspector, select the **Use as Button** checkbox.
13. Use the **Style** drop-down menu to apply the **FluidButtonStyle** style to the new button.
14. In the **Actions** tab of the **Properties** inspector, make sure that the **On Success** action of the new button is set to **Go to the next slide**.
15. Move and resize the button so it integrates nicely with the rest of the slide.
16. Save the file when done.
17. Use the **Preview | Project** icon on the toolbar to test the entire project.

In this exercise, you have inserted a PowerPoint slide in the middle of an existing Captivate project. This presentation is available in the **Library** of the project and can be edited using the same Round Tripping workflow discussed earlier in this chapter.

This exercise also demonstrates the ability to add standard Captivate objects on top of the imported PowerPoint slides.

Controlling the user experience

Importing the PowerPoint slides with the **Advance Automatically** feature and adding your own buttons on top of the imported slides, allows you to better control the user experience of the imported projects. Lots of Captivate developers adopt the workflow described in this exercise rather than letting Captivate create a Click box on top of every single PowerPoint slide, as you did in the first exercise of this chapter when choosing **Advance On a Mouse Click**.

This concludes your overview of the integration between Microsoft PowerPoint and Adobe Captivate. Before moving on, it is time to emphasize the key points of what has been covered. They are as follows:

- It is possible to convert an entire PowerPoint presentation into a Captivate project.
- Captivate can import both, a .ppt or a .pptx file. A .ppt file can be imported in Captivate, even if PowerPoint is not installed on the computer. When importing a .pptx file, however, PowerPoint must be installed on the system along with Captivate.
- When converting PowerPoint to Captivate, most animations, effects, and triggers are carried over, even if they are not natively supported by Captivate.
- Each PowerPoint slide is imported as a single animation. It is not possible to access each individual object of the original PowerPoint slide in Captivate.
- An imported presentation cannot be updated in Captivate. To update a presentation, it is necessary to use PowerPoint.
- An imported PowerPoint presentation is either an Embedded presentation or a Linked presentation. An Embedded presentation is entirely integrated into the Captivate project. A Linked presentation is also integrated in the Captivate project, but maintains a link with the original PowerPoint presentation. This link can be used to keep the PowerPoint presentation and the Captivate project in sync.
- **Round Tripping** is a concept that enables you to invoke PowerPoint from within Captivate, update the presentation in PowerPoint, and import the changes back into Captivate.
- The actual Round Tripping experience depends on the operating system in use (Mac or Windows).
- It is also possible to insert only a few PowerPoint slides in the middle of an existing Captivate project.
- All the objects of Captivate can be inserted on top of the imported PowerPoint slide(s).

In the next section, you will use a workflow that involves Captivate and Microsoft Word to localize a Captivate project.

Importing PowerPoint versus animating native Captivate objects
In the early versions of Captivate, the **Effects** panel did not exist. As it was impossible to animate objects directly into Captivate, it was very common to create slides in PowerPoint and insert them in Captivate. Since the introduction of the **Effects** panel in Captivate 5, any native Captivate object can be animated in ways that are very similar to what is found in PowerPoint. In our opinion, the PowerPoint integration is a great tool to recycle existing content made in PowerPoint, or to involve non-Captivate developers in the production process. That being said, we think that new content should be developed entirely in Captivate whenever possible because it offers far more flexibility and does not require constant back and forth between two heavy applications.

Localizing a Captivate project using Microsoft Word

In this section, you will create the French version of the takeTheTrain course (but don't worry if you don't know French!). To produce the French version of the project, there are two basic things to do. They are as follows:

- Translate the Text Captions and the Slide Notes
- Localize the other assets (such as the video file, narration, or additional imported images)

In the following exercise, you will concentrate on the first step of this process and see how Microsoft Word can help you translate the Text Captions and the Slide Notes of your Captivate project using the following steps:

1. Open the `Chapter11/takeTheTrain_English.cptx` file.
2. You need to make a copy of this project for the French version. To do so, use the **File | Save As** option.
3. Navigate to the `chapter11` folder and change the name of the CPTX file to `takeTheTrain_French.cptx` and click **Save**.

The file is now ready for translation of the Text Captions and the Slide Notes in Microsoft Word using the following steps.

 The following exercise requires Microsoft Word to be installed on the computer along with Captivate.

4. Make sure you are still in the Chapter11/takeTheTrain_French.cptx file.
5. Use the **File | Export | Project Captions and Closed Captions...** menu item to export the Text Captions and the Slide Notes to a Word document.
6. Save the file as Chapter11/takeTheTrain_French Captions.doc. Notice that Captivate exports the Word file to .doc and not .docx format.

 After exporting and before importing the captions, do not change the name of the Captivate or Word file. Also, do not make any text changes to the Captivate file. It might result in either the import not working, or incorrect placement of translated captions.

When the export is complete, Captivate displays a message, asking if you want to see the generated Word document.

7. Click **Yes** to open Microsoft Word and view the generated document.

The generated Word document should look like the following screenshot:

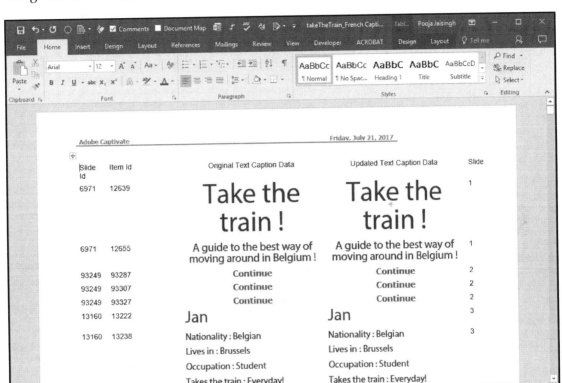

The generated Word document is a five-column table. The first two columns contain the **Slide ID** and **Item ID**. **Do not change anything in the first two columns**. When the translated text will be imported back into the project, these two pieces of information will be used by Captivate to uniquely identify the object into which the text needs to be imported.

The third column is the original text as written in the source language. The fourth column is where the translator will do his job. **The translated text should be entered in the fourth column of the table**.

The last column is the slide number on which the object is found.

If you have used white font for the Text Captions in your Captivate project, you might not be able to see them in the Word document, as the background of the Word file is also white. To see the text clearly, change the page background color of the Word file to a shade of grey, so that both black and white text is visible in the document.

8. Change the text in the fourth column of the Word document.

If you don't know French, don't worry. For the sake of this exercise, you can translate the first few captions in any language you want (or just update the text in any way!). After completing this task, save and close the Word document.

You will now import the updated Text Captions and Slide Notes back into the Captivate project.

9. Return to Captivate in the `takeTheTrain_French.cptx` file.
10. Use the **File | Import | Project Captions and Closed Captions...** menu item.
11. Import the updated `Chapter11/takeTheTrain_French Captions.doc` file.

Captivate imports the Word document, reads the data it contains, and updates the Text Captions, the Slide Notes, and the Closed Captions of the project. This process can be quite lengthy, so be patient. When the import process is complete, use the **Filmstrip** to browse through the slides of the project, and see the updated Text Captions and Slide Notes.

If you are on the Windows platform, and don't see the updated captions after importing the Word file, try running Adobe Captivate as an Administrator and then import the captions again. To run Captivate as an administrator, right-click the **AdobeCaptivate 2017** icon on your toolbar or in the installation folder and select **Run as administrator**.

12. Don't forget to save the `takeTheTrain_French.cptx` file when done.

This simple workflow is only one step in the translation of an eLearning project into a foreign language. At this point of the exercise, the Text Captions, the Smart Shapes with text, the Slide Notes, and the Closed Captions have been updated. However, the localization work is not over. The videos, images, and text used in Learning Interactions, and all the narration must be re-recorded in French and replaced in the project.

These remaining actions are beyond the scope of this book, but all the techniques needed to complete them have been discussed in the previous chapters.

Importing a Photoshop file into Captivate

Photoshop is one of the most famous and widely used Adobe applications. It is an amazing image editing tool aimed at the professional designer. Many design companies around the world use Photoshop as one of their primary tools to develop the look and feel of the projects they work on.

Therefore it is common to have a designer make use of Photoshop to create the look and feel of a Captivate project. This is why the Captivate engineering team came up with a specific feature to import a Photoshop file into Captivate.

In Photoshop, each piece of the image is stored on a separate **layer**. The layers are arranged in a way that is similar to what is found in the **Timeline** of Captivate.

The **Import from Photoshop** feature is able to retain the layers and layers comps of the original Photoshop file during the import process creating separate images for each of the layers contained in the Photoshop document. You will see the benefit of this approach during the next exercise.

Examine the file in Photoshop
If Photoshop is available on your system, don't hesitate to open the `Chapter11/DiDaXoTitlePage.psd` file in Photoshop and to further examine its content. Just make sure you don't make any changes to the file.

The following screenshot is the Photoshop file, as seen in Photoshop CC 2017:

Notice that this image has one layer and three layer groups. They are as follows:

- At the bottom of the stack, the Background Image layer is the image of the train with some effects applied to it
- Above it is the Footer layer group, which includes the footer background frame and the Dark Blue color border

- Above the Footer layer group is the Header layer group, which is composed of the background frame, the Dark Blue color border, and the logo visible in the top left corner of the image
- At the top of the stack is the Title layer group, which includes the background frame, Dark Blue borders for top and bottom of the title bar, and the blue semi circle on the right of the slide

You will now import this Photoshop document in a blank Captivate project to create a title slide.

Close every open project before starting the following exercise:

1. On the **Welcome** screen, select the **Blank Project** thumbnail.
2. Select the **1024 x 627** canvas size and click **Create**.
3. When the project is open, use the **Window | Master Slide** menu item to switch to Master Slide view.
4. Use the **Master Slide** panel on the left side of the screen to select the **Title** Master Slide.
5. Delete the Placeholder Title Text from the slide.

The Title Master Slide should now be completely blank. Next, you will insert the Photoshop file described on the previous page to this Master slide.

6. Still on the Title Master Slide, use the **File | Import | Photoshop File** menu item to start the procedure.
7. Import the `Chapter11/DiDaXoTitlePage.psd` Photoshop file of the exercises folder (notice that the file extension of a Photoshop file is `.psd`, which stands for PhotoShop Document).

Captivate opens the **Import "DiDaXoTitlePage.psd"** dialog box.

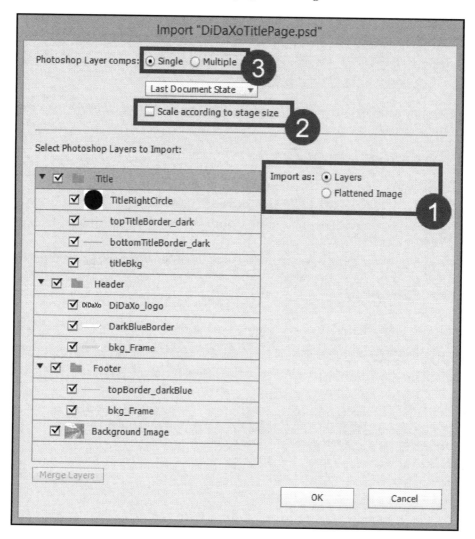

First of all, notice that you can import all the **Layers** of the original Photoshop file or import a **Flattened Image** (1). A **flattened image** is an image where all the layers have been combined into one single image.

Notice also the **Scale according to stage size** checkbox (2). If selected, the Photoshop image will be automatically enlarged or reduced to fit the size of the Captivate project.

Photoshop users should notice the **Photoshop Layer comps** option at the top of the dialog (**3**).

8. Make sure that **Import as Layers** (**1**) is selected.
9. Make sure all the layer groups and layers are selected in the left panel.
10. Click the **OK** button to import all the Photoshop layers in Captivate.
11. When the import is complete, click the **Timeline** button at the bottom of the screen to open the **Timeline** panel.

This is where the import from Photoshop feature shows its awesomeness. 10 images have been imported on the new Master Slide. This means that **a separate image has been created for each of the imported layers**.

12. Select the DiDaXo logo on the Master Slide.
13. Go to the **Timing** inspector, and apply a **Fade In Only** transition to the logo.

This illustrates that in Captivate, these images can be treated as entirely separate objects. Transitions, effects, and other treatments can be applied to each image separately. On regular slides, you can even arrange each component of the imported Photoshop file on the Timeline. This capability is not available on Master Slides though.

14. While on the **Title** Master Slide, use the **Insert** | **Placeholder Objects** | **Title** menu item to insert a Title Smart Shape placeholder on the Master Slide.
15. Use the **Properties** inspector to change the font style and properties.
16. Arrange the objects of the Master Slide as you see fit. The goal is to come up with the greatest title slide ever created in the entire universe!

Inserting a Photoshop file in Captivate is that easy. The last step of the process is to use this new Master Slide in the Project.

17. Use the **Window** | **Filmstrip** menu item to return to the main project.
18. You will see that the Title Master Slide is applied to the slide. Now you can change the title of the slide, as required.
19. Use the **File** | **Save** option to save this project as a `Chapter11/DiDaXoTitlePage.cptx` file.

In the next section, you will examine the round tripping workflow between Captivate and Photoshop.

Round Tripping between Captivate and Photoshop

Now that the Photoshop file has been imported into the Captivate project, let's pretend you want to modify the Photoshop file a little bit. The Round Trip editing workflow that exists between Captivate and Photoshop allows you to do it without reimporting the whole Photoshop document again. Let's examine this workflow hands-on, using the following steps:

 The following exercise requires Photoshop to be installed on your system along with Captivate. If Photoshop is not available on your computer, just read through the steps to have an idea of the workflow. You can also download a trial version of Adobe Photoshop, which is a part of Adobe Creative Cloud: http://www.adobe.com/products/photoshop.html.

1. Still in the Chapter11/DiDaXoTitlePage.cptx file, click the **Library** icon on the Toolbar to open the **Library** panel.
2. In the **Library** inspector, you will see the **DiDaXoTitlePage.psd** folder.
3. Use the disclose triangle to toggle the folder open, if necessary.

In the **Library** panel, the imported Photoshop file is seen as a folder and each of the imported layers is seen as an image within that folder. This is shown in the following screenshot:

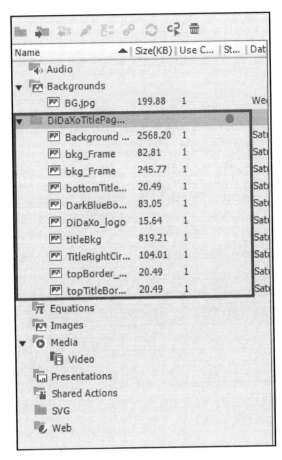

4. Right click the **DiDaXoTitlePage.psd** folder or on any of the images it contains and choose the **Edit PSD Source File** item of the contextual menu.

This action opens the `.psd` file in Photoshop. Note that all the layers of the `.psd` document are available in Photoshop, not only the one you right clicked on in Captivate. From here, you can use all the tools of Photoshop to modify your image.

5. Feel free to modify the image using the tools of Photoshop.
6. When done, save and close the Photoshop file.
7. Captivate automatically updates the components of the `.psd` document.

This simple procedure illustrates the tight integration that exists between Captivate and Photoshop. If you have Photoshop available on your system, this Round Trip editing workflow will greatly enhance your authoring experience.

In the next section, you will explore the integration between Captivate and Adobe Audition, but before that, let's quickly summarize what has been covered in this section:

- Photoshop is a professional image editing application developed by Adobe.
- Photoshop uses a layer based system to create complex compositions.
- Captivate contains a specific tool to import Photoshop files into the project.
- You can import a flattened image into Captivate or maintain the layers found in the Photoshop file during the import process.
- If the Photoshop layers are maintained, each layer is imported as a separate image in Captivate. This allows you to arrange these images on the **Timeline** and apply different effects to the different parts of the imported image.
- You can edit the original .psd file using the round trip editing workflow between Captivate and Photoshop.
- In the **Library** panel, the Photoshop document is a folder.

Editing audio with Adobe Audition

Adobe Audition (formerly CoolEdit) is the audio editing and mixing application of the Creative Cloud. It allows you to manipulate your audio clips in ways that are impossible in Captivate. Thanks to Audition, you can apply effects and filters to your audio clips and create sophisticated multitrack sessions. Audition is also particularly good at sound restoration, so if you have a background noise, a pop or a hiss to remove, Audition is the way to go!

 The following exercise requires that Adobe Audition CC be installed on your computer alongside Captivate. If you don't have access to Audition, which is a part of Adobe Creative Cloud, you will not be able to complete this exercise. In that case, just read through the steps to have an idea of the workflow. You can also download a trial version of Adobe Audition, which is a part of Adobe Creative Cloud:
http://www.adobe.com/products/audition.html

If Audition is installed on your computer alongside Captivate, you can take advantage of some special workflows that unite the two applications. You will now discover these workflows hands-on using the following steps:

1. Return to the Chapter11/takeTheTrain_English.cptx file.
2. Use the **Filmstrip** to go to slide 3 of the project.

3. Open the **Timeline** panel and notice that there is an audio track attached to the slide.
4. Double click the audio track in the **Timeline**. This will open the Slide Audio dialog box for you, with the contents for the **Edit** tab visible.

The **Object Audio** dialog has been covered in `Chapter 3`, *Working with Multimedia*. It allows you to change and modify the audio clip using the tools of Captivate. However, sometimes, the audio editing tools of Captivate are not enough. If Adobe Audition is installed on the same computer as Captivate, an Adobe Audition button will become available at the bottom of the **Object Audio** window.

5. Click the **Adobe Audition** button in the bottom area of the **Object Audio** window.

A dialog box appears in Captivate stating **Edit and Save Audio in Adobe Audition. Click OK in this dialog to import changes**. Don't press any button in this dialog yet. You will need to take action once you finish the edits in Adobe Audition.

Along with this dialog, an Adobe Audition window opens and loads the audio clip from slide 3. The following screenshot shows the audio clip as seen in Adobe Audition CC 2017:

6. Edit the audio clip in Adobe Audition using all the tools, filters, and presets that you want to. When done, save and close the file in Audition and return to Captivate.

7. Click **OK** in the dialog box.

Captivate will now pick up all the changes and update the audio clip.

8. Click the **Save** button on the bottom right corner of the **Object Audio** dialog and close the dialog.

Thanks to this simple workflow, Adobe Audition is only one click away when working in Captivate. Your students will certainly enjoy the crystal-clear noise free audio clips that you will produce for them. Note that this workflow also works with audio clips associated with an object, or with the background audio associated with the entire project.

You will now return to the **Library** panel of Captivate and explore yet another way to use Audition from within Captivate.

9. Make sure the `Chapter11/takeTheTrain_English.cptx` file is still open.
10. Use the **Filmstrip** to go to slide 4 of the project.
11. Open the **Timeline** panel, if needed.
12. When in the **Timeline** panel, right click the sound clip associated with the slide.
13. Choose the **Find in Library** menu item.

This action opens the **Library** panel and automatically selects the audio clip you right clicked on (in this case, the **slide03.wav** audio clip, which is being used for Slide 4 in this project).

14. Right click the **Slide03.wav** item of the **Library**.
15. Choose **Edit With...** in the contextual menu.
16. Browse to the Adobe Audition executable file. On the Mac, look for the `/Applications/Adobe Audition CC 2017/Adobe Audition CC 2017.app` file. On Windows, look for the `C:\Program Files\Adobe\Adobe Audition CC 2017\Adobe Audition CC.exe` file.
17. The selected audio clip opens in Adobe Audition. You can now use the tools, filters, and presets of Audition to edit this audio clips in many ways not available in Captivate. When done, save and close the audio file.
18. Captivate should automatically pick up the changes and load a new version of the audio clip in the Library.

This simple exercise concludes the overview of the integration between Adobe Captivate and Adobe Audition. Let's quickly summarize what has been covered in this section:

- Adobe Audition is the professional audio editing application of the Creative Cloud.
- If Captivate and Audition are both installed on the same computer, the **Adobe Audition** button of the Audio Edit dialog box will be active.
- This button allows you to open Audition from within Captivate. You can then use the advanced tools of Audition to manipulate your audio file in many ways not possible in Captivate.

- When you save the file in Audition, Captivate automatically picks up the changes and adapts your eLearning project accordingly.
- Right click an element of the **Library** and choose the **Edit With...** menu item to open it in an external application.

Editing SVGs with Adobe Illustrator

Adobe Illustrator is a vector graphic design application that allows you to create icons, logos, typography, and complex illustrations. It also allows you to create Scalable Vector Graphics, also known as SVGs. Adding SVGs in Captivate projects has been covered in Chapter 2, *Working with Standard Objects*.

Adobe Captivate allows you to insert SVGs in your courses, which is especially beneficial for responsive courses, as the SVGs scale beautifully in the project, without any loss of quality. The SVG images that you insert in Captivate can be edited by Adobe Illustrator using the same kind of round tripping workflow that you used with Audition and Photoshop in the previous sections.

 The following exercise requires that Adobe Illustrator CC be installed on your computer alongside Captivate. If you don't have access to Illustrator, which is a part of Adobe Creative Cloud, you will not be able to complete this exercise. In that case, just read through the steps to have an idea of the workflow. You can also download the trial version of Adobe Illustrator, which is a part of Adobe Creative Cloud:
http://www.adobe.com/products/illustrator.html.

Now you will learn how to edit the already added SVG in Captivate using the round tripping feature with Adobe Illustrator:

1. Return to the Chapter11/takeTheTrain_English.cptx file.
2. Use the **Filmstrip** to go to slide 5 of the project.
3. Select one of the pins on the map, which is an SVG.
4. In the **Properties** inspector, notice the name of the pin mentioned as mapSymbolPin.svg. To see the entire filename, you may need to drag the library column to make it larger.

5. Select the other two pins and notice that they are also linked to the same SVG. You will modify this SVG in Adobe Illustrator, which will apply the changes to all three pins on this slide.

6. To make edits to the SVG file in Adobe Illustrator, select **Edit with Adobe Illustrator** and then click **Edit SVG** in the **Properties** inspector.

7. This opens the SVG file in Adobe Illustrator CC, as shown in the following screenshot:

8. Make the required changes to the SVG file. For this pin, let's change the red color to green. Select the pin in the Illustrator window.

9. Use the **Edit** menu and select **Edit Colors | Recolor Artwork**.

10. In the **Recolor Artwork** dialog box, double click the Red color below the **New** section.

11. In the **Color Picker** dialog box, select the dark green color and click **OK**.

12. Click **OK** to close the **Recolor Artwork** dialog box.

13. You will see the new color applied to the pin. Now save the changes to the Illustrator document and close it.

14. The changes will immediately be reflected in your Adobe Captivate project on all three pins.

15. This brings us to the end of the round tripping workflow between Captivate and Illustrator to edit the SVG files added to Captivate projects.

Exporting the project to XML

In this section, you will export the project as an XML file. Exporting the Captivate project to `.xml` gives you access to a much wider range of properties and content than the Export to Microsoft Word feature you used earlier in this chapter. According to the official Adobe Captivate blog, the exported XML file contains the following:

> *Text Captions, Text Animations, Rollover Captions, Default text and correct entries in Text Entry Box, Success/Failure/Hint Captions and button text for all interactive objects, Text Buttons, Slide Notes, Text and Rollover Captions in Rollover Slidelets, Quiz Buttons and Feedback captions, Project Info, Project Start and End options, text messages for password and Expiry Messages*

 See the original post at `https://elearning.adobe.com/2009/05/quick_editing_of_text_using_xm_1/`.

Here are the steps to export your project to an XML file:

1. If needed, return to the `chapter11/takeTheTrain_English.cptx` file.
2. You need to make a copy of this project for the French version. To do so, use the **File | Save As** option.
3. Navigate to the `chapter11` folder and change the name of the CPTX file to `takeTheTrain_French_xml.cptx` and click **Save**.
4. Use the **File | Export | To XML** menu option.
5. Export the project as `chapter11/takeTheTrain_French_xml.xml` in the exercises folder.

When the export is finished, Captivate asks if you want to open the resulting XML file.

6. Click **No** to close the message box and return to Captivate.

The resulting XML can be opened and updated with any XML editor. When the editing is done, the **File | Import | From XML...** menu item can be used to import the updated data back into Captivate.

Summary

In this chapter, you have learned some of the workflows that integrate Captivate with other applications. Some of these applications, such as Photoshop, Illustrator, and Audition are a part of the Adobe product line, and others, such as Microsoft Word and Microsoft PowerPoint, are third-party applications.

By using the PowerPoint workflows, you are able to reuse existing content made in PowerPoint. When it comes to localization, you can export the Text Captions and the Slide Notes to a Microsoft Word document, send it to a translation service, and import it back into Captivate. There is no need for the translators to know anything about Captivate to make this workflow work. When importing a Photoshop file into Captivate, you can decide to maintain the layers of the original Photoshop file, which gives you a great deal of flexibility to further customize the imported images using the tools and effects of Captivate. Exporting to Audition allows you to tweak your audio files in many ways. And the round tripping workflow between Captivate and Illustrator will help you edit the SVG files added to Captivate projects.

When used correctly, these workflows are huge time savers that help you streamline the production process of your eLearning content.

In the next chapter, you will learn how to make your eLearning courses accessible for people with special needs.

Meet the community

In this section, meet *Shambu Nashi*. Shambu is a product manager for Adobe. He is in charge of the eLearning Community Portal. This is the website available under the *Community* icon on the Toolbar of Adobe Captivate. He is the one who distributes the incentives when you reach a certain number of points for participating in the community. But that's not why everyone wants to be nice to Shambu; he is simply a nice person!

Shambhu Nashi

Shambhu Nashi is the Product manager for eLearning community. Passionate about solving problems that matter to customers, he loves to dive deep into numbers to uncover the core problem, and recommend strategies to create a seamless and amazing customer experience!

Before this, he has been working on different products in different roles, and he is now celebrating a decade working at Adobe!

Through the years he, and his team have heard from customers needing a single platform to connect with all eLearning users, in order to voice their opinion, engage and learn from other passionate users in eLearning space. In August 2016, Shambu launched the all-new Adobe eLearning Community portal. He wants to take this opportunity to thank all the users who are supporting the building of this community.

This would be a one stop for all eLearning professionals to familiarise themselves with the latest in Adobe eLearning tools and the eLearning industry! This also helps you create your portfolio by showcasing your expertise!
Come and engage, learn, and contribute.

Contact details

- **Adobe eLearning Community**: http://elearning.adobe.com
- **Blog**: http://elearning.adobe.com/profile/shambunashi
- **LinkedIn page**: http://www.linkedin.com/in/shambunashi/
- **Facebook page**: https://www.facebook.com/AELCOMM/

12
Creating Accessible eLearning

When you need to deliver your eLearning courses to a large group of people, you have to be mindful of how the course experience would be for people with different abilities. Learning is the right of every individual. You need to design your content in a way that benefits everybody and gives the best possible experience to all the eager learners.

An accessible project is a project that can be accessed in good conditions by people with disabilities. These particular students use some specific input and output devices (such as Braille readers, text-to-speech utilities, screen readers, such as JAWS, and so on). These devices work better if you take the time to enter some extra metadata in your projects.

Many countries around the world have adopted some kind of accessibility standards, rules, and even laws. Most of the time, these standards are based on the **Web Accessibility Initiative** (**WAI**, see `https://www.w3.org/WAI/`), a document developed by the **World Wide Web Consortium** (**W3C**). In the US legislation, these standards are implemented as an amendment of the US Rehabilitation Act of 1973. This amendment is commonly known as Section 508. When a project is 508 compliant, it simply means that it complies with the accessibility requirements of this legal document.

To learn about the accessibility laws followed in the different parts of the world, visit this web page created by **WebAIM**: `http://webaim.org/articles/laws/world/`.

Thankfully, Captivate allows you to create accessible eLearning courses by adding accessibility text, closed captions, keyboard shortcuts, tabbing order, and so on, to the slide content and help you make it accessible for people with special needs.

In this chapter, you will:

- Enable accessibility for Captivate projects
- Add project information for the course
- Add accessibility text for slides and objects
- Assign keyboard shortcuts to interactive objects
- Set the tab order for interactive objects on the screen
- Add Closed Captions for slide narration and multi-slide synchronized videos
- Add a CC button to the playbar

Preparing your work

At the beginning of this chapter, it is a good idea to take some time and reset the Captivate interface to default. If you are using the default interface mode, just close and restart Captivate. If you use the advanced interface mode, use the **Window | Workspace | Reset 'Classic'** menu item to reset Captivate to default. In this chapter, you will use the exercises stored in the Chapter12 folder. If you get confused by any of the step-by-step instructions, take a look at the Chapter12/final folder, which contains a copy of the files as they will be at the end of this chapter.

Enabling accessibility in Captivate projects

In this section, you will learn how to enable accessibility for Captivate courses, at a project level, by following these steps:

1. Open the Chapter12/takeTheTrain.cptx file.
2. Open the **Preferences** dialog of Captivate by using the **Edit | Preferences** (Windows) menu item or the **Adobe Captivate | Preferences** (Mac) menu item.
3. In the **Preferences** dialog, navigate to the **Publish Settings** category, under the **Project** section.
4. In this section, make sure the **Enable Accessibility** option is selected.

This will ensure that the screen readers are able to read the slides and the objects in your course. If this option is not selected, the accessibility options that you set throughout the project will be useless.

5. Below the **Enable Accessibility** option is the **Restrict keyboard tabbing to slide items only** option. Select this option as well.

While previewing your course modules, you will have certainly noticed the playbar at the bottom of your project. This playbar is one of the elements that is automatically added by Captivate. In `Chapter 14`, *Finishing Touches and Publishing*, you will also activate a Table of Contents as well as borders. The option you just selected restricts the tabbing order inside the slide rather than going to the table of contents and playbar.

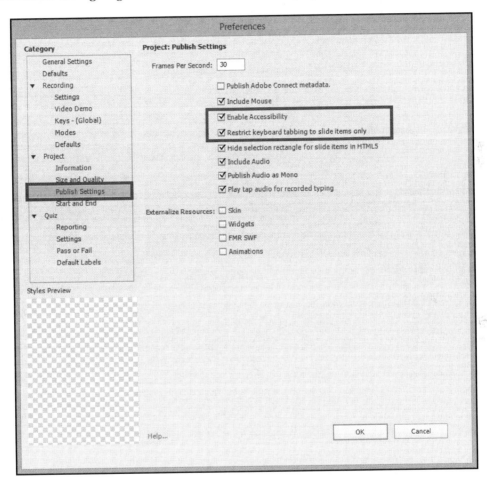

6. Now switch to the **Information** category, under the **Project** section.

In this section, you will need to fill out the project information. The screen readers will be able to fetch this information and read it out for the learners. It also helps in indexing the content in search engines.

7. Type `DiDaXo` in the **Company** field.

8. Type `2017-DiDaXo` in the **Copyright** field.

9. Enter `Take the Train` in the **Project Name** field.

10. Type `This is a short training on how to take the train in Belgium.` in the **Description** field.

11. Fill the remaining fields (**Author**, **Email**, and **Website**) with your own name, email address, and website URL. Note that none of these fields are mandatory. If you do not have a website, just leave the field blank.

Your screen should now look like the following screenshot:

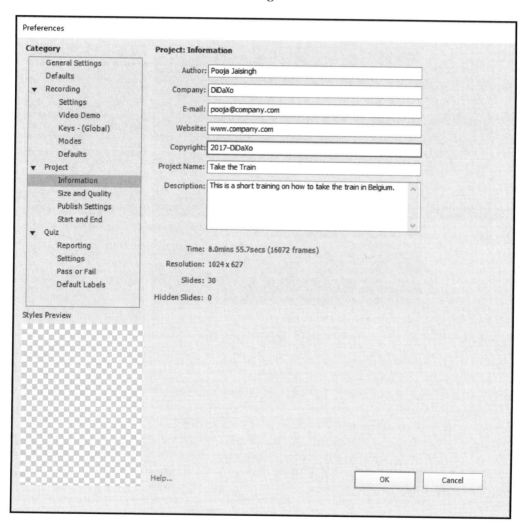

12. Click the **OK** button when done to close the **Preferences** dialog.

By entering the project information and enabling accessibility, you have taken the first important step towards making the project 508 compliant. This is a very good point, but there is a lot more that can be done throughout Captivate to further enhance the accessibility of the project. In the next sections, let's look at these enhancement workflows.

Adding accessibility text for slides

After completing the first critical step of enabling accessibility for your course, the next step is to add accessibility text to the slides and objects. Remember that this accessibility text will be read aloud by the screen readers of the visually impaired students. Let's look at the workflow to add slide-level accessibility text first.

1. If needed, return to the `Chapter12/takeTheTrain.cptx` file.
2. Use the **Filmstrip** panel to go to slide 3.
3. Click the **Properties** icon on the Toolbar to open the **Properties** inspector.
4. Click the button on the right side of the Name field, and select **Accessibility**.

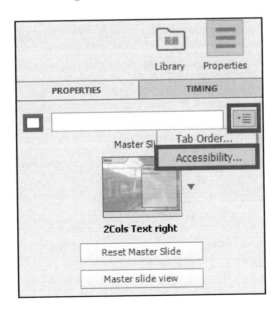

5. This will open the **Slide Accessibility** dialog. You can enter the text in the field, or if you have slide notes added for the slide, you can click the **Import Slide Notes** button.

You currently don't have any slide notes added for this slide, so let's close this dialog and add the slide notes.

6. Click **OK** to close the dialog.
7. Use the **Window | Slide Notes** menu item to open the **Slide Notes** panel.
8. The **Slide Notes** panel appears next to the **Timeline** panel.
9. Then browse the `Chapter12/Slide3_Notes.txt` file and open it with Notepad (Windows) or Text Edit (Mac).
10. Copy the first line of text from the `Slide3_Notes.txt` file.
11. Then go back to the Captivate project and click the + icon in the **Slide Notes** panel to add a slide note.
12. Copy the second line of text from the `Slide3_Notes.txt` file.
13. In the Captivate project, click the + icon in the **Slide Notes** panel and paste the second line.
14. Similarly, copy and paste the remaining three lines of text.

The **Slide Notes** panel should now look like the following screenshot:

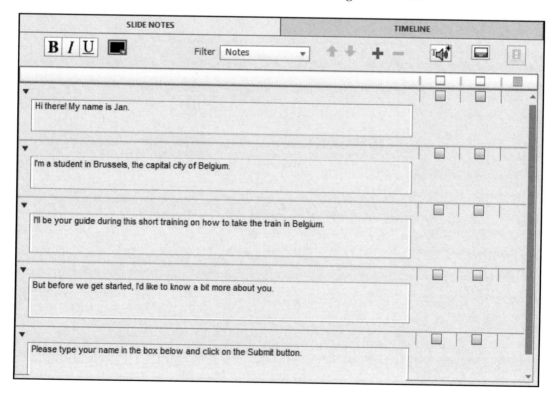

Now that you have added notes for this slide, let's import these notes as Accessibility text.

15. In the **Properties** inspector, click the button on the right side of the Name field, and select **Accessibility**.
16. In the **Slide Accessibility** dialog, click **Import Slide Notes**.

This will add the slide notes to the field, and you can use them as Accessibility text. You can also edit this text, if required.

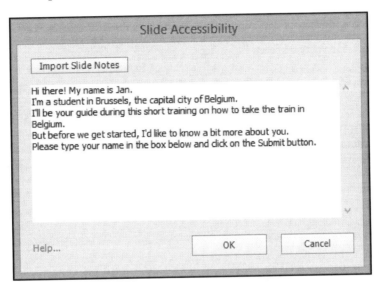

17. Click **OK** to confirm the addition of notes and close the dialog.

You can follow the same steps to add accessibility text to each of the slides in the project.

Adding accessibility text for objects

After you have finished adding accessibility text to the slides, you can add accessibility text to the objects on the slide.

Let's begin adding accessibility text to the objects on slide 3:

1. Select Jan's picture on the slide.
2. In the **Properties** inspector, click the button on the right side of the Name field, and select **Accessibility**.

This will open the **Item Accessibility** dialog. Notice that the **Auto Label** option that is selected by default and the **Accessibility Name** and **Accessibility Description** sections are greyed out. The **Auto Label** option will automatically label the objects based on their name in the Name field.

3. Deselect the **Auto Label** option to add meaningful information about this image.
4. This will allow you to add details in the **Accessibility Name** and **Accessibility Description** fields. Enter the name for the object and add the description. For this image, type Jan in the **Accessibility Name** field and Picture of Jan. in the **Accessibility Description** field.
5. Click **OK** to confirm the addition of the details and close the dialog.

And that's how you add accessibility text to the objects in Captivate projects. Select the other objects on the screen, and add the accessibility text to them. Make sure you follow the best practices listed earlier in this section.

Here are some of the best practices you should follow while adding accessibility text for the objects on the screen:

- Keep the accessibility information about the objects to the point. Do not add extra information or duplicate information for the accessibility text.
- All objects that contribute in providing textual or non-textual information should have accessibility text assigned to them.

- As far as possible, avoid using the Auto Label option for graphical elements, and provide a meaningful description for them.
- If you have any decorative objects on the slide, which do not contribute to the information being provided on the screen, leave the description blank so that the screen reader excludes it from the slide.
- If you have several objects on the screen which are placed together to create a single visual on the screen, add accessibility text to only one of the objects of the group, which provides the main idea of the content for the entire group of objects. This will help you avoid repetition of information.

 For more accessibility best practices, visit the official Captivate documentation page for creating accessible courses in Adobe Captivate at `https://helpx.adobe.com/captivate/using/creating-accessible-proj ects.html`.

Adding accessibility text is certainly a tedious process, but you are sure to create a meaningful learning experience for all your learners and bring smiles to their faces!

Assigning keyboard shortcuts

When you are designing interactions for your courses, which need to be accessible, avoid using hover- and drag-based interaction. The only types of interactions which support accessibility are click-based interactions. Similarly, when adding quiz questions, you can choose from Multiple Choice, True/False, and Rating Scale questions, as they support accessibility.

Now let's talk about making interactive objects accessible. Apart from adding accessibility text, you need to follow a few more steps to make the interactive objects truly accessible. The first and the most important step is to assign keyboard shortcuts, so that your learners are able to complete the course without using a mouse.

Here are the steps to assign keyboard shortcuts to buttons in Captivate projects:

1. If needed, return to the `Chapter12/takeTheTrain.cptx` file.
2. Use the **Filmstrip** panel to go to slide 2.
3. Select the **Continue** button on the bottom right corner of the slide.
4. Click the **Properties** icon on the Toolbar to open the **Properties** inspector.
5. In the **Properties** inspector, open the **Actions** tab.

Notice the **Shortcut** option under the **Actions** tab. This option lets you choose the keyboard key (or shortcut) the learners can use to execute the action attached to the button.

6. The **Shortcut** option for the interactive objects is disabled by default. Select the radio button under the Shortcut section to enable it.

7. Use your keyboard to press a key or key combination to assign that shortcut to the button.

8. After assigning a shortcut to the button, make sure you add the information about the shortcut key to the accessibility text for the button.

Setting the tab order

When your learners are using screen readers to access the course, they can use the tab key to navigate through the interactive objects. If you have multiple interactive objects on your screen, you might want to check the tab order for these objects and place the objects in the desired order.

Here are the steps for setting the tab order of the interactive objects on the slide:

1. Make sure you are still on slide 2 of the `takeTheTrain.cptx` file.

2. If you have any object selected on the slide, click the slide 2 thumbnail on the **Filmstrip**, or click anywhere on the scrap area around the stage to make the slide the active object.

3. Open the **Properties** inspector.
4. In the **Properties** inspector, click the button on the right side of the Name field and select **Tab Order**.

You will see the Interaction widget and the button listed in the **Tab Order** dialog. Notice that the button is placed above the widget in the tab order.

5. To change the order, so that the widget interaction is active before the **Continue** button, select the **SmartShape_86** item. Notice that when you select it, the **Continue** button is selected on the slide as well.
6. Then click the **Move Selected Row Down** arrow. This changes the order for the interactive objects on the slide.
7. Click **OK** to confirm the changes and close the dialog.

You can follow the same steps on other slides with more than one interactive object to change the tab order.

Here's a quick summary of what you have learned so far:

- Captivate helps you create accessible courses for learners with special needs.
- You can make the courses accessible by adding accessibility text, Closed Captions, keyboard shortcuts, tabbing order, and so on.
- You need to enable accessibility for the project to ensure that the screen readers are able to read the slides and the objects in your course.
- You can add accessibility text to slides as well as objects. The accessibility text, added throughout the project are read aloud by the screen readers of visually impaired students, which will dramatically enhance their experience of the course content.
- Avoid using hover- and drag-based interaction for the courses that need to be accessible.
- You can choose from Multiple Choice, True/False, and Rating Scale questions for a quiz.
- For interactive objects, you need to add keyboard shortcuts as well as set the tab order.

Adding Closed Captions for slide narration

You have done a good job so far to make your course accessible. So don't forget to give yourself a pat on your back!

The last thing you need to ensure is to have Closed Captions for the slides with narration. Closed Captions make your eLearning content more accessible and more interesting for the learners. There are many situations where the Closed Captions are useful:

- They make your Captivate projects accessible for hearing impaired students.
- They make the project easier to understand for foreign students.
- They are useful for the learners that have to take the online course in an office and don't want to bother their colleagues with the voice-over narrations.

For these reasons (plus the ones not listed here), it is a good idea to use Closed Captions each time you add voice-over narration to a slide.

In Captivate, Closed Captions are always associated with a slide level audio clip or with a **Multi-Slide Synchronized Video** inserted with the **Video | Insert Video** menu item.

In the next exercise, you will add Closed Captions to the Take the Train course, by performing the following steps:

1. Return to the `Chapter12/takeTheTrain.cptx` file.
2. Use the **Filmstrip** panel to go to slide 3.
3. If needed, use the **Window | Slide Notes** menu item to reopen the **Slide Notes** panel.

Slide 3 is the first slide of the course to which you added narration. There are five notes in the **Slide Notes** panel. They exactly reflect what is said in the audio file associated with the slide.

4. At the top right corner of the **Slide Notes** panel, click the **Audio CC** checkbox next to the Text-to-Speech checkbox. This operation is shown in the following screenshot:

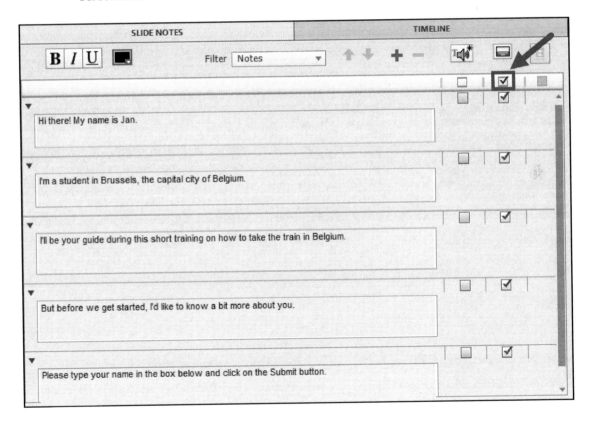

This action selects all the Slide Notes for Closed Captioning. Note that the **Audio CC** checkbox is available only if an audio file is associated with the slide.

5. In the top right corner of the **Slide Notes** panel, click the **Closed Captioning** button.

The **Slide Audio** dialog opens, with the **Closed Captioning** tab (**1**) active:

6. Use the zoom slider (**2**) to reduce the zoom level so you can see the entire sound clip.

Each of the vertical bars (**3**) represents one of the **Slide Notes** you marked for Closed Captioning.

7. Click the **Play** button. While the audio is playing, note the current position of the yellow vertical bars as compared to the audio file.

8. If needed, adjust the position of the vertical bars and test again until all the Closed Captions are in sync with the audio.

9. Now it's time to make some formatting changes to the Closed Captions. Click the **CC Settings** button (**4**) at the center right of the dialog.

The **CC Settings** dialog appears which lets you define the formatting of the Closed Captions. In the previous version of Captivate, you had limited customization options available for Closed Captions but, with the 2017 versions, you have a lot of customization options for formatting and displaying the Closed Captions in your Captivate courses. If required, you can also have a different look and feel and placement for Closed Captions on each slide.

In the top section of the **CC Settings** dialog, you will see a live preview of how the Closed Captions will appear on the screen. In the bottom section, you will find all the alignment and formatting options.

10. You will make some formatting changes to the Closed Captions area. To apply these changes to the entire project, open the dropdown which has **Slide 3** selected, and change it to **Project**.

11. Notice that the Closed Captions are currently set to appear at the bottom center of the screen. Open the drop-down list for the Align option and switch to the bottom left. This moves the captions to start from the bottom left corner.

12. Open the drop-down list again and select **Custom**.

This option will help you decide the starting point of the closed caption by modifying the **X** and **Y** coordinates, and size of Closed Captions area by modifying the Width and Height properties.

13. Set the Width of the Closed Captions area to 100%, so that it covers the slide end-to-end.

14. Then reduce the height to 9%, so that the Closed Captions appear exactly inside the bottom bar area.

15. Then set the **X** and **Y** properties to 0% and 91% respectively, so that it covers the entire bottom area. You can also drag and drop the Closed Caption area in the slide preview area to change the **X** and **Y** coordinates. Unfortunately it does not work with size.

16. Change the font and background properties, if required.
17. If you want to show the Closed Captions as soon as this slide loads, select **Show Closed Captions**. For this exercise, let's leave it unchecked, so that you can see another workflow to turn on the Closed Captions in the course.

18. When you are satisfied with the result, click the **Apply** button on the bottom right corner and then click the **Close** button.
19. Click the **Save** button at the bottom right corner of the **Slide Audio** dialog.
20. Close the **Slide Audio** dialog.

Don't forget to save the file when you are done!

Viewing the Closed Captions

Now that Closed Captions have been added to slide 3 of the project, you will test it in the preview pane and control the newly inserted Closed Captions:

1. Still in the `takeTheTrain.cptx` file, use the **Filmstrip** to return to slide 1.
2. Use the **Preview** icon on the Toolbar to test the **Next 5 Slides**.
3. When the preview reaches the third slide (the first one with audio and Closed Captions) notice that the Closed Captions do not appear.

By default, the Closed Captions do not appear in the resulting Captivate output. It is up to the student to turn them on or leave them off while watching the project.

To let the student turn them on, you need to add a closed captioning button on the playback controls bar that appears at the bottom of the project. To add this button, you need to use the **Skin Editor**.

In `Chapter 13`, *Working with Variables and Advanced Actions*, you will use an advanced action to create a custom toggle button for Closed Captions.

This chapter only shows how to use the Skin Editor to add a Closed Captions toggle button to the playback controls bar. You will study the other features of the Skin Editor in `Chapter 14`, *Finishing Touches and Publishing*.

4. Close the **Preview** pane.
5. Use the **Project | Skin Editor** menu to open the floating **Skin Editor** panel.
6. On the left side of the **Skin Editor**, select the **Closed Captioning** checkbox to add a CC button on the playback controls bar.

7. You can also click the **Settings** button below the Closed Captions checkbox to access the Closed Captions settings, and make any modifications. This is the same dialog that you accessed while adding the Closed Captions in the previous section.

Everything is now ready to test the Closed Captions you have added to the project.

8. Make sure you are still on slide 1 of the project and use the **Preview | Next 5 Slides** icon on the Toolbar to test the new CC button in the preview pane.

9. When the project opens in the preview pane, click the **CC** button on the right of the playback controls bar to turn the Closed Captions on.

10. When the preview reaches slide 3, you should see the associated Closed Captions displayed in sync with the audio.

You have successfully added Closed Captions for this slide and it will help in making the project accessible to the students with disabilities.

Closed captioning a video file

The last thing that you will do in this chapter is to add Closed Captions to the video file you imported on slide 22 of the takeTheTrain.cptx project. Note that you can add Closed Captions to a video file only if it has been imported as a **Multi-Slide Synchronized Video**.

1. Still in the Chapter12/takeTheTrain.cptx project, use the **Filmstrip** to return to slide 22. It is the slide where you imported the video file in Chapter 3, *Working with Multimedia*.

2. Go to the **Slide Notes** panel. If it is not open, use the **Window | Slide Notes** option to open it.

3. Click the + sign to add a new note.

4. Type Now, it is time for the departure using a very precise procedure.

5. Click the + sign one more time and type First the train attendant whistles and closes all the doors but one.

6. Click the + sign for the third and last time and type If you are late, this is your very last chance to board the train.

This video is a lot longer and requires more Closed Captions. For this exercise, we will add captions for a small portion of the video. You can follow the same steps to add captions to the rest of the video.

7. Select the **Video CC** checkbox on the top right corner of the **Slide Notes** panel.
8. Then click the **Video CC** button located above the checkbox. The **Edit Video Timing** dialog opens.

The **Edit Video Timing** dialog can be used to edit the imported video file. In this exercise, that's not what you want to do. You only want to add Closed Caption to the video.

9. Click the **Closed Captioning** tab at the top left corner of the **Edit Video Timing** dialog.

Notice that the three yellow vertical bars appear in the upper area of the **Edit Video Timing** dialog.

Watch out! It is possible that these three bars sit on top of each other at the same location, giving the false impression that there is only one vertical bar.

10. Move these vertical bars to synchronize the Closed Captions with the video file. This is the exact same procedure as for the Closed Captions associated with the slide audio.
11. Click the **Play** button in the top left corner of the **Edit Video Timing** box to test the synchronization between the video and the Closed Captions. It will probably be necessary to adjust the position of the vertical bars and to retest the video a few times before the yellow bars are properly positioned.

At the end of this exercise, the **Edit Video Timing** dialog should look like the following screenshot:

12. When done, click **OK** to validate the changes and close the **Edit Video Timing** dialog.
13. Use the **Preview | Next 5 Slides** icon on the Toolbar to test your new Closed Captions.
14. When the **Preview** pane appears, click the **CC** icon of the playback controls bar to turn the Closed Captions on. Confirm that Closed Captions have been successfully added to the video file of slide 22.
15. Save the file when finished.

This exercise concludes your overview of the Closed Captioning system of Captivate. Here is a quick summary of what has been covered.

- Closed Captions are associated either with a slide-level audio clip or with a Multi-Slide synchronized Video.
- The text of the Closed Captions is found in the **Slide Notes** Panel.
- The **Slide Notes** panel is not displayed by default. Use the **Window | Slide Notes** menu item to turn it on and off.
- Use the **Skin Editor** to add the **CC** button to the playback controls bar. The **CC** button is used by the learners to turn the Closed Captions ON or OFF.

Summary

In this chapter, you learned how to add accessibility text to slides and to the objects of the slides. Remember that this text is read aloud by the screen readers for the students with disabilities. Then, you learned how to make the interactive objects of Captivate accessible by assigning a shortcut key and by fine-tuning the tab order.

These options are a little tedious to set, but taking the time to do it dramatically enhances the experience of the student with disabilities. Learning is a right everyone has, so it is part of our duty, as teachers, to ensure that students with disabilities can access our course content in a comfortable fashion.

In some countries, making course content accessible is a legal requirement. The accessibility guidelines and standards are commonly known as Section 508 in reference to an amendment of the US Rehabilitation Act of 1973.

In the next chapter, you will discover some of the most powerful and advanced features of Captivate. Thanks to the variables and the advanced actions, you will be able to add an even higher degree of interactivity and customization to your projects.

Meet the community

In this section, we want to introduce you to Kevin Siegel. Kevin is an awesome technical writer and has written several Adobe Captivate books and developed several courses. Kevin regularly speaks at various Adobe and eLearning related events throughout the United States. Look for one of his sessions during your next conference!

Damien

As an Adobe Captivate Certified Instructor, I teach a lot of Captivate classes. Before I had my own book, I used Kevin's courseware for my teaching. So I can tell you, with no hesitation, that these are great resources if you want to learn Captivate.

Pooja

I have known Kevin for several years, but got to spend quality time with him a few years back during my first trip to Washington DC. He, along with his wife, took me and my colleague for a tour of Washington DC's monuments. It was a day full of history, humor, and excitement. In the last one year, I also got a chance to work closely with Kevin on developing some eLearning courses and conducting training at IconLogic, and it's been a pleasure working with him.

Kevin Siegel

Kevin Siegel is the founder and president of IconLogic, Inc. He has written hundreds of step-by-step computer training books on applications such as Adobe Captivate, Articulate Storyline, Adobe RoboHelp, Adobe Presenter, Adobe Technical Communication Suite, Adobe Dreamweaver, Adobe InDesign, Microsoft Word, Microsoft PowerPoint, QuarkXPress, and TechSmith Camtasia Studio.

Kevin spent five years in the US Coast Guard as an award-winning photojournalist and has nearly three decades of experience as a print publisher, technical writer, instructional designer, and eLearning developer. He is a certified technical trainer, a veteran classroom instructor, certified master online trainer, and a frequent speaker at trade shows and conventions.

Kevin holds multiple certifications from companies such as Adobe, CompTIA, and the International Council for Certified Online Trainers.

IconLogic offers online classes on Captivate that are attended by students worldwide. The company also offers full development and one-on-one mentoring on Captivate and other eLearning development tools.

Contact details

- **Kevin's email**: ksiegel@iconlogic.com
- **IconLogic's website**: http://www.iconlogic.com/
- **IconLogic's blog**: http://www.iconlogic.blogs.com/

13
Working with Variables and Advanced Actions

In this chapter, you will take advantage of the scripting capabilities of HTML5 and Flash. The Flash technology includes a programming language named **ActionScript**. When publishing a Captivate project in Flash, a lot of ActionScript code is generated behind the scenes. It is the Flash Player that executes this ActionScript at runtime. If you decide to publish your projects in HTML5, Captivate generates a lot of JavaScript code instead. It is the browser that executes this JavaScript code at runtime.

Captivate exposes part of this scripting technology to the eLearning developer. Now let's be honest, most eLearning developers won't actually be writing real JavaScript or ActionScript in Captivate (being an ActionScript or JavaScript developer requires proper training and solid programming skills), but you will be able to create some simple scripts, using buttons, drop-down lists, and dialog boxes. In Captivate, these small scripts are called **Advanced Actions**.

Thanks to Advanced Actions, you will be able to dramatically enhance the eLearning experience of the students. For example, you can:

- Dynamically generate text in Text Captions based on student input
- Show and hide objects in response to system or user events
- Trigger a sequence of actions instead of a single action when a Click Box or a Button is clicked to make one interaction accomplish more than one thing
- Evaluate if a condition is true or false before executing an action and so on

Most of the time, Advanced Actions need to store and read data in the memory of the computer, so you need a robust system to manage these pieces of data. This task is handled by **Variables**. Basically, a variable is a named space in the memory of the computer in which you can store pieces of data. When referencing the name of a variable, you can access the data it holds and manipulate this data with Advanced Actions.

In this chapter, you will:

- Learn about and use System Variables
- Store student input in a User Variable
- Use variables to generate text dynamically
- Create Standard and Conditional Advanced Actions
- Create and use Shared Actions
- Create and use a Geolocation variable

Preparing your work

Before getting started with this new chapter, take some time and reset the Captivate interface to default. If you are using the default interface mode, just close and restart Captivate. If you use the advanced interface mode, use the **Window | Workspace | Reset 'Classic'** menu item to reset Captivate to default. In this chapter, you will use the exercises stored in the Chapter13 folder. If you get confused by any of the step-by-step instructions, take a look at the Chapter13/final folder, which contains a copy of the files, as they will be at the end of this chapter.

Working with Variables

Every single programming language in the world makes use of **Variables** to store and retrieve data to and from the memory of the computer. JavaScript and ActionScript are no exception! In Captivate, it is enough to know that a variable is a named space in the memory of the computer in which data can be read or written.

To cut a long story short, a variable is made of two things:

- **A name**: This name must comply with strict naming rules and conventions. In ActionScript for instance, the name of a variable cannot contain any spaces or special characters (such as @, é, è, ç, à, #, ?, /, and so on). When writing a script, the programmer uses the name of the variable to access the data it contains.
- **A value**: The value is the piece of data that the variable contains. This value can change (vary) during the execution of the script or each time the script is executed, hence the name *variable*.

For example, `v_firstName = "Damien"` defines a variable:

- `v_firstName`: This is the name of the variable
- `Damien`: This is the value of the variable

Next time the script is executed, you might have `v_firstName = "Bill"` or `v_firstName = "Pooja"`, depending on the first name of the student taking the course.

In most programming languages, when a variable is created (the proper word is *Declared*), the programmer must specify the type of data that the variable will contain (data types include Text String, Integer, Date, Boolean, and so on), but Captivate has decided to keep things simple, so you won't have to worry about data types in your Captivate scripts.

System and user-defined Variables

In Captivate, there are two types of Variables:

- **System Variables**: These Variables are automatically created by Captivate. You can use them in your scripts to retrieve information about the project, about the system, or to control various aspects of the project.
- **User Variables**: These Variables are your own custom Variables that you create for your own specific use.

Exploring System Variables

Enough talking for now! Let's go back to Captivate to start your hands-on exploration of Variables by performing the following steps:

1. Open the `Chapter13/takeTheTrain.cptx` file.
2. Use the **Project | Variables** menu item to open the **Variables** dialog box.
3. Open the **Type** dropdown, and choose **System** (see **1** in the following screenshot):

When selecting **System** in the **Type** dropdown, the list of the available System Variables appears in the main area of the **Variables** dialog (marked as **2** in the preceding screenshot). Notice the **View By** dropdown (see the arrow in the preceding screenshot) that filters the Variables by their category.

4. Open the **View By** dropdown, and take some time to examine the available items. When you are done, select the **Movie Information** category.

Only the Variables pertaining to the **Movie Information** category are now displayed in the **Variables** dialog.

5. Select the **CaptivateVersion** variable.

The upper area of the **Variables** dialog now displays the information for the **CaptivateVersion** variable. The **CaptivateVersion** variable gives you access to the version number of your Captivate installation.

6. Take some time to review the other **System** Variables available.
7. When you are done, click **Close** to close the **Variables** dialog.

Now that you have a better idea of the available System Variables, you will use one of them to dynamically generate the content of a Text Caption.

You can find more information about the variables available in Captivate at the following URL:
`https://helpx.adobe.com/captivate/using/captivate-variables-list`
`.html`

Generating text dynamically

In Captivate, you can include Variables pretty much anywhere text is supported, typically within Text Captions and Smart Shapes. To be more exact, you will use the names of the Variables to specify the piece of data you want to show on the screen. At runtime, the web browser (if the project is published in HTML5) or the Flash Player (if the project is published in Flash) will replace the name of the Variable with the current value of that variable.

In the next exercise, you will use the following steps to create a small note on the last slide containing the version of Captivate used to create the project:

1. Still in the `Chapter13/takeTheTrain.cptx` file use the **Filmstrip** to go to the last slide of the project (slide 30).
2. Insert a new Text Caption on the last slide. Type `This project is powered by Captivate` in the Text Caption.
3. In the **Timing** or in the **Timeline** panel, make the Text Caption **Appear After 0 sec** and **Display for** the **Rest of** the **Slide**.
4. Feel free to further customize the formatting of this object.
5. Move and resize the Text Caption so it fits on top of the white placard held by the Character. Remember that you can rotate an object using the icon just above the Text Caption, or the **Options** tab of the **Properties** inspector.

So far, so good! This is just about inserting a new Text Caption. Now, what you want is to automatically insert the version number of Captivate at the end of the Text Caption.

6. Double-click the new Text Caption, and place your cursor at the end of the text, after the word **Captivate**.
7. Add a space in the Text Caption after the word **Captivate**.
8. On the **Style** tab of the **Properties** inspector, go to the **Character** section and click the **Insert Variable** icon as shown in the following screenshot:

This action opens the **Insert Variable** dialog. You use this dialog to choose the variable whose value is to be inserted in the Text Caption.

    9. In the **Insert Variable** dialog, change **Variable Type** from **User** to **System** if necessary.

    10. In the **View By** dropdown, choose the **Movie Information** category.

    11. Open the **Variables** dropdown, and choose the **CaptivateVersion** variable in the list of available variables.

    12. Click **OK** to append the Variable to the Text Caption.

Thanks to this sequence of actions, you have added the **CaptivateVersion** system variable to the end of the new Text Caption. Actually, it is the name of the variable that has been added to the Text Caption. The Text Caption now reads **This project is powered by Captivate $$CaptivateVersion$$**. At runtime, the **$$CaptivateVersion$$** part of the sentence will be automatically replaced by the value of the `CaptivateVersion` variable.

It is now time to test the new Text Caption in the **Preview** pane.

    13. Use the **Filmstrip** to return to slide 29.

    14. Use the **Preview | From This Slide** icon on the Toolbar to preview your sequence in the **Preview** pane.

    15. When the last slide appears in the **Preview** pane, pay close attention to the newly added Text Caption.

    16. Close the **Preview** pane when you are done and save the file.

Normally, the Text Caption should read something like **This project is powered by Captivate 10.0.0**!

This first experience with Variables teaches you what **Dynamic Text** is. It is a piece of text that is generated dynamically at runtime.

Using user-defined Variables

What is true for System Variables is also true for User Variables. In this section, you will create a User Variable to store the first name of the student taking the course. To capture the value of that variable, you will use the Text Entry Box that you've added at the beginning of the project in `Chapter 5`, *Working with Interactive Objects*.

Creating a User Variable

First, you will create your own User Variable using the following steps:

1. Return to the `Chapter13/takeTheTrain.cptx` file.
2. Use the **Project | Variables** menu item to open the **Variables** dialog.
3. Make sure that **User** is selected in the **Type** dropdown.

Note that Captivate has already generated a few User Variables for you. Two of these variables expose the name and the ID of the student when the course is hosted on an LMS (This data is transmitted from the LMS to your course module using the SCORM, AICC, or xAPI standard).

4. Click the **Add New** button to create a new variable.
5. Type `v_name` in the **Name** field.

This will be the name of your new variable. Remember that the name of a variable must comply with a strict set of rules and conventions, which are as follow:

- A variable name cannot contain any spaces
- A variable name cannot contain any special characters

In addition to these rules, some names are reserved by ActionScript/JavaScript and cannot be used as the names of your user-defined variables.

See the Captivate Help at `https://helpx.adobe.com/captivate/using/create-user-defined-vari able.html` for a complete list of ActionScript reserved names.

6. Leave the **Value** field empty.
7. Optionally, add a meaningful **Description** to the new variable.
8. Click **Save** to create the variable and **Close** the **Variables** dialog.

Now that the variable exists, you will use the Text Entry Box you added on slide 3 earlier in this book to capture the value to be stored in it.

Capturing values with Text Entry Boxes

Back in `Chapter 5`, *Working with Interactive Objects*, you added a Text Entry Box on slide 3 of this project. In this section, you will assign your new User Variable to this object. Whatever the student types in the Text Entry Box becomes the value of your `v_name` custom variable.

1. Use the **Filmstrip** to go to slide 3 of the `takeTheTrain.cptx` project.
2. Select the Text Entry Box on the right side of the slide.
3. If needed, click the **Properties** icon on the Toolbar to open the **Properties** inspector.
4. In the **Style** tab of the **Properties** inspector, make sure the **Validate User Input** checkbox is *not* selected.

Remember that a Text Entry Box can be used for two very different purposes. You can use it in a Quiz and ask your students to type something specific. In this case, you have correct and incorrect answers, and the value typed in the Text Entry Box must be validated.

But in this case, you want to use a Text Entry Box to grab a piece of data (the name of the learner). There are, therefore, no correct or incorrect answers. So there is no need to validate what the user types in the Text Entry Box. Instead, you will associate this Text Entry Box with the custom `v_name` variable you created in the previous section.

5. Still in the **Style** tab of the **Properties** inspector, open the **Variable** dropdown.
6. Select the `v_name` variable from the list of available variables.

Your Text Entry Box is now associated with the `v_name` variable. It means that whatever the student types in the Text Entry Box at runtime becomes the value of the `v_name` variable.

Using the right variables

When creating the Text Entry Box, Captivate has automatically created the `Text_Entry_Box_1` user variable. We suggest you don't use these automatically created variables. Instead, take the necessary time to create your own variables and to give them meaningful names. This is critical for developing and maintaining your projects over time, especially when working in a team. Note that you can create your custom variable directly from the **Properties** inspector by clicking the [x] icon next to the **Variables** dropdown in the **Style** tab. You can also safely delete the `Text_Entry_Box_1` using the **Project | Variables** menu item.

The Text Entry Box is now ready to capture the first name of the student and to store that value in the `v_name` variable.

Using user-defined variables to dynamically generate text

The last step of this sequence is to use the v_name variable and its associated value to dynamically generate the title of slide 4 using the following steps:

1. Use the **Filmstrip** to go to slide 4 of the takeTheTrain.cptx project.
2. Double-click the title placeholder and type Welcome followed by a space.
3. In the **Character** section of the **Style** tab of the **Properties** inspector, click the **Insert Variable** icon.
4. In the **Insert Variable** dialog, choose the v_name **User** variable.
5. Change the **Maximum length** value to 30 characters to accommodate longer first names.
6. When the **Insert Variable** dialog looks similar to the following screenshot, click the **OK** button:

This action inserts the v_name variable in the title of slide 4 and encloses it in double **$** signs. The full text of the Caption now is **Welcome $$v_name$$**. Remember that at runtime, the **$$v_name$$** part of the sentence is automatically replaced by the first name of the student as typed in the Text Entry Box of the previous slide.

7. When you are done, save the file and return to the first slide of the project.
8. Use the **Preview | Next 5 Slides** icon on the Toolbar to preview the first few slides.

On the third slide, type your first name in the Text Entry Box, and click the **Submit** button. On slide 4, your name should be displayed in the title. If your name was longer than the 30 characters maximum length you defined, it will be truncated. You can always increase that value.

9. Close the **Preview** pane and save the file when you are done.

This exercise concludes your first exploration of System and User Variables. Before moving on to creating more variables and using them in Advanced Actions, let's quickly summarize what you have learned so far.

- A variable is a named space in the memory of the computer. When referencing the *name* of a variable, you can access the *data* that the variable contains.
- There are two types of variables in Captivate. The System Variables are automatically created by Captivate. The User Variables are yours to create.
- It is possible to insert Variables in Text Captions and in Smart Shapes to add dynamic text into the project.
- A dynamic text is a text that is generated at runtime. The Flash Player or the JavaScript engine of the browser retrieves the current value of a given variable to generate the content of a Text Caption/Smart Shape.
- A Text Entry box can be associated with a User Variable. Whatever value typed by the student in the Text Entry Box becomes the value of the associated variable. Once captured and stored in a variable, that piece of data can be used later in the project for various purposes, including generating dynamic text.

Working with Advanced Actions

An Advanced Action is a small program that is executed at runtime by the JavaScript engine of the web browser or the Flash Player. These Advanced Actions can be used to manipulate the data contained in Variables, and to manipulate the objects of Captivate or even the project itself.

In Captivate, there are three families of Advanced Actions:

- **Standard Actions**: These actions are simple procedures that are always executed the same way in a linear fashion.
- **Conditional Actions**: These actions are a bit more complex. They can evaluate if a given condition is true or false and act accordingly. Consequently, they do not always perform the same set of actions each time they are executed.
- **Shared Actions**: These actions can be reused throughout a given project or even shared across projects.

In the next exercise, you will create a couple of Standard Actions to get a sense of what they can achieve.

Using Standard Action

The Standard Action is the simplest form of Advanced Actions that can be created in Captivate. A Standard Action is simply a list of instructions that the JavaScript engine of the browser or the Flash Player executes one by one and in order in response to an event.

Using a button to mute and unmute the audio

In this section, you will use an advanced action to mute and unmute the audio of the project. The goal is to provide the student with a button in the top left corner of the slide to toggle the audio on and off. To do so, you first need to prepare and identify all the ingredients that will make up this action.

Step 1 - Creating the Mute button

The first ingredient is the Mute button itself, which you will create using the following steps.

1. Still in the `Chapter13/takeTheTrain.cptx` file, use the **Filmstrip** to return to the first slide of the project.
2. Use the **Shapes** icon on the Toolbar to create a new oval anywhere on the slide.
3. With the new shape selected, look at the **Properties** inspector.

4. In the **Options** tab, give your oval a Width and a Height of 35 px. This is the best way to ensure that the oval is actually a circle. Note that you must deselect the **Constrain proportions** checkbox to be able to set the Width and the Height of the object independently from each other.

5. In the **Style** tab, Change the **Fill** type to **Image Fill**.

6. Click the **Fill** button (1) and choose to use a custom image (2). This operation is illustrated in the following screenshot:

7. In the **Select Image/Audio from Library** dialog, click the **Import** button.

8. Navigate to the `Chapter13/images/Mute_Button_up.png` image file and use it as the image fill of the circle shape.

9. At the top of the **Properties** inspector, select the **Use as Button** checkbox.

10. Click the **State View** button to switch to the States view.

Notice that three built-in states have been automatically generated by Captivate when selecting the **Use as Button** checkbox. You will now customize these states and add an additional custom state using the following steps:

11. In the **Object State** panel, on the left side of the screen, select the **RollOver** state.

12. In the **Style** tab, change the **Fill** type to **Image Fill**.

13. Click the **Fill** button and choose to use a custom image. Navigate to the `Chapter13/images/Mute_Button_over.png` image file and use it as the image fill of the circle shape in the **RollOver** state.

14. 14. Repeat the same operations to change the image used in the **Down** state. Use the `Chapter13/images/Mute_Button_down.png`.

15. In the **Object State** panel, right click the **Down** state and choose the **Duplicate State** menu item.

16. Duplicate the **Down** state as a **Custom** state named `Active`.

You should now have four different states for your Mute button. The **Normal, Rollover,** and **Down** states are three built-in states created automatically by Captivate. You simply customized them by changing the background image of the button in each state. On top of that, you have created an additional custom state called **Active**. This last state is simply a copy of the built-in **down** state.

17. Use the **Exit State** icon on the Toolbar to return to the standard Captivate interface.

18. Move the button in the header area of the slide next to the **DiDaXo** logo.

19. At the top of the **Properties** inspector, give your button a meaningful name such as `btn_mute`. Don't forget to validate the button name with the *Enter* or with the *Tab* key.

20. Switch to the **Timing** panel.

21. Make sure your button **Appears After 0 sec.**

22. Deselect the **Pause After** checkbox.

23. In the **Display For** drop-down menu select the **Rest of Project** option. This ensures that the button will be displayed at this exact same location throughout the whole project.

24. Select the **Place Object on Top** checkbox. Since this button is displayed during the whole project, you want to make sure that it is always on top of whatever object you could add on the other slides of the project.

The first piece of your action is now in place. It should look like the following screenshot:

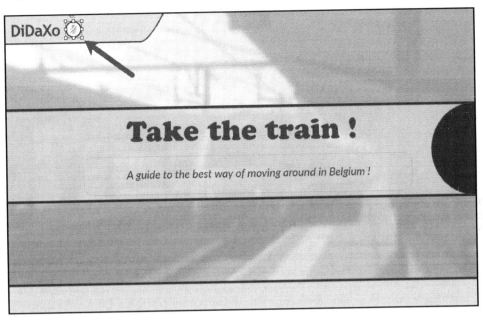

Step 2 - Finding out the action to create

The second ingredient that you need is the name of the system variable that you want to manipulate. Let's find it using the following steps:

1. Use the **Project | Variables** menu item to open the **Variables** dialog.
2. In the **Type** drop-down menu choose the **System** variables.
3. In the **View By** drop-down menu, choose the **Movie Control** category.
4. Select the **cpCmndMute** variable.

This is the system variable that you need to use to mute and unmute the audio. Take some time to read its description. Take good note of the fact that this variable accepts only two values. If it is set to 1, the audio is muted and if it is set to 0, the audio is un-muted. For you techies, this is an example of a Boolean variable in Adobe Captivate.

Step 3 - Creating the action

Now the third ingredient is the action itself. It should mute the audio and change the state of the button. Use the following steps to create this standard Advanced Action:

1. Still in the `Chapter13/takeTheTrain.cptx` file, use the **Project | Advanced Actions** menu item to open the **Advanced Actions** dialog.
2. In the top left corner of the dialog, type `muteAudio` in the **Action Name** field.

Note that the name of the action must comply with the same strict rules as the name of the variables (no spaces, no special characters, no reserved names).

3. In the **Actions** area of the dialog, double-click the first line of the table.

This adds a first step to the Advanced Action. In the first column, a yellow warning sign indicates that the action is invalid in its current state. In the second column, you find a dropdown menu containing a list of possible actions.

4. Open the **Select Action...** dropdown, and take some time to inspect the list of possible actions.
5. When done, choose the **Assign** action in the list (unfortunately, these actions are not alphabetized).
6. Open the **Select Variable** dropdown, and take some time to inspect the available Variables.

The **Select Variable** dropdown proposes a list of Variables whose value can be changed. (For instance, the `CaptivateVersion` variable you used earlier is not listed, because you cannot change the value of this variable. It is a read-only variable).

7. Select the `cpCmndMute` variable.
8. Open the second **Variable** dropdown and choose **Literal**.
9. Type `1` in the field that appears, and press *Enter*.

The whole sentence becomes `Assign cpCmndMute with 1`. In plain English, it translates to *Turn off the audio*. Notice that the yellow warning sign in front of the action changed into a green checkmark. This is an indication that Captivate understands the first instruction of your Advanced Action, which is very good news!

10. Double-click the second line of the table to add a second step into the action.
11. In the **Select Action...** dropdown, choose the **Change State Of** action.
12. In the next dropdown, choose the object you want to change the state of. In this example, choose your **bnt_mute** button.
13. In the third and final dropdown, choose the custom state of the selected object you want to go to. In this case, you need the **Active** state.

Notice that only the **Normal** state and whatever custom states you created for the selected object are displayed in the list. The other built-in states (in this case the *RollOver* and the *Down* states) are not listed. This is the reason why you had to duplicate the Down state as a custom state (that you decided to name *Active*) earlier in this procedure.

Make sure the **Advanced Actions** dialog looks like the following screenshot before continuing with this exercise:

14. Click the **Save As Action** button at the bottom of the dialog to save the Advanced Action.
15. Acknowledge the successful saving of the Advanced Action, and **Close** the **Advanced Action** dialog.

Your Advanced Action is now ready, but one last piece of the puzzle is still missing. You need to tell Captivate *when* you want your action to be executed. In other words, you need to attach the action to the **event** that will trigger it.

Step 4 - Assigning the action to an event

In Captivate, there are lots of events you can attach actions to. Some of them are **system events** (for example, the start of a course, the beginning of a slide, etc.), and some of them are **student-driven events** (typically, clicking a button). In this case, you will ask Captivate to execute the action when the student clicks the Mute button you created earlier in this chapter.

1. Still on slide 1 of the `Chapter13/takeTheTrain.cptx` project, make sure that the **Properties** inspector displays the properties of the mute button.
2. In the **Actions** tab of the **Properties** inspector, change the **On Success** action to **Execute Advanced Actions**.
3. In the **Script** dropdown that appears just below, make sure the **muteAudio** action is selected.
4. Save the file and use the **Preview | Project** icon on the Toolbar to test the project.

When the **Preview** pane opens, there are a few things to test in order to make sure that the action works properly:

- First, make sure your mute button appears on the first slide and stays visible on the other slides of the project.
- When the audio narration starts (on slide 3), click the Mute button. Confirm that the audio stops and that the button switches to the Active state.

This first example illustrates how an Advanced Action can be used to manipulate a System Variable and how to attach an action to an event. By providing a way to mute the audio, you enhance the overall experience of your students.

Note that your advanced action is actually performing two things: it mutes the audio *and* it changes the state of your Mute button. In other words, clicking the Mute button does not trigger only one action, but a whole bunch of actions as defined in the *muteAudio* Advanced Action. The ability to perform multiple actions as a response to a single event (in this case, clicking the Mute button) is the real power of those Advanced Actions.

Now, there is one more problem to solve. When you click the Mute button, you turn the audio off, but there is currently no way of turning the audio back on (in other words, to unmute the audio). In the next section, you will use a conditional advanced action to turn your mute button into a toggle button that has the ability to turn the audio on, if it is currently off, and to turn the audio off, if it is currently on.

Using Conditional actions

A Conditional Action is a bit more complex than a Standard Action as it is able to evaluate if a condition is true or false and act accordingly.

To illustrate this capability, you will now turn the Mute button you created in the previous section into a toggle button. This means that you want your button to be able to do two entirely different things:

- Firstly it needs to be able to mute the audio and to change the state of the Mute button to Active.
- Secondly, it needs to be able to unmute the audio and to change the state of the Mute button back to Normal.

In order to choose which set of actions to perform, your button needs to evaluate if a condition is true or false. In this example, you first need to verify if the audio is currently on or off. This is what will decide which set of actions to perform.

You will now update the standard advanced action you created in the previous section and make it a conditional action using the following steps:

1. Still in the `Chapter13/takeTheTrain.cptx` project, use the **Project | Advanced Actions** to reopen the **Advanced Actions** dialog.
2. In the upper right corner of the dialog, open the **Existing Actions** drop-down menu and choose the **Mute Audio** action. This is how you can update an existing action instead of creating a new one.
3. Just above the main area of the dialog box, select the **Conditional Tab** checkbox (see **1** in the following screenshot).

This turns your action into a Conditional Action. The **Advanced Actions** dialog updates and shows the interface that you use to create the Conditional Advanced Action.

Notice that you now have two main sections in the **Advanced Actions** dialog.

- At the top of the dialog, you have the **If** section (see **2** in the following screenshot). This is where you define the condition(s) to check before performing an action.
- The bottom half of the dialog (see **3** in the following screenshot) is used to define the actions to perform if the condition(s) defined above is (are) true. Note that the set of actions you defined earlier in this chapter have been moved to that section.

At the very bottom of the box, notice the optional **Else** section (see 4 in the following screenshot) that allows you to optionally provide an alternative set of actions to perform if the condition(s) evaluate to *false*.

In this example, you want to execute the actions defined in the Actions section (**3** in the above screenshot) only if the audio is turned on when the student clicks the Mute button.

4. In the **If** part of the box, double-click the first line of the table to add the first condition.
5. Open the **Variable** dropdown and select the **Variable** option from the list. Then, open the list again to select the `cpCmndMute` system variable.
6. Open the **Select comparison operator** dropdown, and choose the **is equal to** option from the list of available operators.
7. Open the last dropdown and choose **Literal** from the list. Then type 0 in the field that appears.

The whole expression now reads `cpCmndMute is equal to 0` and a green checkmark appears in the first column of the table. In plain English, this translates to *If the audio is currently not muted.*

Notice the **AND** word at the end of the condition. It tells you that you can add more conditions and that these would be united by an AND operator. In other words, every individual condition should be true for the entire condition to be true.

8. Open the **All conditions are true** dropdown, and choose the **Any of the conditions true** option from the list.

Note that the **AND** keyword switches to **OR**. In this case, the entire condition is true if any one of the individual conditions is true.

9. Open the **Any of the conditions true** dropdown and choose the **Custom** option from the list.

In this situation, it is up to the developer to choose between **AND** and **OR** at the end of every condition. This allows you to create very complex conditions. In this exercise, you only have a single condition, so the choice between **AND** and **OR** is not relevant.

10. Open the **Custom** dropdown one last time, and revert to the **All conditions are true** option to return to the initial situation.
11. Click the **Else** button (marked as 4 on the preceding screenshot) to open the list of actions to perform if the condition evaluates to *false*.
12. Double-click the first row of the **Else** action pane.
13. Open the **Select Action...** dropdown and choose the **Assign** action in the list.
14. Open the next dropdown and select the `cpCmndMute` variable.

15. Open the second **Variable** drop-down list, and choose **Literal**.
16. Type 0 in the field that appears, and press *Enter*. This is the action that turns the audio back on if it is already muted when the student clicks the button.
17. Double-click the second line of the table to add a second step into the action.
18. In the **Select Action...** dropdown, choose the **Change State Of** action.
19. In the next dropdown menu, choose your **bnt_mute** button.
20. In the third and final dropdown list, choose the **Normal** state.

The **Else** part of your Advanced Action should look like the following screenshot:

You will now update the name of your advanced action to better reflect what it actually does, and save it using the following steps.

21. In the **Action Name** field, in the top left corner of the dialog, change the name of the action to toggleAudio.
22. At the very bottom of the dialog, click the **Update Action** button.
23. Acknowledge the successful update and close the **Advanced Actions** dialog.

Your advanced action has been updated and is now much more sophisticated than before. It is now a conditional action that is able to execute different sets of actions based on whether a condition is *true* or *false*. Let's test it out using the following steps:

24. Save the file and use the **Preview | Project** icon on the Toolbar to test the project.

When the **Preview** pane opens, test the following things:

- When the audio narration starts (on slide 3), click the Mute button. Confirm that the audio stops and that the button switches to the Active state.
- Click the same button again and confirm that the audio switches back on and that the button reverts to the Normal state.

Congratulations! You now have a toggle button in your project that your student can use to mute and unmute the audio.

Extra credit: Creating a Closed Captions toggle button

In this Extra Credit section, you will create an additional button next to the **Mute** button you created in the previous sections and develop a Conditional Advanced Action to turn the Closed Captions on and off. The main difference between this button and the mute button is the System Variable you need to manipulate. In this example, use the cpCmndCC variable to turn the Closed Captions on and off. The general steps of the procedure go as follows:

- Create a Closed Captions button using the images stored in the Chapter13/images folder. Make sure you create a custom **Active** state for the button and place it next to the **Mute** button. Don't forget to give this new button a name in the topmost section of the **Properties** inspector.
- Use the **Timing** panel to make the button visible for the whole project on top of any other elements.
- Use the **Project | Variables** dialog to read the description of the cpCmndCC system variable.
- Create a conditional advanced action to determine the current value of the cpCmndCC Variable and act accordingly.
- Assign your Advanced Action to the click event of your new button.
- Test your button in the Preview pane of Captivate.

This concludes your first exploration of Conditional Advanced Actions in Captivate. In the next section, you will discover Shared Actions.

Using Shared Actions

A Shared Actions is an Advanced Action (standard or conditional) that can be reused multiple times in a single project or shared across multiple projects.

Shared Actions make sharing actions across projects easy. But there are other ways to share actions across projects. Dr Pooja Jaisingh has written a great blog post about this. You can find it at https://elearning.adobe.com/2013/12/the-most-awaited-enhancements-in-advanced-actions-and-variables-are-here/.

In Chapter 5, *Working with Interactive Objects*, you created a sequence of slides to teach the different types of train tickets available in Belgium:

- On slide 13 of your takeTheTrain.cptx project, you have three buttons, one for each ticket type. Each of these buttons takes you to the corresponding slide of the sequence.
- Slides 14, 15, and 16 are the three destination slides of the buttons defined on slide 13. Remember that at the end of each of these three slides, the playhead jumps back to slide 13.
- Also remember that you used the Visited state of the buttons to add a checkmark next to the ticket type that has already been viewed by the student.

In this section, you will make sure that the student goes through the three ticket types before clicking the **Continue** button that you have added in the bottom right corner of slide 13.

To do so, you will first hide the **Continue** button. Then, you will create three User Variables in order to track which ticket type has been viewed by the student.

When the student will have viewed each ticket type at least once, you will reveal the **Continue** button on slide 13, allowing the student to jump to the next sequence and continue with the rest of the course.

Step 1 - Creating the necessary variables

The first step towards creating this advanced interactive sequence is to create the variables that you will need to track the ticket types visited by the students.

1. Still in the Chapter13/takeTheTrain.cptx file, use the **Project | Variables** menu item to open the **Variables** dialog box.
2. At the top of the **Variables** dialog, click the **Add New** button.

3. Type `v_standardTicket_visited` as the variable name.
4. Type `0` as the initial value of the variable.
5. Optionally type a meaningful description in the **Description** field.
6. Click the **Save** button to save the new variable.
7. Repeat the above process to create the `v_pass_visited` and the `v_subscription_visited` variables.

Make sure that the **Variables** dialog looks like the following screenshot before moving on:

Each of these three variables has an initial value of 0, indicating that the corresponding slides have not yet been viewed by the student. You will use an action to turn the value of these variables to 1 when the student clicks the buttons of slide 13.

About naming variables

You already know that the name of a variable must comply with strict naming rules (no space, no special characters, and so on). That being said, any name that complies with these rules is not necessarily right. When naming variables, it is important to stick to **conventions** in addition to complying with the rules, especially when working in a team. If no naming convention exists among the developers of a team, everyone ends up with his own naming rules and habits. In such a case, it is nearly impossible to keep track of the variables and to maintain the projects over time. In this chapter, you use the `v_` prefix to mark your custom variables. It also helps in finding your custom variables amongst the alphabetically ordered list of variables in Captivate. This is one of the possible naming conventions, but any other convention will do! The bottom line is: complying with the technical rules is not enough!

Step 2 - Creating the Shared Action

You will now create the actions that will update the value of the variables created in the preceding section to 1 and jump the playhead to a different slide when the student clicks the buttons of slide 13.

If you think about it, you have three buttons on slide 13 to which you want to apply a similar behavior (changing the value of a variable to 1 and jumping to a slide). The only differences between the actions to create are the specific variable to update and the specific slide to jump to. Thanks to Shared Actions, you will create a single Advanced Action that you will reuse multiple times, only changing some parameters each time you use the action.

In this exercise, you will use the following steps to create a Conditional Advanced Action that updates the value of the `v_standardTicket_visited` variable to 1 and jumps the user to slide 14.

1. Still in the `Chapter13/takeTheTrain.cptx` file, use the **Project | Advanced Actions** menu item to open the **Advanced Actions** dialog.
2. Type `viewTicketType` in the **Action Name** field.
3. Double-click the first line of the **Actions** list.
4. Choose **Assign** in the list of available actions.
5. Open the **Variables** dropdown and click the **Variables** item.
6. Choose the `v_standartTicket_visited` variable in the list.
7. Open the second **Variable** dropdown and choose the **literal** item.
8. Type *1* in the field that appears and validate with the *Enter* key.
9. Double-click the second row of the **Actions** list to add a second action.
10. Choose **Jump to Slide** in the list of available actions.
11. In the next dropdown menu, choose the **14 Using standard tickets** slide.

Your Advanced Action is now complete. The two actions should read: *Assign the v_standardTicket_visited variable with 1, and Jump to slide 14.* This is illustrated in the following screenshot:

So far, creating the Shared Action is no different to creating a regular action. You will now save your new Advanced Action as a Shared Action using the following steps:

12. Click the **Save As Shared Action** button at the bottom of the dialog.

This action opens the **Save As Shared Action** box. In this box, you need to define the parameters of the Shared Action. Remember that a Shared Action is meant to be reused multiple times in the project (or even across projects). The parameters of the Shared Action are the elements that differ each time the action is executed. In this case, you need two parameters: the variable to update and the slide to jump to.

Note that Captivate has automatically identified the potential parameters. It has already selected one of those parameters automatically, and that there is no way to deselect the checkbox that Captivate has selected for you. The Variables and their values are not mandatory to parameterize in shared actions, as opposed to the objects and their states. This explains why, in this example, the *Slide to Jump to* parameter is mandatory, while the other two are optional.

You will now create those two parameters using the following steps:

13. Select the checkbox associated with the **v_standardTicket_visited** parameter.
14. Type `Variable to update` in the associated **Parameter Description** field.

15. Type `Slide to jump to` in the **Parameter Description** field associated with the **14 Using Standard Ticket** slide.

16. Take some time to type a meaningful **Description** as it will help you use this same action in other situations later.

Make sure the **Save As Shared Action** box looks like the following screenshot before continuing:

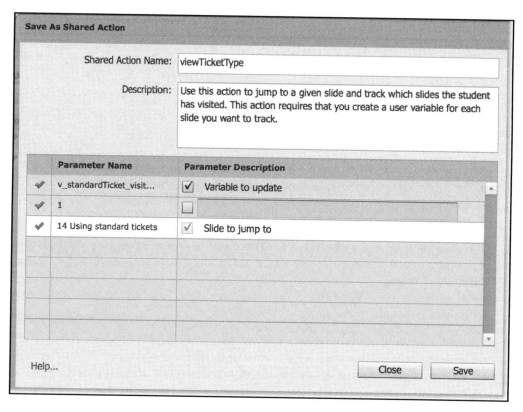

17. When you are done, click the **Save** button of the **Save As Shared Action** dialog.

18. Clear the information message and **Close** the **Advanced Actions** dialog.

The Shared Action is now complete and saved in the project. The next step is to attach this action to an event. In this case, the event is a click that the transparent buttons associated with each ticket type.

Step 3 - Using and reusing the Shared Action

The last step of the process is to use and reuse your shared action. As with any other action, you have to attach your shared action to an event. Only this time, you will attach the same Shared Action to many different events and set different action parameters each time. You will test it out on the *Using Standard Ticket* button using the following steps:

1. Still in the `takeTheTrain.cptx` file, use the **Filmstrip** panel to go to slide 13.
2. Select the transparent button on top of the **Using Standard Ticket** image. (Remember this requires two clicks. The first click selects the group of objects and the second click subselects the button within the group).

You can check that the selected object is indeed the intended transparent button by looking at the **Properties** inspector. If you see an **Actions** tab, it means that the selected object is a button! When the learner clicks this button, the value of the v_standartTicket_visited variable must change to 1 and the student must jump to slide 14.

3. In the **Actions** tab of the **Properties** inspector, open the **On Success** dropdown list.
4. Choose the **Execute Shared Action** item.
5. Make sure the **viewTicketType** action is selected in the dropdown that appears just below.
6. Click the little {P} icon next to the name of the action. This opens the **Shared Action Parameters** dialog.
7. Choose **v_standardTicket_visited** as the value of the **Variable to update** parameter.
8. Choose **14 Using standard tickets** as the value of the **Slide to jump to** parameter.

These actions are illustrated in the following screenshot:

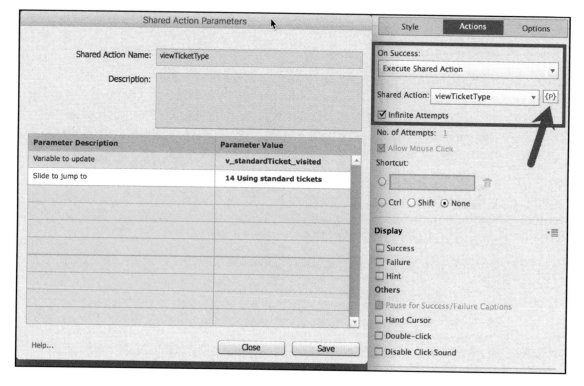

9. Click the **Save** button of the **Shared Action Parameters** dialog to finalize the process.

Extra Credit: reusing the Shared Action

All you need to do now is to attach the same Shared Action to the **On Success** event of the other transparent buttons of slide 13. For each button, the same Shared Action will be executed but using different parameters. These are the general steps to follow:

- Select the transparent button associated with one of the remaining ticket types
- In the **Actions** tab of the **Properties** inspector, attach the `viewTicketType` Shared Action to the **On Success** event of the selected button
- Click the {P} icon and choose the parameters pertaining to the selected button
- When you are done, use the **Project | Next 5 slides** icon on the Toolbar to test your sequence and make sure you jump to the correct slide when clicking the buttons

Refer to the following table for choosing the right parameters for the Shared Action:

Button	Variable to update	Slide to jump to
Using passes	v_pass_visited	15 Using passes
Using Subscriptions	v_subscription_visited	16 Using subscriptions

Reusing shared actions across projects

In the previous section you created a shared action and used it three times in the same project. It is also possible to share actions across projects using two different techniques.

- First, take a look at the **Library** panel and notice the **Shared Actions** section toward the bottom of the panel. In Chapter 4, *Working with the Timeline and Other Useful Tools,* you learned how to open the **Library** of another project in the current project in order to share assets (including Shared Actions) across projects.
- The second technique is to use the icons located in the top right corner of the Advanced Actions dialog. Using these icons, you can Import Shared Actions in the project or Export shared actions from the project. Captivate uses a file with the .cpaa extension to save a shared action externally.

Shared Advanced Actions is a very powerful and advanced feature of Captivate. If you want to know more about it, consult the official Captivate help page on Shared Actions at
http://helpx.adobe.com/captivate/using/shared-actions.html.

Hiding and showing objects using advanced actions

The reason why you have created the Shared action of the previous section is to be able to track which ticket type the students have visited. In this section, you will use that information to show the **Continue** button on slide 13 only when all three ticket types have been visited at least once. The first step is to hide the **Continue** button and to give it a name.

1. Use the **Filmstrip** to go to slide 13 of the `Chapter 13/takeTheTrain.cptx` file.
2. Select the **Continue** button in the bottom right corner of the slide.
3. At the top of the **Properties** inspector, give this button a meaningful name (for example, `btn_continue`) and press *Enter* to validate.
4. Use the **Timeline** panel or the **Timing** inspector to make sure the **Continue** button **Appears After** 0 sec and stays visible for the **Rest of the Slide**.
5. Click the eye icon in the topmost section of the **Properties** inspector to hide this object from the student in the published project.

Make sure the topmost section of the **Properties** inspector looks like the following screenshot:

Visibility versus Visibility

Notice that the **Continue** button is still visible on the stage, even though you have clicked the eye icon at the top of the **Properties** inspector. This is because the eye icon you clicked controls the visibility of the object *in the published project only*, but not in the authoring environment of Captivate. Use the **Preview | Next 5 slides** icon of the Toolbar to confirm that the **Continue** button is *not* displayed to the student. Remember that you have another eye icon located in the **Timeline** panel, that controls the visibility of the object in the Captivate authoring environment only.

Now that the **Continue** button is hidden, you will create a Conditional Advanced action that will check if the three slides associated with each ticket type have been visited. If all three slides have been visited, the action should turn the visibility of the **Continue** button back on.

6. Use the **Project | Advanced Actions** menu item to open the **Advanced Actions** dialog.
7. Type showContinueButton in the **Action Name** field.
8. Select the **Conditional Tab** checkbox.
9. In the **If** area of the **Advanced Actions** dialog, check if the v_standardTicket_visited variable **is equal to 1**.
10. Add two more conditions in the If section to check if the v_pass_visited variable **is equal to 1** and if the v_subscription_visited variable **is equal to 1**. All three variables should be equal to 1 for the whole condition to be true.
11. In the **Actions** section of the **Advanced Action** dialog, add the **Show btn_continue** action.

In this case there is no need to specify an action in the **Else** section. Make sure your **Advanced Actions** dialog looks like the following screenshot before moving on.

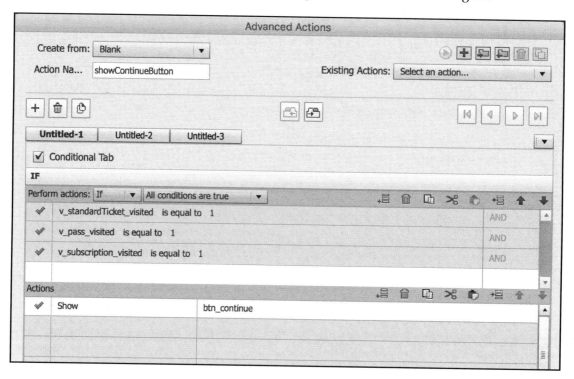

12. Save this as an action and close the **Advanced Actions** dialog.

The last step of this process is to attach this action to the **On Enter** event of slide 13. Since the student goes back to slide 13 multiple times, your action will be executed multiple times as well. But it is only when all three variables will be equal to 1 (in other words when the student visited all three ticket types) that the **Continue** button will appear on the slide.

13. Still on slide 13 of the `Chapter13/takeTheTrain.cptx` file, click once in the grey scrap area around the slide to select the slide itself. After this operation, the **Properties** inspector should display the properties of the slide.
14. Switch to the **Actions** tab of the **Properties** inspector.
15. Open the **On Enter** dropdown and choose the **Execute Advanced Action** item.
16. Choose the **showContinueButton** action in the **Script** dropdown menu.
17. Use the **Preview | Next 5 slides** icon on the Toolbar to test your new action. Make sure the **Continue** button displays only when you have visited the three ticket types.

In this section, you have used Advanced Actions to show an object when certain conditions are met. Using Advanced Actions to show and hide objects is another very common use case found in many Captivate projects.

While there is still so much more to say about Advanced Actions (they probably deserve their own book), let's consider your first exploration of the Advanced Actions of Captivate complete. It is time to quickly summarize what has been covered before moving on to the next section.

- There are three kinds of Advanced Actions in Captivate: Standard Actions, Conditional Actions, and Shared Actions.
- A Standard Action is a simple list of instructions executed one by one and in order at runtime.
- A Conditional Action checks if a condition is met before executing an action.
- A Shared Action is an Advanced Action that can be reused multiple times in a project or even across multiple projects.
- Use the **Conditional Tab** checkbox of the **Advanced Actions** dialog to decide if your action is a Standard Action or a Conditional Action.
- The Advanced Actions can be used to manipulate system or user-defined Variables, to manipulate the objects of the project or to manipulate the project itself.
- It is possible to give a name to any objects of Captivate. This makes it easier to manipulate these objects with Advanced Actions or to use them as parameters of Shared Actions.
- Make sure you create and name all the variables you need before creating your Advanced Actions.
- It is necessary to attach an action to an event in order to instruct Captivate about when an action should be executed.
- There are two kinds of events in Captivate: system events and student-driven events.
- System events are triggered automatically by the project. Examples of system events include the beginning or the end of a slide, or the start of the project, etc.
- Student-driven events are triggered by an action performed by the student. The typical student-driven event is clicking a Button, but it can also be clicking a Click Box, or answering a Question Slide, etc.

Variables and Advanced Actions are among the most advanced topics found in Captivate. You've only scratched the surface of this powerful feature in this book. With time and experience, you'll be able to take full advantage of this most powerful tool.

For more on Advanced Actions, make sure you subscribe to the Blog of Lieve Weymeis, aka Lilybiri, at `http://blog.lilybiri.com/`. She is a world-class specialist of Advanced Actions, and her blog is second to none when it comes to Variables, Advanced Actions, and other advanced tips and tricks on Captivate.

Geolocation in Adobe Captivate

What makes mobile learning so exciting and promising are the unique capabilities of the mobile devices used by the students when taking their online courses. One such capability is called **Geolocation**. It is the ability to detect where the learner is located while using his/her mobile device. Many apps take advantage of this ability to provide different content based on the user's location. For example, you can ask your mobile device to look for a restaurant within a 5-mile radius of your current location.

Captivate allows you to leverage that power in your eLearning course. You can now access the location of the learner and provide content based on where the learner is located.

For the `takeTheTrain.cptx` file, the target audience is foreigners who want to visit Belgium. In other words, this project is not aimed at Belgian residents. In the next exercise, you will use the Geolocation capabilities of Captivate to detect the location of the learner taking the course. If you detect that the learner is in Belgium, you should display a warning message and give the learner the opportunity to skip the course. In every other situation, the course will run normally.

Inserting an extra slide

First you need to insert a new slide in the project. To speed you up, this slide has already been created for you. All you need to do is to copy-paste it using the following steps:

1. Still in the `chapter13/takeTheTrain.cptx` project, use the **Filmstrip** to return to the first slide of the project.
2. Open the `Chapter13/geolocation.cptx` file.
3. In the **Filmstrip**, select and copy the first and only slide of the project.

4. Return to the `takeTheTrain.cptx.cptx` file and paste the slide just after the first slide of the project. The new slide is inserted as slide 2.

5. Select the **No I will Skip It** button.

6. In the **Actions** tab of the **Properties** inspector, change the action of the button to **Jump To Slide**.

7. Select the last slide of the project (**Slide 31**) in the **Slide** dropdown that appears just below.

8. Make sure that the **Action** of the other button is set to **Go to the next slide**.

This new slide should be displayed to Belgian learners only. In the next section, you will learn how you can access the location of the learner taking the course.

Detecting the location of the learner

One of the System Variables of Adobe Captivate 2017 returns the position (the latitude and the longitude) of the learner taking the course. Use the following steps to inspect this variable and understand how it works:

1. Still in the `takeTheTrain.cptx` project, use the **Project | Variables** menu item to open the **Variables** dialog.

2. At the top of the **Variables** dialog, change the **Type** to **System**.

3. Open the **View By** dropdown.

4. Scroll to the end of the list and choose the **Mobile** item.

5. Select the **cpInfoGeolocation** variable.

As explained in the **Description** field, the `cpInfoGeoLocation` variable returns the geographic coordinates of the learner taking the course. It actually returns the Latitude and the Longitude coordinate of the learner (as well as the Accuracy, which is the range of the detected location). This ability is based on the Geolocation capabilities of the device used when taking the course.

Note that desktop and laptop computers can also be geolocalized based on the network they are connected to and on their IP address. So Geolocation is not specific to mobile devices. That being said, the accuracy of the Geolocation data largely depends on the device and the data connectivity used.

Geolocation and privacy

Many users (including us!) decide to disable the geolocation capabilities of their devices for privacy reasons. This means that you may not have access to this data even if the learner uses a geolocation-aware device. You must respect this decision of the learner and always provide a default scenario that does not depend on the learner's location.

Creating a custom Geolocation variable

Now that you have a way to detect the user location, you will create a new User Variable in which you will store the geolocation coordinates of Belgium. At runtime, you will compare the `cpInfoGeolocation` system variable to your custom Belgium variable. If you detect that the learner is in Belgium, you should display the slide that you inserted in the project earlier in this section. Use the following steps to create a custom Belgium variable:

1. Still in the **Variables** dialog of the `takeTheTrain.cptx` file, use the **Type** dropdown to return to the **User** Variables.
2. Click the **Add New** button to create a new **User Variable**.
3. Type `v_locationBelgium` in the **Name** field.
4. Select the **Geolocation** checkbox below the **Unused Items** button.

By selecting this checkbox, you tell Captivate that you want to create a custom Geolocation variable. The difference between a Geolocation variable and a standard variable is in the way you express the value of the variable. When defining a standard variable, you simply type its initial value in the **Value** field of the **Variable** dialog. When defining a Geolocation variable, you must supply the **Latitude**, the **Longitude,** and the **Accuracy,** as shown in the following screenshot.

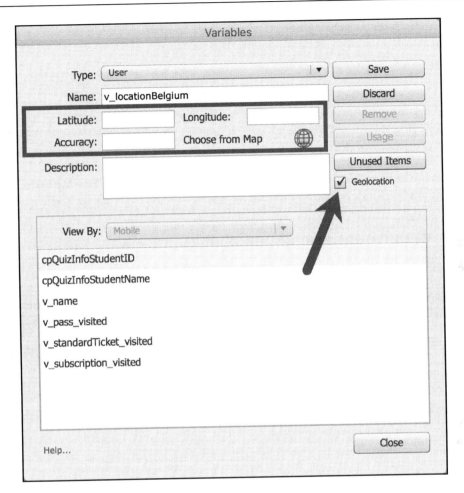

The **Latitude** and the **Longitude** are used to define a precise spot on Earth. The **Accuracy** is measured in meters. It defines the radius of a circle whose center is the precise spot defined by the **Latitude** and the **Longitude** coordinates. If the location of the learner as returned by the `cpInfoGeolocation` system variable is within that circle, the learner is considered to be at the custom location.

5. Click the **Choose From Map** icon to find out the **Latitude**, **Longitude**, and **Accuracy** values that you need.

The box that opens is based on Google Maps, which explains why you must be connected to the internet to make it work. Note that a circle and two points are present on the top of the Google Map.

6. Type `Belgium` in the search field in the top area of the window.
7. Eventually, adjust the position of the two points so that the circle more or less covers Belgium on the map.
8. When you are done, click the **Submit** button just below the Search field.

Note that the **Latitude, Longitude,** and **Accuracy** values of the Geolocation variable have been automatically filled in. The center of the circle is used to define the **Latitude** and the **Longitude** values; the radius of the circle is used for the **Accuracy** value of the variable.

9. Click the **Save** button to save the new variable and close the **Variables** dialog.

In the next section, you will use this new variable to check if the learner is in Belgium or not and act accordingly.

Altering the content based on learner's location

The `cpInfoGeolocation` variable gives you access to the location of the learner and your custom `v_locationBelgium` variable defines what area of the world you consider as *Belgium*. In this section you will create a conditional Advanced Action that will compare these two variables and decide if slide 2 must be displayed to the learner or skipped using the following steps:

1. Use the **Project | Advanced Actions** to open the **Advanced Actions** dialog.
2. Type `checkBeLocation` as the name of the action.
3. Select the **Conditional Tab** checkbox.
4. In the **If** part of the action, check if the `cpInfoGeolocation` variable **is equal to** the `v_locationBelgium` variable.
5. In the **Action** section of the dialog box, double-click the first line and choose the **Continue** action.
6. Click the **Else** button at the bottom of the dialog box.
7. Double-click the first line of the **Else** panel and choose the **Go to Next Slide** action.
8. Click the **Save As Action** button at the end of the dialog box.
9. Acknowledge the successful creation of the script and close the **Advanced Actions** dialog.

The last piece of the puzzle is to decide *when* the action needs to be performed. In this case, you want to attach this action to a system event using the following steps:

10. Use the **Filmstrip** to go to slide 2 if necessary.
11. In the **Actions** tab of the **Properties** inspector, open the **On Enter** dropdown.
12. Choose the **Execute Advanced Action** item in the list.
13. Select the **checkBeLocation** action in the **Script** dropdown menu.

The advanced action is executed when the playhead enters slide 2. If the geolocation of the learner is within the circle defined by the `v_locationBelgium` variable, the playhead continues normally. In the other situation, the playhead directly jumps to the next slide and skips slide 2.

14. Return to the first slide of the project and use the **Preview | HTML5 In Browser** icon to test your project.

When the project appears in the browser, notice the **Emulate Geolocation** dropdown menu. Use it to test your project, as if you were in Belgium, and confirm that slide 2 is displayed (use the first icon of the playbar to rewind your project and test the Advanced Action). Test your project a second time, leaving the **Emulate Geolocation** option to its default value of **<nowhere>** and confirm that slide 2 is skipped.

This exercise illustrates how you can use the Geolocation capabilities of Captivate to modify the content that is supplied to the learner based on its location.

Blog Post

Dr. Allen Partridge, Adobe eLearning evangelist, has written an excellent blog post that illustrates another use case for these Geolocation capabilities. Even though this blog post was written with Captivate 8, it is still very relevant to Captivate 2017. See this blog post and download the sample files at

`https://elearning.adobe.com/2014/06/location-aware-learning-exam`
`ple-with-complete-source-files-for-the-australia-zoo-app/`.

This concludes your exploration of the geolocation capabilities of Captivate. Let's list the main takeaways:

- Adobe Captivate 2017 leverages the geolocation capabilities of the devices used by the learner to take the course and gives you access to that information using a System Variable.

- The `cpInfoGeolocation` System Variable exposes the learner's location when taking the course. This ability depends on the device used by the learner and on his/her privacy settings.

- Select the **Geolocation** checkbox in the **Variables** dialog to create custom user variables that define a location. These variables define a circle on the globe. If the user is in the circle, Captivate considers that the user is at the custom-defined location.

- The center of this circle is a point defined by Latitude and Longitude coordinates. The radius of the circle is defined by the Accuracy parameter expressed in meters.

- You can use the Geolocation variables (System or User-defined) in any Advanced Actions, the same way you use standard variables.

Summary

Thanks to Advanced Actions and Variables, you have been able to add a whole new level of interactivity and sophistication to your projects. The good news is that you only saw the tip of the iceberg in this book. The possibilities are virtually endless, and your imagination is the ultimate limit to what can be achieved.

To implement Advanced Actions and Variables, Captivate takes advantage of the scripting capabilities included in both the HTML5 and the Flash technologies. Advanced Actions and Variables can be used to create dynamic Text Captions, to turn the visibility of objects on and off, to control the course, to access information about the course, and much, much more.

With the completion of this chapter your project can now be considered complete. Starting with the Captivate production workflow described at the very beginning of the book, you have now completed the second part of the process: the post-production phase. As anticipated, this has been the most time-consuming and feature-rich part of the whole course development process.

In the next chapter, you will finally make your work available to your learners by performing the last part of the process. The publishing step will allow you to publish your projects in various formats so that your students will be able to start watching and learning from your Captivate eLearning course!

Meet the community

In this section, we want to introduce you to Lieve Weymeis. Lieve is a legend in the Captivate community and one of the most active members. Her blog has become one of the most primary resources on Variables and Advanced Actions. She certainly deserves her title of "Captivate Queen".

Damien

Lieve and I share our Belgian nationality. I first met her in the summer of 2013 in San Jose, California, during an Adobe event. There, she celebrated her 10,000th answer on the Captivate forums with the rest of the Adobe Education team. I was fortunate enough to be part of the celebration and to have my share of the fantastic chocolate cake made for the occasion. Full respect, Lieve!

Pooja

Lieve is a powerhouse of knowledge on Captivate, and I salute her of it! I've always admired her for helping Captivate users troubleshoot issues and use Captivate in the best possible manner. Whenever I see her at conferences, she makes sure to give me a big hug and my favorite Belgian chocolate!

Lieve Weymeis

Lieve is civil engineer (Ir) and professional musician. After years of teaching and research (project management and eLearning), she is now a freelance consultant/trainer specialized in advanced Adobe Captivate. Her blog (`http://blog.lilybiri.com`) is a reference for Captivate users worldwide.

In 2009, she was invited to the Advisory Board for Captivate. As an Adobe Certified Expert, Adobe Community Professional, and Adobe Education Leader, she presented about Captivate and Flipped classes, both online and Live (Adobe Summits, DevLearn, Media and Learning, and so on). Since 2015, she has been the moderator of Adobe forums. In the Captivate community (forums/portal) and on social media, she has established herself as a well-known and much-appreciated expert.

Contact details

- **Twitter**: `@Lilybiri`
- **Website**: `http://www.lilybiri.com`
- **Blog**: `http://blog.lilybiri.com`
- **LinkedIn**: `be.linkedin.com/in/lieveweymeis`
- **E-mail**: `info@lilybiri.com`

14
Finishing Touches and Publishing

With the work done in the previous chapters, your time in the post-production studio is almost over. There are just a couple of things left to be done before the project can finally be published.

Most of these final changes are options and features that you will set for the entire project. They include checking the spelling, choosing how the project starts and ends, and so on. The most important of these final changes is probably the creation of a skin in the Skin Editor. A Skin allows you to customize the playback controls bar and create the table of contents for the project, among other things.

In the second part of this chapter, you will focus on the third and last step of the Captivate production process: publishing the project. Publishing is the process by which you make your Captivate projects available to the target audience. Most of the time, you'll publish your courses in the HTML5 format or in the Adobe Flash format so that any student can enjoy the content of your online course across different devices. However, Captivate can also publish courses in many other formats, which you will also learn about.

In this chapter, you will perform the following actions:

- Check the spelling of the entire project
- Set the Start and End preferences of the project
- Export the properties of a project and import them into another project
- Customize the project Skin
- Add a Table of Contents
- Publish the project in various formats
- Publish a SCORM package

- Use the Multi-SCORM Packager
- Convert your HTML5 project into a native application using the Adobe PhoneGap Build service

At the end of this chapter, your work as an eLearning developer will be finished and your content will be ready to be pushed online.

Preparing your work

Before getting started with this chapter, take some time to reset the Captivate interface to the defaults. If you are using the default interface mode, just close and restart Captivate. If you are using the advanced interface mode, use the **Window | Workspace | Reset 'Classic'** menu item to reset Captivate to the default. In this chapter, you will use the exercises stored in the `Chapter14` folder. If you get confused by any of the step-by-step instructions, take a look at the `Chapter14/final` folder-which contains a copy of the files-at the end of this chapter.

Finishing touches

With the completion of `Chapter 13`, *Working with Variables and Advanced Actions*, you can consider your project finished. There are, however, a few more things to do before the project can be published. In this section, you will focus on these small finishing touches.

Checking the spelling

Checking the spelling is probably one of the most fundamental finishing touches. The Spell Checker of Captivate works like any other Spell Checker found in any text authoring application.

In Captivate, the Spell Checker has the ability to check the text typed in various locations throughout the project. This includes the text typed in Text Captions, Smart Shapes, Slide Notes, Text Animations, Buttons, and the Table of Contents.

Before using the Spell Checker, you will take a quick look at its options using the following steps:

1. Open the `Chapter14/encoderDemo_800.cptx` project.
2. Open the **Preferences** dialog of Captivate by using the **Edit | Preferences** (Windows) menu item or the **Adobe Captivate | Preferences** (Mac) menu item.

3. On the left side of the **Preferences** dialog, click the **General Settings** category.

4. Click the **Spelling Preferences...** button to open the **Spelling Options** dialog, as shown in the following screenshot:

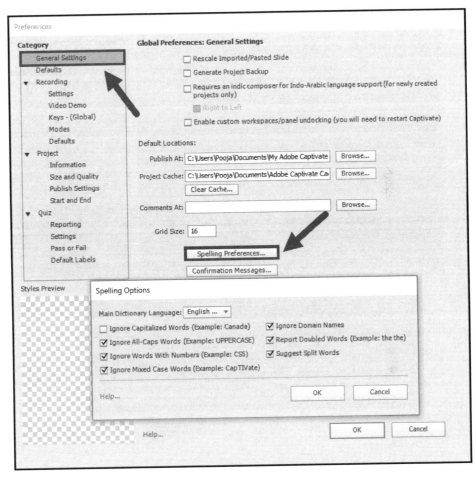

The main option of this box is the **Main Dictionary Language**. Note that, by default, most of the checkboxes of the **Spelling Options** dialog are selected.

1. Open the **Main Dictionary Language** drop-down list and take some time to inspect the available languages.

2. For this exercise, make sure you choose **English (United States)** as the **Main Dictionary Language**.

3. Take some time to inspect the other options in the dialog. They should be self-explanatory. Make sure they are all selected before moving on.

4. Click the **OK** button to close the **Spelling Options** dialog. Then click **OK** again to validate the changes and close the **Preferences** dialog.

Now that you have a better idea of the available Spell Checker options, you will use this feature to check the spelling of the Encoder Demonstration.

9. Use the **Project | Check Spelling...** menu item (or press the *F7* shortcut key) to launch the Spell Checker.

Some spelling errors have been left behind in this project. Each time a spelling mistake is found, the Spell Checker stops and proposes replacement words. Let the Spell Checker go through the whole project and handle each spelling mistake; they are detected using the dialog box shown in the following screenshot:

At the bottom of the **Check Spelling** window are two important buttons.

10. Click the **Options...** button at the end of the **Check Spelling...** dialog.

The same **Spelling Options** dialog you accessed through the **Preferences** dialog opens.

11. Leave all the **Spelling Options** at their current settings and click **OK** to close the **Spelling Options** dialog.
12. In the bottom left corner of the **Check Spelling...** dialog, click the **Help...** link.

Such a **Help...** link can be found in the bottom left corner of many dialog boxes throughout Captivate. It opens the default browser and displays the **Adobe Captivate Help** page that specifically explains the options of the current dialog box. The **Help...** link is an easy and fast way to access specific help content.

13. Take some time to review the currently opened help page. When done, close your browser and return to Captivate.

When the spell check is finished, a message appears stating that the spell check is complete and that a certain number of corrections have been made.

14. Click the **OK** button to discard the information box.
15. Make sure you save the file before moving on.

Now that you've finished spell-checking, you can advance to the other steps in your post-production work. Checking the spelling in Captivate is as easy as checking the spelling in any other text authoring application. Just remember that it is an essential part of any professional eLearning project.

Here's is a quick summary of what has been covered in this section:

- Captivate contains a Spell Checker that works the same way as any other Spell Checker found in virtually every text authoring application.
- The Spell Checker of Captivate has the ability to check the spelling of all the text typed throughout the application. This includes the text typed in Text Captions, Slide Notes, Text Animations, Buttons, and Table of Contents.

- The **Spelling Options** can be accessed through the **Preferences** dialog or directly from the **Check Spelling** dialog.
- The **Help...** link found at the bottom left corner of many dialog boxes opens the default browser and displays the help page specifically dedicated to that dialog box. It is a quick and easy way to access specific help content.
- Checking the spelling is an essential part of any professional eLearning project.

Exploring Start and End preferences

The next final touch you will focus on lets you decide how the course should start and how it should end. This is very important to fine tune a student's experience and to optimize the performance of the project when viewed over the internet.

In the following exercise, you will explore the available Start and End preferences using the following steps:

1. If needed, return to the `Chapter14/encoderDemo_800.cptx` file.
2. Use the **Edit | Preferences** (Windows) menu item or **Adobe Captivate | Preferences** (Mac) menu item to open the **Preferences** dialog.
3. On the leftside of the **Preferences** dialog, select the **Start and End** category in the **Project** section.

The preferences pertaining to the **Project** section of the **Preferences** dialog are specific to the current project only. Your screen should now display the dialog shown in the following screenshot:

The **Start and End** preference page is divided into two sections. At the top of the page is **Project Start Options**, shown as (**1**) in the previous screenshot. At the bottom of the page is **Project End Options**, shown as (**2**) in the previous screenshot.

The following options are available under the **Project Start** section:

- **Auto Play**: If this option is selected, the project starts playing as soon as it finishes loading. If it is not selected, the student will have to click the **Play** button to view the project. In this situation, you can use the **Browse** button to choose a static image that is displayed until the student clicks the **Play** button (such an image is often called a poster image).

- **Preloader**: The **Preloader** checkbox is an image or an animation that is displayed while the movie is loading. If **Preloader** is selected and no preloader file is supplied, Captivate uses its default preloader. You can also create your own custom preloader or choose one from the gallery.

- **Preloader %**: This is, to us, the most important option of this **Preferences** pane. It represents the percentage of the file that has to be downloaded before the course starts to play. If it is set to 50 percent, it means that the movie starts playing when 50 percent of the entire file is downloaded. The remaining 50 percent is loaded while the beginning of the movie is being played. Use this option when the project is large and contains lots of audio or video; it reduces the waiting time for the student, and provides a much smoother learning experience.

 There is an interesting blog post from the Icon logic' blog in which Kevin Siegel gives you more details about the Preloader and Preloader % options. It is available at
`http://iconlogic.blogs.com/weblog/2014/05/adobe-captivate-preloa`
`ders.html`.

- **Password Protect Project**: This option is self-explanatory. Share the password only with those individuals who should be granted access to the project. Use this option if the project contains confidential information, or if you want to share a beta release of the project with a limited team of reviewers.

- **Project Expiry Date**: Use this option to set an expiration date for the project. The project will not be accessible if a student wants to access it after the expiration date.

- **Fade In on the First Slide**: This provides a smoother transition when the student enters the course. This option is turned off by default.

The following options are available under the **Project End Options** section:

- **Action**: The **Action** drop-down list is used to select an action that will be activated when the project is complete. By default, the **Stop project** action is selected.

- **Fade Out on the Last Slide**: This option is turned off by default, and allows the course to smoothly fade out at the end.

Now that you have had an in-depth overview of the available options, you can set the **Start and End** preferences of this particular project.

    4. Set the **Preloader %** option to 50.

This particular course contains a lot of sound, and sound takes a lot of time to download. With the **Preloader %** option set to 50, the time spent by a student waiting for the course to download is cut in half. You will have to test what preloader percentage works best on your own projects.

    5. Leave the remaining options at their default settings, and click **OK**.

    6. Don't forget to save the file when done.

This concludes your overview of the **Start and End** preferences. Here's what we have learned so far:

- In the **Preferences** dialog, the pages pertaining to the **Project** section are specific to the current project only.
- In the **Start and End** category, Captivate shows options and features to let you decide how the project should start and what happens when it has finished playing.
- Use these options to enhance the user experience, enforce some basic security, and optimize the loading time of the movie.

Exploring other project preferences

There are some more project preferences available in Captivate that are worth exploring before publishing. Most of the time, the default settings for these particular options work just fine, so we won't modify any of these options in the Encoder Demonstration Project.

In the following exercises, we will simply take a look at these preferences and briefly discuss some of them:

    1. If needed, return to the `Chapter14/encoderDemo_800.cptx` file.

    2. Use the **Edit | Preferences** (Windows) menu item or the **Adobe Captivate | Preferences** (Mac) menu item to open the **Preferences** dialog.

    3. Open the **Size and Quality** category in the **Project** section.

This particular **Preferences** page provides options to control how the Captivate project is converted into HTML5 or Flash upon publication. If you want more information about any one of these options, don't hesitate to click the **Help...** link in the bottom left corner of the **Preferences** dialog.

4. Click the **Publish Settings** category in the **Project** section in the left column of the **Preferences** dialog.

This **Preferences** page displays additional options about how the project will be converted to HTML5 or Flash. Once again, the default options work just fine for the vast majority of projects. Let's briefly discuss some of these options:

- **Frames Per Second**: Use this option if you want to embed your Captivate project in a Flash project that has a different frame rate than 30 frames per second (FPS), or if you want to insert a video in your project that was created with a different FPS value. Otherwise, leave this option at its default value of 30 fps.
- **Publish Adobe Connect metadata**: This option adds some metadata to the project, thus producing a slightly larger file. This metadata is designed to facilitate the integration of the Captivate project in Adobe Connect. If you do not have access to an Adobe Connect server, there is no need to turn this option on.

 Read this great blog post by Michael Lund (also known as the Captivate Guru) about how Adobe Connect metadata affects the size of the resulting file. It is available at
`http://www.cpguru.com/2008/12/30/reducing-the-file-size-of-your-captivate-projects/`.

- **Enable Accessibility**: This option makes the project 508 compliant. It is covered in detail in Chapter 12, *Creating Accessible eLearning*.
- **Externalize Resources**: When publishing to Flash, Captivate produces a single SWF file containing the whole project by default. Consequently, this file can be very large and hard to download based on your IT infrastructure. Externalizing resources tells Captivate to generate many smaller SWF files that reference each other. This option may help in optimizing the download time of a large project, but it makes it more difficult to push the Captivate project online once published. Note that some assets (such as inserted video files) are always externalized. Also note that when publishing to HTML5, all the resources are always externalized.

Other options on the **Preferences** page should be self-explanatory. Don't hesitate to click the **Help...** link if you need more information.

> 5. Click the **Cancel** button to close the **Preferences** dialog and discard the changes you've made along the way.

This concludes our tour of project preferences. You will now export the preferences of this project and import them into another project.

Exporting project preferences

Remember that the options pertaining to the **Project** section of the **Preferences** dialog are specific to the current project only.

If you want to apply the same set of **Preferences** to another project, Captivate lets you export the preferences of the current project and reimport them in another project. In the following exercise, you will export the preferences of the Encoder demonstration and apply them to the Encoder simulation:

> 1. If needed, return to the `Chapter14/encoderDemo_800.cptx` file.
> 2. Use the **File | Export | Preferences...** menu item to export the preferences of the demonstration.
> 3. Save the preferences file as `Chapter14/encoderDemo_800_Preferences.cpr`. It should be the default name proposed by Captivate.
> 4. Click **OK** to acknowledge the information box telling you that the export is successful.

Note that the file extension of such a preference file is `.cpr`, which stands for **C**aptivate **PR**eferences.

You will now open the simulation and import the preferences of the demonstration. At the end of this process, both files will share the exact same project preferences.

> 5. Open the `Chapter14/encoderSim_800.cptx` file.

This is the simulation you created back in Chapter 8, *Capturing Onscreen Action.*

6. Use the **File | Import | Preferences** menu item to import a preference file in the project.

7. Browse to the encoderDemo_800_Preferences.cpr file that you created earlier in this exercise and click **Open**.

After a short while, an information box should appear on the screen telling you that the preferences were successfully imported.

8. Click **OK** to discard the information box.

9. Use the **Edit | Preferences** menu item (Windows) or the **Adobe Captivate | Preferences** menu item (Mac) to open the **Preferences** dialog of the encoderSim_800.cptx file.

10. Open the **Start and End**category in the **Project** section of the **Preferences** dialog.

11. Verify that the **Preloader %** is set to 50.

12. Click the **Cancel** button to close the **Preferences** dialog.

13. Use the **File | Save All** menu item to save both the Encoder demonstration and the Encoder simulation in one action.

The following list is a quick summary of what you have learned about the remaining project preferences:

- Most of the time, the default settings of the **SWF Size and Quality** and **Publish Settings** pages of the **Preferences** dialog work just fine.

- These settings help you control the size of the published HTML5 or Flash application and optimize the download time of the project. On the other hand, they can be quite technical, and require some knowledge of Flash and HTML5 to be used efficiently.

- It is possible to export the preferences of one project and import them back into another project.

Preferences and templates
Templates offer another convenient way to share preferences across projects. Remember that the preferences defined in a template become the default preferences of all future projects based on this template.

Customizing the project Skin

The Skin of a project is a collection of elements that are, for the most part, displayed around slides. It means that the elements of the Skin are not a part of the actual eLearning content. Learners use them to interact with the Captivate content, which enhances the overall user experience. A Skin is made of the following three elements:

- **The Playback Controls bar**: This is the most visible element of a Skin. It contains the necessary buttons and switches used by the student to control the playback of the course. It also contains a progress bar that tracks the student's progression in the Captivate project.
- **The Borders**: The Skin Editor lets you create Borders around your projects. You can turn each of the four Borders on and/or off, and choose their width, color, and texture.
- **The Table of Contents**: The last element of a Skin is the Table of Contents. By default, it is turned off, but it is very easy to turn it on and generate a Table of Contents for the project.

By default, Captivate contains a handful of predefined Skins that you can apply as-is to your projects for rapid development. However, you also have the option of customizing any of the existing skins and saving that skin with your own unique Skin name.

Also remember that the color scheme of the Skin is the third element of a Theme. The other two elements are Styles and Master Slides. This has already been covered in `Chapter 6`, *Crafting the Graphical Experience with Styles and Themes*.

In this section, each of the three elements of the Skin will be discussed one by one. Following along, you will slowly create a unique Skin design that you will save and apply to other projects. Some more features of Captivate will be uncovered along the way.

Customizing the Playback Controls bar

The first and most visible element of the Skin is the Playback Controls bar. By default, it appears below the project and contains the necessary buttons and switches to let the student control the playback of the project.

In the following exercise, you will explore the available options and create a customized Playback Controls bar for your project:

1. Return to the `Chapter14/encoderSim_800.cptx` file.
2. Use the **Project | Skin Editor** menu item to open the **Skin Editor** floating pane.

The **Skin Editor** floating pane should look similar to what is shown in the following screenshot:

The **Skin Editor** floating pane is divided into two main areas. On the left side are the swatches, checkboxes, and buttons you use to customize the various elements of the Skin. On the right side is a live preview of the first slide of the project. This area of the **Skin Editor** is automatically updated as you turn the options of the left area on and off.

Note two important controls in the upper-left area of the **Skin Editor** floating pane. The **Skin** drop-down list (marked as (1) in the previous screenshot) is used to choose and apply one of the predefined Skins of Captivate to the project. Right below this, there are three icons (marked as (2) in the preceding screenshot). Each of them represents one of the elements of the skin: the Playback Control, the Borders, and the Table of Contents.

3. Open the **Skin** drop-down list and choose any Skin you want.

4. The chosen Skin is applied to the project, and the preview area of the **Skin Editor** is updated.

5. Open the **Skin** drop-down list again and reapply the **Theme Default** Skin to the project.

The **Theme Default** Skin is the one that is stored in the Theme applied to the project. As you can see, the colors of the Theme Default skin are yet to be defined given that the look and feel of the project have not yet been decided.

6. Make sure the **Playback Colors** option is checked. Then, click the **Background Color** color picker in the **Theme** section of the left column.

7. Click the eyedropper icon in the top-center area of the color chooser.

8. Take a close look at your mouse pointer. It should look like an eyedropper. With this pointer active, click anywhere on the brown background where the **Adobe Media Encoder - The Demonstration** title is located.

The eyedropper tool takes the color of the pixel you click on and applies it to the **Background Color** property of the Playback Controls bar. This tool is an incredibly fast and easy way to make two different elements share the same color.

9. Customize the other colors of the Playback Controls bar to your taste.

 Remember that the Swatches Manager offers the ability to import a custom set of color swatches into the project. Don't hesitate to use this ability to choose the colors of the playback controls and give them the same look and feel as the rest of the project.

You will now remove the Playback Controls bar and see how the Skin updates.

10. Deselect the **Show Playback Control** checkbox.

When the preview updates, note that the playback controls are not displayed anymore, and that a border appears at the bottom of the project where the Playback Controls used to be. This is shown in the following screenshot:

This is very interesting and deserves further investigation.

By default, when a Playback Controls bar is applied, a bottom border that has the same width as the Playback Controls bar is also automatically applied to the project. The idea is to put the Playback Controls bar on top of that bottom border so that it does not overlap with the content. This is a very good thing, and, most of the time, it works just fine. That being said, this system increases the overall height of the project. If you remember the discussion we had in Chapter 8, *Capturing Onscreen Action* about the resolution of the movie, this can be quite a problem in some situations.

You will now set the Skin so that the Playback Controls are displayed without adding a single pixel to the height of the movie.

11. Select the **Show Playback Control** checkbox to turn the Playback Controls back on.
12. Right below the **Show Playback Control** checkbox, select the **Playbar Overlay** checkbox.

In the preview area of the **Skin Editor**, you should see that the Playback Controls bar now overlaps the slide. You can now safely turn off the border using the following steps:

13. Click the **Borders** icon. It is the second of the three icons just below the **Skin** drop-down list.
14. Deselect the **Show Border** checkbox.

This is how you can accommodate Playback Controls without adding a single pixel to the height of the movie. The advantage of this is that the height of the project, as defined when creating it, is now respected. The disadvantage is that the Playback Controls might now sit on top of some important information displayed at the bottom of the slides.

15. Close the **Skin Editor** floating pane.
16. Use the **Preview | Next 5 Slides** icon on the Toolbar to test the new Playback Controls configuration.
17. When the preview is over, close the **Preview** pane.

In this example, you want the Playback Controls to be located outside the actual eLearning content. You will now return to the **Skin Editor** floating pane to revert to your latest changes before further exploring the other available options.

18. Use the **Project | Skin Editor** menu item to reopen the floating **Skin Editor** pane.
19. Deselect the **Playbar Overlay** checkbox.
20. Deselect the **Rewind, Forward, Back, Close,** and **Fast Forward** checkboxes.
21. Make sure the **Play, Mute, Progress Bar,** and **Closed Captioning** checkboxes are selected.
22. After this operation, the Playback Controls bar should contain only three buttons, along with the Progress bar. Take some time to inspect the remaining options of the Playback Controls bar. Make sure you do not change any of them before moving on to the next step.

With the completion of this exercise, you can consider the Playback Controls bar as definitive. Let's give it a try by using the **Preview** pane.

23. Close the floating **Skin Editor** pane.
24. Use the **Preview | Project** icon on the Toolbar to preview the entire project.

When the course starts to play, take a look at the Playback Controls bar below the project. It contains three buttons and the progress bar as specified in the **Skin Editor** floating pane during the preceding exercise.

25. Close the **Preview** pane.

In the next section, you will discover the second element of a Captivate Skin: Borders.

Working with Borders

Borders are the second main element of a Captivate Skin. As discussed in the previous section, *Customizing the Playback Controls bar*, adding a Playback Controls bar automatically adds a corresponding bottom border so that the Playback Controls do not overlap with the slide elements. Please note that Borders are not supported in the HTML5 published output. Also, for responsive projects, the Borders option is disabled.

In the following exercise, you will further experiment with the Borders and discover some more of their properties:

1. While still in the `encoderSim_800.cptx` file, use the **Project | Skin Editor** menu item to return to the **Skin Editor** floating pane.
2. Click the **Borders** icon below the **Skin** drop-down list.
3. Select the **Show Borders** checkbox to turn borders back on.

In the **Borders** tab of the **Skin Editor** floating pane, note that the Bottom Border is currently turned on, as shown in the following screenshot:

The bottom border is currently situated below the Playback Controls bar, which explains why you don't see it even if it is turned on. You will now turn all four borders on and explore the available formatting options.

4. Click the Left border, Right border, and Top border icons to turn the corresponding borders on.

5. In the **Style** drop-down list, choose the **Rounded Corners** style.

6. Note how the edges change from square to rounded. Now switch it back to **Square Edge**.

7. Click the **Color** chooser. Use the eyedropper tool in the top right corner of the color chooser to give your border the same dark-gold color as the background of the slide.

8. Open the **Texture** drop-down list and choose any texture you want.

9. Change the **Width** option of the borders to 80.

10. Change the **HTML Background** color to a shade of gray.

The previous steps illustrate the available options of the Borders. You will now arrange these options to fit the particular needs of the Encoder simulation.

Let's start with the most obvious change to be made: turning off this texture!

11. Open the **Texture** drop-down list again and choose **None** at the very top of the list.

This action turns the **Texture** off. With the **Texture** option turned off, the dark-gold border reappears.

12. Turn the Top, Left, and Right borders off. Leave only the Bottom border on.
13. Reduce the **Width** option of the border to 30 pixels.
14. Change the **HTML Background** color to white.
15. Close the floating **Skin Editor** pane and save the file.

With the completion of the preceding exercises, the first two elements of the Skin (Playback Controls and Borders) are now in place. In the next section, you will focus on the third and last element of the Skin: the Table of Contents.

Adding a Table of Contents

The Table of Contents is the third and last element of the Skin. By default, the Table of Contents is turned off.

In the following exercise, you will turn the Table of Contents on and explore the available options:

1. While still in the `Chapter14/encoderSim_800.cptx` file, use the **Project | Table of Contents...** menu item to open the floating **Skin Editor** pane on the **Table of Contents** page.
2. Click the **Show TOC** checkbox to turn the Table of Contents on.

By default, the Table of Contents appears on the left side of the project and lists every single slide. At this moment, the slides are named **Slide 1**, **Slide 2**, and so on. In the next section of this exercise, you will experiment with two ways of changing the names of the slides in the Table of Contents.

The first way is to change the name of the slide directly in the **Skin Editor** floating pane using the following steps:

3. Right below the **Show TOC** checkbox, double-click the **Slide 1** title.
4. Change the name of the slide to `Title` and press the Enter key.

After a short while, the preview area displays the updated Table of Contents.

The second way of changing the slide name involves closing the **Skin Editor** floating pane and using the **Properties**inspector of each slide to specify a slide label.

5. Close the floating **Skin Editor** panel.
6. Use the **Filmstrip** panel to select slide 2. Make sure the **Properties** inspector shows the properties of the slide and not the properties of any of the slide's elements.
7. At the top of the **Properties** inspector, type `Introduction` in the **Label** field.
8. Press *Enter* to validate the change.

When you are done, take another look at the **Filmstrip** panel. The slide label should be displayed below the corresponding thumbnail.

9. Use the same technique to enter a label for other slides of the project:
   - **Slide 3**: Change the label to `Beginning of the Simulation`.
   - **Slide 17**: Change the label to `Ending slide`.
   - Leave the **Label** field of the other slides empty.

10. Use the **Project | Table of Content** menu item to reopen the floating **Skin Editor** pane on the **Table of Contents** page.

11. Click the **Reset TOC** icon below the list of TOC entries, as shown in the following screenshot:

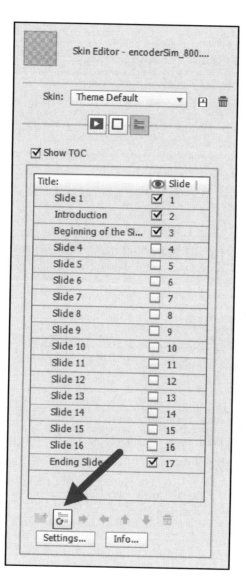

When you click this icon, Captivate inspects the slides of the project and regenerates the entries of the Table of Contents. Note that the slide label, if any, is used as the title of the corresponding TOC entry.

Also note that there is no longer a label for slide 1. This tells you that manually changing the name of the slide in the TOC editor does *NOT* add a corresponding label to the slide.

About slide labels

In the current exercise, you are using slide labels to generate the entries of the Table of Contents, but adding labels to slides serves many other purposes as well. First of all, it makes the project easier to use and maintain, but the main benefit of a slide label is probably the enhanced accessibility it provides. The slide label is yet another piece of metadata used by the assistive devices of those with disabilities, and its use is mandatory to make the eLearning project 508 compliant.

You will now re-enter a name for slide 1 and hide the unnecessary slides from the Table of Contents.

12. In the **Skin Editor** floating pane, double-click the **Slide 1** title in the list of TOC entries. Retype `Title` and press the Enter key.

13. Uncheck the visibility checkbox for slides 4 through 16.

In the preview area of the **Skin Editor** floating pane, the corresponding slides disappear from the Table of Contents. At this point, there should be only four slides mentioned in the Table of Contents.

You will now finalize the look and feel of the Table of Contents.

14. Click the **Info...** button at the bottom of the **Skin Editor** floating pane, below the list of TOC entries. The **TOC Information** dialog opens.

15. In the **TOC Information** dialog, click the **Project Information** button.

This last action copies the available project metadata to the corresponding fields of the **TOC Information** box.

16. Type `Adobe Media Encoder - Simulation` in the **Title** field of the **TOC Information** dialog.

17. At the bottom of the **TOC Information** dialog, open the **Font Settings** dropdown, and select **Title:**.

18. Change the Font to **Verdana**. You can also change the font color and size, if required.

19. Click the **OK** button to validate your choices and close the **TOC Information** dialog.

At this point, the Table of Contents is almost ready. One of the remaining problems is the extra space the Table of Contents requires in order to be displayed properly. To address this problem, you will ask Captivate to position the Table of Contents on top of the slide and to provide a way to toggle its visibility on and off.

20. Click the **Settings...** button at the bottom of the **Skin Editor** floating pane, below the list of TOC entries.

21. At the top of the **TOC Settings** dialog, change the **Style** option to **Overlay**.

22. In the **Color** section, click the **Background** color and use the eyedropper tool to apply the dark brown color from the slide.

23. Use the same technique to customize the other colors of the Table Of Contents to your taste.

24. Change the **Alpha** value to 65% to create a semi-transparent Table of Contents:

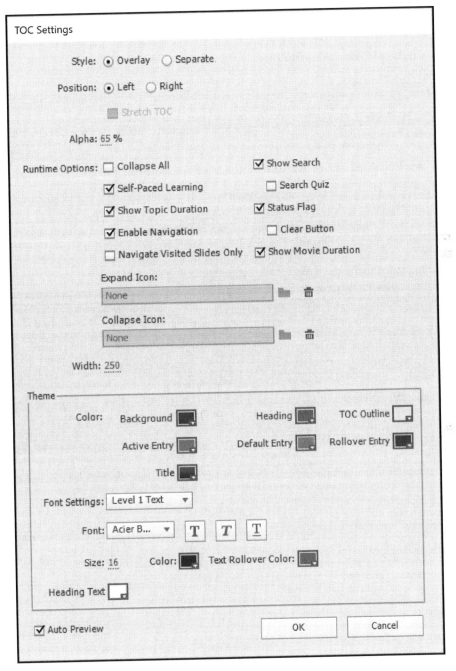

Take some time to explore the other available options, and feel free to modify them at will.

TIP To learn more about the TOC Settings, visit the TOC in Adobe Captivate Help page at
`https://helpx.adobe.com/captivate/using/table-contents-toc.html`.

When done, your screen should look similar to what is shown in the following screenshot:

25. When you are happy with your Table of Contents, click **OK** to validate your choices and close the **TOC Settings** dialog.
26. Close the floating **Skin Editor** pane and save the file.

Your Table of Contents is now ready. It is time to give it a try in the **Preview** pane.

27. Use the **Preview | Project** icon in the toolbar to preview the entire project.

When the **Preview** pane opens, note the small double-arrow in the top-left corner of the slide.

28. Click that small double-arrow to reveal the Table of Contents.
29. Click the same icon to turn off the Table of Contents.

Note the new **TOC** button at the right edge of the Playback Controls bar.

30. Click the **TOC** icon at the right edge of the Playback Controls bar to reveal the Table of Contents.
31. Click the **TOC** icon again to turn off the visibility of the Table of Contents.
32. Close the **Preview** pane and save the file.

With the addition of the Table of Contents, the Skin of your project is now definitive. It looks so great (no kidding!) that you want to apply it to other projects you are working on.

Applying the same Skin to other projects

To create a Skin for the Encoder simulation, you started from the **Theme Default** Skin and you customized it. In this section, you will make the current Skin the **Theme Default** Skin, save the Theme, and apply it to other projects using the following steps:

1. While still in the `encoderSim_800.cptx` file, use the **Project | Skin Editor** menu item to reopen the floating **Skin Editor** pane.

The **Skin** dropdown indicates that the **Theme Default (Modified)** Skin is currently in use.

2. Next to the **Skin** drop-down list, click the **Save As** icon.
3. In the **Save As** box that pops up, leave the **Theme Default** name as it is and click **OK**.
4. Confirm that you want to replace the existing **Theme Default** Skin with a new one.
5. Close the floating **Skin Editor** pane.

The new Skin is now saved as the Default Skin of the applied Theme. You will now save the Theme in a new file and apply that theme to the Encoder demonstration.

6. Use the **Theme | Save Theme As** menu item to save the current theme as a new file.

7. Save the Theme in your exercise folder as `Chapter14/encoderSim_800 Theme.cptm`.

8. Switch to (or open) the `Chapter14/encoderDemo_800.cptx` file.

9. When in the demonstration project, click the **Themes** icon in the Toolbar to open the Themes picker.

10. Click the **Browse** link at the bottom-left corner of the Themes picker.

11. Apply the `Chapter14/encoderSim_800 Theme.cptm` theme that you created earlier in this exercise to the current project.

12. Click **Yes** to confirm that you want to apply the new Theme to the demonstration.

13. Go through the slides of your project, as some styles and Master Slides must be reapplied after applying the Theme to the project.

Both your demonstration and your simulation now share the very same theme. This means that they share the same set of Styles, the same Master Slides, and the very same Skin.

14. Use the **Project | Skin** menu item to open the **Skin Editor** of the `Chapter14/encoderDemo_800.cptx` file.

15. On the **Playback Controls** page of the **Skin Editor** floating pane, click the **TOC** icon below the **Skin** drop-down menu to jump to the **TOC** page of the Skin.

16. Click the **Show TOC** checkbox to turn the TOC on.

By default, the Table of Contents is not activated. When turned on, note that the TOC has the exact same look and feel as in the simulation project.

17. Deselect the **Show TOC** checkbox to turn the TOC off.

18. Close the floating **Skin Editor** panel.

19. Save the file when done.

Apply this Skin to future projects
If you want to apply this Skin by default to future projects, one of the possible approaches is to apply the Theme that contains the Skin to a Captivate template (a `.cptl` file). All Captivate Projects made from that template would, therefore, inherit the Skin applied to that template.

Here is a quick summary of what has been covered in the Skin Editor section of this chapter:

- A Skin is a collection of three elements: Playback Controls, Borders, and a Table of Contents.
- By default, adding a Playback Controls bar to the project automatically adds a corresponding border. The idea is to place Playback Controls on top of the border to avoid overlapping between the Playback Controls and the project. You can customize the Playback Controls bar in many ways using the Skin Editor panel.
- You can also turn the Borders on and off, change their width, their color, and their texture.
- Borders are not supported in HTML5-published output and responsive projects.
- By default, the Table of Contents is turned off.
- It is possible to add labels to slides. Slide labels serve many purposes--for example, they make it easier for the developer to work with the project, they provide enhanced accessibility, and they are used to automatically generate the TOC. It is recommended that you add the slide labels before enabling the TOC.
- The **Skin Editor** floating pane provides many options to fine-tune the Table of Contents.
- Captivate contains default predefined Skins for rapid development.
- When you modify one of the predefined Skins, you actually create a new Skin that can be saved and reapplied to another project.
- The Skin of a project is one of the elements of the applied Theme. All the projects that have the same Theme inherit the same Skin.

Now that all *Finishing Touches* have been taken care of, you will move on to the final phase of the general Captivate production workflow and make your eLearning content available to your students.

Publishing a Captivate project

So far, you have been working with `.cptx` files, which is the default native file type of Captivate. The `.cptx` file format is great when creating and designing projects, but it has two major disadvantages:

- It can become very large. Consequently, it is difficult for you to upload the file on a website and for the student to download and view it.
- Opening a `.cptx` file requires Captivate to be installed on the computer system.

Publishing a Captivate project means converting (the proper word is *compiling*) the `.cptx` file into a format that can be easily deployed on a web server (or on an LMS), downloaded, and viewed by the students.

HTML5 and Flash are the two primary formats in which to publish your projects. The Flash format (also called the `.swf`-pronounced swiff-format) stands for ShockWave Flash. It is the file format used by the free Adobe Flash Player plugin. It has two advantages compared to the `.cptx` file:

- A `.swf` file is usually much smaller in size than its `.cptx` counterpart, making it much easier to upload and download across the Internet.
- Any browser equipped with the free Adobe Flash plugin is able to open and play a `.swf` file. This makes it incredibly easy to deploy the courses made with Captivate.

That being said, the `.swf` format has some major disadvantages of its own:

- It requires the Adobe Flash Player plugin to be installed. If, for whatever reason, the plugin is not available, the `.swf` file cannot be played back.
- It cannot be modified. To modify a `.swf` file, you need to reopen the corresponding `.cptx` file, modify it in Captivate, and publish another version of the `.swf` file.
- The Flash Player plugin is no longer available on mobile devices. Consequently, a `.swf` file cannot be played back on a smartphone or on a tablet device.

- As per the recent announcement from Adobe, Flash Player will be discontinued in 2020: see `https://blogs.adobe.com/conversations/2017/07/adobe-flash-update.html` for more information.

To overcome those limitations, other publishing formats are available in Captivate. The most popular alternative to the `.swf` format is the HTML5 format. When published in HTML5, the project can be played back in any modern browser without the need for an extra plugin. A HTML5-enabled project can also be played back on mobile devices, such as iOS and Android devices. Also remember that Responsive Projects can only be published in HTML5.

HTML5 also has its caveats. HTML5 cannot reproduce every single feature, animation, and interaction that Flash has made us accustomed to. That's why certain features of Captivate (such as Rollover Objects and Text Animations) are not supported when you publish your file in HTML5.

 For a complete list of unsupported features in HTML5, see the following page of the Captivate help files:
`http://helpx.adobe.com/captivate/using/publish-projects-html5-fi`
`les.html.`

In this section, you will explore the various publishing options available in Captivate.

Publishing to Flash

In the history of Captivate, publishing to Flash has always been the primary publishing option. Even though HTML5 publishing is now taking the lead, publishing to Flash is still an important capability of Captivate.

In the following exercise, you will publish the Encoder Demonstration project to Flash using the default options:

1. Return to the `Chapter14/encoderDemo_800.cptx` file.
2. Click the **Publish | Publish to Computer** icon in the Toolbar. Alternatively, you can also use the **File | Publish** menu item.
3. In the **Publish to My Computer** dialog, change the **Project Title** to `encoderDemo_800_swf`.
4. Click the folder icon next to the **Location** field.
5. Select the `Chapter14/publish` folder from your exercises as the publish location.
6. Select the **Output Format** as **SWF**. Make sure **HTML 5** is not selected.
7. Select the **Publish to Folder** option below the Location section.

The **Publish to My Computer** dialog should now look like the following screenshot:

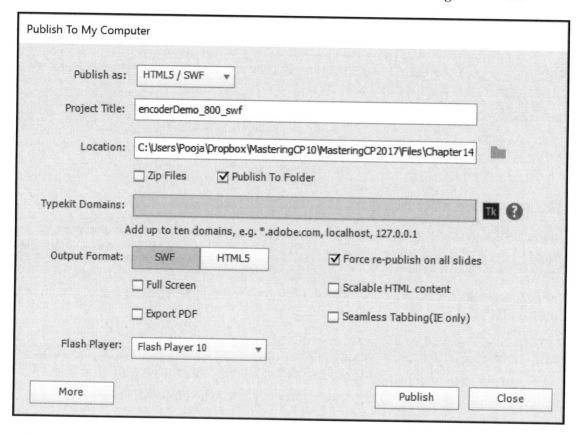

Take a quick look at the remaining options, but leave them all at their current value.

8. Click the **Publish** button in the bottom-right corner of the **Publish** dialog box.

When Captivate has finished publishing the project, an information box appears on the screen asking whether you want to view the output.

9. Click **No** to discard the information box and return to Captivate.

You will now use the Finder (Mac) or Windows Explorer (Windows) to take a look at the files Captivate has generated.

10. Use the Finder (Mac) or Windows Explorer (Window) to browse to the Chapter14/publish folder of your exercises.

Because you selected the **Publish to Folder** checkbox in the **Publish** dialog, Captivate will have automatically created the `encoderDemo_800_swf` subfolder of the `Chapter14/publish` folder.

11. Open the `encoderDemo_800_swf` subfolder to inspect its content.

There should be four files stored in this location:

- `encoderDemo_800_swf.swf`: This is the main Flash file containing the compiled version of the `.cptx` project
- `encoderDemo_800_swf.htm`: This file is an HTML page used to wrap the Flash file
- `standard.js`: This is a JavaScript file used to make the Flash Player work well within the HTML page
- `captivate.css`: This file provides the necessary style rules to ensure the proper formatting of the HTML page

If you want to embed the compiled Captivate movie in an existing HTML page, only the `.swf` file is needed. The HTML editor (such as Adobe Dreamweaver) will recreate the necessary HTML, JavaScript, and CSS files.

Captivate and Dreamweaver

Adobe Dreamweaver CC (2017) is the HTML editor of the Creative Cloud and the industry's leading solution for authoring professional web pages. Inserting a Captivate file in a Dreamweaver page is really easy! First, move or copy the main Flash file (`.swf`) as well as the required support files, if any, somewhere in the root folder of the Dreamweaver site. When done, use the Files panel of Dreamweaver to drag and drop the `.swf` file onto the HTML page. That's it! More information on Dreamweaver can be found at `http://www.adobe.com/products/dreamweaver.html`.

You will now test the compiled project in a web browser. This is an important test as it closely recreates the conditions in which the students will experience the course once uploaded on a web server.

12. Double click the `encoderDemo_800_swf.htm` file to open it in a web browser.
13. Enjoy the final version of the demonstration you have created!

Now that you have experienced the workflow for publishing the project to Flash with the default options, you will explore some additional publishing options.

Using the Scalable HTML content option

Back in Chapter 8, *Capturing Onscreen Action*, there was a discussion about choosing the correct size for the project. One of the solutions was to use the **Scalable HTML content** option of Captivate. Thanks to this option, the eLearning content is automatically resized to fit the screen on which it is viewed. Let's experiment with this option hands-on by going through the following steps:

1. If needed, return to the Chapter14/encoderDemo_800.cptx file.
2. Click the **Publish | Publish to Computer** icon in the Toolbar to reopen the **Publish** dialog. The publishing options you defined in the previous section should have been maintained.
3. Change the **Project Title** to encoderDemo_800_swfScalable.
4. Ensure that the publish **Location**is still the Chapter14/publish folder of the exercise, that the **Publish to Folder** checkbox is still selected, and that the selected **Output Format** is still **SWF**.
5. Select the **Scalable HTML content** checkbox in the lower right area of the **Publish** dialog.
6. Leave the remaining options at their current value and click the **Publish** button at the bottom right corner of the **Publish** dialog box.

When Captivate has finished publishing the project, an information box appears on the screen asking whether you want to view the output.

7. Click **Yes** to discard the information box and open the published project in the default web browser.

During the playback, use your mouse to resize your browser window and note how the movie is resized and always fits the available space without being distorted.

The Scalable HTML Content option also works when the project is published in HTML5 format. It is very different from an actual Responsive Project, though. Here, the project is simply scaled up or down to fit the screen, but the layout itself is not adapted. A Responsive Project goes way beyond a simple scaling of the project as it provides a way to actually modify the layout itself based on the screen on which the content is viewed.

Publishing to HTML5

One of the main goals of HTML5 is to provide a plugin-free paradigm. It means that the interactivity and strong visual experience pioneered by the plugins (such as Adobe Flash) should be supported natively by browsers and their underlying technologies (mainly HTML, CSS, and JavaScript) without the need for an extra third-party plugin.

Because plugins are no longer necessary to deliver rich interactive content, any modern browser should be capable of rendering the interactive eLearning courses created by Captivate. This includes the browsers installed on mobile devices, such as tablets and smartphones.

This is an enormous change, not only for the industry but also for Captivate users and eLearning developers. Thanks to HTML5, your students are able to enjoy your eLearning content across all their devices, and with the option to create Responsive Projects, it gives a much better screen experience to learners. The ability to create Responsive Projects is one of the few Captivate features that work in HTML5 only, with no Flash equivalent. This fact demonstrates that HTML5 publishing is taking the lead over the original Flash-based publishing. It also clearly shows that the future of Captivate and of eLearning is HTML5.

Using the HTML5 Tracker panel

Because HTML5 and Flash are two different technologies, everything possible in Flash is not always possible in HTML5. Consequently, some features of Captivate that are supported in Flash are not supported in HTML5. When planning a project, it is necessary to decide up front on the format (Flash or HTML5) in which the project will be published and only use the objects supported by the chosen publication format.

In the following exercise, you will use the **HTML5 Tracker** to better understand what features of the Encoder demonstration are (un)supported in HTML5:

1. If needed, return to the `encoderDemo_800.cptx` file.
2. Use the **Window** | **HTML5 Tracker** menu item to open the **HTML5 Tracker** floating panel.

The **HTML5 Tracker** floating panel informs you that one of the features used in this project is not supported in HTML5, as shown in the following screenshot:

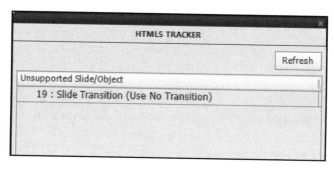

On slide 19, the slide transition is not supported, so let's remove the transition.

3. In the **HTML5 Tracker** panel, select **19 : Slide Transition (Use No Transition)**.
4. This takes you directly to slide 19. With the **HTML5 Tracker** still open, go to the **Timing** inspector.
5. Note that the current transition for this slide is set to **Fade**. Open the drop-down list and change it to **No Transition**.
6. In the **HTML5 Tracker**, click **Refresh** in the top right corner of the dialog. This removes slide 19 from the Unsupported Slide/Object list.
7. Close the **HTML5 Tracker** panel.

A comprehensive list of all the objects and features that are not supported in the HTML5 output is available in the official Captivate Help pages at `http://helpx.adobe.com/captivate/using/publish-projects-html5-files.html`. Make sure you read this page before publishing your projects in HTML5.

In the next exercise, you will publish the Encoder demonstration in the HTML5 publishing format.

Publishing the project in HTML5

The process of publishing the project in HTML5 is very similar to the process of publishing the project in Flash. Perform the following steps to publish the project in HTML5:

1. If needed, return to the `encoderDemo_800.cptx` file.
2. Click the **Publish | Publish to Computer** icon in the toolbar to reopen the **Publish** dialog.

3. Change the **Project Title** to `encoderDemo_800_HTML5`.

4. Ensure that the publish location is still the `Chapter14/publish` folder from your exercises.

5. In the **Output Format Option** section, select the **HTML5** button and then deselect the **SWF** button.

6. Deselect the **Scalable HTML content** checkbox.

7. Leave the other options at their current value and click the **Publish** button.

If you still have some unsupported slides/objects in your project, Captivate informs you that some features used in this project are not supported in HTML5.

8. Click **Yes** to discard the message and start the publication to HTML5.

When the publishing process is complete, a message appears asking if you want to view the output.

9. Click **No** to discard the message and return to the standard Captivate interface.

You will now use Windows Explorer (Windows) or the Finder (Mac) to take a closer look at the generated files.

10. Use Windows Explorer (Windows) or the Finder (Mac) to go to the `Chapter14/publish/encoderDemo_800_HTML5` folder of the exercises.

You should find a bunch of files and folders in the `encoderDemo_800_HTML5` folder. These are as follows:

- `index.html`: This file is the main HTML file. This is the file to load in the web browser to play the course.
- `goodbye.html`: This file is executed when the learner exits the course.
- `project.txt`: This file publishes the metadata for the course.
- `/ar`: This folder contains the required audio assets in `.mp3` format.
- `/dr`: This folder contains the required images.
- `/vr`: This folder contains the required video files in `.mp4` format.
- `/assets`: This folder contains the required CSS and JavaScript files.

- `/callees`: If your project contains a link to another Captivate project, you can copy the project to this folder.

You will now test this version of the project in a web browser.

11. Double-click the `index.html` file to open it in the default web browser.

Note that Captivate does a pretty good job of converting the demonstration to HTML5.

Publishing to Flash AND HTML5
When in the **Publish** dialog, it is possible to select both the **SWF** and the **HTML5 Output Formats** at the same time. When publishing in both formats, Captivate generates the assets of both the Flash and the HTML5 application in the same folder. It also generates one extra file called `multiscreen.html`. This file is used to detect the device used to visit the course. If a desktop / laptop computer is detected (with Flash Player installed), it redirects the student to the Flash version of the course, but if a mobile device is detected, it redirects the student to the HTML5 version. Don't hesitate to test it out by selecting both the **SWF** and the **HTML5 Output Formats** before publishing the project.

Publishing a Responsive Project

The process of publishing a responsive project is very similar to the process of publishing a standard project to HTML5. But because a responsive project is designed to be viewed on a mobile device right from the start, there are a few interesting options that can be fine-tuned before publication.

Using the Mobile Palette

One of the things that characterize the mobile experience (versus the desktop/laptop experience) is the touch screen. Owners of tablets and smartphones use their fingers to interact with their devices by performing various multitouch gestures. These gestures include swipes, taps, double-taps, pinches, and so on. The Mobile Palette feature in Captivate gives you the ability to leverage the power of those mobile gestures in your projects. This is what you will examine right now using the following steps:

1. Open the `Chapter14/FluidBoxes.cptx` project. This is the responsive project you created in `Chapter 10`, *Creating a Responsive Project*.
2. Use the **Window | Mobile Palette** menu item to open the **Mobile Palette** floating panel.

As described in the following screenshots, the **Mobile Palette** allows you to enable mobile **Gestures** and **Geolocation** services for that project:

3. Make sure the **Gesture Configuration** checkbox is selected for this project.

Since this project does not use any **Geolocation** capabilities, there is no need to select the **Geolocation** option.

4. Deselect the **Geolocation** checkbox, if needed.

Note that you can enable or disable gestures at the project level from this dialog. If you have a branched course and you wish to disable gestures for the decision screens, you can do so in the slide properties. Let's take a look at that workflow now.

5. Click **OK** to validate the changes and to close the **Mobile Palette** panel.
6. To disable gestures for the first slide of this project, use the **Filmstrip** to go to the first slide.
7. Click the **Properties** icon in the Toolbar to open the **Properties** inspector.
8. In the **Properties** inspector, uncheck **Allow Gesture Navigation**.

You can follow the same steps to disable gestures for any other slide in the project.

This option in Captivate is yet another mobile-only option that has no equivalent in Flash. Note that these options are not limited to Responsive Projects. You can use Gestures and Geolocations on any standard project as well.

Publishing a Responsive Project

The actual publication process is the same as for a standard project published in HTML5. Let's check it out using the following steps:

1. Still in the `Chapter14/FluidBoxes.cptx` file, click the **Publish | Publish for Devices** icon in the Toolbar to reopen the **Publish** dialog.

At the top of the **Publish** dialog, note that the **Publish as** option is set to **HTML5**, without any options to turn it off or choose another publishing format.

2. If needed, change the **Project Title** to `Fluid Boxes`.
3. Use the folder icon to choose the `Chapter14/publish` folder from your exercise as the publish **Location**.
4. Make sure the **Zip Files** checkbox is deselected.

The **Publish** dialog should now look like the following screenshot:

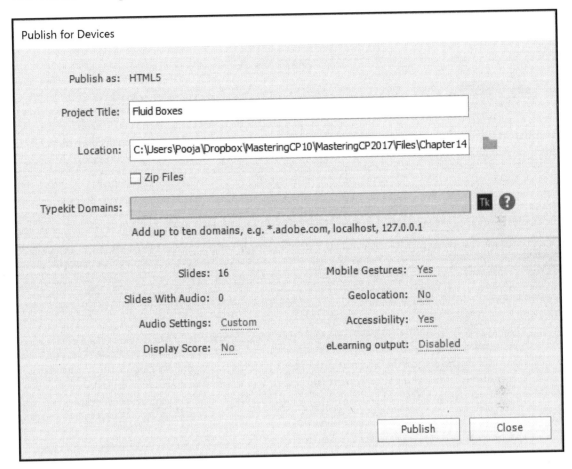

Note that the bottom part of the dialog box displays information about the project being published. Also note that you can use the blue links to access various panels and preferences should you need to perform some last-minute changes before publishing.

5. Click the **Publish** button at the bottom right corner of the dialog box.

When the publishing process is complete, a second message appears asking whether you want to view the output.

6. Click **Yes** to discard the message and view the published project in a web browser.

That's it! Apart from the fact that a Responsive Project can only be published in HTML5, the process is actually the same as for a standard project published in HTML5. Before moving on to the next section, take some time to inspect the published files on your computer. They should be in the `Chapter14/publish/Fluid Boxes` folder of your exercises.

Publishing an eLearning-enabled project

As a Captivate user, publishing an eLearning-enabled project is not very different from publishing a normal project in Flash or HTML5. Behind the scenes, however, Captivate generates a whole bunch of files to enable SCORM, AICC, or xAPI compliance. In this section, you will publish your SCORM-enabled *Take The Train* project.

Publishing the SCORM package in HTML5

In this section, you will publish your SCORM-enabled project in HTML5 format using the following steps:

1. Still in the `Chapter14/takeTheTrain.cptx` file, use the **Publish | Publish to Computer** icon in the Toolbar to open the **Publish** dialog.
2. As Typekit fonts have been used in the project, you will get a message that the fonts might look slightly different. While creating the Captivate project, you used Typekit Sync fonts, but the published files will use the corresponding web fonts, which may result in minor differences. Read the message and click **Next**.
3. In the **Publish to My Computer** dialog, change the **Project Title** to `takeTheTrain_HTML5_SCORM`.
4. Ensure that the publish **Location** is the `Chapter14/publish` folder of your exercises.
5. In the Typekit Domains section, type the domain name of the LMS or web server you will host your course on. You can add up to ten domains to this field.
6. Click the **More** button in the bottom left corner of the **Publish** dialog.

Take good note of the information revealed by the **More** button. Note that the eLearning Output is set to **Disabled**. Let's change it to SCORM 1.2.

7. Click the **Disabled** link. This opens the **Preferences** dialog with the Quiz Reporting section visible.
8. Select **Enable reporting for this project**. This enables all LMS-related settings in the dialog.

9. Make sure **Standard** is set to **SCORM 1.2**.

10. Click **OK** to confirm the changes and close the **Preferences** dialog:

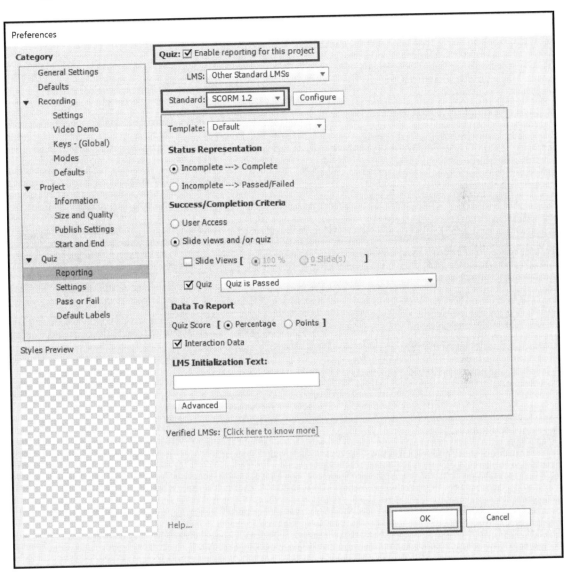

This takes you back to the **Publish To My Computer** dialog. Note that the **Zip Files** option has been automatically selected by Captivate. This is the default behavior when reporting options are enabled. You should leave this checkbox selected when publishing an eLearning-enabled project. After it has been published, you have to upload that single .zip file to the LMS as-is. A SCORM-compliant LMS is able to unzip the package and properly deploy the files it contains.

11. In the **Output Format** section, make sure the **HTML5** option is the only one selected.

12. Click the **Publish** button in the bottom right corner of the **Publish** dialog.

A dialog box should warn you that negative scoring is not supported in SCORM 1.2. This means that some of the scoring properties that have been set for your quiz will not be enforced by the LMS because they are not supported in SCORM 1.2. These unsupported scoring options include negative scoring, penalties, and partial scoring.

13. Click **Yes** to acknowledge the message and move on with publishing the project anyway.

14. Acknowledge the **Publish Complete** message by clicking the **OK** button.

You will now take a look at the generated .zip file.

15. Use the Finder (Mac) or Windows Explorer (Windows) to navigate to the published folder of the exercises files.

You should find the takeTheTrain_HTML5_SCORM file in this folder.

16. Unzip the file to take a closer look at its content.

This is where the magic takes place! In the unzipped version of the file, you should find the same files as when you published a regular non-SCORM project in HTML5. However, because you decided to produce a SCORM-compliant package, Captivate has generated lots of extra files. These extra files are used to enable communication between the LMS and the eLearning content produced by Captivate.

The most important of these extra files is the imsmanifest.xml file. This file is the SCORM Manifest file. It must be stored at the root of the SCORM package. Feel free to open this file in your favorite text editor to take a look at its content (but make sure you do not modify it). The manifest file describes the course structure to the LMS using a SCORM-compliant XML format.

Note that the actual extra files that Captivate generates depend on the standard being used (SCORM, AICC, or xAPI) and on the chosen version of SCORM.

Extra credit - Publishing the Flash version of the SCORM package

In this extra credit section, you will publish the Flash version of your eLearning-enabled project as a SCORM package. The general steps go as follows:

- Use the **Publish | Publish to Computer** icon in the toolbar to open the **Publish** dialog.
- Make sure the **Output Format** is set to **SWF** and that the **Location** is the Chapter14/publish folder of the exercises.
- Change the name of the project to takeTheTrain_SWF_SCORM.
- Publish the file.

Captivate should generate the takeTheTrain_SWF_SCORM.zip file in the Chapter14/publish folder. Don't hesitate to unzip that file and inspect its contents.

Working with the MultiSCO packager

In Chapter 7, *Working with Quizzes*, you discovered that the concept of the **Sharable Content Object (SCO)** is at the heart of the SCORM specification. As far as SCORM is concerned, the two eLearning-enabled projects you published in the previous section are both considered as SCOs. Each of these SCOs contains its own manifest file. One of the key pieces of information contained in the imsmanifest.xml file is the unique SCO identifier of this particular package, as entered in the **Manifest** dialog of Captivate.

One of the most interesting aspects of SCORM is the ability to take different SCOs, arrange them in a course, and publish them as a single SCORM package. This is precisely what the MultiSCO packager enables you to do.

In the next exercise, you will create one more SCO and use the MultiSCO packager to package multiple SCOs into a single package.

Creating SCOs

Captivate is not the only eLearning authoring tool that can produce valid SCORM packages. You can therefore use the MultiSCO packager to include multiple eLearning modules developed by different authoring tools in a single course package.

Creating a SCORM package from the Video Demo project

A Video Demo is a project using the `.cpvc` file extension. As discussed earlier in `Chapter 9`, *Producing a Video Demo*, such a project can only be published as an `.mp4` video file. The publishing options available for a Video Demo project do not allow for the creation of a SCORM package. But there is a trick! In the next exercise, you will import a `.cpvc` Video Demo project inside a standard Captivate project and publish it as a SCORM package using the following steps:

1. Return to Captivate and close every open file.
2. Use the **File** | **New Project** | **Blank Project** menu item to create a new Blank Captivate project.
3. In the **New Blank Project** dialog, select the predefined size of **1024 x 768** and click **OK**.

Captivate creates a new project that is 1024 pixels in width and 768 pixels in height. The next step is to insert the Video Demo CPVC project inside this new project.

4. Use the **Insert** | **CPVC Slide** menu item to insert the Video Demo into the current project.
5. Browse to the `Chapter14/encoderVideo.cpvc` file and click **Open**.
6. In the **Filmstrip** panel, right click slide 1 and delete it.
7. Save the file as `Chapter14/EncoderVideo.cptx`.

Thanks to the **Insert** | **CPCV Slide** menu item, you have inserted the Video Demo as a new slide in a regular project. As far as Captivate is concerned, this project is a standard project that uses the `.cptx` file extension. The Video Demo project can therefore be published as a SCORM package.

8. Use the **Quiz** | **Quiz Preferences** menu item to open the **Preferences** dialog on the **Quiz Reporting** page.
9. At the top of the page, select the **Enable reporting for this project** checkbox.
10. Open the **LMS** drop-down menu and choose **Moodle** as the LMS.
11. Click the **Configure** button to create a SCORM Manifest.

12. Enter the following values in the **Manifest** dialog:

Field	Content
Course Identifier	encoderVideo
Course Title	The Adobe Media Encoder Video Demo
Course Description	This video shows the student how to convert a Quick Time movie into an MP4 video.
SCO Identifier	encoderVideo
SCO Title	The Adobe Media Encoder Video Demo

13. Click **OK** to validate and close the **Manifest** dialog.

There is no Quiz in this particular file, but it does not mean that you have nothing to track! In a Quiz-less project, SCORM can be used to track the project's completion status by the students.

14. In the **Status Representation** section, make sure that the **Incomplete ---> Complete** option is selected.
15. In the **Success/Completion Criteria** section, select the **Slide Views** checkbox and deselect the **Quiz** checkbox.
16. Since there is no Quiz in this project, deselect the **Interaction Data** checkbox in the **Data To Report** section.
17. Click **OK** to validate and close the **Quiz Preferences** dialog.

Now that Quiz Reporting Preferences have been correctly entered, the last step is to publish this project as a SCORM package.

18. Use the **Publish | Publish to Computer** icon in the Toolbar to open the **Publish** dialog.
19. If needed, change the **Project Title** to encoderVideo.
20. Use the Chapter14/publish folder of the exercise as the publish **Location**.
21. Select **SWF** as the only option in the **Output Format**.
22. Make sure that the **Zip Files** option is selected.
23. Leave all the other options at their default values and click **Publish**.
24. When the publication process is finished, use the Finder (Mac) or Windows Explorer (Windows) to browse to the publish folder of your exercises.

You should see another SCORM package named encoderVideo.zip. This ZIP file contains all the assets that are necessary to integrate the Video Demo project into a SCORM 1.2-compliant LMS, such as Moodle.

Creating a single course package from multiple SCOs

The publish folder of your exercises should now contain three separate SCORM packages: takeTheTrain_HTML5_SCORM.zip, takeTheTrain_SWF_SCORM.zip (from the Extra Credit section), and encoderVideo.zip, created in the previous section. Each of these packages has a unique SCO identifier defined in the imsManifest.xml file inside each package.

Using the MultiSCO packager, you will now combine these SCOs into a single SCORM course. At the end of this procedure, you will have a single .zip file containing all three modules. This single .zip file can be uploaded as-is into a SCORM-compliant LMS, such as Moodle.

Perform the following steps to create the SCORM package:

1. Return to Captivate and use the **File | New Project | Multi-SCORM Packager** menu item to open the **Adobe Multi SCO Packager** AIR application.

The **Multi SCO Packager** application is an external AIR application that is part of your Captivate installation. As shown in the following screenshot, the **Multi SCO Packager** proposes three course templates, the leftmost template being the simplest one:

In Chapter 7, *Working with Quizzes,* you learned that Moodle is SCORM 1.2-compliant. This means that you need to generate a SCORM 1.2-compliant package if you want to upload your course to Moodle. In the **Multi SCO Packager** application, only the simplest template is SCORM 1.2-compliant, and the other two templates are SCORM 2004-compatible.

1. Click the first (leftmost) template named **Multiple SCOs**.

2. In the **Course Manifest Details** dialog, perform the following steps:
   - Select **1.2** in the **Version** drop-down menu under **SCORM Version**.
   - Type `DiDaXo_bestOfSeries` in the **Identifier** field.
   - Type `The best of DiDaXo` in the **Title** field.
   - Type `Experience the best courses of the DiDaXocompany in this sample Course package` in the **Description** field.
   - Type `1` in the **Version** field.

3. Click **OK** to validate the changes and close the **Course Manifest Details** dialog.

The information you just typed in the **Course Manifest Details** dialog box will be merged with the Manifest files of each individual SCO contained in this course in order to create a single SCORM manifest for the entire course. The next step is to add multiple SCOs into the course.

5. Click the **+** icon in the top-right corner of the **Multi SCO Packager** application (identified by the tooltip).

6. Browse to the `Chapter14/publish` folder from your exercise and select the `takeTheTrain_HTML5_SCORM.zip` package. Click **Open** to add the package to the course.

7. Repeat the same operation to add the `takeTheTrain_SWF_SCORM.zip` and the `encoderVideo.zip` package of your publish folder to the course.

You can add as many SCORM packages as needed into the course. Note the icons at the bottom right corner of the **Multi SCO Packager** application. They allow you to reorder or delete the SCOs inside the course:

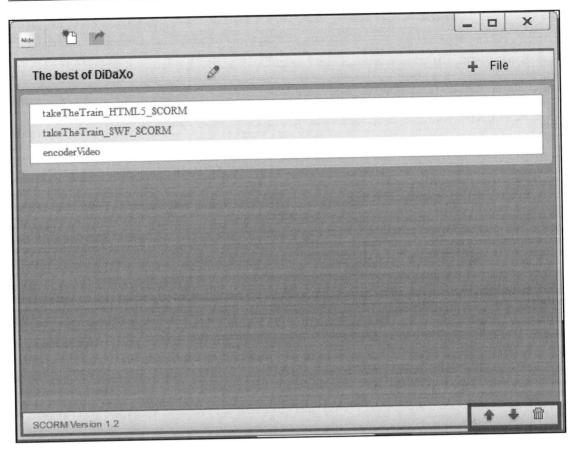

Now that every SCO has been added to the course, the last step is to publish the course as a single SCORM package that contains all three SCOs.

8. Click the **Publish Course** icon at the top left corner of the **Multi SCO Packager** application.

9. In the **Publish SCO package** dialog, use the **Publish Folder** field to choose the Chapter14/publish folder of the exercises as the output folder of the package.

10. Click the **Publish** button. When the process is complete, click **OK** to acknowledge the successful creation of the SCORM package.

11. Close the **Multi SCO Packager** application.

12. Use the Finder (Mac) or Windows Explorer (Windows) to browse to the publish folder of your exercises.

You should see the new `DiDaXo_bestOfSeries.zip` package that has been created by the Multi SCO Packager application. This package contains the three modules that you added in the Multi SCO Packager in the previous section. Feel free to unzip the package to check its content out. You should be able to locate a single `imsManifest.xml` file, as well as the assets pertaining to each of the three modules you added to the course.

When using the MultiSCO Packager, remember the following points:

- Each individual component needs to be published as a SCORM package that contains a valid `imsManifest.xml` file. Such a package is called a **Sharable Content Object (SCO)**.
- A single SCO can be used in many different course packages.
- A single course can contain an unlimited number of SCOs.
- The generated course package can be uploaded as a single unit to a SCORM-compliant LMS.
- There are different versions of SCORM. Make sure you create course packages that are compliant with whatever SCORM version your LMS supports.
- The MultiSCORM Packager of Captivate proposes three course templates to choose from. Make sure the chosen Template can be used with the version of SCORM that you are targeting.

This concludes your exploration of the MultiSCORM packager of Captivate.

 For more information on the MultiSCORM Packager, refer to this help article on the Adobe website at `https://helpx.adobe.com/captivate/using/multi-scorm-packager.html`.

Publishing to PDF

Another publishing option available in Captivate is to publish the project as an Adobe PDF document. This process is tied to the Flash publishing process covered previously. When converting to PDF, Captivate first converts the project to Flash and then embeds the resulting `.swf` file inside a PDF document. To read the Flash file embedded in the PDF document, the free Adobe Acrobat Reader relies on the Flash Player plugin that is installed on the student's computer. This is why this option does not work on a mobile device, even if the Adobe Reader app is installed.

Publishing the Captivate project to PDF is a great way to make the eLearning course available offline. The students can, for example, download the PDF file from a website and take the course on a train or on an airplane where no Internet connection is available. However, be aware that, if the course is viewed offline or outside an LMS, quiz scores and the course completion status cannot be tracked.

In the following exercise, you will publish the Encoder Demonstration to PDF:

1. Return to the `Chapter14/encoderDemo_800.cptx` file.
2. Click the **Publish | Publish to Computer** icon on the Toolbar.
3. In the central area, change the **Project Title** to `encoderDemo_800_PDF`.
4. Make sure the **Location** field still points to the `Chapter14/publish` folder of the exercises.
5. Choose **SWF** as the only **Output Format**.
6. Make sure the **Publish to Folder** checkbox is selected.
7. In the bottom left area of the **Publish** dialog, select the **Export PDF** checkbox.
8. Click the **Publish** button in the lower right corner of the **Publish** dialog.

When the publishing process is complete, a message tells you that Acrobat 9 or higher is required to read the generated PDF file.

9. Click **OK** to acknowledge the message. A second information box will open.
10. Click **No** to discard the second message and close the **Publish** dialog.
11. Use the Finder (Mac) or Windows Explorer (Windows) to browse to the `Chapter14/publish/encoderDemo_800_PDF` folder of the exercises.

There should be five files in the `encoderDemo_800_PDF` folder. Actually, publishing to PDF is an extra option of the standard ability to publish to Flash.

12. Delete all but the PDF file from the `encoderDemo_800_PDF` folder.
13. Double-click the `encoderDemo_800_PDF.pdf` file to open it in Adobe Acrobat.
14. Note that the file plays normally in Adobe Acrobat. This proves that all the necessary files and assets have been correctly embedded into the PDF file.

In the next section, you will explore another option of Captivate: publishing the project as a standalone application.

Publishing as a standalone application

When publishing as a standalone application, Captivate generates an .exe file for playback on Windows or an .app file for playback on the Macintosh. The .exe (Windows) or .app (Mac) file contains the compiled .swf file, plus a light version of the Flash Player.

The advantages and disadvantages of a standalone application are similar to those of a PDF file. That is, the file can be viewed offline on a train, on an airplane, or elsewhere, but features requiring an Internet connection will not work.

In the following exercise, you will publish the Captivate file as a standalone application for Mac or Windows using the following steps:

1. If needed, return to the Chapter14/encoderDemo_800.cptx file.
2. Click the **Publish | Publish to Computer** icon on the Toolbar.
3. At the top of the **Publish** dialog, open the **Publish As** drop-down menu.
4. Choose the **Executable** menu item.
5. Open the **Publish Type** drop-down menu.
6. If you are on a Windows PC, choose **Windows Executable (*.exe)**. If you are using a Mac, choose **MAC Executable (*.app)**.
7. If needed, change the **Project Title** to encoderDemo_800.
8. Make sure that the Chapter14/publish folder of the exercises is still the current publish **Location**.

Take some time to inspect the other options of the **Publish** dialog. One of them allows you to choose a custom icon for the generated .exe (Windows) or .app (Mac) file.

9. Leave the other options at their current value and click the **Publish** button.

When the publish process is complete, an information box will ask whether you want to see the generated output.

10. Click **No** to clear the information message and to close the **Publish** dialog.

Now that the standalone application has been generated, you will use the Finder (Mac) or Windows Explorer (Windows) to take a look at the Chapter14/publish folder and test the newly created applications.

11. Use the Finder (Mac) or Windows Explorer (Windows) to browse to the Chapter14/publish folder of the exercises.

12. Double click the `encoderDemo_800.exe` (Windows) or the `encoderDemo_800.app` (Mac) to open the generated application.

The Captivate project opens as a standalone application in its own window. Note that no browser is necessary to play the project.

This publish format is particularly useful when you want to burn the course module to a CD-ROM. When generating a Windows executable (`.exe`), Captivate can even generate an `autorun.ini` file so that the project automatically plays when the CD-ROM is inserted into the computer.

Publishing as an .mp4 video file

When publishing a project as a video, Captivate generates an `.mp4` file and suggests various video presets for the conversion. Actually, Captivate first generates a `.swf` file and then converts it into an `.mp4` video file.

After the conversion, the video file can be played with any media player that is capable of reading the `.mp4` format. It is an ideal solution if you want to upload the resulting movie to YouTube or if you want to make it available to non-Flash devices. On the other hand, the generated `.mp4` video file permits only a linear experience-that is, no more interaction and no more branching is possible. The student experiences the video from the beginning to the end in a linear fashion, as is the case while watching a motion picture in a movie theater or on TV. Consequently, converting a Captivate project to a video file is well suited for a demonstration, but does not work well with simulations.

In the following exercise, you will convert the Encoder Demonstration into an `.mp4` video using the following steps:

1. If needed, return to the `Chapter14/encoderDemo_800.cptx` file.
2. Click the **Publish | Publish to Computer** icon in the Toolbar.
3. Open the **Publish As** drop-down menu and choose the **Video** item.
4. If needed, change the **Project Title** to `encoderDemo_800`.
5. Ensure that the **Location** field still points to the `Chapter14/publish` folder of the exercises.
6. Open the **Select Preset** drop-down list. Take some time to inspect the available options and choose **YouTube Widescreen HD**.
7. Click the **Publish** button in the bottom right corner of the **Publish** dialog.

Publishing to a video file can be quite a lengthy process, so be patient. First, you will see that Captivate converts the project into a .swf file. When that first conversion is over, Captivate opens a second box named **SWF to Video Conversion** and converts the .swf file to an .mp4 video. At the end of the whole process, the **Video** dialog proposes to publish the generated video to YouTube or to open it.

8. Close the **Video** window.

9. As usual, use the Finder (Mac) or Windows Explorer (Windows) to take a look at the Chapter14/publish folder of your exercises.

10. Double-click the encoderDemo_800.mp4 file. The video opens in the default media player.

The generated video file can be uploaded to YouTube, Vimeo, DailyMotion, or any other video hosting service. You can also host the video on your own internal video streaming server (such as an Adobe Media Server) if you have one available.

Publishing to YouTube

Captivate includes a workflow that allows you to publish your Captivate movie to a video file and upload it to your YouTube account even without leaving Captivate.

In the following exercise, you will convert your Captivate file to a video and upload it to YouTube.

 This exercise requires a YouTube account. If you do not have a YouTube account, you can create one for free at https://support.google.com/youtube/answer/161805 or read through the steps of the exercise.

Perform the following steps to upload the video to YouTube:

1. Return to the Chapter14/encoderDemo_800.cptx file.

2. Use the **File | Publish to YouTube** menu item to start the process.

When using that menu item, Captivate generates the slides as if you were publishing the movie in Flash format. When that first conversion is complete, Captivate opens the **SWF to Video Conversion** window and converts the .swf file to .mp4. So far, the process is exactly the same as the one used in the previous section. At the end of the process, however, Captivate opens another window.

3. In the **Publish to YouTube** window, click **Log in**.

4. Enter your YouTube account credentials.

5. You will get a message that Adobe Captivate wants to manage your YouTube account and your YouTube videos. Click **Allow** to give access to Captivate.

6. Once logged in, enter the relevant project information.
   - Enter the title of the movie in the **Title** field.
   - Enter a description in the **Description** field.
   - Choose the level of **Privacy** (Public, Private, or Unlisted).
   - Select the **I have read the terms & conditions** checkbox and click the **Upload** button.

Captivate will then upload the video to YouTube. When the process is complete, you can see a preview of the video in the same dialog. To go to the YouTube page and view the video, click the **YouTube** button on the bottom right corner of the video.

7. Click the **Close** button to close the **Publish to YouTube** window.

As you can see, Captivate makes it incredibly easy to publish a project to YouTube!

For more information on YouTube's privacy settings and the difference between a public and private video, visit
`https://support.google.com/youtube/answer/157177?hl=en`.

Publishing to Microsoft Word

Another important publishing option is publishing a Captivate project as a Microsoft Word document. There are four formats available: Handout, Lesson, Step-by-Step guide, and Storyboard.

This publication option requires that both Adobe Captivate and Microsoft Word are installed on the same system. If you do not have Microsoft Word installed on your computer, just read through the steps of this exercise to have an idea of the workflow.

Use the following steps to publish your Captivate project as a Microsoft Word file using the Handout template.

1. Return to the `Chapter14/encoderDemo_800.cptx` file.

2. Use the **File | Print** menu item to open the **Print** dialog box.

3. In the left column, change the **Project Title** to encoderDemo_800_handout.

4. Make sure the **Folder** field still points to the Chapter14/publish folder of the exercises.

5. In the **Export Range** section, make sure that **All** is selected. You could publish a smaller selection of slides if needed.

That's it for the usual options. Before clicking on the **Publish** button, you have a few more options available in the right column of the **Print** dialog.

6. Open the **Type** drop-down list. Inspect the available options and choose the **Handouts** type.

7. In the **Handout Layout Options** section, select the **Use table in the output** option.

8. Open the **Slides Per Page** dropdown and choose to have two slides on each page of the Word document.

9. Select the **Caption Text**, **Slide Notes**, and **Include mouse Path** checkboxes.

10. Take some time to inspect the remaining options, but leave them all at their current value.

11. When ready, click the **Publish** button.

Captivate generates the Word document according to the options defined in the **Publish** dialog. When done, an information box appears asking whether you want to view the generated file.

12. Click **No** to discard the information box and close the **Print** dialog.

13. Use the Finder (Mac) or Windows Explorer (Windows) to browse to the published folder of your exercises.

14. Double click the newly created encoderDemo_800_handout.doc file.

The file will open in Microsoft Word. Take some time to inspect the generated Word document. Can you find the effect of each of the boxes you selected in the **Print** dialog?

Extra credit - publishing to Word

In this section, you will test the remaining Microsoft Word publishing options by generating a Lesson, Step-by-Step guide, and Storyboard. These are the general steps to follow:

1. Use the **File | Print** menu item to open the **Print** dialog box.

2. Give the project a meaningful Project Title.

3. In the right area of the **Print** dialog, change **Type** as **Lesson**, **Step by Step**, or **Storyboard**.

4. Experiment with the other options as well. Each Type has a specific set of options available, which are, for the most part, self-explanatory.

5. When ready, click the **Publish** button.

6. Use the Finder (Mac) or Windows Explorer (Windows) to browse to the `Chapter14/publish` folder and test your files in Microsoft Word.

Publishing for devices

When publishing an HTML5 application, you rely on the web browser installed on the computer (or device) of the student to render the course. That is, if the course is viewed on a tablet, your student needs to open the web browser installed on the tablet to see the course.

When using the **Publish for Devices (app)** feature of Captivate, you can generate a native mobile application from your eLearning content. This means that your course could be distributed by an app store (such as the Apple App Store for iOS or the Google Playstore for Android) and will install as yet another app on the device of your learners.

To convert your course into a native application, Captivate relies on the Adobe **PhoneGap Build** service. This online service can convert any HTML5/CSS/JavaScript web application into a native mobile application. PhoneGap Build supports many mobile platforms, including iOS, Android, and Windows Phone.

More information on the Adobe PhoneGap Build service can be found at `https://build.phonegap.com/`.

When using this option, Captivate first publishes the project in HTML5 and then uploads the HTML5 application to the PhoneGap Build service, where it is compiled into a native iOS and/or Android application. Because this system relies on HTML5, all the capabilities and limitations of regular HTML5 projects also apply to projects published as apps.

Note that if you want to compile your eLearning course as an iOS application, you need to be registered as an Apple developer, pay the annual Apple Developer fee, and create an Apple-approved security certificate for your app. Android also requires a certificate, but this certificate is not mandatory to compile the application for testing purposes.

Visit the Captivate Help page at
`https://helpx.adobe.com/captivate/using/preview-publishing.html` to learn how to publish apps using PhoneGap Build.

This last section concludes your overview of the publishing options of Captivate. So let's do a quick summary of what has been covered so far:

- Publishing is the third and last step of the Captivate workflow. The goal is to make the content available to learners in a variety of formats.
- The main publishing formats of Captivate are the HTML5 format and the Flash (SWF) format.
- When publishing in Flash format, Captivate generates a `.swf` file that can be played back by the free Adobe Flash Player plugin.
- The generated `.swf` file can be embedded in a PDF document for offline viewing. This option requires Adobe Acrobat, Adobe Reader 9, or later versions.
- A project published in HTML5 can be played back on virtually any mobile device, including iOS and Android devices.
- Not every feature of Captivate is supported in HTML5. Use the **HTML5 Tracker** to find out which slides/objects of your project are not supported.
- It is possible to hide and show slides. A hidden slide is not part of the published project, even though it is still in the `.cptx` file.
- **Mobile Palette** allows you to enable Gestures and Geolocation services.
- When publishing as a standalone application, Captivate produces either an `.exe` file for playback on Windows or an `.app` file for playback on a Mac.
- Captivate can produce an `.mp4` video that can be optimized for YouTube and for playback on a mobile device.
- When publishing as a PDF file or standalone application, the published project can no longer connect to the Internet. Consequently, some features that require an Internet connection (such as communicating with an LMS) do not work.
- When the project is published as a video file, it can only be experienced as a linear video that plays from the beginning to the end. Consequently, interactivity and branching are not supported.
- Use the **File | Print** menu item to publish your files as Microsoft Word documents.

- It is possible to publish your eLearning content as native Android and/or iOS applications. This capability relies on the PhoneGap Build service from Adobe.

Summary

At the end of this final chapter, you can proudly turn off the lights and leave the post-production studio. You have gone through the three major steps of the production process, uncovering lots of Captivate features, tools, and objects along the way!

In this chapter, you first focused on the final fine-tuning you can apply to the project before the actual publishing phase. You checked the spelling, decided how the movie should start and end, added metadata to the project, and created a unique Skin, among other things. When all these final changes had been taken care of, the course module was finally ready for publication.

In the second part of this chapter, you concentrated on the **Publish** dialog, where you gained experience of the main publishing features of Captivate. Publishing is the process by which the course is made available to your target audience.

Publishing to Flash is the first (and legacy) publishing option of Captivate. When published in HTML5, the project can be played back on any device equipped with a modern web browser. This includes the vast majority of mobile devices, such as iOS and Android smartphones and tablets.

Other publishing formats of Captivate include publishing as a standalone application, publishing as an .mp4 video file, and publishing as a Microsoft Word document. The .mp4 video files produced by Captivate can be easily uploaded to YouTube without even leaving the application.

Congratulations on achieving this important milestone! With the completion of this chapter comes the end of the book. We hope you have enjoyed reading these pages, and have acquired the knowledge you need to create the next generation of eLearning content with Adobe Captivate.

As for us, we would like to thank you for reading our book. We are already looking forward to your feedback or meeting you in person during an eLearning or Captivate event somewhere in the world.

Until then, have fun with Adobe Captivate!

Meet the community

Rick Zanotti is a legend in the eLearning community. Everyone knows him and he knows everyone! This is probably due to his numerous video podcasts that he makes, with a wide number of eLearning influences from all over the world. I strongly recommend that you subscribe to his Vimeo channels to get the latest and greatest from the best minds in our industry.

Rick Zanotti

Rick Zanotti is the president of RELATE, a well-known multimedia and eLearning development firm. Rick has a long career in information systems and over 20 years of eLearning and media design. He's been a systems analyst, instructional designer, programmer, web developer, and voice talent. He runs a number of technical and industry-specific Internet broadcasts on the RELATECASTS channel. For 10 years, Rick was on the advisory board for RoboDemo / Adobe Captivate.

Contact details

Website: http://www.relate.com/

Twitter: @rickzanotti

Facebook: rickzanotti

Google+: rickzanotti

Shows: video netcasts

- **eLearnChat**: http://vimeo.com/channels/elearnchat
- **SchreckTeck**: http://vimeo.com/channels/schreckteck
- **RELATE**: http://vimeo.com/channels/relate

Index

Made in the USA
Lexington, KY
08 March 2018